celebrate!

cele

sheila lukins

with Peter Kaminsky

Photography by Melanie Acevedo

brate!

cookbook

Workman Publishing · New York

Library of Congress Cataloging-in-Publication Data
Lukins, Sheila.
   Celebrate! / by Sheila Lukins; photographs by
Melanie Acevedo.
      p. cm.
   Includes index.
   ISBN 0-7611-2372-5 (alk. paper)—ISBN 0-7611-3185-X
      1. Holiday cookery. 2. Cookery, International. 3. Menus.
   I. Title
   TX739.L76 2003
   641.5'68—dc21   2003056387

Cover design by Paul Hanson
Book design by Paul Hanson and Lisa Hollander with
   Sophia Stravropoulos and Lori Malkin
Art direction of photography by Elizabeth Johnsboen
Photography by Melanie Acevedo
Back cover author photograph by Gwendolen Cates
Food styling by Alison Attenborough
Prop styling by Robyn Glaser

Workman books are available at special discounts when
purchased in bulk for premiums and sales promotions as
well as for fund-raising or educational use. Special editions
can also be created to specification. For details, contact
the Special Sales Director at the address below.

Workman Publishing Company, Inc.
708 Broadway
New York, NY 10003-9555

Printed in the U.S.A.
First printing October 2003
10 9 8 7 6 5 4 3 2 1

To Laurie Griffith,
a wonderful person.
I could never have written
this book without
her help and style.
She is like honey in the kitchen.
After all these years and
books together,
we work in perfect harmony.

It takes a special magic to celebrate with flair. Enthusiastic friends and colleagues have joined in the festivities from the inception, sharing their talents and support in order to bring *Celebrate!* to life.

Since 1981, when I first met Peter Workman, my brilliant publisher, I have been in awe of him, and am constantly thankful for his support of my books and my ideas, often before they are completely formed.

None of this would be possible without my beloved, one-of-a-kind editor, Suzanne Rafer, who has also become my dear friend. I could not imagine doing a book without her. Thanks, too, to copy editors Kathie Ness and Ann ffolliott; Barbara Peragine in prepress; and Elizabeth Gaynor in production.

Then of course there is the Renoir of Workman Publishing, Art Director Paul Hanson, who always creates a simply gorgeous book, and this time in living color! The creative Lisa Hollander pulled it all together, as always, along with Elizabeth Johnsboen, who took such care at the photo shoots. Melanie Acevedo's magnificent photographs, with food styling by Alison Attenborough and prop styling by Robyn Glaser, make the book a sheer pleasure to look at. Special thanks, as well, goes to Molly Burke for her stylish photo suggestions.

I am very grateful to so many others at Workman. There's Jim Eber and Kate Tyler—the best publicists going; an unbeatable sales team, including Bruce Harris, James Wehrle, Jodi Weiss, Jenny Mandel, and Heather Carroll; Carolan Workman, who sends all my books off around the world; and an energetic, imaginative marketing crew headed by Katie Workman and Claudia Boutote.

Of course, in the Could-Not-Do-Without category comes my dear friend and agent, Arthur Klebanoff. Thank you for your constant words of wisdom. And then there is my *Parade* family, led by Walter Anderson, who is always one-hundred-percent supportive of my publishing efforts. I thank everyone at *Parade,* especially editor Lee Kravitz and my editor at the magazine, Fran Carpentier.

My heartfelt thanks to my creative colleagues, beginning with my indispensable kitchen soulmate, Laurie Griffith, whom I could not do without. Next, my writing collaborator, Peter Kaminsky, for his eloquent and humorous way with words. He escorted Laurie and me to some great meals on Atlantic Avenue, an especially memorable one after we smoked the pork shoulder in his backyard in Brooklyn. The final results of long, hard work are a book I am very proud of.

Then there are the sugar plum fairies whose confections delight the most discerning sweet tooth. Lynnia Milliun and her brilliant Devil's Food Cake and Lemon-Glazed Angel Food Cake, Amanda Ross and those summer fruit desserts, Laura Donnelly and her Luscious Strawberry Shortcake to go to heaven for. These women, along with Maureen Luchejko, shared their talents with me, making life a little bit sweeter, and I am so very grateful! I also thank Graham Murtough for the help he gave me with the flowers. As gardening is a passion, two green thumbs are better than one. Daniel Johnnes and his unexcelled jeroboamwines.com put together our stylish selections, making menu planning easier now that most people are serving a bottle of wine with meals, especially when celebrating.

My musical muses were lyrical and so right for every menu. Many thanks to Laurie Griffith, Brian Burke, and Annabel Lukins.

What a book! Number six and it was still a thrilling, new experience. How many authors can say that? If that's not reason enough to celebrate I don't know what is!

a year of celebrations

Our calendar year offers up dozens of reasons to celebrate. Choose your favorite traditional and not-so-traditional holidays and annual events—New Year's Day, the Academy Awards, Mother's Day, Midsummer's Eve, Thanksgiving—and share them and an abundance of good food with friends and family.

celebrating our lives

Life is full of surprises, full of joy. A new job, a new bride-to-be, a new graduate, a return from a wonderful vacation. Good fortune and good feelings are meant to be shared with others, whether it's a candlelit dinner with one special person, or a day-long festive family reunion. New neighbors next door? Celebrate! Plump blueberries are in season? Celebrate! Just got a big raise? Absolutely Celebrate!

let's

I'm in the mood to celebrate! It's the kind of joyous mood that makes me happy to phone friends and family and invite them over for good food, good conversation, and good cheer! It's the kind of mood that makes needing a reason to celebrate unnecessary. . . . Well, almost.

celebrate!

Actually, I like having a reason, and am never at a loss to find one. There are so many occasions to choose from—big and small, traditional and quirky—that selecting the right one is easy. A cousin's graduation, a friend's engagement, the pleasures of a summer garden, the warmth of a winter hearth, a passion for Italian food—the choices are unlimited. I love planning the menu, shopping for ingredients, cooking the recipes, and decorating the table. And most of all, I get great pleasure in sharing my celebratory mood with others!

I believe the most memorable celebrations take place at home. In mine, all celebrations begin in the kitchen, and part of the fun is deciding what to prepare, creating a menu with appeal, start to finish. Forty-three of my favorites (yes, I have many more than that!) are included in this book, which I've divided into two sections. The first, A Year of Celebrations, marks the annual celebrations we all look forward to; some are holidays, some popular events. Christmas, the Super Bowl, Valentine's Day, the Academy Awards, Mother's Day, the Fourth of July, Thanksgiving—all heartfelt traditions to enjoy with food, friends, and family.

In addition to the big occasions, there are special moments that cry out for a get-together. The selection in Celebrating Our Lives includes the kinds of events that inspire us to really pull out all the stops. You're thrilled to have bought a new house? Inaugurate the kitchen with an aromatic Slow-Roasted Tomato and

Fennel Soup and a sweet-tangy meltingly tender chicken casserole. Birthday coming up? Highlight your bash with a seductive Honey-Lime Roast Pork and a gorgeous Chocolate Birthday Cake. Just got a big raise? Blushing Lobster Cocktails and Rich Man's Burgers say it all. Home from an exotic vacation in Morocco? Tempt friends to your table with a tantalizing, succulent Lamb Tagine, and a palate-cooling, fragrant Orange-Blossom Sorbet, and they'll be happy to ooh and ahh over all your photos and your tales of adventure. Roll up the rug for a bridal shower (complete with a Coconut Trousseau Cake), a graduation (slice up a New York Strip Steak Lavished with Tomatoes and Olives), a big family reunion (no one will want to miss the Sherried Shrimp Salad and Roasted Salmon Salad). Plus, enjoy a Saturday dinner with friends, an Anytime Sunday Brunch, Pool Party, A Cozy Dinner for Two—there are menus for all occasions and for any reason.

All the menus, whether they're for a Fresh Blueberry Breakfast to celebrate summer, a New Year's Day open house, or a sit-down Thanksgiving Dinner with all the traditional trimmings, include recipes for several courses—sometimes I've suggested alternative appetizers or entrees—along with suggestions for the appropriate wines or other drinks. I've left the coffee and tea up to you—brew or steep a pot of your favorite freshly ground beans or loose (if possible) leaves to enjoy with dessert at the end of a meal.

With each of the menus, there is a small list of "Extras," some key equipment or tableware that is needed either to prepare the recipes (barbecue equipment, an ice-cream maker) or to serve the food (a pedestal cake stand, pretty baskets). I've also shared some ideas about setting the scene, offering suggestions for creating an attractive table. I'm a big fan of all kinds of dinnerware and table linens, and enjoy using what I have as often as I can. Vases of fresh flowers, lots of candles in various holders, pretty serving bowls

and platters, all add to the celebration. I know that no one has a warehouse of dishes and linens, or a greenhouse full of breathtaking blooms, so just use these ideas as inspiration, a way to start thinking about the things you have that might help to make an occasion all the more special.

Music adds to the party atmosphere, so I've offered up recommendations—some mine, some from music-loving friends; some fun, some joyous, some romantic. Sometimes it's just a favorite musician or singer, sometimes it's a specific collection of tunes or a movie soundtrack or a classical piece. Whether you go with these suggestions or with your own favorites, remember to keep the music low—conversation is what counts at any celebration.

As in all my books, special occasions and special recipes do not have to be difficult or fussy. My great hope has always been to interest as many cooks as possible by creating new recipes usi ng the freshest and newest ingredients available today. Each menu is impressionistic and enchanting. The dishes all work together as a piece, yet I've left room for your imagination. Choose your favorites from them—or join me in the magic

of making them all, because I believe that the home-cooked meal is, in fact, the greatest celebration.

I hope this collection sparks your enthusiasm and that you'll look forward to each celebration with excitement. Enjoy the fanciful and share the feast! Get creative and move dishes around to suit your own taste. Add your own personality to the menus and let's pop the cork together!

COOKING INSIDE AND OUTSIDE THE MENU

Each dish in each celebration was composed to serve the number of people noted at the top of its menu page. So, for example, if you are preparing the Mother's Day Luncheon, which was designed to serve eight people, rest assured that all the dishes in that menu will serve eight. But, please don't wait until a particular holiday to prepare a dish that sparks your interest. By all means, make that luscious Potato Leek Soup from the St. Patrick's Day menu, even though the holiday is six months away. Just be sure to check the serving amount on the menu page so you know you're preparing enough for your family or friends.

A Year of

Celebrations

Ring in the New

Year

Ican remember New Year's Days that were cold and still, with the winter sun bright and clear in the deepest blue sky; when the breath of every man, woman, child, dog, and cat passing on the street puffed like little white clouds. And then there were the New Year's that were warm as early April, when people walked in Central Park in shirtsleeves and the wet smell in the air promised spring. New Year's weather is unpredictable and changeable. But as the first day in a family of 365 (or 366), it is the one that so many look to for a taste of what's to come. My tradition? Have a big open house with food that will stay delicious all day, so guests can drop in casually. It's a wonderful low-key party.

MENU

N ew Year's cries out for a bountiful buffet laid out on a pretty tablecloth-covered table. Stack the plates at the head, and because it's tough to juggle a plate and silverware while helping yourself through a buffet line, roll the knives and forks in large napkins, and tie them with ribbon. Place the rolled napkins in a basket at the end of the table.

The pork tenderloins are the star of this meal. Present them on a large platter and surround them with plenty of fresh kumquats and watercress. Slice the beef tenderloin before serving it, so guests can easily help themselves. The stunning Platter of Plenty, laden with gemlike vegetables, is so gorgeous that it deserves a prominent place, too. A hot plate or chafing dish will keep the black-eyed peas nice and warm, and the two salads go in large attractive bowls.

Ring in the New Year

BUFFET FOR TWENTY-FOUR

Party Pork Tenderloins

Roasted Tenderloin of Beef

Platter of Plenty

Good Luck Black-Eyed Peas

Basil Cream Potato Salad

Savory Fruit Salad

Pineapple Upside-Down Cake

Butter Balls

After all these pungent flavors, offer two choices of good old-fashioned sweetness for dessert—a glorious upside-down cake and irresistible Butter Balls.

Now is the time to remove the tired Christmas poinsettias. Think white and fresh for the New Year—buy some pots of paperwhites or even white orchids. You may still have your beautiful tree up—no need to remove it. A green and white color scheme will be very festive and a change from the red of Christmas. Happy New Year!

THE MUSIC

Duke Ellington
New Orleans zydeco

THE WINE

Alsace Pinot Gris
California Pinot Noir

THE EXTRAS

Several large platters or silver trays
Decorative bowls
Baskets
Chafing dish

PARTY PORK TENDERLOINS

Pork tenderloin is a stylish choice for a New Year's buffet. Overnight marinating and high-heat roasting brings out the pork's refined flavor—it's the perfect partner for the tangy, fruity, and herbaceous sauces offered alongside. (Try them all!) Serve the pork at room temperature.

FOR THE PORK AND MARINADE

5 pork tenderloins
 (about 1 pound each)
1 cup sherry vinegar
⅔ cup fresh orange juice
¼ cup honey
8 cloves garlic, finely minced
2 tablespoons tiny capers,
 drained, plus 2 tablespoons brine
2 tablespoons extra-virgin olive oil
2 tablespoons ground cumin
1 tablespoon dried oregano

FOR COOKING AND SERVING

4 tablespoons extra-virgin olive oil
Several bunches fresh kumquats with leaves,
 for garnish
4 bunches watercress, rinsed and patted dry,
 for garnish
Pebre (recipe follows), for serving
Lemon-Garlic Aïoli (recipe follows),
 for serving
Romesco Mayonnaise (recipe follows),
 for serving

1. Wipe the pork tenderloins with damp paper towels and place them in two large bowls or plastic containers.

2. Combine all the marinade ingredients with 1 cup water in a bowl and pour it over the tenderloins. Cover and marinate in the refrigerator overnight.

3. Transfer the tenderloins to a colander, wipe them clean of any marinade pieces, and let them drain for 15 minutes. Then pat them dry with paper towels. Strain the marinade, reserving 2 cups of the liquid.

4. Preheat the oven to 400°F.

5. Heat 2 tablespoons of the olive oil in each of two large nonstick skillets over medium-high heat. Sear the tenderloins well all over, in batches, if necessary, turning the meat as it browns. It will take about 10 minutes per batch. Transfer the pork to two 15 x 10-inch shallow roasting pans (2 tenderloins in one pan and 3 in the other), and add 1 cup of the reserved marinade to each pan.

6. Roast the tenderloins until slightly pink in the center, 10 minutes. (If you prefer to lose the pinkness, cook 2 minutes more.) Place the tenderloins on a cutting board and let them rest for 10 to 20 minutes. (They will continue to cook as they rest.)

7. Cut the tenderloins into ½-inch-thick slices and arrange them on a large round platter, overlapping the slices slightly. Garnish decoratively with the kumquats and watercress. Place the three sauces in decorative bowls and serve them alongside.

PEBRE (FRESH SALSA VERDE)

Herbs, onions, salt, and garlic make up the basic ingredients of savory *pebre*. I think of it as the Chilean cousin of the more famous Argentinean chimichurri. Peter Kaminsky brought this recipe for *pebre* back from a fly-fishing trip to the camp of his friend Carlos Hernandez on the Rio Paloma. Peter reports that for a week he doused his *chancho* (roast pork), *costilla* (short ribs), and *cordero* (whole roasted lamb) with it. His conclusion: "If it's meat, *pebre* goes with it."

3 large sweet onions, such as Vidalia
    or Walla Walla, finely diced
3 cloves garlic, finely minced
3 green jalapeño peppers, seeds and
    ribs removed, finely chopped
¾ teaspoon coarse (kosher) salt
4½ cups chopped fresh cilantro
1½ teaspoons dried oregano
¾ teaspoon ground coriander
Pinch of cayenne pepper
6 tablespoons olive oil
6 tablespoons red wine vinegar

1. Place the onions in a large bowl, cover with cold water, and allow to soak for 15 to 20 minutes. Drain, rinse under cold water, drain again, and pat dry.

2. Place the garlic and jalapeños on a cutting board. Sprinkle with the coarse salt and chop as fine as possible, mashing the mixture

---

In Mexico's Yucatán, the Maya say the weather in the first twelve days of the year tells you what the weather will be like in each of the twelve months. Similarly in Wales, the farm folk used to carry a burning hawthorn bush over twelve hills; if the fire did not go out before they reached the end of the course, the crops would be good in the coming year. Down on Bank Street, in Greenwich Village, I have a friend who follows the African American custom of cooking up a pot of black-eyed peas because her grandmother taught her that this would ensure good luck in the New Year. A recipe for this good-luck dish is on page 8.

---

into a paste with the side of a large sharp knife. Place the paste in a bowl and add the cilantro, oregano, coriander, cayenne, olive oil, and vinegar. Stir well. Add the onions and toss to combine. Adjust the seasonings to taste. Serve within 2 to 3 hours.

MAKES ABOUT 4½ CUPS

LEMON-GARLIC AIOLI

This aïoli has a creamy texture balanced by a lemony tang and plenty of pungent garlic. It will coax the best flavor out of the pork—and add a Provençal accent to the vegetables farther down the buffet line.

6 slices white bread, crusts removed,
    torn into large pieces
1½ cups whole milk
6 cloves garlic, minced
Finely grated zest of 6 lemons
4½ cups prepared mayonnaise,
    such as Hellmann's
¾ cup extra-virgin olive oil
Salt and freshly ground black pepper,
    to taste

1. Soak the bread in the milk in a bowl for 1 minute. Squeeze the bread well to remove as much milk as possible and place it in a food processor along with the garlic and lemon zest. Pulse the machine on and off about 5 times to combine the ingredients.

2. Add the mayonnaise and process until smooth.

3. With the motor running, drizzle the olive oil through the feed tube and process until smooth.

4. Transfer the mixture to a bowl and season with salt and pepper. Cover and refrigerate. This will keep for up to 2 days.

MAKES 4½ CUPS

ROMESCO MAYONNAISE

Romesco is a Catalan sauce that is made with bell peppers, almonds, tomatoes, garlic, and usually some bread. In my version, mayonnaise provides body and the orange juice adds some zing. The result is a condiment that is superb not only with pork but also with fish, poultry, and Spain's traditional prosciutto-like Serrano ham.

> 6 tablespoons olive oil
> 2 large cloves garlic, thinly sliced
> ½ cup coarsely chopped blanched almonds
> 2 red bell peppers, stemmed, seeded, and
>   chopped
> 2 small onions, halved and slivered
> 2 cups diced and seeded ripe plum tomatoes
> 2 teaspoons finely grated orange zest
> 6 tablespoons fresh orange juice
> Salt and freshly ground black pepper, to taste
> 2 cups prepared mayonnaise,
>   such as Hellmann's

1. Heat 4 tablespoons of the olive oil in a saucepan over low heat. Add the garlic and cook until pale gold, 5 to 7 minutes. Remove the garlic with a mesh skimmer and set aside in a small bowl. Add the almonds to the pan, raise the heat slightly, and cook, stirring, until golden, about 3 minutes. Add the almonds to the garlic.

2. Add the remaining 2 tablespoons oil to the pan. Add the bell peppers and onions and cook, stirring, over medium-low heat until they are very soft, 15 minutes. Add the tomatoes, orange zest, and orange juice. Season with salt and pepper. Cook for 5 minutes to blend the flavors. Add the garlic and almonds and cook for 2 minutes more. Remove from the heat and allow to cool, then puree in a food processor or blender.

3. Stir this mixture into the mayonnaise and refrigerate, covered, until ready to use. It will keep for up to 3 days.

MAKES 4 CUPS

ROASTED TENDERLOIN OF BEEF

Nothing develops the deep beefy flavor of a tenderloin more fully than roasting it. And all the sauces you've made for the pork are delicious companions for it, too. If anyone happens to bring you caviar as a present, an extravagant but totally scrumptious treat is to dollop some right on the meat. It's a more expensive way to salt it, certainly, but after all, New Year's comes just once a year.

> 2 oven-ready beef tenderloins (about
>   4½ pounds each), prime center cut
> 6 to 8 cloves garlic, cut into thin slivers
> 4 to 6 tablespoons olive oil
> 2 teaspoons dried thyme
> Coarse (kosher) salt and freshly ground
>   black pepper, to taste
> Garden cress, for garnish (optional)

1. Position a rack in the center of the oven and preheat the oven to 425°F.

2. With the tip of a sharp knife, cut small slits all over both tenderloins and insert the garlic slivers in them.

3. Lightly brush the meat with the olive oil. Sprinkle it with the thyme and a generous amount of coarse salt and pepper. Set the meat in a shallow pan that is just large enough to hold both of them comfortably and place it in the oven.

4. Roast the tenderloins for 10 minutes. Then reduce the heat to 350°F and continue to roast for another 40 minutes for rare meat, or 50 minutes for medium-rare. (Rare registers 125°F on a meat thermometer; medium-rare is 130°F.)

5. Let the roasts rest for 10 to 12 minutes, then carve into ½-inch-thick slices. Arrange overlapping on platters and garnish with garden cress, if desired.

PLATTER OF PLENTY

Anytime a large group is expected, there will be guests who are on a meatless, low-fat, or vegetarian regimen—guaranteed. Others may have overdone it during the round of holiday banquets and crave something light and simple. The vegetables here are either roasted or lightly blanched, enhancing their luminous colors and popping the flavors. You can prepare them and the eggs a day ahead, and then refrigerate everything overnight in separate covered containers. The Lemon-Garlic Aïoli served with the pork is the perfect dollop for these vegetables. If you're making the vegetables but not the pork, you should still make the same amount of aïoli.

16 small red-skinned new potatoes, scrubbed
4 pounds slim carrots, peeled and
    cut in half crosswise on the diagonal
2 heads cauliflower, cored and
    broken into small florets
2 pounds green beans, ends trimmed
8 roasted red bell peppers (page 399),
    cut in quarters
16 roasted small beets (page 399),
    cut in half or quarters
4 cans (19 ounces each) chickpeas
    (garbanzo beans), rinsed and drained
16 hard-cooked eggs (see box, facing page),
    cut in half
4 to 6 tablespoons extra-virgin olive oil
6 tablespoons fresh lemon juice
Salt and freshly ground black pepper, to taste
1/3 cup coarsely chopped fresh flat-leaf
    parsley, for garnish
Chive blossoms, if available, for garnish
Lemon-Garlic Aïoli (page 6), for serving

1. Bring a large pot of lightly salted water to a boil.

2. Cut the potatoes in half if necessary to make them uniform in size. Add them to the boiling water and cook until tender, 15 minutes. Using a slotted spoon, transfer the potatoes to a colander to drain. Then run them under cold water to stop the cooking, drain again, and pat dry. Set aside.

3. Add the carrots to the boiling water and cook until tender, 8 to 10 minutes. Using tongs, transfer them to a colander to drain and repeat the cooling and drying process. Set them aside separately from the potatoes.

4. Add the cauliflower florets to the boiling water and cook until tender, 2 to 3 minutes. Using a slotted spoon, transfer them to a colander to drain and repeat the cooling and drying process. Set them aside separately from the other vegetables.

5. Add the green beans to the boiling water and cook until tender, 3 to 4 minutes. Drain them in a colander and repeat the cooling and drying process.

6. Arrange the vegetables, the chickpeas, and the eggs in individual groupings decoratively on one or two platters. Drizzle all with the olive oil and lemon juice and season lightly with salt and pepper. Sprinkle the parsley over all, and add the chive blossoms if available. Spoon the Lemon-Garlic Aïoli into a decorative bowl and serve it alongside.

GOOD LUCK BLACK-EYED PEAS

The black-eyed pea, also known as the cowpea, was probably brought to the Americas by African slaves. Like so many other legumes, it is a potent source of protein. This recipe, in many variations, has come to be a Southern tradition on New Year's Day, a harbinger of good luck in the year to come.

HOW TO HARD-COOK EGGS

Place room-temperature eggs in a saucepan. Cover with cold water, place over medium-high heat, and bring to a boil. Reduce the heat to a gentle simmer and cook for exactly 13 minutes. Drain the eggs, rinse under cold water, and then peel. Use as directed in recipes.

Platter of Plenty

1½ pounds dried black-eyed peas
2 smoked ham hocks
3 tablespoons olive oil, or more if needed
1½ pounds andouille sausage, each
  quartered lengthwise, and cut into
  ¼-inch-thick slices
2 large onions, cut into ¼-inch dice
6 cloves garlic, lightly crushed
2 small green bell peppers, stemmed,
  seeded, and cut into ¼-inch dice
2 small red bell peppers, stemmed,
  seeded, and cut into ¼-inch dice
6 sprigs fresh thyme
6 bay leaves
½ cup chopped fresh flat-leaf parsley
Salt and freshly ground black pepper,
  to taste

1. Pick over the beans, discarding any debris. Place them in a bowl, add cold water to cover by 2 inches, and soak overnight (or see box at right).

2. Drain the beans in several changes of cold water to cover and place them in a large heavy pot.

QUICK-SOAKING BEANS

Place the picked-over beans in a large heavy pot and add cold water to cover by 2 inches. Bring to a boil over medium-high heat and boil for 2 minutes. Remove the pot from the heat and let it stand for 1 hour, covered. Then drain the beans, rinse them in several changes of water, and drain again. The beans are now ready to use in a recipe.

3. Place the ham hocks in a large saucepan and add water to cover. Bring to a boil over high heat, reduce the heat to medium-low, and simmer for 4 minutes. Drain, rinse, and add them to the beans.

4. Heat the olive oil in a nonstick skillet over medium heat. Add the sausage and cook, stirring, until browned, about 10 minutes. Using a slotted spoon, transfer the sausage to the beans. Add the onions, garlic, and bell peppers to the same skillet and cook over medium-low heat, stirring, until wilted, about 15 minutes, adding more olive oil if necessary. Add this mixture to the beans.

5. Add 12 cups water and the thyme sprigs and bay leaves to the beans. Bring the mixture to a boil over high heat, skimming off any foam that rises to the surface. Reduce the heat to medium-low and simmer the beans, partially covered, until they are tender but not mushy, 35 to 40 minutes. Remove the ham hocks and set them aside to cool. Discard the thyme sprigs and bay leaves.

6. When the ham hocks are cool, remove the meat from the bones and cut it into small dice. Add the meat to the beans along with the parsley and season with salt and pepper (see Note).

Note: This is best served the same day, but you can make it a day ahead. Add a little heated broth to the beans before reheating them, covered, in a 350°F oven for 15 to 20 minutes.

Good Luck Black-Eyed Peas

BASIL-CREAM POTATO SALAD

This salad has plenty of zip and crunch to complement the other big flavors in this New Year's spread. The mayonnaise is tangy, with watercress, shallots, and Mediterranean flavors like capers and anchovies making for a fresh-tasting and colorful buffet dish.

FOR THE SAUCE

2 cups fresh watercress leaves
½ cup (packed) fresh basil leaves
1 tablespoon coarsely chopped shallots
3 cloves garlic, coarsely chopped
3 anchovy fillets, drained
2 teaspoons tiny capers, drained
6 tablespoons fresh lemon juice
½ cup extra-virgin olive oil
2 cups prepared mayonnaise,
*   such as Hellmann's*
Salt and freshly ground black pepper,
*   to taste*

FOR THE POTATOES

4 pounds small red-skinned new potatoes,
*   unpeeled, scrubbed and quartered*
8 scallions, including 3 inches green,
*   thinly sliced*
Salt and freshly ground black pepper,
*   to taste*
¼ cup slivered fresh basil leaves, for garnish

1. Prepare the sauce: Place the watercress, basil, and shallots in a food processor and process until finely minced. Add the garlic, anchovies, capers, and lemon juice and process until smooth.

2. With the motor running, add the olive oil in a steady stream through the feed tube. Process until smooth. Add the mayonnaise and process until smooth. Season the sauce with salt and pepper, and set it aside in a small bowl.

3. Cook the potatoes in a large pot of salted water over medium-high heat until just tender, about 10 minutes. Then drain the potatoes well and allow them to cool to room temperature.

4. Combine the potatoes and scallions in a large bowl and season with salt and pepper. Using a large rubber spatula, fold in the sauce. Transfer the salad to a serving dish and sprinkle the slivered basil over it. Serve at room temperature. (If making in advance, refrigerate, covered, for up to 24 hours. Bring to room temperature and garnish with the basil before serving.)

SAVORY FRUIT SALAD

Combine some favorite salad ingredients with tropical fruits, add the snap of garlic and chiles, and you have a gorgeous, stylish, salsa-type salad that partners exceptionally well with the pork.

6 cups diced fresh pineapple
*   (2 pineapples; ¼-inch dice)*
6 cups diced ripe cantaloupe
*   (2 cantaloupes; ¼-inch dice)*
6 cups diced peeled hothouse (seedless)
*   cucumbers (3 cucumbers; ¼-inch dice)*
8 ripe plum tomatoes, seeded and
*   cut into ¼-inch dice*
4 ribs celery, cut into ¼-inch dice
⅔ cup diced red onion (¼-inch dice)
1½ tablespoons finely minced garlic
2 to 3 teaspoons finely minced red
*   jalapeño, serrano, or other fresh red*
*   chile pepper*
4 teaspoons finely grated lime zest
⅓ cup fresh lime juice (from 2 to 3 limes)
⅔ cup small fresh mint leaves

1. Combine the pineapple, cantaloupe, cucumber, tomatoes, celery, and onion in a large bowl.

2. Using a rubber spatula, gently fold in the garlic, chile, lime zest, and lime juice. Refrigerate, covered, for up to 4 hours before serving.

3. Arrange the salad in a decorative bowl and scatter the mint leaves over the top just before serving.

PINEAPPLE UPSIDE-DOWN CAKE

I f dessert is playful in general, it's doubly so for one that's turned upside down. Cooking the topping on the bottom of the pan heightens the sweetness and fruitiness of the pineapple and infuses the cake with its sweet tropical moistness. Normally one of these cakes serves eight as an ending to a sit-down dinner. As part of a buffet, it will serve twelve or so. If you're expecting a houseful, prepare two or three cakes.

FOR THE TOPPING

7 tablespoons unsalted butter
1 cup (packed) light brown sugar
1 tablespoon white rum
1 can (20 ounces) whole pineapple
   slices packed in juice, drained,
   juices reserved

FOR THE CAKE

1⅔ cups all-purpose flour
2 teaspoons baking powder
½ teaspoon salt
8 tablespoons (1 stick) unsalted butter,
   at room temperature
1½ teaspoons pure vanilla extract
1 cup granulated sugar
3 large eggs, separated
½ cup whole milk
1 tablespoon white rum

1. Position a rack in the lower third of the oven, and preheat the oven to 350°F.

2. Prepare the topping: Melt the butter in a flameproof 9-inch round cake pan on the stovetop over low heat. Raise the heat to medium, add the brown sugar, and swirl the pan until the mixture is smooth and bubbly, about 2 minutes. Add the rum and swirl again to mix. Remove the pan from the heat. Arrange whole pineapple slices around the edge of the pan and place one in the middle. Cut the remaining slices in half and distribute them evenly on top of the whole pieces. Set the pan aside.

3. Prepare the cake: Sift the flour, baking powder, and salt together in a medium-size bowl. Set it aside.

4. Cream the butter in a mixing bowl with an electric mixer until light and fluffy, about 2 minutes. Add the vanilla and ¾ cup of the granulated sugar and beat on high speed until very light, about 5 minutes. Add the egg yolks, one at a time, scraping down the sides of the bowl and beating well after each addition until combined.

5. Stir the milk, rum, and 3 tablespoons of the reserved pineapple juice together in a small bowl.

6. Add one third of the flour mixture to the butter mixture and mix on low speed until combined. Add half of the milk mixture and mix on low speed, scraping down the sides of the bowl, until combined. Repeat with half of the remaining flour, the remaining milk mixture, and then the remaining flour. Set the batter aside.

7. Place the egg whites in a bowl and beat until foamy. Add the remaining ¼ cup granulated sugar, a tablespoon at a time, and continue mixing until the whites hold soft peaks. Stir one quarter of the whites into the batter until smooth. Add the remaining whites and fold gently with a large rubber spatula until completely incorporated.

8. Spoon the batter over the pineapple in the cake pan and smooth the top. Bake until the center springs back when touched and a knife inserted into the center comes out clean, 25 to 35 minutes.

9. Cool the cake in the pan on a rack for 10 minutes. While it is still warm, carefully unmold the cake onto a decorative serving plate.

MAKES 1 CAKE (SEE HEADNOTE)

BUTTER BALLS

This classic holiday cookie—light, buttery, crunchy—goes by many names. In some places they are called Noel Balls; in others, Mexican Wedding Cakes. I find that the addition of a little "holiday cheer"—namely bourbon—makes them particularly memorable. My prediction: You won't stop after eating one. Serve them mounded on an ornate paper doily in a shallow bowl or on a delicate silver tray.

1 cup all-purpose flour
½ cup blanched almonds, coarsely chopped
1½ teaspoons finely grated orange zest
½ cup pecans, toasted (see box, page 104)
*   and cooled*
8 tablespoons (1 stick) unsalted butter,
*   at room temperature*
3 tablespoons granulated sugar
½ teaspoon pure vanilla extract
2 tablespoons bourbon
About 2 cups confectioners' sugar, for dusting

1. Position a rack in the center of the oven, and preheat the oven to 350°F. Line two baking sheets with parchment paper (see Note).

2. Place the flour, almonds, and orange zest in a food processor and process until the mixture is very finely ground. Transfer it to a bowl.

3. Place the pecans in the food processor and chop medium-fine. Add to the flour mixture and set aside.

4. Cream the butter with an electric mixer, until light and fluffy, about 2 minutes. Add the granulated sugar, vanilla, and bourbon and beat on medium speed, scraping the sides of the bowl occasionally, until the mixture is well combined, 5 minutes.

5. Add the flour and nut mixture to the butter mixture and mix on low speed until just incorporated.

6. Form the dough into 1-inch balls, rolling them between the palms of your hands, and place them ½ inch apart on the prepared baking sheets. Bake until they are just beginning to turn golden, 12 to 18 minutes. Let the cookies cool slightly on the baking sheets on wire racks.

7. Place 1½ cups of the confectioners' sugar in a shallow bowl. While the cookies are still warm, roll them in the confectioners' sugar and then place them on a plate and let them cool completely. Just before serving, dust the cookies with the remaining ½ cup confectioners' sugar.

MAKES ABOUT **60** COOKIES

Note: Although these cookies don't spread, you don't want to crowd them when baking. Better to bake in two batches. If you have a third baking sheet, use it, having it ready to go into the oven when the first batch of cookies comes out.

Super

No longer is New Year's Day the only start-of-the-year celebration. Less dressy, but certainly festive, the Super Bowl comes fast on its heels. Why not take the name literally and make super dishes to serve in bowls? Most people watch the big game sitting or standing around the television. Bowls are practical because they are much easier to handle than trying to balance a plate, the silverware, plus a glass and a napkin—especially if all of a sudden you jump out of your seat to cheer your team on to a touchdown.

Bowls

MENU

Whether you've invited over a small or a large group of fans, it's all about watching the game. So once it gets started, the fewer interruptions the better.

First of all, have enough comfy chairs, ottomans, and giant cushions for all to plop onto. If you're in a cold climate, a few warm throws are always fun and practical. Most important, make sure the television (or televisions) offers easy viewing for all.

After greeting your guests with a spicy Bloody Mary, just point them toward the setup on the kitchen island or at the buffet table. This hearty spread will provide plenty of fuel for the excitement ahead.

Have the drinks in a big cooling tub (it can be a galvanized metal tub filled with ice) or on a few shelves in the fridge—with openers close at hand—so everybody can help themselves. Roll silverware up in good-looking cotton dish towels that are large enough to cover laps while doubling as napkins. (Look for inexpensive ones on sale; they're so practical and handy to have around anyway.) Place durable stemmed goblets, tumblers, or glass mugs nearby. Set out medium-size ceramic bowls—about the size of pasta bowls—instead of plates. Wooden bowls or napkin-lined baskets can be filled with chips and pretzels. For decoration, feature a pitcher arranged with masses of large yellow mums.

Hot trays or chafing dishes are useful for the chili, ribs, and penne, all of which are best served in oven-to-table casseroles. The salad and the shrimp can go in large decorative serving bowls. Make up cookie baskets and set up the coffee pot ahead of time, so they're ready to go for the third and fourth quarters.

Just keep it coming, keep it casual, and keep the bets small!

Super Bowls

SUPPER FOR EIGHT

MISS WENDE SASSE'S
CITRON BLOODY MARY

SAUCY SHRIMP COCKTAIL WITH
KNOCKOUT COCKTAIL SAUCE

RODEO RIBS WITH
RODEO BARBECUE SAUCE

EL CID CHILI

CHOPPED COBB SALAD

PEPPER STEW AND PENNE, TOO

A COOKIE BASKET:
Molasses Cookies,
Chocolate Chip Cookies,
Chocolate Chunk Brownies

THE MUSIC

Fats Domino
Allman Brothers
Bruce Springsteen

THE DRINKS

Bloody Marys
Microbrews
Cider

THE EXTRAS

Wide shallow bowls
Hot tray
Colorful dish towels

MISS WENDE SASSE'S CITRON BLOODY MARY

Poor Mary Tudor. In her short reign on England's throne, she killed only a handful of people, which was very good behavior for a monarch in those days. Still, it was enough for her enemies to nickname her Bloody Mary, and the name has stuck. The original Bloody Mary cocktail was served up by the legendary bartender Pete Petoit at Harry's New York Bar in Paris in the 1920s. When Harry transplanted himself to New York City in the 1930s, he brought the recipe with him. He called it a Red Snapper, but Bloody Mary, as it later came to be called, is so much more memorable. My friend Wende Sasse, who always has an original flair, dreamed up the delicious idea of using Absolut Citron, with its lemony accent.

> 2 quarts tomato juice
> 24 ounces Absolut Citron vodka
> 1/2 cup fresh lemon juice (from 6 lemons)
> 4 teaspoons prepared white horseradish, drained
> 4 teaspoons Worcestershire sauce
> 3/4 to 1 teaspoon Tabasco sauce, to taste
> Celery salt, to taste
> Freshly ground black pepper, to taste
> 8 small lemon wedges
> 8 celery ribs with leaves, for garnish

1. Combine the tomato juice, vodka, lemon juice, horseradish, Worcestershire sauce, Tabasco sauce, celery salt, and pepper in a large pitcher. Stir well.

2. Fill eight highball glasses with ice and pour in the Bloody Mary mixture. Squeeze a lemon wedge into each and garnish each with a celery rib. Serve immediately.

SAUCY SHRIMP COCKTAIL

No question: The hands-down, all-time favorite American appetizer is shrimp cocktail. And for favorite dip, it is probably guacamole. Why not combine the best of both worlds? Poach the shrimp in a well seasoned white wine and vegetable broth and then toss them with a bright and tangy avocado and tomato salad. Of course, a shrimp cocktail is only as good as its cocktail sauce. This one will provide a great fanfare for the taste buds.

FOR THE SHRIMP
> 1/2 cup dry white wine
> 2 ribs celery with leaves, coarsely chopped
> 4 sprigs fresh parsley
> 6 whole black peppercorns
> 1 1/4 pounds medium-size shrimp, peeled, deveined, and well rinsed

FOR THE COCKTAIL
> 2 1/2 ripe avocados, preferably Hass, peeled, pitted, and cut into 1/2-inch pieces
> 2 1/2 tablespoons fresh lime juice
> 4 ripe plum tomatoes, cut into 1/2-inch pieces
> 1/4 cup finely diced red onion
> 1 teaspoon finely diced and seeded green jalapeño pepper
> 1 1/2 tablespoons extra-virgin olive oil
> 1 1/4 teaspoons red wine vinegar
> Salt and freshly ground black pepper, to taste
> 1/4 cup coarsely chopped fresh cilantro or flat-leaf parsley
> Knockout Cocktail Sauce (recipe follows)
> 8 large sprigs fresh cilantro or flat-leaf parsley, for garnish

1. Fill a medium-size saucepan half full with water and add the wine, celery, parsley, and

KNOCKOUT COCKTAIL SAUCE

This cocktail sauce packs just the right punch; it's sweet-tart, with a flavorful bite from the horseradish. Dip Cheddar cheese cubes and raw vegetables in it, as well as shrimp, scallops, and other chilled seafood.

1/3 cup ketchup
2 tablespoons chili sauce, such as Heinz
2 tablespoons well-drained prepared
   white horseradish
1/2 teaspoon fresh lemon juice

Combine all the ingredients in a small bowl. Cover and refrigerate for up to 1 week.
MAKES 1/2 CUP

RODEO RIBS

The Dallas Cowboys were in so many Super Bowls when my friends and I first started to gather for the game that it seemed the state of Texas needed some recognition in a Super Bowl meal. Because Texas is the home of the longhorn, no pork ribs are allowed. Instead, this recipe calls for meaty, succulent beef short ribs. Slather them with a spicy, tangy barbecue sauce with that distinctive zip typical of sauces from the Alamo to the Oklahoma border. Be sure to make the sauce at least two days before you plan to cook the ribs, to allow the flavors to develop. If you're inclined to adjust the tang or the sweetness, add more lemon juice first, and then brown sugar, a teaspoon at a time. You want to be sure to ask the butcher to cut the ribs in 2½-inch lengths so you can pick them up with your hands and just eat the meat right off the bone. If they are too long they'll be too messy, and face it—ribs are messy enough to begin with.

Saucy Shrimp Cocktail

peppercorns. Bring to a boil over high heat, reduce the heat to medium-low, add the shrimp, and simmer until the shrimp are cooked through, about 3 minutes. Drain the shrimp, run them under cold water to stop the cooking, then drain well again.

2. Toss the avocados with the lime juice in a large bowl. Using a rubber spatula, gently fold in the tomatoes, red onion, and jalapeño. Add the shrimp, olive oil and vinegar and toss. Season generously with salt and pepper, and add the chopped cilantro.

3. Serve the shrimp in a large decorative bowl, with a bowl of the sauce alongside. Garnish with sprigs of cilantro.

5. Remove the pot from the oven and stir in 2 cups of the Rodeo Barbecue Sauce. Then spoon the mixture over the ribs. Return the pot to the oven and cook, uncovered, basting the ribs once or twice, until the meat is tender and succulent, 40 minutes.

6. Remove the pot from the oven and skim off the fat. Serve the ribs, with the remaining barbecue sauce alongside.

RODEO BARBECUE SAUCE

This barbecue sauce has the kick and tang of Texas sauces. It goes with almost anything you cook on a grill, so think of it for steaks, burgers, chicken—you name it.

4 pounds beef short
  ribs, cut into 2- to
  2¹/₂-inch lengths
Coarse (kosher) salt and coarsely
  ground black pepper, to taste
2 tablespoons olive oil
1 large onion, halved lengthwise
  and slivered
1 cup Beef Broth (page 397)
Rodeo Barbecue Sauce
  (recipe follows)

2 cups ketchup
1 cup cider vinegar
¹/₄ cup Worcestershire sauce
Juice of 1 large lemon
¹/₄ cup (packed) dark brown sugar
¹/₄ cup chili powder
2 tablespoons paprika
3 cloves garlic, minced with
  ¹/₂ teaspoon coarse (kosher) salt

1. Preheat the oven to 350°F.

2. Sprinkle the ribs generously with coarse salt and pepper. Place the olive oil in a heavy Dutch oven and heat it over medium heat. Add the ribs, in batches, and brown them well on all sides, about 8 minutes per batch. Transfer the ribs to a plate.

3. Add the onion to the Dutch oven and cook over low heat until wilted, scraping up any browned bits, 8 to 10 minutes. Return the ribs to the Dutch oven, arranging them on top of the onions. Cover the pot and transfer it to the oven.

4. Bake for 30 minutes, then add the beef broth, stir, and continue to cook, covered, for another 45 minutes.

1. Combine all the ingredients plus 4 cups water in a heavy saucepan. Bring to a slow rolling boil over medium heat and cook, stirring regularly to prevent the sauce from scorching, until thickened, 25 to 30 minutes.

2. Pour the sauce through a fine-mesh strainer into a bowl to remove the garlic. Let the sauce cool to room temperature. Then transfer it to a container and refrigerate for 2 days for the flavors to blend.

MAKES 4¹/₂ CUPS

EL CID CHILI

Every year at *Parade* magazine, where I am the food editor, we hold a recipe contest for our readers. In 2000, the contest was for the "Best Chili in the USA." We received over 21,000 entries and tested and tasted hundreds, looking for Numero Uno. Here it is—Cid Prevost's winner. Each bowlful presents a generous range of textures: steak in cubes, ground beef, slices of spicy, salty chorizo sausage. And then the spices! Cumin (it isn't chili if it doesn't have cumin) and cinnamon (which is surprising yet fragrantly satisfying). And no beans—just spices, meat, onions, tomatoes, and as much peppery heat as you can stand.

2 tablespoons olive oil
2 pounds boneless sirloin steak,
   cut into 1-inch cubes
8 ounces lean ground beef
12 ounces chorizo sausage, casings removed,
   cut into 1/2-inch cubes
1 large onion, coarsely chopped
1/4 cup chili powder
1 tablespoon garlic salt
2 teaspoons ground cumin
1 teaspoon dried basil
2 cans (14.5 ounces each) peeled whole
   tomatoes, undrained
2 cans (14.5 ounces each) beef broth
1 cup chopped fresh cilantro
1 cinnamon stick (3 inches long)
3 bay leaves
2 green jalapeño peppers, each slit
   lengthwise in 3 places
1 tablespoon yellow cornmeal
Salt and freshly ground black pepper,
   to taste
Freshly grated Cheddar cheese, for garnish
Sour cream, for garnish
4 scallions, including 3 inches green,
   thinly sliced on the diagonal,
   for garnish

1. Heat the olive oil in a large heavy pot over medium heat. Add the sirloin cubes, in batches, and brown them on all sides, about 6 minutes per batch. Use a slotted spoon to transfer the browned cubes to a bowl. Add the ground beef, chorizo, and onion to the pot and cook, breaking up the ground beef with the back of the spoon, until the beef is browned, about 8 minutes. Return the sirloin cubes to the pot.

2. Stir in the chili powder, garlic salt, cumin, and basil. Add the tomatoes, broth, cilantro, cinnamon stick, bay leaves, jalapeños, and cornmeal and stir. Season with salt and pepper.

3. Bring the chili to a boil, then reduce the heat to medium-low and simmer, uncovered, for 2 hours. Stir the chili occasionally, breaking up the tomatoes with a spoon. The consistency will be chunky and the aroma fragrant.

4. Before serving, remove and discard the cinnamon stick, bay leaves, and jalapeños. Place the grated cheese, sour cream, and scallions in small bowls near the chili so your guests can garnish their servings as they like.

CHOPPED COBB SALAD

If the Super Bowl is the all-American TV show, the Cobb salad is equally the all-American salad. The legend is that Robert Cobb, the owner of Hollywood's famous Brown Derby (where Clark Gable proposed to Carole Lombard), created this dish for Sid Grauman, of Grauman's Chinese Theater. When the two Hollywood old-timers were hungry late one night, Cobb opened the refrigerator at his nightspot and proceeded to chop up everything at hand—the first Cobb salad. I've expanded the mixture even further by adding some ham and crunchy radishes.

FOR THE VINAIGRETTE

1/4 cup red wine vinegar
2 tablespoons fresh lemon juice
2 teaspoons sugar
1/4 teaspoon dry mustard
Salt and freshly ground black pepper, to taste
1 teaspoon finely minced garlic
1/2 cup extra-virgin olive oil

FOR THE SALAD

2 heads romaine lettuce, trimmed, rinsed,
   patted dry, and cut into 1/2-inch pieces
6 ripe plum tomatoes, seeded and cut into
   1/4-inch dice
12 red radishes, trimmed and cut into
   1/4-inch dice
6 scallions, including 3 inches green,
   thinly sliced on the diagonal
8 ounces baked Virginia ham,
   in 1 slice, cut into 1/4-inch dice
2 cooked whole skinless, boneless chicken
   breasts (see Note, page 260), cut into
   1/4-inch dice
4 hard-cooked eggs (page 9), quartered
   and sliced
2 ripe avocados, preferably Hass, peeled,
   pitted, and chopped
24 slices cooked bacon, crumbled
1/2 cup snipped fresh chives (1-inch pieces)
Salt and freshly ground black pepper, to taste
8 ounces Roquefort cheese, crumbled

1. Prepare the vinaigrette: Whisk the vinegar, lemon juice, sugar, mustard, salt and pepper, and garlic in a small bowl. Whisking constantly, drizzle in the olive oil. Continue whisking until the dressing has thickened slightly. Set aside.

2. Combine the lettuce, tomatoes, radishes, scallions, ham, chicken, eggs, avocados, bacon, and 1/4 cup of the chives in a large serving bowl. Season with salt and pepper.

3. Just before serving, toss the salad with the vinaigrette and scatter the Roquefort over it. Sprinkle with the remaining 1/4 cup chives.

Note: If you're serving this at a sit-down dinner, cut the avocados into 12 thin slices instead of chopping them, and leave the cooked bacon slices whole. Combine the salad, minus the avocados and bacon, and toss it with the dressing. Mound the salad in individual bowls, and surround each serving with 3 strips of bacon and 3 slices of avocado, arranged alternately on edge to form a rim around the salad. Place a spoonful of the cheese on top of each salad, and sprinkle with the remaining 1/4 cup chives.

PEPPER STEW AND PENNE, TOO

There are three good reasons to serve pasta as part of a party spread. First, just about everybody loves it. Second, meatless sauces offer something for the vegetarians in the group. And third, nearly every youngster will, when all else fails, dive into a bowl of pasta. The bell peppers and tomatoes are slow-cooked to coax out their deep sweetness for a flavor that is full and powerful but pleasantly light on the tummy.

1/2 cup extra-virgin olive oil,
   plus extra for drizzling
8 cloves garlic, thinly sliced lengthwise
2 cans (14 ounces each) peeled Italian
   plum tomatoes, chopped, with their juices
2 teaspoons sugar
8 red bell peppers, stemmed, seeded,
   and cut into generous 1-inch pieces
8 yellow bell peppers, stemmed, seeded,
   and cut into generous 1-inch pieces
1 cup dry red wine
2 cups torn fresh basil leaves, plus
   1 large sprig fresh basil
Salt and freshly ground black pepper, to taste
1 1/2 pounds dried penne
Freshly grated Parmesan cheese, for serving

1. Heat ¼ cup of the olive oil in a heavy saucepan over low heat. Add half the garlic and cook until soft, stirring occasionally, 3 minutes. Add the tomatoes and sugar and cook until thickened, about 30 minutes. Set the tomato sauce aside.

2. Heat the remaining ¼ cup oil in another heavy saucepan over medium-low heat and add all the remaining garlic and the bell peppers. Cook, stirring occasionally, until soft, 30 minutes.

3. Add the tomato sauce, wine, torn basil, and the basil sprig to the peppers. Cook over medium-low heat, partially covered, stirring occasionally, to blend the flavors, 30 minutes. Add a bit of water if the sauce gets too thick. Remove the sprig of basil and season the sauce with salt and pepper.

4. Meanwhile, bring a large pot of salted water to a boil over high heat. Add the penne to the boiling water and cook until just tender, 10 to 12 minutes. Drain the pasta well and toss it with the sauce. Drizzle with a little olive oil and serve in a large bowl, with the grated Parmesan cheese alongside.

MOLASSES COOKIES

For nearly two centuries (until it was replaced by refined sugar), molasses was the sweetener of choice for most American homemakers. Dark, rich, sweet, this is the comforting cookie to enjoy in front of an equally warming fireplace. The combination of aromatic spices and sweet cookie dough is traditional all over Europe during the holidays, and who knows, this cookie could have been the inspiration for the term "sugar and spice and everything nice."

A COOKIE BASKET

Consider the cookie. Most culinary histories say it was an afterthought to cake making. You made your cake and from what was left of the batter or pastry, you baked a few little cakes for the children. Some afterthought! Maybe the attraction is partly psychological. With a cake, you are committing yourself to the whole piece. With cookies, you can tell yourself that you're just going to have one. Never mind that you don't have a prayer of following through on that resolve. Another virtue is that there is no better way to soothe jittery nerves when rooting for your team to win the Super Bowl. Munching on a homemade cookie or brownie will ease you through the game. Psychology apart, cookies are sweet and crunchy, which are two of the finest virtues of any food. Here are cookies to please every cookie-crunching palate—and a brownie, too?

12 tablespoons (1½ sticks) unsalted butter
2 cups plus 2 tablespoons sugar
¼ cup molasses, preferably "light"
1 large egg, beaten
1¾ cups all-purpose flour
1 teaspoon ground cinnamon
½ teaspoon ground cloves
½ teaspoon ground ginger
½ teaspoon salt
½ teaspoon baking soda

1. Melt the butter in a small saucepan over medium heat. Pour the butter into a mixing bowl, and add 1 cup plus 2 tablespoons of the sugar and the molasses. Beat with an electric mixer until smooth, 2 to 3 minutes. Allow to cool to room temperature. Then add the egg and beat on medium speed until well combined, 2 minutes.

2. Sift the flour, spices, salt, and baking soda together in another bowl. Add the flour mixture to the butter mixture and beat on low speed until just incorporated. Gather the dough into a ball, flatten it into a disk, wrap in plastic wrap, and refrigerate it for 30 minutes.

3. Meanwhile, preheat the oven to 375°F. Line two baking sheets with parchment paper.

4. Form the dough into walnut-size balls, rolling them between the palms of your hands. Fill one small bowl with water and another with the remaining 1 cup sugar. Lightly dip half of each ball into the water and then into the sugar. Place the dough balls on the prepared baking sheets, sugar side up. Flatten them slightly with the bottom of a glass. They should be ½ inch thick.

5. Bake until the cookies are just turning golden brown at the edges, 10 to 15 minutes. Allow the cookies to cool on the baking sheets on a wire rack for 3 minutes. Then use a spatula to transfer the cookies to wire racks to cool completely.

MAKES 24 COOKIES

CHOCOLATE CHIP COOKIES

Here is a legend. In 1930 Ruth and Kenneth Wakefield bought an old inn on the road that runs from Boston to New Bedford. It was called the Toll House Inn and it had a reputation for scrumptious food. Ruth was quite the baker, and one day she decided to make chocolate cookies by adapting an old colonial-era butter cookie recipe. Ruth didn't have any cocoa on hand, so she chopped up a Nestlé chocolate bar and put the bits in the dough. Rather than melting and disappearing during the baking, they held their shape. And thus was born the chocolate chip cookie, the all-time number-one favorite homemade American cookie (the Oreo is the favorite store-bought).

> 1 cup (2 sticks) unsalted butter, at room temperature
> 1½ cups (packed) light brown sugar
> 6 tablespoons sugar
> 2 large eggs, beaten
> 2 teaspoons pure vanilla extract
> ½ teaspoon salt
> 1 teaspoon baking soda, dissolved in 1 teaspoon boiling water
> 2 cups all-purpose flour
> 1 cup semisweet chocolate chips
> 1 cup pecans, toasted (see box, page 104) and coarsely chopped

1. Position a rack in the center of the oven, and preheat the oven to 350°F. Lightly butter two or three baking sheets, or line them with parchment paper.

2. Cream the butter in a large bowl with an electric mixer until light, 4 minutes. Add both sugars and continue to beat until light and fluffy, 5 to 8 minutes. With the mixer on low speed, add the eggs and beat until creamy, about 5 minutes more.

3. Add the vanilla, salt, and dissolved baking soda, and mix on low speed to combine. Add the flour, still on low speed, scraping down the bowl once or twice. Stir in the chocolate chips and pecans.

4. Drop the dough by heaping tablespoons, 2 inches apart, on the prepared baking sheets. Bake, rotating the baking sheets as necessary for even baking, until the cookies no longer look raw in the center and are golden brown, 8 to 10 minutes. Cool the cookies on the baking sheets for 5 minutes. Then, using a spatula, transfer them to wire racks to cool completely. Store these cookies in an airtight container for up to 5 days.

MAKES 24 COOKIES

CHOCOLATE CHUNK BROWNIES

These brownies are what you would expect from the perfect brownie in texture, taste, and size. Fill up a basket, serve with a glass of cold milk—one of those great fifties striped glasses—or mix them in with the cookies. Bake them a little fudgy!

1 cup (2 sticks) unsalted butter

6 ounces semisweet chocolate, coarsely chopped

2 ounces unsweetened chocolate, coarsely chopped

3 cups (packed) light brown sugar

6 large eggs, lightly beaten

1½ cups coarsely chopped bittersweet chocolate

1 teaspoon pure vanilla extract

1 tablespoon cognac

2 cups all-purpose flour

¾ teaspoon salt

1 teaspoon baking powder

¼ teaspoon ground cinnamon

1. Position a rack in the center of the oven and preheat the oven to 350°F. Butter a 17 x 12 x 1-inch sheet pan, and line the bottom with a piece of wax or parchment paper. Butter the paper and then dust the pan with flour, tapping out any excess.

2. Melt the butter in a large saucepan over low heat. Add the semisweet and unsweetened chocolate. Stir occasionally until melted. Add the brown sugar and stir to combine. Remove the pan from the heat and scrape the mixture into a large bowl. Add the eggs and mix with an electric mixer on low speed until just incorporated. Stir in the bittersweet chocolate, vanilla, and cognac.

3. Sift the flour, salt, baking powder, and cinnamon together in a large bowl. Add the flour mixture to the chocolate mixture, beating with an electric mixer on low speed until just combined.

4. Scrape the batter into the prepared sheet pan and smooth the top with a spatula. Bake until a wooden toothpick inserted into the center comes out just clean, 20 to 25 minutes. Do not overbake. Let the brownies cool completely in the pan on a wire rack. Once they have cooled, cut them into pieces. (For very cleanly cut brownies, chill them before cutting.)

MAKES 24 BROWNIES

Valentines Served

Like most people, I am in love with love . . . and with food, so I could not conceive of love's special day without a romantic, sensual, and exciting meal. Did St. Valentine have a Mrs. St. Valentine? The history books are unclear on this. In those days priests could marry, so I like to think that Valentine, Bishop of Terni, had someone special in his life before he was martyred in A.D. 27. In any event, he became the patron saint of lovers, and all over the world his feast day, February 14, is associated with

romance. So bring on the champagne and chocolates and here's to love!

MENU

Valentines Served with Love

DINNER FOR FOUR

Kir Royale

Oysters with Mignonette Sauce

Lobster Potpie

A Romantic Little Salad

Mini Coeurs à la Crème

Raspberry Linzer Hearts

Dinner for a Valentine's Day celebration needs to be romantic, but need not only be for two. Invite your newly engaged daughter and her fiancé over to share in this indulgence. A Kir Royale is a beautiful blush color, so immediately we're there. Word is that oysters are an aphrodisiac. Whether that can be proved scientifically doesn't matter—in the right setting they are just the food for the mood. The pièce de résistance is Lobster Potpie, all pink and yummy. End the dinner as romantically as it began with heart-shaped Mini Coeurs à la Crème and Fresh Strawberry Sauce.

For the table, think pink: Find the prettiest pink plates you can—ones with decorative rims or an all-over pattern of cabbage roses or tiny flowers. Pull out the crystal or other heavy candlesticks—as ornate and dangly as possible. Use a white damask cloth and drape antique lace on top. Hit the flea markets for silver napkin rings and cranberry glass. Cut-glass wineglasses have a particularly lovely sparkly effect. Add an arrangement of sweet peas or pink carnations. Next to each plate, set a tiny nosegay of double narcissi, with their lovely, creamy fragrance, tied with pink streamers on a paper doily, because you can never be too romantic.

THE MUSIC

Frank Sinatra's
Songs for Young Lovers
Chopin Preludes

THE DRINKS

Kir Royale
Premier or Grand Cru Chablis

THE EXTRAS

Champagne flutes
Oyster forks
Individual soufflé dishes
Coeur à la crème molds
Heart-shaped cookie cutters

KIR ROYALE

The deep ruby color of the black currant syrup the French call *cassis* and the bubbly gold of the champagne make for as romantic a drink as ever was poured. Rubies and gold for Valentine's Day.

> *4 ounces crème de cassis or raspberry syrup*
> *4 splits (6.34 ounces each) or*
> *   1 bottle chilled champagne*
> *8 fresh raspberries*

Pour 1 ounce crème de cassis into each of four champagne flutes. Top each flute off with chilled champagne, and garnish with the raspberries.

OYSTERS WITH MIGNONETTE SAUCE

Oysters and love—why do they seem to go together? It hardly matters how they got their romantic reputation, oysters are hard to leave out of a Valentine's menu. Mignonette sauce, with its sharp tang, is traditional with briny oysters.

> *1/2 cup sherry vinegar*
> *1/4 cup very finely chopped shallots*
> *Freshly ground white pepper, to taste*
> *Coarse (kosher) salt, fresh seaweed,*
> *   or crushed ice, for nesting the oysters*
> *24 assorted oysters, shucked*
> *   (see Note)*
> *2 lemons, cut in half, seeds removed*

1. Combine the vinegar, shallots, and white pepper in a small bowl and set it aside.

American servicemen helped spread this very American celebration in Europe right after World War II. In Japan, schoolgirls sometimes give special candies as a consolation prize to boys who don't have a girlfriend. When those girls grow up, they are the ones who buy the chocolates for their loves.

2. Neatly spread a thick bed of coarse salt, seaweed, or crushed ice on a large pretty platter. Nest the oysters attractively on the bed (when it comes to serving oysters, presentation is most important!). Arrange the lemon halves on the platter, as well. If they don't fit, place them in a small bowl.

3. Place the platter of oysters in the center of the table with the mignonette sauce (and lemons, if serving separately) at its side. And don't forget the delicate oyster forks and small spoons for spooning some of the sauce on each oyster.

Note: A few favorite oysters include Pacific Kumamoto, belon, and Maine bluepoint. Have the fishmonger shuck the oysters, placing each variety in its own marked container. The shells should also be stored separately and marked. This way you will be able to reassemble them correctly for serving.

LOBSTER POTPIE

As long as we're serving the most luxurious foods of the ocean, we have to include lobster—sweet, rich, buttery tasting. Baked in a crisp crust with a creamy sauce and the same vegetables you would put in a chicken potpie, this is a sensuous variation on the traditional.

1 tablespoon unsalted butter

1 tablespoon olive oil

1 cup diced onion ($1/4$-inch dice)

1 tablespoon minced garlic

3 tablespoons all-purpose flour

2 carrots, peeled and cut into $1/2$-inch dice

1 cup diced peeled russet potato ($1/2$-inch dice)

$1^{1}/2$ cups Basic Chicken Broth (page 397),
*   or more if needed*

$1/2$ cup heavy (whipping) cream

$1/2$ cup green peas, thawed if frozen

$1/2$ cup corn kernels, thawed if frozen

$1/2$ cup diced seeded plum tomatoes

3 tablespoons chopped fresh tarragon leaves

2 teaspoons finely grated orange zest

2 cups cooked lobster meat (see Note)
*   cut into chunks*

Salt and freshly ground black pepper, to taste

1 large egg

14 ounces frozen puff pastry, thawed in
*   the refrigerator*

Tarragon sprigs, for garnish

1. Melt the butter in the olive oil in a large heavy pot over low heat. Add the onion and cook, stirring, until soft, 5 minutes. Add the garlic and cook for another 3 minutes. Sprinkle with the flour, stir, and cook to form a paste, 1 minute longer.

2. Stir in the carrots, potatoes, broth, and cream. Increase the heat to medium and bring to a boil. Reduce to medium-low and simmer, partially covered, until the vegetables are tender and the sauce has thickened, 20 minutes. Add the peas, corn, tomatoes, tarragon, orange zest, and lobster. Simmer for 5 minutes to blend the flavors. If the mixture is too thick, add 2 more tablespoons broth. Season with salt and pepper and set aside.

3. Preheat the oven to 350°F.

4. Beat the egg and 1 tablespoon water together in a small bowl. Place $1^{1}/2$ cups of the lobster mixture in each of four individual (13.5-ounce) soufflé dishes.

5. Lay a sheet of puff pastry on a lightly floured surface and roll it out $1/8$ inch thick. Cut out four

rounds of puff pastry, each 2 inches larger than the diameter of the soufflé dishes. Brush the egg wash over the inside and outside rim of the soufflé dishes. Lay the pastry over the top of each dish, trim the overhang to 1 inch, and crimp the edges around the rim to form a tight seal. Cut several slits in the center of the pastry to allow the steam to escape and brush it with the remaining egg wash.

6. Place the dishes on a baking sheet and bake until the crust is golden and puffed, 40 to 45 minutes. Serve immediately, garnished with the tarragon sprigs.

Note: Generally a $1^{1}/2$-pound lobster will yield 1 cup of meat. For cooking instructions, see Steamed Lobsters, page 152.

A ROMANTIC LITTLE SALAD

In love and salad, a light touch often succeeds where coming on strong fails. When a romantic dinner calls for a kiss of a salad, crisp light greens and a touch of fruit is the solution, and in the middle of February there is nothing nicer than a clementine orange and mâche. Garnish the servings with delicate pink rose petals for a romantic flourish.

6 cups frisée lettuce leaves, separated, rinsed,
*   and patted dry*

2 cups (loosely packed) mâche leaves

1 cup diced peeled hothouse (seedless)
*   cucumber ($1/4$-inch dice)*

6 clementines, peeled and segmented,
*   membranes completely removed*

Salt and freshly ground black pepper,
*   to taste*

6 tablespoons Sherry Vinaigrette (page 263)
*   or Tangerine Vinaigrette (page 227)*

1 cup small pink edible fresh rose petals
*   (optional)*

Lobster Potpie

Combine the frisée, mâche, cucumber, and clementines in a large bowl and toss gently. Just before serving, season with salt and pepper and toss with the vinaigrette. Garnish with the rose petals if desired.

Mâche, also known as corn salad, is a delicate green favored by gourmet chefs of the last decade or so. It is also known as lamb's lettuce—some say because its small leaves resemble lamb's tongues. Others think the name stems from the lambs' preference for this tender green while grazing in the pasture.

MINI COEURS A LA CREME

Literally "a little heart of cream"—surely a dessert invented by a poet and lover. In the United States, it is a traditional Valentine's Day dessert because of its heart shape. In France, where it originated, every day is for lovers, so they just serve it when they are in the mood, which, rumor has it, is most of the time. Creamy, sweet, with what the wine tasters call "a long finish," it is just the kind of dessert to linger over and savor.

4 ounces cottage cheese, drained (see Note)
6 ounces cream cheese,
  at room temperature
1½ tablespoons crumbled soft mild goat
  cheese, such as Montrachet (without ash)
1½ tablespoons confectioners' sugar
½ cup heavy (whipping) cream
Fresh Strawberry Sauce (recipe follows),
  for serving

1. At least 1 day before serving, blend the cheeses together in a food processor until smooth. Add the confectioners' sugar and process until smooth. With the machine running, slowly add the cream through the feed tube and process until thoroughly incorporated.

2. Place four ⅓-cup ceramic *coeur* molds on a large rimmed baking sheet or in a large baking pan. Line the molds with a single layer of slightly dampened cheesecloth, allowing for a 1-inch overhang.

3. Fill the molds with the cheese mixture and refrigerate until the cheese is firmly set, about 24 hours. (Discard the watery drippings.)

4. About an hour before serving, unmold the *coeurs* onto individual dessert plates. (This gives them time to return to room temperature.) Just before serving, spoon some Fresh Strawberry Sauce over the tops.

Note: Place the cottage cheese in a strainer and tap or press it lightly with a spoon to get rid of the excess liquid.

FRESH STRAWBERRY SAUCE

Not so long ago, fresh strawberries would have been impossible to find in February. Not so anymore. If they aren't available in your area, however, the whole frozen berries found in bags in the supermarket make a fine sauce. Thaw the berries before getting started.

3 cups ripe strawberries
2 tablespoons sugar
1 tablespoon fresh lemon juice

Hull, then lightly rinse the berries and drain them well. Cut the berries into coarse ½-inch pieces and place them in a large bowl. Add the sugar and lemon juice and toss gently. Let rest at room temperature for 2 to 3 hours for the juices to form. Refrigerate, covered, for up to 6 hours.

RASPBERRY LINZER HEARTS

These delicate confections are ideal to serve alongside any cup of coffee or tea, and they always dazzle as a dessert. Try to find a good-quality raspberry jam for the filling. Apricot jam is lovely too—but save it for a non-red occasion.

> 8 tablespoons (1 stick) unsalted butter, at room temperature
> ¹/₂ cup confectioners' sugar, plus extra for dusting
> ¹/₂ teaspoon pure vanilla extract
> 1 cup all-purpose flour
> ¹/₄ cup ground blanched almonds
> 1 teaspoon finely grated lemon zest
> ¹/₄ teaspoon ground cinnamon
> About ¹/₂ cup seedless raspberry jam

Mini Coeurs à la Crème with Fresh Strawberry Sauce

1. Lightly butter two baking sheets, or line them with parchment paper.

2. Cream the butter with the confectioners' sugar and vanilla in a bowl with an electric mixer on medium speed until the mixture is light and fluffy, about 2 minutes.

3. Place the flour, almonds, and lemon zest in a food processor and process until completely smooth. Add this to the butter mixture along with the cinnamon and mix on low speed until just combined.

4. Form the dough into a ¹/₂-inch-thick disk on a piece of plastic wrap, wrap it well, and chill for 1 hour.

5. Place the dough between two pieces of floured wax or parchment paper and roll it out to ¹/₈ inch thick. Using a 3¹/₂-inch heart-shaped cookie cutter, cut out 20 hearts. Use a smaller, 1³/₄-inch heart-shaped cutter to cut out the center of 10 of the cookies.

6. Using a spatula, gently transfer the cookies to the prepared baking sheets, spacing them about ¹/₂ inch apart. Refrigerate the cookies for 30 minutes.

7. Meanwhile, position a rack in the center of the oven, and preheat the oven to 325°F.

8. Bake the cookies, rotating the baking sheets to ensure even baking, until they are just turning golden brown, 15 to 20 minutes.

9. Let the cookies cool on the sheets for about 5 minutes, then transfer them to a wire rack to cool completely.

10. Melt the raspberry jam in a small saucepan over low heat. Spread the jam evenly over the top of the 10 whole hearts. Cover them with the cookies with the cut-out centers, bottom (flat) side up, to make a sandwich. Liberally sift confectioners' sugar over the cookies. Store, flat, covered with plastic wrap, for up to 2 days.

MAKES 10 COOKIES

St. Patrick's

Day Feast

Surprisingly—or maybe not so surprisingly—St. Patrick's Day is a bigger deal in the United States than it is in Ireland. True, the evangelizing monk is the patron saint of the Emerald Isle, but it was in America that Irish immigrants made March 17 a day of celebration, as a show of national pride. According to historians, the tradition was first observed in 1737 by the Charitable Irish Society of Boston.

In my hometown, New York City, St. Patrick's Day is marked by a huge parade on Fifth Avenue, and all of Manhattan—the streets, the restaurants, the subways and buses—is a sea of green. Everyone, it seems, is Irish for the day, and a celebratory gathering is appreciated even by those only temporarily touched by a leprechaun.

MENU

I n New York, St. Patrick's Day also often marks the opening of flounder season. Fishermen and -women look forward to reeling up a glistening fresh one from our beautiful coastal waters. So it seems only natural to include a flounder on the menu. The soothing Potato Leek Soup is welcome, especially if the day has a chill to it and appetites are running hearty. Corned beef and cabbage—so traditional— is a must. Pistachio ice cream and oatmeal cookies (made with Irish oatmeal, of course) offer a tasty, not-too- heavy ending.

The color scheme is easy— St. Patrick's Day means green. But there's no need to rush out and buy green plates, or to resort to the local party store's selection. Use whatever china you have, and maybe a tablecloth with green accents. Of course white Irish linen would be very elegant. Because beer is the drink of choice with this menu, set out cut-glass tumblers or hefty stemmed goblets.

For floral decorations, try young

lush spring grasses potted in small clay pots or wooden boxes. Look, too, for the delicate pots of shamrocks that are often sold in flower shops around St. Patrick's Day. Choose what suits your room—formal or informal—or just mix them all up.

For a cheerful final touch, serve bowls of green candy-coated after-dinner mints with the coffee.

St. Patrick's Day Feast

DINNER FOR EIGHT

Potato Leek Soup

Lemon-Mustard Broiled Flounder

Corned Beef and Cabbage
with Horseradish Cream and Cumberland Sauce

A Bouquet of Root Vegetables

Irish Soda Bread Rolls

Pistachio Ice-Cream Sundae with Silky Chocolate Sauce

Little Oatmeal Cookies

Irish Coffee

THE MUSIC

Van Morrison
The Chieftains
James Galway

THE DRINKS

Harp Lager
Harpoon Hibernian Style Ale
Killian's Irish Red
Irish Coffee

THE EXTRAS

Irish coffee mugs or glasses
Ice-cream maker

POTATO LEEK SOUP

Served cold, creamy, smooth potato and leek soup is known as vichyssoise, which would lead you to think that the recipe is French. It is, sort of. The basic soup—potato and leek—is well loved in the French countryside, but French chef Louis Diat didn't swirl cream into it until 1917, when he was in New York, working at the Ritz Hotel. Diat created vichyssoise for the party that celebrated the first issue of *Vanity Fair* magazine.

Once the potatoes are sliced, keep them submerged in cold water until you add them to the pan, so they don't discolor. This soup is rich, so small portions are recommended. The green accent of chives gives the soup its St. Paddy's Day feel.

4 leeks
2 tablespoons distilled white vinegar
2 tablespoons unsalted butter
2 tablespoons extra-virgin olive oil
2 onions, halved and thinly sliced
2 large cloves garlic, chopped
4 russet potatoes (about 8 ounces each),
   peeled and thinly sliced
5 cups Basic Chicken Broth (page 397)
2 tablespoons fresh lemon juice
Salt and freshly ground black pepper,
   to taste
2½ cups heavy (whipping) cream
2 cups whole milk
¼ cup snipped fresh chives, for garnish
Chive blossoms, if available, for garnish

1. Trim the roots and tough outer leaves from the leeks and discard them. Trim the remaining leaves to about 2 inches. Cut the leeks in half lengthwise. Stir the vinegar into a large bowl of water, add the leeks, and soak for 30 minutes. Then rinse, drain, and dice the leeks.

Legend has it that Patrick, who was originally called Maewyn, preached to the accompaniment of spirited drumming. The combination of his fiery sermons and the loud drumming is said to have frightened every last serpent out of Ireland.

2. Melt the butter in the olive oil in a large heavy pot over low heat. Add the leeks, onions, and garlic and cook, stirring occasionally, until well softened, 15 minutes.

3. Add the potatoes, broth, and lemon juice. Raise the heat to medium-high and bring to a boil. Then reduce the heat to medium-low and simmer, partially covered, until the potatoes are tender, 40 minutes. Season with salt and pepper and allow to cool slightly.

4. Puree the soup, in batches, in a blender, leaving a bit of texture. Transfer the pureed soup to a clean pot and stir in the cream and milk. Season to taste. If serving the soup hot, reheat it very slowly over low heat; do not boil. If serving it cold, chill it well. Serve the soup garnished with chives and chive blossoms, if available.

LEMON-MUSTARD BROILED FLOUNDER

Whether you catch it or buy it, flounder and all other white-fleshed flatfishes (halibut, fluke, and sole, for example) are almost magically transformed when broiled with a flavored butter. Here the butter has a browned nuttiness that combines with lemon zest, mustard, and garlic to make for a delicate dish with forceful flavor.

6 tablespoons (³/₄ stick) unsalted butter,
  at room temperature
4 teaspoons Dijon mustard
2 teaspoons finely grated lemon zest
2 tablespoons chopped fresh flat-leaf parsley
8 flounder fillets (4 ounces each)
Clover or alfalfa sprouts, for garnish
2 lemons, quartered, for serving

1. Place the butter in a small bowl and mix in the mustard, lemon zest, and parsley. Set it aside.

2. Position the oven or broiler rack 4 inches from the heat and preheat the broiler.

3. Line two baking sheets with aluminum foil. Oil the foil lightly. Arrange 4 flounder fillets on each baking sheet, spacing them evenly.

4. Spread 2 to 3 teaspoons of the butter mixture over each fillet. Broil until the fish is lightly browned on top and just cooked through, 4 to 5 minutes. Do not let it overcook.

5. Serve immediately, each portion garnished with a flourish of clover sprouts and a lemon wedge.

CORNED BEEF AND CABBAGE

Originally an Easter meal in Ireland, corned beef and cabbage is now the traditional St. Patrick's Day feast. Root vegetables and cured beef, slowly simmered to coax out the flavors, makes for a deep, delicate combination of tastes. Horseradish sauce offers a colorful contrast with the dark red meat, but don't ignore the festive Cumberland Sauce—it's just too delicious with corned beef.

14 carrots
3 ribs celery, with leaves
1 fresh first-cut corned beef (4 to 5 pounds)
2 onions, unpeeled
8 whole cloves
4 large cloves garlic
6 sprigs fresh flat-leaf parsley
Zest of 1 orange, removed in 1 long strip
  with a paring knife (see Note)
8 leeks
2 tablespoons distilled white vinegar
1 green cabbage (3 to 3¹/₂ pounds)
16 small red-skinned new potatoes,
  unpeeled, scrubbed
Salt and freshly ground black pepper,
  to taste
4 tablespoons coarsely chopped fresh
  flat-leaf parsley
Horseradish Cream (recipe follows),
  for serving
Dijon mustard, for serving
Cumberland Sauce (recipe follows),
  for serving

1. Peel 6 of the carrots and cut them in half. Cut the celery into thirds.

2. Gently rinse the corned beef and pat it dry. Place it in a large flameproof casserole. Stud the onions with the cloves and add them to the casserole along with the carrot halves, the celery, and the garlic, parsley sprigs, and orange zest. Cover all with cold water and bring to a boil over high heat. Reduce the heat to medium and simmer, partially covered, until the meat is very tender, 3 hours. While it is cooking, skim off any foam and turn the meat every 30 minutes.

3. Meanwhile, trim the roots and the tough outer leaves from the leeks and discard. Trim the remaining leaves to about 2 inches, and cut the leeks in half lengthwise. Stir the vinegar into a large bowl of water, add the leeks, and leave for 30 minutes. Then rinse and drain the leeks.

4. Core the cabbage and remove the tough outer leaves. Cut the cabbage into 8 wedges. Peel the remaining 8 carrots and cut them into 2¹/₂-inch lengths.

5. When the meat can be easily pierced with a fork, transfer it to a plate and cover it with aluminum foil to keep it warm.

6. Strain the broth, discarding the vegetables, and return it to the casserole. Add the potatoes, leeks, cabbage, and remaining carrots. Season with salt and pepper. Bring to a boil over high heat, reduce the heat to medium-low, and simmer, uncovered, until the vegetables are tender, 25 to 30 minutes. Stir in 2 tablespoons of the chopped parsley.

7. To serve, slice the corned beef. Place the slices on a large decorative serving platter and arrange the vegetables around them. Ladle some of the hot broth over all and sprinkle with the remaining 2 tablespoons parsley. Serve with the Horseradish Cream, mustard, and Cumberland Sauce alongside.

Note: Use a paring knife to remove the orange zest in one long strip, working your way from the top around the orange to the bottom.

HORSERADISH CREAM

This sauce is one of the most versatile. Served with both meat and fish, it is de rigueur on my table when I serve a standing rib roast, corned beef and cabbage, or smoked trout.

³/₄ cup heavy (whipping) cream
¹/₂ cup prepared mayonnaise,
  such as Hellmann's
¹/₂ cup prepared white horseradish, drained
2 tablespoons Dijon mustard
¹/₈ teaspoon sugar
Salt and freshly ground black pepper,
  to taste

1. Whip the cream in a bowl with an electric mixer until it forms soft peaks.

2. Combine the mayonnaise, horseradish, and mustard in another bowl; stir well. Add the sugar and the salt and pepper and stir well. Using a rubber spatula, fold in the whipped cream. Transfer to a serving bowl. This sauce will keep in the refrigerator, covered, for up to 2 days.

MAKES 2 CUPS

CUMBERLAND SAUCE

This luscious sauce is to corned beef what mint jelly is to lamb. The English and Irish enjoy their fruit sauces with many savory dishes, and Cumberland Sauce, all rosy with its appealing combination of ruby port and red currant jelly, is also delicious served alongside platters of cold meats and poultry. Oranges and lemons are always a part of the recipe, but crystallized ginger is a bit untraditional. The sauce thickens as it chills.

1¹/₂ cups red currant jelly
1 cup ruby port
Finely grated zest and juice of 1 orange
Finely grated zest and juice of 1 lemon
1 large shallot, very finely minced
1 tablespoon English mustard powder
1¹/₂ teaspoons ground ginger
1 teaspoon finely minced crystallized
  ginger
Salt and freshly ground black pepper,
  to taste
1 tablespoon cornstarch
1 tablespoon water

1. Combine the jelly, port, orange zest and juice, lemon zest and juice, shallot, mustard, both gingers, and salt and pepper in a saucepan. Bring to a boil over high heat, then reduce the heat to medium-low and cook, stirring, until the jelly melts, about 5 minutes.

2. Meanwhile, mix the cornstarch and water together. Whisking constantly over medium heat, drizzle the cornstarch mixture into the jelly mixture. Continue whisking until the mixture thickens slightly, about 5 minutes.

3. Remove the sauce from the heat and allow it to cool to room temperature. Let it rest for about 30 minutes longer, then cover and refrigerate. It will keep for up to 1 week.

MAKES ABOUT 2 CUPS

A BOUQUET OF ROOT VEGETABLES

Don't be fooled by the unspectacular looks of root vegetables. When roasted, they develop a deep, nutty, caramelized intensity that is focused and heightened by a dusting of herbs from the Mediterranean kitchen. Serve this versatile platter with any major roast—meat or poultry. It's good with salmon, too, for that matter. And it's a special treat for your vegetarian guests.

8 parsnips, peeled and cut in half lengthwise and into thirds crosswise
8 carrots, peeled and cut in half lengthwise and into thirds crosswise
6 white turnips, peeled and cut into 1-inch cubes
4 beets, peeled and cut into 1-inch cubes
¼ cup olive oil
2 teaspoons herbes de Provence
Salt and freshly ground black pepper, to taste
3 tablespoons sugar
2 to 3 tablespoons snipped fresh chives

Corned Beef and Cabbage

1. Preheat the oven to 450°F. Fit a large pot with a vegetable steamer, add water to reach just below the bottom of the steamer, and bring to a boil over high heat.

2. Steam the parsnips until tender, 8 to 10 minutes. Transfer them to a large bowl. Repeat with the carrots, turnips, and beets, steaming each vegetable separately for 8 to 10 minutes.

3. Toss the vegetables with the olive oil, herbes de Provence, and salt and pepper.

4. Spread the vegetables in a single layer on two baking sheets and sprinkle them with the sugar. Roast, shaking the pans occasionally, until the vegetables are golden brown and fork-tender, 30 minutes. Serve immediately on a platter, garnished with the chives.

IRISH SODA BREAD ROLLS

Irish soda bread is made with baking soda rather than yeast for leavening. The buttermilk gives it that deep, sweet aroma that Southerners love in their biscuits. Traditionally the soda bread roll has a cross cut in the top. The explanation may be practical—it allows the inside to bake evenly and quickly—or it may be because, as many believe, the sign of the cross scares away the devil. And since St. Patrick scared the devil away from Ireland, it seems appropriate to serve these tasty rolls on his day.

2 1/2 cups all-purpose flour
1 cup quick-cooking oats (preferably McCann's)
1 1/2 teaspoons salt
1 teaspoon baking soda
1/2 cup golden raisins or 6 tablespoons
   dried currants
1 teaspoon caraway seeds (optional)
1 1/2 cups buttermilk

1. Position a rack in the center of the oven, and preheat the oven to 350°F. Line a baking sheet with parchment paper.

2. Combine the flour, oats, salt, baking soda, raisins, and caraway seeds in a bowl and mix well. Add the buttermilk and stir with a wooden spoon until just combined; do not overmix. The dough should hold together and be slightly sticky.

3. Transfer the dough to a lightly floured surface. Form it into a ball, kneading it once or twice, just until smooth. Cut the dough into 8 pieces and form rough balls—it is okay if they are not perfectly round. Place them on the prepared baking sheet. Using scissors dipped into cold water, cut a 1/2-inch-deep X in the top of each roll.

4. Bake, rotating the baking sheet to ensure even browning, until the rolls are golden brown, 40 to 45 minutes. Serve hot (see Note).

MAKES 8 ROLLS

Note: If you've made the rolls in advance, warm them in a 350°F oven for about 10 minutes before serving. Tuck them in an Irish linen napkin–lined basket to keep them warm.

PISTACHIO ICE-CREAM SUNDAE

I never think of pistachio ice cream without three colors in my mind's eye: the green of the ice cream, and the orange and blue of Howard Johnson's, where, as a child, I enjoyed stunningly green pistachio ice-cream cones. Maybe green food coloring is best left to the less *au naturel* days of the 1950s, but where would St. Paddy's Day be without a touch of green in the meal? So do add a few drops here.

FOR THE ICE CREAM
6 cups heavy (whipping) cream
2 cups whole milk
2/3 cup sugar
10 tablespoons pistachio paste
   (see Note)
4 drops green food coloring (optional)
8 large egg yolks
2/3 cup shelled pistachio nuts, preferably
   unsalted, skinned and halved

FOR THE SUNDAE
1 cup Silky Chocolate Sauce
   (recipe follows), warm
Sweetened Whipped Cream
   (page 403)
8 red maraschino cherries
   with stems

1. Prepare the ice cream: Combine the cream, milk, sugar, and pistachio paste in a heavy

> "*May the frost never afflict your spuds.*
>
> *May the outside leaves of your cabbage be free from worms.*
>
> *May the crows never pick at your haystack,*
>
> *And may your donkey always be in foal.*"
>
> —*Traditional Irish Toast*

saucepan. Cook over medium heat until the mixture is hot but not boiling and the sugar has dissolved, 8 to 10 minutes. Remove the pan from the heat and whisk in the food coloring if using.

2. Place the egg yolks in a small bowl and whisk to mix. Whisking constantly, slowly pour 1 cup of the hot milk mixture into the eggs. Continue to whisk until smooth.

3. Slowly pour the egg mixture into the saucepan, whisking constantly until well combined. Place the saucepan over medium heat and cook, stirring constantly, until the mixture is thick enough to coat the back of a spoon, 6 to 8 minutes. The mixture should never boil.

4. Strain the mixture into a bowl and allow it to cool to room temperature.

5. Freeze in an ice-cream maker (in batches if necessary) according to the manufacturer's instructions. During the last 7 minutes, add the nuts. Transfer the ice cream to a container, cover, and freeze.

6. Place 2 scoops of the ice cream in each of eight sundae dishes or small bowls, and drizzle each serving with 2 tablespoons of the chocolate sauce. Top each with a generous dollop of whipped cream and a cherry. Serve immediately.

Note: Pistachio paste is available from several specialty food markets and by mail order. See Sources, page 405.

SILKY CHOCOLATE SAUCE

There are all kinds of chocolate sauces, and I truly love them all, including the fudgy sort that hardens the minute it touches the ice cream. This is a silky version, which pours easily and carries a sweet, refined, powerful dark chocolate flavor. Spoon it over ice cream, stir it into milk shakes, dip fruit into it, or just lick it off your finger.

8 ounces best-quality bittersweet chocolate
1 cup heavy (whipping) cream
2 tablespoons sugar
2 tablespoons unsalted butter

1. Chop the chocolate into small pieces.

2. Combine the cream and the sugar in a small saucepan and heat it over medium heat. When the mixture is just about to boil, remove the pan from the heat and stir in the chocolate and the butter. Stir until the sauce is smooth and all the chocolate has melted. Let it cool slightly, then whisk briefly. The sauce is best served warm (see Note).

MAKES 2 CUPS

Note: This chocolate sauce can be made ahead and reheated in a double boiler before serving. It will keep for up to 2 weeks in the refrigerator.

LITTLE OATMEAL COOKIES

Oats are, to my way of thinking, what they had in mind when they invented the term "comfort food." They're warm, filling, slightly nutty, with a wonderful affinity for sweet, salty, and savory flavors. They are really the universal dancing partner for just about every flavor in the Irish larder. And when you bake them into these cookies, they add a wonderfully pleasing crunch. The cookies are bite-size, by the way, so you can eat them alongside your pistachio sundae and not feel as if you're gobbling up two desserts.

*8 tablespoons (1 stick) unsalted butter,
    at room temperature*
1 cup (packed) light brown sugar
1 large egg, slightly beaten
2 teaspoons pure vanilla extract
*1½ cups quick-cooking oats
    (preferably McCann's)*
¾ cup all-purpose flour
½ teaspoon baking soda
½ teaspoon baking powder
¼ teaspoon ground cinnamon
¾ cup golden raisins

1. Position a rack in the center of the oven, and preheat the oven to 350°F. Lightly butter a baking sheet.

2. Place the butter in a bowl and beat it with an electric mixer until light and fluffy, 2 minutes. Add the brown sugar and continue beating on medium speed until fluffy, about 5 minutes.

3. Add the egg and vanilla and beat until the batter is light and smooth, 5 minutes.

4. Place the oats in a bowl. Sift the flour, baking soda, baking powder, and cinnamon together over the oats. Add the raisins and stir to combine.

5. Add the flour mixture to the butter mixture and beat on low speed until just incorporated.

6. Drop the dough by teaspoons, 2 inches apart, onto the prepared baking sheet. Bake, rotating the baking sheet as necessary to ensure even baking, until lightly golden brown, 8 to 10 minutes. Cool the cookies on the baking sheet for 5 minutes. Then use a spatula to transfer them to wire racks to cool completely (see Note).

MAKES ABOUT 48 COOKIES

Note: The cookies will keep in an airtight container for up to 4 days.

IRISH COFFEE

Although spring has started to show in some parts of the country by St. Patrick's Day, there still is something to be said for a warm fire and a mug of strong coffee laced with good Irish whisky and topped with a dollop of sweet whipped cream. And then maybe a nice cozy nap to the sound of the hisses and pops of the fire.

12 ounces Irish whisky
About 6 tablespoons sugar
8 cups (64 ounces) hot black coffee
Sweetened Whipped Cream (page 403)

1. Stir 1 jigger (1½ ounces) whisky with 1 to 2 teaspoons sugar in each of eight tall coffee cups or heat-resistant stemmed glasses.

2. Pour in hot coffee to ½ inch from the top. Top with whipped cream and serve immediately.

An Academy

Awards Bash

There may be more dinner parties in America (and maybe the world) for the Academy Awards than for any other event. Gathered around the television, you ooh at the beautiful and daring gowns (and of course trash the ones that never should have made it off the sketchpad), ahh the gorgeous guys, and argue the fine points of every nominee in every major category. Like most TV-oriented gatherings, the food should be as manageable as finger food or served in small bowls. For years, my tradition—in fact a lot of people's tradition—was to order in Chinese food. If you'd rather order in, go right ahead, but then you'll miss the oohs and ahhs these Chinese-inspired recipes will elicit from your fans.

MENU

This is a meal meant to be eaten in front of the TV, so it's organized as a buffet. In planning, I started with some familiar Chinese restaurant dishes and added the influences of Vietnam, Thailand, and Bali to modernize the preparations. So, light summer rolls with irresistible dipping sauces take the place of the heavier egg rolls. Spicy Sesame Noodles are included because they are a perennial favorite. The ribs are sticky, crispy, and meaty—yes, it's possible—and go nicely with fried rice. The vegetables are not necessarily a choice you'd find on a Chinese restaurant menu, but they complement the chicken roasted in Balinese spices. After this big feast and with all the awards excitement, a gooey sundae is just the thing to accompany a lot of good gossip and gown-gazing.

Set out blue-and-white Asian bowls for your guests, with bright red lacquered chopsticks—and forks for those who prefer them. The serving dishes should vary in size, shape, and color. Look for half moons, small cups, fish shapes, and deep bowls. Intermingle small Chinese figurines among the dishes. Buy a batch of fortune cookies and fill a pretty little lacquer basket with them.

Create large flower arrangements of dark blue or purple irises. A blue-and-white bowl filled with blue hyacinths would also be beautiful. Once you set up, take it easy and enjoy the show: Only the nominees are supposed to be nervous!

An Academy Awards Bash

BUFFET FOR EIGHT

Starlet Summer Rolls
with Sweet Chile Sauce and Spiced Chile Sauce

Shrimp and Vegetable Fried Rice

Spicy Sesame Noodles

A Honey of a Spare Rib

Bali Chicken

Star Slaw

Stir-Fried Baby Bok Choy

Outrageous Brownie Sundaes
with Double Vanilla-Bean Ice Cream

THE MUSIC

Hooray for Hollywood
movie tune compilation

Soundtrack from *There's No Business Like Show Business*

THE WINE

Off-dry German Riesling

Côtes de Castillon

THE EXTRAS

Chopsticks

Blue-and-white Asian dishes

Ice-cream maker

STARLET SUMMER ROLLS

First came the fried egg roll (heavy and kind of wintry in feel), then we got the spring roll (a thinner, lighter, but still fried version of the egg roll). Now we have the guilt-free, unfried summer roll. Best known in its Vietnamese incarnation, it is usually a refreshing mix of fresh herbs, pork or shrimp, and shredded or julienned raw vegetables wrapped in a silky rice crepe and dipped in a spicy sauce. Here they are at their lightest—a filling of just vegetables and herbs—with two contrasting sauces, one spicy, one sweet. It's said you should be able to eat the whole thing in four comfortable bites.

2 heads Boston lettuce
3 carrots, peeled
4 scallions, including 3 inches green
1 red bell pepper, stemmed and seeded
16 rice paper (spring roll) wrappers
    (8½ inches in diameter; see Sources,
    page 405)
32 fresh mint leaves
32 small sprigs fresh cilantro
Sweet Chile Sauce (recipe follows)
Spiced Chile Sauce (recipe follows)

1. Discard any damaged outer leaves of the lettuce. Separate the remaining leaves, rinse them, and pat them dry. Tear out any tough center ribs in the leaves and discard them. Set the lettuce aside.

2. Cut the carrots, scallions, and bell pepper into 4-inch-long matchstick pieces.

3. Dip a rice paper into a bowl of water for 5 seconds. Shake off the excess water and place it on a flat surface. (I like to work on a clean kitchen towel.) Stack a couple of lettuce leaves on the bottom third of the rice paper. Top the lettuce with a few carrot, scallion, and bell pepper matchsticks, followed by 2 mint leaves and 2 cilantro sprigs.

4. Fold the bottom of the rice paper up over the vegetables. Fold in the sides, and then roll it up. Repeat with the remaining rice paper, lettuce, vegetables, and herbs. Arrange the rolls on a serving platter. Keep the rolls covered with a damp paper towel until serving time if you prepare them in advance (they will keep for about 2 hours). Serve the rolls with bowls of the dipping sauces.
MAKES 16

SWEET CHILE SAUCE

Forget about the bottled red stuff in the condiment aisle of the supermarket. The inspiration here is the pungent, tangy, spicy, sweet, salty sauces of Thailand. Sauces are often considered the most important elements in the Thai dining experience, their varied layered flavors and hues weaving a flavor tapestry that unites magnificently with fish, meat, and salads. While Thai food may be on the hot side, the sauces cool the palate. This Sweet Chile Sauce is similar to the ubiquitous sweet dipping sauce sold in markets all over Thailand.

½ cup rice vinegar
⅓ cup sugar
¼ cup ketchup
2 tablespoons Chinese plum sauce
1 tablespoon finely minced fresh ginger
2 teaspoons finely minced garlic
2 teaspoons finely chopped fresh
    red serrano chile with seeds,
    or to taste
½ teaspoon salt
1 teaspoon cornstarch, mixed with
    1 teaspoon cold water

Combine all the ingredients in a small heavy saucepan. Bring the mixture to a boil over medium-high heat, reduce the heat to medium-low, and simmer, stirring constantly, to blend the flavors, 5 minutes. Remove from the heat and cool to room temperature. Puree the mixture in a food processor until nearly smooth. Store, covered, in the refrigerator for up to 2 weeks.

MAKES ABOUT 1 CUP

SPICED CHILE SAUCE

Well spiced but not overwhelming, this sauce has just the right amount of bite to excite the palate. Jalapeños are not terribly hot, so if you wish to turn up the fire, seek out a hotter chile. Lime and vinegar brighten the tastes, and fresh mint—which often accompanies chiles in Southeast Asian cuisine—pulls out all the flavor in the Starlet Summer Rolls.

¼ cup finely diced shallots
1 ripe plum tomato, seeded and cut into
  ⅛-inch dice
1 to 2 teaspoons minced red or
  green jalapeño chile, seeds removed
  according to desired hotness
½ cup fresh lime juice
¼ cup rice vinegar
1 teaspoon sugar
Salt and freshly ground black pepper, to taste
1 tablespoon chopped fresh mint

Combine all of the ingredients in a small bowl and serve within 2 to 3 hours. For the freshest taste, serve within 1 hour.

MAKES 1 CUP

SHRIMP AND VEGETABLE FRIED RICE

Fried rice can be a mundane dish, but not here. I like it lavish, so I've loaded up on the vegetables and added plenty of small

HOW TO COOK SHRIMP

Peel and devein the shrimp and then rinse them under cold water. Drain well. Bring a pot of water to a boil and cook the shrimp until they are pink all over and just cooked through, 2 to 3 minutes, depending on size. Drain and use as directed.

shrimp. The only thing missing from the standard take-out fried rice is the quick scrambled egg that's usually whisked in at the end—but I don't think you'll miss it. Serve this hot on a platter, so you can see the puffs of steam rising off the rice.

1 cup finely diced carrots
½ cup diced red bell pepper
2 tablespoons corn oil
1 cup slivered onions
1 tablespoon finely minced garlic
1 tablespoon minced fresh ginger
½ green cabbage, cored and coarsely
  chopped (1-inch pieces)
2½ cups cooked white rice
6 tablespoons soy sauce
¼ cup dry sherry
¼ cup Basic Chicken Broth
  (page 397)
1 cup frozen thawed peas
12 ounces small shrimp, cooked
  (see box above)
½ cup frozen thawed corn kernels
¼ cup chopped fresh cilantro
4 scallions, including 3 inches green,
  thinly sliced on the diagonal

1. Bring a small saucepan of lightly salted water to a boil over high heat. Add the carrots and cook until just tender, 1½ minutes. Using a slotted spoon, transfer the carrots to a colander to drain, then pat dry and transfer them to a bowl.

2. Add the bell pepper to the boiling water and cook until just tender, 1 minute. Transfer the pepper to the colander to drain, then pat dry and add to the carrots.

3. Heat the oil in a large skillet or wok over medium-low heat. Add the onions, garlic, and ginger and cook, stirring, until the onion softens, 5 minutes. Add the cabbage and cook, stirring, until softened, 10 minutes more.

4. Stir in the rice, soy sauce, sherry, and broth. Cook, stirring constantly to combine, 3 minutes. Then add the peas, shrimp, corn, and the carrots and peppers and cook for 1 minute more.

5. Fold in the cilantro, using a fork to keep the rice fluffy. Transfer the mixture to a platter and serve immediately, garnished with the scallions.

SPICY SESAME NOODLES

Sesame noodles are meant to be slurped up! They are prepared here with more sauce than is traditional because the wetter they are, the easier to slurp. The vegetables add a nice crunch.

1½ pounds dried linguine
3 cups Hot-Stuff Dunk (page 71)
4 carrots, peeled and cut into 3-inch-long
 matchstick pieces
1 hothouse (seedless) cucumber,
 unpeeled, halved lengthwise, center
 scooped out, and cut into 3-inch-long
 matchstick pieces
8 scallions, including 3 inches green,
 cut into 3-inch-long matchstick pieces
2 tablespoons chopped fresh cilantro,
 for garnish

1. Bring a large pot of salted water to a boil over high heat. Add the linguine and cook until cooked through, but still firm to the bite, about 11 minutes. Drain well, and place in a large bowl.

2. Add the Hot-Stuff Dunk to the bowl and toss well.

3. Place the noodles in a large shallow serving bowl. Arrange the carrots, cucumber, and scallions decoratively in little piles around the rim of the dish. Sprinkle with the cilantro and serve.

A BIT OF TRIVIA

The Question: Can you name the years that James Dean, Marilyn Monroe, Lauren Bacall, Marlene Dietrich, and Richard Burton won their Oscars? And for what films?

The Answer: As a matter of fact, none of these megastars ever won an Oscar! Which is really surprising because they are surely among the all-time favorites.

Spicy Sesame Noodles

A HONEY OF A SPARE RIB

The secret to great Chinese spare ribs—salty and smoky—lies in two ingredients that are fairly widely available today. Hoisin sauce is one. It is sweet, pungent, tangy, and irresistible. The other, five spice powder, usually consists of more than five spices, but five is a lucky number for health in traditional Chinese belief. The powder combines anise, cinnamon, cloves, Szechwan pepper, and sometimes fennel, ground ginger, and licorice roots. These make for sublime ribs for a great party dish. Don't forget to have plenty of napkins on hand.

FOR THE SAUCE

$1/2$ cup hoisin sauce
6 tablespoons soy sauce
6 tablespoons sherry vinegar
6 tablespoons honey
3 tablespoons Asian sesame oil
3 tablespoons finely minced
    fresh ginger
4 teaspoons finely minced garlic
2 teaspoons Chinese five spice powder
Salt, to taste

FOR THE SPARERIBS

2 sides pork spareribs (2 to $2^1/2$ pounds
    each), or 4 sides baby back ribs
    (about 1 pound each)
6 scallions, including 3 inches green,
    thinly sliced on the diagonal,
    for garnish

1. Preheat the oven to 350°F.

2. Combine all the sauce ingredients in a bowl and mix well.

3. Lay the ribs in a shallow baking pan, meat side up. Slather them with two thirds of the sauce. Bake, covered loosely with aluminum foil, for 30 minutes. Uncover and bake, basting every 15 minutes with the pan juices and the remaining sauce, until the ribs are cooked through, 45 minutes more.

4. Cut the ribs apart and serve them on a platter, garnished with scallions. These are delicious hot, warm, or even at room temperature.

Note: The ribs can be prepared a day in advance and reheated, covered loosely in foil, in a 350°F oven for 15 to 20 minutes.

BALI CHICKEN

Bali spices and herbs influence this moist marinated chicken. It's delicious with the fried rice alongside.

2 chickens (3 to $3^1/2$ pounds each),
    each cut into 8 pieces
2 tablespoons soy sauce
2 tablespoons fresh lemon juice
2 tablespoons extra-virgin olive oil
4 teaspoons ground cumin
2 teaspoons ground turmeric
1 teaspoon salt
$1/2$ cup dry white wine
$1/2$ cup small fresh mint leaves (optional),
    for garnish
$1/4$ cup chopped fresh cilantro,
    for garnish

1. Remove all excess fat from the chicken and rinse the pieces well under cold water. Pat dry and place them in a large bowl.

2. Combine the soy sauce, lemon juice, olive oil, cumin, turmeric, and salt in a small bowl. Rub this well into the chicken pieces and let them rest, covered in the refrigerator, for 2 to 3 hours or as long as overnight.

3. Remove the chicken from the refrigerator 30 minutes before cooking. Arrange the pieces in a large baking dish and pour the wine into the dish.

4. Meanwhile, preheat the oven to 350°F.

5. Bake the chicken, basting it occasionally, for 45 minutes. Raise the heat to 375°F and bake for another 15 minutes, continuing to baste. The chicken will be cooked through and fragrant.

6. Serve the chicken sprinkled with the mint leaves and the cilantro, with the pan juices on the side.

STAR SLAW

A crisp slaw adds flourish to any menu, especially when it's dressed with whispers of sesame oil and orange. This one deserves the Oscar for best supporting salad.

*8 ounces snow peas, thinly slivered
    lengthwise*
*1 large head green cabbage
    (about 2½ pounds), tough outer
    leaves removed, halved, cored, and
    finely shredded*
1 head radicchio, cored and finely shredded
½ cup diced red onion (¼-inch dice)
⅓ cup rice vinegar
1 tablespoon light soy sauce
1 teaspoon sugar
1 teaspoon salt, or to taste
¼ cup canola oil
1 teaspoon Asian sesame oil
1 tablespoon finely grated orange zest
¼ cup coarsely chopped fresh mint

1. Bring a saucepan of lightly salted water to a boil over high heat. Add the snow peas and cook for just 45 seconds. Drain, and rinse under cold water to stop the cooking. Drain again.

2. Toss the cabbage and radicchio in a large bowl. Add the red onion and the snow peas and toss to combine.

3. In a small bowl, whisk together the vinegar, soy sauce, sugar, and salt. Whisking constantly,

drizzle in both oils. Continue to whisk until thickened. Stir in the orange zest and adjust the seasonings.

4. Add the dressing and the chopped mint to the cabbage and radicchio, toss thoroughly. Let rest for at least 1 hour before serving.

STIR-FRIED BABY BOK CHOY

Do as the Chinese do for special occasions and look for tender young bok choy with leaves no longer than 4 inches. If you can't find baby bok choy, then go with the grown-up version, but slice the leaves crosswise into 2-inch widths before cooking. The trick with stir-frying is to use intense heat and cook quickly, so that the greens remain bright and the stalks are tender.

2 pounds baby bok choy
6 tablespoons Asian sesame oil
2 teaspoons hot chili oil
*1 piece (4 inches) fresh ginger,
    very thinly sliced*
2 tablespoons finely minced garlic
*16 scallions, including 3 inches green,
    thinly sliced on the diagonal*
¼ cup light soy sauce
½ cup chopped fresh cilantro
Freshly ground black pepper, to taste

1. Trim the bottom ½ inch off the bok choy, separating the leaves. Rinse, pat dry, and set aside.

2. Place 3 tablespoons of the sesame oil and 1 teaspoon of the hot chili oil in each of two non-stick skillets and set them over low heat. Add half the ginger and garlic to each skillet. Cook, stirring, for 2 minutes to mellow the flavors. Divide the scallions and bok choy between the skillets. Raise the heat to medium-high and cook, shaking the pans, until just tender, 2 to 3 minutes.

3. Add half the soy sauce and cilantro to each skillet and toss with the bok choy. Remove from the heat, season to taste with pepper, and serve immediately.

OUTRAGEOUS BROWNIE SUNDAES

This dessert is as over-the-top as some of the jewelry on the most ambitious starlets. Rich homemade vanilla ice cream, rich chocolate brownies with chocolate chunks, and dark chocolate sauce—when you've gone this far, go ahead and dollop it with whipped cream. And, in the interest of being classically correct, top it off with a firehouse-red maraschino cherry.

8 Chocolate Chunk Brownies (page 25),
* each 3 inches square*
2 batches Double Vanilla-Bean Ice Cream
* (recipe follows)*
1 cup Silky Chocolate Sauce (page 42)
Sweetened Whipped Cream (page 403)
8 maraschino cherries with stems

1. Carefully cut each brownie in half horizontally, using a serrated knife, creating two layers. Then place the bottom half of each brownie in each of eight small dessert bowls.

2. Place a scoop of ice cream on top of each brownie, and drizzle each with a tablespoon of the chocolate sauce. Top with a dollop of whipped cream.

3. Cover with the remaining brownie halves, pressing them down slightly. Top each with another scoop of ice cream, a tablespoon

of chocolate sauce, and a dollop of whipped cream. Crown with a cherry.

DOUBLE VANILLA-BEAN ICE CREAM

In this recipe, the vanilla seeds are scraped out of their pod and added to the ice-cream mix. They give the dessert a distinct, rich flavor—this is what real vanilla ice cream should taste like.

3 cups heavy (whipping) cream
1 cup whole milk
½ cup sugar
1 tablespoon pure vanilla extract
2 vanilla beans, split in half lengthwise
4 large egg yolks

1. Combine the cream, milk, sugar, and vanilla extract in a heavy saucepan. Scrape the seeds out of the vanilla bean pods with the tip of a sharp knife, and add the seeds and the pods to the cream mixture. Place the pan over medium heat and cook until the mixture is hot but not boiling and the sugar has dissolved, about 10 minutes. Remove the pan from the heat.

2. Place the egg yolks in a small bowl and whisk to mix. Whisking constantly, slowly pour 1 cup of the hot cream mixture into the eggs. Continue to whisk until smooth.

3. Slowly pour the egg mixture into the saucepan, whisking constantly until well combined. Place the saucepan over medium heat and stir the mixture constantly until it is thick enough to coat the back of a spoon, 6 to 8 minutes. The mixture should never boil.

4. Strain the mixture into a bowl and allow it to cool to room temperature. Discard vanilla beans.

5. Freeze in an ice-cream maker according to the manufacturer's instructions. Transfer the ice cream to a container, cover, and freeze.

Makes 1 quart

Note: This recipe may be easily doubled.

Sheila's

In the Jewish tradition, Passover is the Main Event: It commemorates the deliverance of the Jews from Egypt. The meal serves as part of the celebration, known as a Seder, and during the festivities families read aloud the story of the Jews' escape from Egypt and their years of

wandering in the desert. Every member of the family takes part in the reading, and each part of the specially prepared Seder plate has a symbolic meaning. Then, when the reading is done, comes the endless, boundless, delicious, lovingly prepared meal, long awaited—followed by singing of celebratory songs and the traditional refrain, "Next year in Jerusalem."

The word *Seder* literally means "order." The exact order of the telling of the Passover story and eating of the meal is written in the Haggadah, a copy of which is given to each person at the Passover table.

MENU

T his Seder menu has tradition in mind but it veers somewhat, especially right at the beginning. Typically gefilte fish is served at the start of the meal, but I chose to make salmon croquettes instead. Rémoulade Sauce dolloped on top is delicious and makes the croquettes decidedly modern. For non–fish-lovers, there's chopped liver, which is traditional and lovely served with crackerlike matzohs. My mother's chicken soup and my niece Marci's matzoh balls make a memorable combination. You can't celebrate the holiday without a haroseth, and the one included here is delicious. Rosy Pot Roast, with its rich paprika-scented sauce, is my choice for a substantial entree. Tzimmes—a combination of carrots, sweet potatoes, and dried fruit—complements the savory asparagus. A flourless chocolate cake blanketed in a sauce made of fresh berries provides a sparkling finish.

While festive, Passover is a holiday steeped in tradition and is not at all casual. The Seder table is traditionally set with a white tablecloth and napkins, the best china and silverware.

Place a Haggadah, a wineglass, and a small bowl of salted water at each setting. The Seder plate goes in front of the leader, along with a silver goblet (reserved for Elijah, the prophet). Place a plate of matzoh, covered with a napkin, at each end of the table.

Now you're set to celebrate the festival of freedom.

Sheila's Seder
DINNER FOR EIGHT

Apple Walnut Haroseth

Salmon Croquettes with Rémoulade Sauce

Holiday Chopped Liver

Chicken Soup
with Marci's Fluffy Matzoh Balls

Rosy Pot Roast

Sheila's Tzimmes

Fresh Asparagus with Shallots and Herbs

Flourless Chocolate Cake
with Fresh Blackberry Sauce

Morning-After Matzoh Brei

THE MUSIC

Richard Tucker's
Passover Seder Festival

THE WINE

Kosher Pinot Blanc
Kosher Côteaux du Languedoc

THE EXTRAS

Decorative Seder plate
Silver goblet
Candlesticks

APPLE WALNUT HAROSETH

I have Nach Waxman, owner of New York's cookbook store, Kitchen Arts & Letters, to thank for this glorious haroseth. When I first called him, knowing he'd have a great recipe, he began by saying, "You must chop everything by hand," and that certainly is the key. The texture adds elegance and allows each ingredient to retain its own integrity.

3 Granny Smith apples, unpeeled,
   cored and halved
2 tablespoons fresh lemon juice
$1/2$ cup walnuts
$1/4$ teaspoon ground cinnamon
$1/2$ teaspoon ground ginger
3 tablespoons sweet Passover wine,
   or more as needed
2 to 3 tablespoons honey (optional)

1. Chop the apples coarsely by hand. Place them in a large bowl and toss them with the lemon juice to prevent discoloration.

2. Chop the walnuts coarsely by hand and add them to the apples (don't add any of the walnut dust that forms). Add the cinnamon and ginger. Pour in the wine and the honey, if using. Let stand, covered, in the refrigerator for up to 6 hours before serving. If the haroseth is dry, add a tablespoon more of the wine just before serving.

3. To serve, place in a decorative bowl with a small serving spoon on the side.

MAKES 1 QUART

I n order to keep strictly kosher for Passover, cupboards in traditional Jewish homes are cleared of all items that do not explicitly say "kosher for Passover" on the label. Happily, there is an abundance of available Passover products, and items like fresh fruits and vegetables remain fair game.

SALMON CROQUETTES

A t Passover it is traditional to serve gefilte fish, which are delicious little quenelles of pike and whitefish, but why not try something different? A variation on the theme of chopped-up fish, the crisp salmon croquettes are flavorful by themselves, and when served with a jazzy rémoulade sauce they are a sublime palate-preparer for the feast to follow.

4 cans (7.5 ounces each) pink salmon,
   drained
1 cup finely diced onions
1 cup finely diced celery
1 teaspoon crushed dried tarragon
Salt and freshly ground black pepper,
   to taste
1 cup prepared pareve mayonnaise,
   such as Hellmann's (see box, page 59)
2 tablespoons Dijon mustard
2 large eggs, lightly beaten
$2^2/3$ cups crushed matzoh crumbs
16 carrots, peeled
Rémoulade Sauce (recipe follows),
   for serving
4 tablespoons ($1/2$ stick) pareve margarine
   (see box, page 59)
4 tablespoons olive oil

1. Carefully flake the salmon into a bowl, discarding any small bones, cartilage, and skin. Add the onions, celery, tarragon, and salt and pepper and fold together with a rubber spatula.

THE SEDER PLATE

At the beginning of the Seder, the family reads through an ancient service contained in a book called the Haggadah, in a ritual that has been handed down for thousands of years. Every Seder plate, no matter how fancy or simple, contains these items: in the center, three whole matzohs; arranged in a circle around the matzohs, a roasted bone, a roasted egg, haroseth, a bitter herb (horseradish), and parsley or another green herb.

Matzoh: Unleavened bread, the bread of affliction. According to tradition, the Hebrews left Egypt in such a hurry that their bread had no time to rise. These crisp wafers were all the refugees had to sustain them as they began their Exodus.

Karpas: Green herbs, usually parsley, symbolic of spring and the renewal of life.

Zeroa: A roasted shank bone as a symbol of the pascal offering at the time of the Exodus.

Haroseth: This mixture of apples, walnuts, wine, and honey symbolizes the mortar that the Hebrew slaves used to hold together the bricks used in building monuments for the Pharaoh.

Salt water: Placed in individual bowls scattered around the table, into which the herbs will be dipped. The salty water represents the bitter tears that the Jews wept in bondage.

Maror: Freshly grated horseradish, symbolizing the bitter life of the Hebrews when they were Pharaoh's slaves.

Roasted egg: Represents the ancient festival sacrifice and is also a symbol of rebirth, as eggs are in many cultures.

---

2. Combine the mayonnaise and mustard in a small bowl, and mix this into the salmon. Still using the rubber spatula, fold in the eggs and ⅔ cup of the matzoh crumbs.

3. Place the remaining 2 cups matzoh, crumbs on a plate or in a shallow bowl.

4. Form the salmon mixture into 16 patties and coat them in the matzoh crumbs. Refrigerate, loosely covered, for 1 hour.

5. Meanwhile, coarsely grate the carrots into a large bowl. Toss with ⅔ cup of the Rémoulade Sauce, using a fork so that they don't clump together.

6. Melt 1 tablespoon of the pareve margarine in 1 tablespoon of the olive oil in a nonstick skillet over medium heat. Cook the croquettes, in several batches, until golden, 3 to 4 minutes per side. Add more margarine and oil for each batch as necessary. Arrange the croquettes on a platter, dollop with some of the remaining Rémoulade Sauce, and place the carrots alongside. Serve immediately.

REMOULADE SAUCE

The French knew what they were doing when they first made rémoulade sauce. This mustard-laced mayonnaise-based sauce enlivens seafood with its tarragon bouquet and kicks in a little bite with capers and Tabasco. No wonder the best of Cajun chefs adopted it in short order.

1½ cups prepared pareve mayonnaise,
  such as Hellmann's (see box, below)
4 teaspoons Dijon mustard
1 tablespoon whole-grain mustard
2 teaspoons tarragon vinegar
½ teaspoon Tabasco sauce
4 teaspoons tiny capers, drained and chopped
2 tablespoons chopped fresh flat-leaf parsley
2 scallions, including 3 inches green,
  very thinly sliced
Salt and freshly ground black pepper, to taste

Combine all the ingredients in a small bowl and mix well. Set aside, covered, in the refrigerator. This will keep for up to 3 days.

MAKES 2 CUPS

In traditional Jewish homes, meat and dairy products are not eaten together in the same sitting in observance of the rules of *kashrut,* or kosher meal preparation, laid out in the Bible. Therefore *pareve,* or non-dairy items, are substituted in recipes usually calling for dairy to produce similar results. Use non-dairy margarine instead of butter and non-dairy creamer instead of cream to produce luscious Passover dishes.

HOLIDAY
CHOPPED LIVER

My mother, Berta, makes a delicious chopped liver. The onions are sautéed to a rich brown in chicken fat and then mixed with the liver. It is heaven on a crisp matzoh. My uncle Alan says a thin slice of raw onion never hurts either. No doubt you have heard the expression "What am I, chopped liver?" This always puzzled me. Apparently it means that to compare someone to chopped liver is to bring him or her down a peg. But once you taste this smooth, creamy, earthy pâté, "chopped liver" will forevermore ring as a compliment in your ears.

1 pound fresh chicken livers
¼ to ⅓ cup rendered chicken fat (see Note)
2 large onions, coarsely chopped
2 hard-cooked eggs (page 9), coarsely
  chopped
Salt and freshly ground black pepper,
  to taste
Matzoh, for serving

1. Wash the chicken livers well, removing any excess fat. Bring a pot of salted water to a boil and add the livers. Reduce the heat and simmer, uncovered, for 10 minutes. Drain, allow to cool slightly, and cut into small pieces. Place the livers in a bowl and set it aside.

2. Heat the chicken fat in a nonstick skillet over medium heat. Add the onions and cook, stirring, until soft and nicely browned, about 20 minutes.

3. Add the onions to the chicken livers, along with the chopped eggs and salt and pepper. Combine well and then transfer the mixture to a food processor. Process briefly, making sure to retain some texture—you should still be able to see the eggs. Adjust the seasonings if needed. Transfer the mixture to a bowl and serve immediately, or refrigerate, covered, for up to 3 days. Remove from the refrigerator 30 minutes before serving.

4. To serve, spread on good-size pieces of broken matzoh.

MAKES 2 CUPS

Note: To render chicken fat, place the fat, cut into small pieces, in a skillet. Cook over low heat, stirring occasionally, until the fat has melted. Cool slightly and then strain, discarding the bits of chicken skin. Store, covered, in the refrigerator for up to 1 week.

CHICKEN SOUP
WITH MARCI'S FLUFFY MATZOH BALLS

Every culture has its dumpling, from our Southern hush puppies to Chinese wontons and Italian gnocchi. And every culture has a way of serving dumplings in broth or soup. Matzoh balls, which soak up the rich bouquet of deep amber chicken soup, are the dumpling of my heritage.

Years ago my Granny Block used to be in charge of matzoh balls for Passover, but when she passed on, so did the responsibility. My niece Marci picked up the mantle beautifully. Her matzoh balls are delicate, yet not at all hazardous to handle while forming (a great virtue!). These should be made in advance; store them in a large plastic container with a lid. Marci says they freeze well for 1 to 2 days.

12 large eggs, separated
³/₄ cup rendered chicken fat
  (see Note, page 59)
2 teaspoons salt
Freshly ground black pepper,
  to taste
3 cups matzoh meal
My Mother's Chicken Soup
  (recipe follows), for serving
8 small sprigs fresh dill, for garnish

1. Combine the egg yolks, chicken fat, salt, and pepper in a bowl and blend with an electric mixer.

2. Place the egg whites in another bowl, and using clean beaters, beat them until they are stiff.

3. Using a large rubber spatula, fold the whites into the yolk mixture.

4. Fold in the matzoh meal, using just enough so that the balls hold together.

5. Form the mixture into 20 balls the size of large plums and place them on a large platter.

6. Bring a large pot of salted water to a boil. Carefully lower the matzoh balls into the water in batches, using a slotted spoon. Reduce the heat to a simmer and cook, uncovered, until the balls float and are enlarged and delicate, about 30 minutes. Using a slotted spoon, remove the balls from the water and drain them on paper towels.

7. When you are ready to serve it, place the chicken soup over medium heat. Add the matzoh balls and heat through for the flavors to blend, 10 to 15 minutes. Using a slotted spoon, place 2 matzoh balls in each soup bowl. Ladle the soup over it, and garnish with a dill sprig.

MY MOTHER'S CHICKEN SOUP

My mother, Berta, is the Chicken Soup Queen of All Time. As would every great cook, she will tell you, "It starts with using the best-quality ingredients." She's right, but it also matters what you do with them. Berta starts with a stewing hen—not a young chicken, but an older one whose flesh would be tough to eat but will impart lots of flavor to the soup. Then those yummy cooked vegetables and their vitamins get pureed through a strainer back into the soup. It takes a little longer and costs a little more to make a soup this way, but what flavor! Marci's Fluffy Matzoh Balls and fresh dill finish it off to perfection.

1 stewing hen (5¹/₂ to 6 pounds), rinsed,
  trimmed of excess fat, and cut into 8 pieces
2 teaspoons coarse (kosher) salt
2 onions, quartered
4 ribs celery with leaves, cut in half
4 parsnips, peeled and quartered
4 carrots, peeled and quartered
12 sprigs fresh dill, tied into a bundle with
  kitchen string
Salt and freshly ground black pepper, to taste
1 to 2 tablespoons chopped fresh dill leaves

Chicken Soup with Marci's Fluffy Matzoh Balls

1. Place the chicken pieces in a large soup pot. Add 10 cups water and the coarse salt and bring to a boil. Skim off any foam that rises to the surface.

2. Add the onions, celery, parsnips, carrots, and dill sprigs. Season with salt and pepper. Simmer, uncovered, until the chicken and vegetables are tender, 1 hour.

3. Transfer the chicken to a bowl and use the meat elsewhere if desired (it will be tough). Strain the broth through a medium-fine strainer into a large bowl, pressing the vegetables and dill through the strainer with the back of a spoon. If not using it immediately, let the soup cool to room temperature and then refrigerate it, covered, for up to 2 days, or freeze it.

4. To serve, first remove any fat that has accumulated on the surface. Then return the soup to a pot and stir in the chopped dill. Heat through.

ROSY POT ROAST

I can never think about pot roast without thinking of my grandmother's pot roast pot. It was cast aluminum and had a kind of pebble grain. The raised part of the grain was shiny because no one can scrub like a grandmother. The rest was blackened from long and constant use. The key thing with a pot roast is to caramelize those onions. That means really browning, not just a light tan. My collaborator, Peter Kaminsky, recalls his grandmother's recipe: "You brown the onions," she would say, "until you can smell them in the candy store." (The store was one flight down in her building.) If you don't have a candy store downstairs, the translation is "Give the onions and the rest of the veggies some good long heat."

1 first-cut beef brisket (4¹/₂ to 5 pounds)
Salt and freshly ground black pepper, to taste
2 tablespoons olive oil
2 large onions, halved lengthwise and slivered
2 tablespoons minced garlic
2 tablespoons paprika
1¹/₂ teaspoons caraway seeds
3 cups diced carrots (¹/₂-inch dice)
1 cup diced red bell peppers (¹/₂-inch dice)
1 cup diced peeled russet potatoes
  (¹/₂-inch dice)
2 bay leaves
2 sprigs fresh thyme
1¹/₄ cups prepared tomato sauce
¹/₄ cup canned or homemade Beef Broth
  (page 397)
¹/₄ cup (packed) dark brown sugar
2 cups dry red wine

1. Preheat the oven to 325°F.

2. Sprinkle the brisket generously with salt and pepper.

3. Heat the oil in a large heavy ovenproof pot over low heat. Add the meat, raise the heat to medium-high, and brown well, 8 to 10 minutes per side. Transfer the meat to a plate.

4. Add the onions to the pot and cook, stirring, over medium-low heat until softened and starting to brown, 10 minutes. Add the garlic and cook 5 minutes more. The onions should be a luscious brown. Add the paprika and caraway seeds and cook over very low heat, stirring, for 1 to 2 minutes.

5. Place the meat, fat side up, on top of the onions, and pour in any accumulated juices. Add the carrots, bell peppers, potatoes, bay leaves, and thyme sprigs.

6. Combine the tomato sauce, broth, and brown sugar in a saucepan and simmer for 5 minutes. Reduce the heat to medium-low and cook, stirring occasionally, for 5 minutes more. Pour this over the beef and vegetables. Pour in the wine. Cover the pot, transfer it to the oven, and cook for 3 hours, basting occasionally with the juices.

7. Remove the pot from the oven but leave the oven on. Scrape the sauce off the brisket and transfer the meat to a cutting board. Let it rest for 15 minutes. Then carve the brisket into thin slices on the diagonal, against the grain. Gather the slices back together and return them to the pot. Cover the meat completely with the sauce, and season with salt and pepper.

8. Bake, uncovered, basting the meat occasionally with the sauce, until it is tender, about 2 hours. Serve immediately.

Note: This can be prepared ahead. To reheat it, bring it to room temperature and then warm it, covered, in a preheated 350°F oven for 30 minutes.

SHEILA'S TZIMMES

A *tzimmes*, literally speaking, is a "fuss." If someone says, "Why are you making such a big tzimmes over this," they mean you are making a big deal out of a simple matter. I suppose this dish is called a tzimmes because it is a mishmash of carrots, sweet potatoes, and dried fruits. While tzimmes can be made with or without meat, mine is completely vegetarian and made rich with honey. My sister-in-law, Cathy, brought me this recipe and I've added my usual gussing-up here and there. Use some of the margarine to oil the baking dish.

> 1 1/2 pounds carrots, peeled and cut into
>   1 1/2-inch pieces
> 4 large sweet potatoes (8 ounces each),
>   peeled and cut into 1 1/2-inch cubes
> 1/2 pound pitted prunes, cut in half crosswise
> 1 cup sugar
> 3/4 cup clover honey
> 3 tablespoons pareve margarine,
>   at room temperature (see box, page 59)
> 3 tablespoons fresh orange juice
> 2 teaspoons ground cinnamon
> 1 teaspoon salt

1. Preheat the oven to 350°F. Lightly oil a 13 x 9-inch oven-to-table baking dish.

2. Bring a pot of salted water to a boil. Add the carrots and cook until just tender, 5 to 7 minutes.

Sheila's Tzimmes

Using a skimmer or a slotted spoon, transfer the carrots to a colander and allow to drain. Then place them in a large bowl.

3. Add the sweet potatoes to the boiling water and cook until tender, 7 minutes. Drain them and add them to the carrots.

4. Add all the remaining ingredients to the vegetables and gently fold them together.

5. Spoon the vegetables into the prepared baking dish, pouring any liquid over them. Cover the dish with aluminum foil and bake until the tzimmes is bubbling, 1 hour, removing the foil for the last 5 minutes. Use a baster to pour some cooking juices over the vegetables and serve hot.

FRESH ASPARAGUS
WITH SHALLOTS AND HERBS

S imple, fresh, and seasonal—those are three good reasons for including this vegetable dish in this celebration. The asparagus and shallots provide a wonderfully savory foil to the sweetness of the tzimmes.

4 tablespoons (½ stick) pareve margarine,
  at room temperature (see box, page 59)
1 tablespoon finely chopped shallots
1½ teaspoons finely minced garlic
1½ teaspoons chopped fresh flat-leaf
  parsley or tarragon
1 pound asparagus, woody ends trimmed

1. Place 1 teaspoon of the margarine in a skillet over low heat. Add the shallots and garlic and cook, stirring, until softened, 3 to 4 minutes.

2. Place the remaining margarine in a small bowl and cream it well. Add the cooked shallot mixture and the parsley and blend well. Set it aside.

3. Bring a pan of salted water to a boil. Add the asparagus, reduce the heat, and simmer for about 3 minutes, depending on the size of the stalks. Drain and toss with the reserved shallot sauce. Serve immediately.

FLOURLESS CHOCOLATE CAKE

Because the Hebrews had no way to make bread in the desert, flour is traditionally banished from the kitchen during Passover. Still, you need a cake to end the meal, and a flourless chocolate cake, which uses ground almonds instead of flour, fits the bill. The blackberry sauce is not to be missed. (For an explanation of *pareve*, see box, page 59.)

FOR THE CAKE

2 ounces pareve unsweetened chocolate,
  broken into small pieces
4 ounces pareve semisweet chocolate,
  broken into small pieces
9 tablespoons, pareve margarine,
  at room temperature

12 tablespoons sugar
3 tablespoons ground almonds
5 large eggs, separated
Pinch of salt

FOR THE CHOCOLATE ICING

4 tablespoons (½ stick) pareve
  margarine
2 ounces pareve unsweetened
  chocolate
2 ounces pareve semisweet chocolate
3 tablespoons non-dairy creamer
⅔ cup sifted confectioners' sugar
1 teaspoon pure vanilla extract

*Fresh Blackberry Sauce, for serving
  (recipe follows)*

1. Preheat the oven to 350°F. Oil the bottom of a 9 x 3-inch round springform pan. Line the bottom with wax paper. Oil and flour the wax paper and shake out the excess flour.

2. Prepare the cake: Place both chocolates in the top of a double boiler over simmering water and stir until melted. Remove the pan from the heat and use a rubber spatula to scrape the chocolate into a medium-size bowl. Allow it to cool for 3 minutes.

3. Gradually add the margarine to the chocolate, stirring well. Then add 9 tablespoons of the sugar and the ground almonds. Stir in the egg yolks, one at a time.

4. Place the egg whites and salt in a bowl and beat with an electric mixer until they form soft peaks. Add the remaining 3 tablespoons sugar and beat until the whites hold their shape but are not too stiff.

5. Fold the whites, in thirds, into the chocolate mixture. Pour the batter into the prepared pan and smooth the top with a rubber spatula. Bake for 35 minutes.

6. Allow the cake to cool in the pan on a wire rack for 15 minutes. Then carefully remove the sides of the springform pan. Cover the top with a wire cake rack and invert the cake and rack together. Carefully remove the bottom of the pan and peel off the wax paper. Place a second wire rack over the bottom of the cake and invert it once again so the top faces up. Allow it to cool completely on the rack.

7. Prepare the icing. Melt the pareve margarine and both of the chocolates in the top of a double boiler over simmering water, whisking constantly. Remove the pan from the heat and whisk in the creamer. Add the confectioners' sugar and the vanilla and whisk until smooth.

8. Place the cake on a rack on top of a baking sheet (to catch the drips) and pour the warm icing over the cake. Spread it with a long thin cake icer or spatula, making sure the sides are iced too. Let the cake rest for 2 hours for the icing to set.

9. Carefully transfer the cake to a serving platter. Serve slices topped with Fresh Blackberry Sauce.

FRESH BLACKBERRY SAUCE

A pool of this blue velvet sauce—tart, sweet— is delightful with this delicious chocolate cake or a freshly baked pound cake.

2 cups fresh blackberries
1/2 cup confectioners' sugar
1/4 cup kirsch (see Note)
1 tablespoon fresh lemon juice

Combine all the ingredients in a food processor or blender and process until pureed. Pass the sauce through a strainer to remove the seeds. Use immediately or refrigerate, covered, for up to 3 days. Bring to room temperature before serving.

MAKES 1 1/2 CUPS

Note: Kosher kirsch (cherry liqueur) is available. Berghof is one brand.

MORNING-AFTER MATZOH BREI

T his is not, technically speaking, part of the Passover Seder. But matzoh brei (which means "matzoh mush") the morning after a Seder is a gastronomic must, because matzohs soaked in water, crumbled up, and cooked with eggs and fried onions is one of the top two or three brunch dishes in the world, bar none. Some people like to eat their matzoh brei with a little salt and pepper and that's it; others go for some jam, or maybe a little sour cream. Go ahead, mix and match. It's all yummy.

4 pieces unsalted matzoh
2 cups boiling water
3 tablespoons unsalted butter
1 onion, cut into 1/4-inch dice
6 large eggs
3 tablespoons whole milk
Salt and freshly ground black pepper,
*   to taste*
Strawberry or cherry jam, for serving
*   (optional)*
Sour cream, for serving (optional)
Chilled applesauce, for serving
*   (optional)*

1. Break the matzoh into large pieces and place them in a bowl. Pour the boiling water over the matzoh and let it soak for 2 to 3 minutes. Drain.

2. Melt the butter in a nonstick skillet over medium-low heat. Add the onion and cook until golden brown, 12 to 15 minutes.

3. Meanwhile, lightly beat the eggs with the milk, salt, and pepper.

4. Add the eggs to the skillet and cook until they are softly set. Adjust the seasonings. Serve immediately with jam, sour cream, or applesauce.

When Spring

Has Sprung

The twenty-first of March is one of only two days in the year when from the North Pole to the South, on every square inch of Earth, the hours of daylight and darkness are equal. Spring has officially arrived, the trees are just starting to shimmer with buds, and there's a whole season of long sunny evenings to look forward to. On its very first day, spring may feel more anticipatory than real. Still, the equinox marking rebirth and renewal is a fine reason to invite friends to dinner.

> "Asparagus inspires gentle thoughts."
> —CHARLES LAMB

MENU

When Spring Has Sprung

DINNER FOR FOUR

Shad Roe
with a Frisée Salad

Creamy
Asparagus Tarragon
Soup

Panko Soft-Shell Crabs
with Hot-Stuff Dunk
and Jicama Slaw (page 169)

Herb-Roasted Rack of Lamb

Beautiful
Baby Beet Salad with
Orange-Mint Mayonnaise

Rhubarb Strawberry Pie

This menu is the very essence of spring ingredients, from shad roe to asparagus, soft-shell crabs, lamb, and of course rhubarb. It is marvelous to eat foods at the height of their season, with the magnificent flavors, colors, and sensations as vibrant as they can be.

There's an old-fashioned softness to vintage bowls and platters that plays well with the crispness of spring and the flavors of its food. So put away the brightly colored dishes; spring suggests a soft, gentle color scheme. Look around for any milk glass you might have inherited or picked up at a garage sale; rinse off the vintage floral plates and platters that you save for delicate fare. Rather than the predictable tulips and daffodils for the dining table, arrange bunches of lilac branches, if possible.

Serve the rosy beets in a pretty pink bowl to complement the color, with a dish of the orange-hued mayonnaise alongside. The lamb will look excellent on a large serving platter with generous bunches of mint for garnish. Finish off the spring palette with a two-tiered candy dish filled with Jordan almonds in pinks, lavenders, and soft greens.

THE MUSIC

Vivaldi's _Four Seasons_

Ella Fitzgerald's _Cole Porter Songbook_

Debussy

THE WINE

Dry Sauvignon Blanc

Chianti

THE EXTRAS

White wine glasses

Small decorative fish plates

SHAD ROE WITH A FRISEE SALAD

A great springtime delicacy, shad roe is traditionally prepared with bacon, which gives the dish a smoky flavor. Here, lovely Italian pancetta, which is cured but not smoked, allows the flavor and delicate texture of the roe to shine through. Surround the roe with frisée dressed in a honey-mellowed sherry vinaigrette.

> 2 pairs shad roe
> 1½ tablespoons sherry vinegar
> 1½ tablespoons extra-virgin olive oil
> ½ teaspoon honey
> 1 teaspoon finely chopped shallot
> 8 thin slices pancetta
> Salt and freshly ground black pepper,
>   to taste
> 6 cups baby frisée lettuce, leaves trimmed,
>   rinsed, and patted dry
> 2 tablespoons chopped fresh flat-leaf parsley,
>   for garnish

1. Gently dip the shad roe in a bowl of ice water to rinse, then transfer them to a paper towel–lined plate. Using small scissors, carefully trim away the membrane joining the two sides of the roe, to separate them into two pieces each.

2. Whisk the vinegar, olive oil, and honey together in a small bowl. Stir in the shallot; set aside.

3. Heat a dry nonstick skillet over medium heat. Add the pancetta, in batches, and cook until crisp, turning once, 6 to 8 minutes total. Transfer the pancetta to paper towels to drain.

4. Place the shad roe in the skillet you used to cook the pancetta, season with salt and pepper, and cook, covered, over low heat until golden brown and cooked through (the interior should by grayish pink), 5 minutes per side.

5. Place a piece of shad roe in the center of each of four plates. Lay 2 slices of pancetta over the shad roe. Lightly dress the frisée with the reserved vinaigrette and divide it equally among the four plates, arranging it alongside the roe. Sprinkle with the parsley and serve immediately.

CREAMY ASPARAGUS TARRAGON SOUP

Spring has not truly sprung until the asparagus have sprouted. After a winter's worth of root vegetables or produce that has traveled three thousand miles to get to your market, something fresh and green from local soil is like the return of a welcome neighbor. Earthy, creamy, with a hint of licorice from the tarragon, the aroma of this soup hints of a forest glade after a gentle spring rain. And the melon balls? They are a surprising but perfectly suited complement to the rich soup.

> 1 large leek, including 2 inches green
> 2 tablespoons distilled white vinegar
> 2 tablespoons unsalted butter
> 2 tablespoons olive oil
> 1 onion, chopped
> 1 parsnip, peeled and cut into small pieces
> 6 cups Basic Chicken Broth (page 397)
> 3 tablespoons chopped fresh tarragon
> 2 pounds fresh asparagus, woody ends
>   trimmed and discarded, cut into pieces
> ⅓ to ½ cup heavy (whipping) cream
> 12 small cantaloupe or watermelon balls,
>   for garnish
> 16 small fresh mint leaves, for garnish
> ⅓ cup sour cream, for garnish

1. Trim the root and tough outer leaves from the leek. Cut the leek in half lengthwise. Stir the vinegar into a bowl of cold water, add the leek, and let soak for 30 minutes to remove any sand.

Shad, a larger relative of the herring, come up the rivers of the East Coast to spawn each spring. Once upon a time there were millions and millions of them in the Delaware, Hudson, and Connecticut rivers. Then dams, overfishing, and pollution severely reduced their numbers. However, in one of the happier conservation stories of recent times, shad have returned to our rivers in force, so we can continue to enjoy this all-American spring tradition.

Then rinse the leek under running water, pat dry with paper towels, and cut into ¼-inch dice.

2. Melt the butter in the olive oil in a heavy pot over low heat. Add the leek, onion, and parsnip and cook, stirring, until softened, about 10 minutes.

3. Add the broth and tarragon and bring to a boil over high heat. Then add the asparagus, reduce the heat to low, cover, and simmer until the asparagus is very tender, 30 minutes. Uncover and allow to cool to room temperature.

4. Puree the soup, in batches, in a blender or food processor. (If the pureed soup seems stringy, pass it through a strainer.) Return the soup to the pot, stir in the cream, and reheat over low heat. Do not boil. Divide the soup among four bowls and place 3 melon balls in the center of each serving, surrounded by 4 mint leaves. Add a small dollop of sour cream on one side of the melon balls. Serve immediately.

Note: The soup may also be served cold: Chill it after adding the cream; add the melon balls, mint leaves, and sour cream just before serving.

PANKO SOFT-SHELL CRABS

About fifteen years ago there was a little Japanese restaurant in Greenwich Village that served soft-shell crabs in the spring. It was one of a number of Japanese restaurants within a few blocks of each other. This one, however, always had a line out the door at soft-shell time. It may have had something to do with the fact that the chef used the coarse Japanese bread crumbs known as panko to achieve an ethereally light crust. Basically, panko is grated bread, or bread shards, and the texture it creates is more granular than the bread crumbs we're used to. Panko is the ideal coating for seafood because it absorbs so little grease and stays so crunchy. The chili oil gives a bite to the sweet crisp crust.

½ cup all-purpose flour
Salt and freshly ground black pepper,
  to taste
Paprika, to taste
2 large eggs
1 teaspoon hot chili oil
1 cup panko (see Sources, page 405)
4 soft-shell crabs, cleaned (see box, facing page)
Peanut oil, for frying
Hot-Stuff Dunk (recipe follows),
  for serving
Jicama Slaw (page 169), for serving

1. Combine the flour, salt and pepper, and paprika in a shallow bowl.

2. In another shallow bowl, beat the eggs together with the chili oil.

3. Place the panko in a third shallow bowl.

4. Dredge the cleaned crabs in the seasoned flour, shaking off any excess. Then dip the crabs in the egg mixture, followed by the panko, covering them completely.

Panko Soft-Shell Crabs

¼ cup light soy sauce
¼ cup rice vinegar
1 tablespoon sugar
½ teaspoon salt
2 teaspoons minced fresh ginger
1 teaspoon minced garlic
6 tablespoons creamy peanut butter,
   at room temperature
3 tablespoons Asian sesame oil
1 teaspoon hot chili oil

1. Place the soy sauce, vinegar, sugar, salt, ginger, garlic, and 6 tablespoons water in a blender or food processor. Process on high speed until the ginger and garlic are pureed, about 1 minute. Add the peanut butter and process for 1 minute longer.

2. Combine the oils in a small pitcher. With the blender running, drizzle the oils into the sauce. Store, covered, in the refrigerator for up to 2 days. Bring to room temperature before serving.

MAKES 1¾ CUPS

5. Pour peanut oil to a depth of ¼ inch into a 10-inch skillet. Place the skillet over medium-high heat.

6. Fry the crabs in the hot oil until golden brown, 2 minutes per side. Drain on paper towels. Serve immediately with Hot-Stuff Dunk and Jicama Slaw.

HOT-STUFF DUNK

Garlic, ginger, and soy sauce, the holy trinity of Asian flavors, are spiced up with a little peppery heat in this dipping sauce—strong tastes in perfect balance, a very Zen combination.

HOW TO CLEAN A SOFT-SHELL CRAB

Place the crab on its stomach on a flat surface. Using a pair of kitchen shears, cut off the front of the crab, just behind the eyes. Lift up the edges of the shell on either side and remove all of the spongy gills. Then turn the crab over and cut off the tail flap, or "apron." Rinse the crab and pat it dry with paper towels. Cleaned crabs will keep in the refrigerator, on a platter covered in plastic wrap, for up to 2 hours.

HOW TO FRENCH A RACK OF LAMB

To french the rib bones of a rack of lamb, place the rack, fat side up, on a flat surface. Using a very sharp knife (a boning knife works well), make a cut across the rack, down to the bone, about 2 inches from the tip of the ribs. From this point, cut off all of the meat and fat from the top and between the bones, scraping the bones clean. If desired, save the meat scraps to be ground for use in a stuffing for a crown roast, or for any other ground lamb dish.

HERB-ROASTED RACK OF LAMB

Lamb is a sensual meat—succulent, tender, rich. A rack is nothing more than a rib roast of lamb, and "frenching" simply refers to the way the rack is trimmed, so that the ends of the bones are cleaned and separated, making them more attractive. Roasting the whole rack helps the lamb develop a much more intense flavor than cooking the chops separately would. Garlic and strong herbs—traditional with lamb all around the shores of the Mediterranean—add the perfect complementary tastes.

¼ cup fresh bread crumbs (see box, below)
4 cloves garlic
½ teaspoon coarse (kosher) salt
¼ cup chopped fresh rosemary
   or thyme, or 1 teaspoon dried
2 teaspoons coarsely ground black
   pepper
6 tablespoons extra-virgin olive oil
2 racks of rib lamb chops
   (8 chops each), bones frenched
   (see box, left)

1. Preheat the oven to 400°F.
2. Place the bread crumbs in a bowl.
3. Mince the garlic together with the salt. Add this to the bread crumbs, along with the rosemary and pepper. Mix in 4 tablespoons of the olive oil.
4. Cut each rack in half so that there are 4 chops to each piece. Brush the fat side and the meat of the end chops with the remaining 2 tablespoons olive oil. Coat the fat side of the racks and the end chops (not the underside), with the crumb mixture, patting it on well.
5. Arrange the racks in a baking dish and roast until medium-rare (140°F on an instant-read thermometer inserted into the meat through an end chop), 20 to 25 minutes. Slice the chops and, if desired, decorate the ends of the bones with paper frills. Serve immediately.

HOW TO MAKE FRESH BREAD CRUMBS

Tear slightly stale or lightly toasted bread into coarse pieces and place them in a food processor. Pulse the machine on and off for coarse crumbs. Store in an airtight container for up to 2 days.

Beautiful Baby Beet Salad

> *"The beet is the most*
> *intense of vegetables.*
> *The radish, admittedly,*
> *is more feverish,*
> *but the fire of the radish*
> *is a cold fire,*
> *the fire of discontent,*
> *not of passion. Tomatoes*
> *are lusty enough,*
> *yet there runs*
> *through tomatoes an*
> *undercurrent of frivolity.*
> *Beets are deadly serious."*
>
> —TOM ROBBINS

BEAUTIFUL BABY BEET SALAD

The combination of pastel and carmine young beets and pale coral mayonnaise echoes the delicate colors of spring.

2 pounds yellow or red baby beets,
  with 1 inch green and $1/2$ inch root left on
2 tablespoons red wine vinegar
Salt and freshly ground black pepper, to taste
3 tablespoons olive oil
$1/3$ cup small fresh mint leaves, for garnish
Orange-Mint Mayonnaise (recipe follows),
  for serving

1. Preheat the oven to 350°F.

2. Scrub the beets well and then wrap them, 3 or 4 together, in little packets of aluminum foil. Place the packets on a baking sheet and bake until the beets are tender when tested with a toothpick, about 1 hour. Open the packets and let the beets cool slightly.

3. Meanwhile, combine the vinegar and salt and pepper in a small bowl. Whisking constantly, slowly drizzle in the olive oil. Continue whisking until thickened. Set aside.

4. When the beets are cool enough to handle, slip off the skins (use rubber gloves to protect your hands). Halve the beets lengthwise (quarter any ones that seem a little too big) and place them in a bowl. Toss them with the dressing.

5. Using a slotted spoon, transfer the beets to a decorative bowl. Sprinkle with the mint leaves. Serve with the Orange-Mint Mayonnaise alongside for dolloping.

ORANGE-MINT MAYONNAISE

The delicate silkiness of mayonnaise enhanced by citrus and freshened by mint complements a whole spectrum of tastes: young beets, spring asparagus, oven-baked fries (the Belgians love mayo on their fries), and steamed mussels as well.

1 cup prepared mayonnaise,
  such as Hellmann's
2 tablespoons finely grated orange
  zest
1 tablespoon fresh orange juice
2 tablespoons chopped fresh mint
Salt and freshly ground black pepper,
  to taste

Combine all the ingredients in a bowl. Adjust the seasonings if needed. Refrigerate, covered, for 2 to 3 hours for the flavors to develop. This will keep for up to 3 days in the refrigerator; however, the flavor is best if the mint is fresh.

MAKES 1 CUP

RHUBARB STRAWBERRY PIE

Strawberry and rhubarb want to go together. For one, they grow at the same time of year, and that is a pretty big hint from nature. Second, fruitiness and tartness, balanced by a good dose of sweetness, is the hallmark of many a great dessert. Third, my mom made it; yours probably did, too; so does everyone's. When that many mothers agree on food, it is another hint from Mother Nature. After all the rich tastes in this meal, a rhubarb strawberry pie is as refreshing to the palate as a sorbet.

1½ pounds fresh rhubarb
2 cups fresh strawberries
½ cup plus 2 tablespoons granulated sugar
¼ cup (packed) light brown sugar
¼ cup all-purpose flour
2 tablespoons fresh lemon juice
Basic Pie Crust (page 401) for a 9-inch
  double-crust pie
1 large egg white, beaten

1. Position a rack in the lower third of the oven, and preheat the oven to 400°F.

2. Trim the rhubarb, then rinse and pat it dry. Cut the stalks into ¾-inch pieces. You should have about 3 cups of pieces.

3. Rinse the strawberries and pat them dry. Hull and quarter the berries.

4. Place the rhubarb and strawberries in a large bowl and toss with the ½ cup granulated sugar, the brown sugar, flour, and lemon juice.

5. Remove the prepared pie shell from the refrigerator. Brush the bottom and sides with the egg white. Spoon the fruit into the shell.

6. Cut the top crust into fourteen ½-inch-wide strips. Weave lattice strips over the top of the pie, folding the ends over the edge and trimming away any excess pastry. Crimp the edge decoratively. Brush the lattice lightly with water and sprinkle with the remaining 2 tablespoons granulated sugar.

7. Place the pie plate on a baking sheet and bake for 15 minutes. Reduce the oven temperature to 350°F and continue baking until the crust is golden brown and the filling is bubbly, about 1 hour more. Let the pie cool on a wire rack for at least 1 hour before serving.

Rhubarb is so closely associated with its use as an ingredient in pie—especially Rhubarb Strawberry Pie—that in many parts of the country it is known as pie plant.

Easter Sunday

Dinner

Easter celebrates rebirth—and what better reason to gather family together than the warmth of a new season? Make dinner an afternoon affair, sometime around two o'clock. The light is brilliant, the crocuses are in flower, and the egg-hunting generation has filled their baskets with a rainbow of home-dyed eggs for all the grown-ups to admire. As the sun pours through the window, the ham fills the house with its meaty fragrance, and if the day is warm enough, windows are open and the street is fragrant with the aromas of family feasts up and down the block.

MENU

Easter Sunday Dinner

FOR EIGHT

Heavenly Deviled Eggs

Glorious Mushroom Soup

All-American Waldorf Salad

Easter Bonnet Ham

Gina's Glazed Ginger Carrots

"Hot" Roasted Asparagus

Coconut Cream Pie

A basket of Easter eggs in cool pastels makes a pretty picture for the table, but when it comes to Easter eggs for the palate, why not add a little heat? In that spirit, start your Easter dinner with a platter of deviled eggs. Early spring mushrooms flavor the soup, and harmonize well with the fresh Waldorf salad and the gussied-up Virginia ham. Serve glazed carrots and roasted springtime asparagus alongside the ham. The Coconut Cream Pie is truly delicious and bridges the season of heavier winter desserts and those made with lighter summer fruit.

This menu might seem a little rich and creamy for today's lifestyle, but it balances out well—and anyway, it's time to splurge a little, with spring having arrived. You can omit the cream in the mushroom soup if you prefer, but oh, that pie! Put a bowl of ripe fruit on the table to assuage any guilt.

Look for a pastel tablecloth and another pastel shade for the napkins, staying within the gentle Easter egg color range—pinks, lavenders, soft greens, buttery yellows. Fill a pretty basket with fluffy Easter grass and dyed eggs for the centerpiece, and either pink and lavender hyacinths or several small daffodils springing up from between the eggs. (Keep the stems in florists' glass or plastic water tubes so they stay fresh.) These colors echo the pink of the Easter Bonnet Ham, the yellow of the deviled eggs, the green of the asparagus, and the overall softness of springtime. And at each place, a little basket filled with pastel jelly beans and chocolate eggs.

THE MUSIC

Oscar Peterson's
Easter Suite

**Soundtrack
from *Easter Parade***

THE WINE

Gewürztraminer

THE EXTRAS

Easter baskets
with Easter grass
and dyed Easter eggs

Asparagus
serving platter
and plates

Silver pie server

HEAVENLY DEVILED EGGS

Rescue some of the eggs from your morning Easter egg hunt and turn them into a delicious and practical hors d'oeuvre for this traditional Easter meal—the deviled egg. Everything about these eggs is devilish—but especially their touch of heat—and in fact that heat helps to make them heavenly. You don't want to run out—these are very popular—so have plenty on hand.

> 12 large eggs
> 2 teaspoons Dijon mustard
> 2 teaspoons pickle relish, drained
> 2 to 4 dashes Tabasco sauce, to taste
> Salt, to taste
> 1/2 teaspoon freshly ground black
>   pepper
> 2 teaspoons finely chopped fresh
>   tarragon leaves
> 2 tablespoons snipped fresh chives
> 6 tablespoons prepared mayonnaise,
>   such as Hellmann's
> Paprika, for garnish
> Whole fresh chives, for garnish

1. If you already have hard-cooked eggs from your egg hunt, just peel them and move on to step 2. If you're starting from scratch, place the eggs in a saucepan. Gently rinse them with warm water and then drain (this keeps them from cracking). Cover with cold water, place over medium-high heat, and bring to a boil. Reduce the heat to a gentle simmer and cook for exactly 13 minutes. Drain the eggs, rinse under cold water, and peel. Let them cool in the refrigerator, loosely covered, for 15 minutes.

2. Halve the eggs lengthwise and carefully scoop out the yolks. Set the whites aside. Place the yolks in a bowl and mash them with a fork. Add the mustard, pickle relish, Tabasco sauce, salt, pepper, tarragon, and snipped chives. Stir in the mayonnaise.

3. Fill the whites with the egg yolk mixture and dust the tops lightly with paprika. Arrange the eggs in a spoke design on a decorative platter, garnished with the whole chives.

MAKES 24 PIECES

GLORIOUS MUSHROOM SOUP

One of the many delights of spring is the mushroom in all its edible forms. Although most of us aren't knowledgeable enough to "shroom" with authority, nowadays there are so many cultivated and wild varieties of mushrooms available in the market, we need not feel deprived. Their great flavor and texture add a smoky, earthy woodiness to this sophisticated take on an old-fashioned soup.

> 2 leeks, including 2 inches green
> 2 tablespoons distilled white vinegar
> 4 tablespoons (1/2 stick) unsalted butter
> 2 tablespoons olive oil
> 1 cup chopped onions
> 2 pounds white mushrooms
> 8 ounces cremini mushrooms
> 5 ounces shiitake mushrooms
> Salt and freshly ground black pepper,
>   to taste
> 5 to 6 cups Basic Chicken Broth
>   (page 397)
> 1/4 cup Madeira wine
> 1 cup heavy (whipping) cream (optional)
> Crème fraîche, for garnish (optional)
> 2 to 3 tablespoons snipped fresh chives,
>   for garnish

1. Trim the root and tough outer leaves off the leeks. Cut them in half lengthwise. Stir the vinegar into a large bowl of cold water, add the leeks, and let them soak for 30 minutes to remove any sand. Then rinse the leeks under running water, pat dry with paper towels, and chop.

2. Melt the butter in the olive oil in a large soup pot over low heat. Add the leeks and onions and cook, stirring, until softened, 12 minutes.

3. Meanwhile, wipe all the mushroom caps clean with damp paper towels. Trim the stems and thinly slice the mushrooms lengthwise.

4. Add the mushrooms to the leeks and onion, season with salt and pepper, and cook, stirring frequently, until the mushrooms soften and release some of their liquid, 5 minutes.

5. Add the broth and Madeira and bring to a boil over high heat. Reduce the heat to low and simmer, partially covered, until the mushrooms are very tender, about 40 minutes.

6. Strain the soup and place the solids in a food processor. Add 1 cup of the strained broth and puree until smooth.

7. Return the puree to the soup pot. Adjust the seasonings if necessary and add the remaining 4 to 5 cups strained broth. Stir in the cream, if desired. Heat through over low heat. Do not boil. Ladle the soup into bowls, garnish with a dollop of crème fraîche, if desired, sprinkle with the snipped chives, and serve.

ALL-AMERICAN WALDORF SALAD

If they gave an Oscar for inventing American classics, it would go not to a chef but to a maître d', the legendary Oscar Tshirky of the Waldorf-Astoria. Though not a chef by training, he understood food. Culinary tradition credits him with the invention of Thousand Island Dressing and this most American of recipes, the Waldorf Salad. The fruit in it goes beautifully with the glaze on the ham. My additions—fennel and yogurt—add bite and tang to this great classic.

1½ cups diced celery (¼-inch dice)
1½ cups diced unpeeled Granny Smith apple
*   (¼-inch dice)*
½ cup diced unpeeled McIntosh apple
*   (¼-inch dice)*
1 cup diced fennel (¼-inch dice)
Finely grated zest of 1 lemon
1 tablespoon fresh lemon juice
½ cup prepared mayonnaise,
*   such as Hellmann's*
½ cup plain nonfat yogurt
Salt and freshly ground black pepper,
*   to taste*
1 cup coarsely chopped walnuts
2 tablespoons chopped fresh
*   flat-leaf parsley*

1. Combine the celery, apples, and fennel in a large bowl. Toss with the lemon zest and juice.

2. Combine the mayonnaise and yogurt in a small bowl and fold into the fruit. Season with salt and pepper. Stir in the walnuts and parsley. Chill the salad for up to 4 hours. Bring it to room temperature before serving.

EASTER BONNET HAM

While lamb has become a popular Easter main course, a good old-fashioned Easter ham is hard to beat. If you grew up in the fifties, you probably ate those hams studded with maraschino cherries and pineapples, but now that we have been through the Food Revolution, some tend to snub those ingredients. Not me—there are beautiful fruity, sweet flavors in pineapple and cherries, and when they are glistening with a ginger and garlic glaze, this colorful ham will look like a bonnet that Carmen Miranda might have worn in the Easter parade!

4 cups pineapple juice
4 cloves garlic, smashed
1 piece (1 inch) fresh ginger,
   sliced
1 bone-in smoked Virginia ham
   (14 to 16 pounds)
12 to 16 whole cloves
¼ cup Dijon mustard
1 cup (packed) light brown
   sugar
About 10 pineapple rings
About 10 maraschino cherries

1. Combine the pineapple juice, garlic, and ginger in a heavy saucepan. Bring to a boil, reduce the heat to medium-low, and simmer until the liquid is reduced by half, 25 minutes. Strain the liquid and set it aside.

2. Preheat the oven to 350°F.

3. Carefully trim the thick rind and all but ¼ inch of the fat from the surface of the ham. With a sharp knife, score a diamond pattern in the fat. Insert the cloves in the centers of the diamonds.

4. Set the ham in a shallow baking pan. Brush the mustard all over the top and then pat the brown sugar over the mustard.

5. Starting at the butt end, decoratively arrange the pineapple rings over the ham, securing cherries in the center with toothpicks. When the surface is covered, pour the reserved pineapple juice into the bottom of the pan and place it in the oven.

6. Bake, basting every 15 minutes, for 1½ hours.

7. Place the ham on a serving platter and let it rest for 15 minutes. Present the ham at the table so everyone can see just how beautiful it is. Then carve it into thin slices, beginning at the butt end. As you carve, remove the pineapple slices and cherries and serve them with the ham. Serve the warm pan sauce alongside.

Easter Bonnet Ham

GINA'S GLAZED GINGER CARROTS

The first time I devoured my friend Gina Fox's glazed ginger carrots, she served them with a baked Virginia ham, and I've been making them with ham ever since. The ginger here is in larger chips than usual, so that when you take a bite you truly get a jolt! Even Gina's children gobbled these carrots down, as did all of the adults.

3 pounds carrots, peeled
1 piece (3 inches) fresh ginger, peeled
1 cup plus 2 tablespoons Basic Chicken Broth
    (page 397)
3 tablespoons unsalted butter
2 tablespoons minced garlic
6 tablespoons (packed) light brown sugar
1/4 cup maple syrup
3 tablespoons molasses
1/4 teaspoon dried red pepper flakes,
    or up to 1/4 teaspoon more, to taste

1. Slice the carrots into bite-size pieces on an irregular diagonal: Starting at the fat end of the carrot, make a diagonal slice, then turn the carrot a half turn and slice on the diagonal again, repeating until you get to the end of the carrot. Place the carrots in a saucepan.

2. Cut the piece of ginger lengthwise into quarters and then crosswise into 1/8-inch-thick pieces. Add the ginger to the carrots along with all the remaining ingredients. Bring the mixture to a boil. Cook, partially covered, over medium-low heat, stirring occasionally, until the liquid has reduced to a thick syrup and the carrots are glazed, 15 to 20 minutes. Uncover and cook, stirring, until the carrots and ginger are tender, about 5 minutes longer. Watch the carrots carefully to avoid scorching.

1/4 cup sherry vinegar
1 teaspoon honey
1/3 cup extra-virgin olive oil, plus more
    for brushing
Coarse (kosher) salt and freshly ground black
    pepper, to taste
2 shallots, very thinly sliced lengthwise
2 pounds asparagus, woody ends trimmed
8 thin slices pancetta

1. Position a rack in the center of the oven, and preheat the oven to 400°F.

2. Place the vinegar and honey in a small bowl and whisk in the 1/3 cup olive oil. Season with coarse salt and pepper and add the shallot slices. Set the vinaigrette aside.

3. Arrange the asparagus on one or two baking sheets in eight groups of 5 or 6 spears. Brush them with olive oil and sprinkle generously with salt and pepper.

4. Bring a small pot of water to a boil, and blanch the pancetta slices in it for 30 seconds. Drain them on paper towels. Then lay a pancetta slice across the bottom half of each asparagus bunch. Roast until the asparagus have browned slightly, 15 minutes.

5. To serve, use a spatula to carefully transfer the pancetta-topped asparagus to eight salad plates. Spoon the vinaigrette over each portion.

"HOT" ROASTED ASPARAGUS

Because asparagus is the first green vegetable of the season, it is often treated like a never-been-kissed debutant who just graduated from a remote all-girls school—very gently and subtly. But when it's roasted to concentrate the flavors and then combined with some un-shy flavors, such as pancetta, vinegar, and honey, asparagus takes on a new dimension. This deb is definitely ready to paint the town.

COCONUT CREAM PIE

In the beginning there were delicious cream pies that were actually cakes, the most renowned being Boston Cream Pie. During the 1950s authentic cream pies—from banana cream to chocolate cream to coconut cream—were extremely popular. And oh how yummy those pies were; every once in a while one just has to find a place on our tables. Easter Sunday dinner is the ideal occasion because we're between seasons of imported winter fruits and the local crop. Never mind, we'll all watch what we eat on Monday!

FOR THE CRUST AND COCONUT CREAM FILLING

Easy Tart or Pie Crust (page 402)
for a single-crust pie
2 tablespoons all-purpose flour
¹⁄₃ cup cornstarch
³⁄₄ cup granulated sugar
2 cans (14 ounces each) unsweetened
coconut milk
5 large egg yolks
3 tablespoons unsalted butter
1 tablespoon white rum
1 tablespoon pure vanilla extract

FOR THE CREAM TOPPING

2 cups heavy (whipping) cream
¹⁄₃ cup confectioners' sugar
1 teaspoon pure vanilla extract
1 cup sweetened shredded coconut,
for garnish

Coconut Cream Pie

1. Roll the pie dough out to form a 12-inch circle. Lay it evenly in a 9-inch pie plate and pat it in to fit. Trim the overhanging dough so it is even with the edge of the pie plate. Chill the pastry, covered, in the refrigerator for 1 hour.

2. Position a rack in the lower two thirds of the oven, and preheat the oven to 425°F.

3. Fit two sheets of heavy-duty aluminum foil directly on the surface of the pie crust to weight it down. Bake the crust until it turns golden brown, about 10 minutes. Remove the foil and bake the crust to firm up, 5 minutes longer. Let the crust cool on a wire rack.

4. Prepare the coconut cream filling: Combine the flour, cornstarch, and granulated sugar in a saucepan. Gradually whisk in 1 can of the coconut milk. Then whisk in 1 cup of the second can (reserve the rest for another use). Bring to a boil over medium heat, stirring constantly. Reduce the heat to low and simmer 2 minutes.

5. Beat the egg yolks in a bowl. Whisk some of the hot filling into the yolks, and then whisk the mixture back into the saucepan. Continue to simmer, whisking constantly over low heat, until slightly thickened, 2 minutes.

6. Remove the pan from the heat and whisk in the butter, rum, and vanilla until smooth. Pour the filling into a bowl and place a piece of plastic wrap directly on the surface of the filling to prevent a skin from forming. Set it aside to cool to room temperature. When the filling is cool, scrape it into the baked pie crust. Cover and chill in the refrigerator until set, about 1 hour.

7. Just before serving, whip the cream with the confectioners' sugar and vanilla until stiff peaks form. Spread the whipped cream over the coconut cream filling, mounding it slightly in the center. Sprinkle the top evenly with the shredded coconut and refrigerate until serving time, up to 4 hours.

Greek Easter with

My friends Wende and Aristide Kambanis are the heads of a food-loving, fun-loving Greek American family. For them, as for Greeks all over the world, Easter is *the* big holiday, like Thanksgiving, Christmas, and Mardi Gras rolled into one. For the first few days of Holy Week, many Greeks fast, then, on the night of Holy Saturday, all gather at the local church. At the stroke of midnight, the reflectiveness of Holy Week is transformed into the joy of Easter. Feasts of lamb and pastries and every vegetable and fruit available culminate in hours of dancing. The celebrations at the Kambanis home are always warm, festive, fun, and delicious.

the Kambanises

MENU

MEZE:
Fennel and Cucumber Tzatziki • Giant Butter Beans
and Roasted Beets • Greek Tarama Slather • Skordalia
• Roasted Baba Ghanoush • Warmed Pita Bread Wedges

———

ROASTED RED PEPPER SOUP

———

CHOPPED GREEK SALAD

———

SAGE-ROASTED LEG OF LAMB

———

HONEY-GLAZED ALMOND CAKE

———

LAVENDER-HONEY ICE CREAM

Greek food is sumptuous and full-bodied, including the *meze,* the small dishes that begin the meal. A basket filled with warm pita triangles is essential for scooping up the delicious spreads—tzatziki, eggplant-laden baba ghanoush, smooth tarama, and skordalia, with its irresistible garlic flavor. These combine with the meaty butter beans and roasted beets for an array of flavors and textures that your family could linger over for hours—as many Greeks do.

A rich Roasted Red Pepper Soup followed by a modern Chopped Greek Salad set the stage for the main event, the herb-infused roast leg of lamb. End with a heavenly Honey-Glazed Almond Cake and a scoop of Lavender-Honey Ice Cream. They'll be smiling upon this meal from Mt. Olympus.

Wende and Steedy set the scene for their Easter dinner true to Greek custom: Small bowls of assorted olives are placed here and there on the table, and the traditional basket of red-dyed Easter eggs acts as a centerpiece. Wende always has plenty of colorful ceramic dishes for the *meze,* and baskets lined with colorful cotton napkins for the warm pita bread. Sometimes she places a basket filled with lemons on the sideboard as a natural decoration—a nice touch.

A plate with some delicious fresh feta and manouri, another Greek cheese, is set out with bouquets of fresh parsley and mint—both important herbs in Greek cuisine.

Warmth and good times are what Greek Easter is all about at the Kambanis house—or in your own home.

THE MUSIC

Nikos Gounaris

Nana Mouskouri

Gouraris

THE DRINKS

Ouzo

Retsina

Santorini or Patras

Naoussa or Château Carras

THE EXTRAS

Baskets

Ice-cream maker

The Meze

FENNEL AND CUCUMBER TZATZIKI

Tzatziki is usually made with yogurt, cucumber, garlic, and mint. Not unlike raita in Indian cuisine, it is a combination that goes beautifully with roasted meats, especially heavily seasoned ones, because it cools and cleans the palate. To the traditional cucumber I have added fennel—it's no stranger to the Greek cook, although not usually found in tzatziki. I find that its crisp bite and perfumed anise flavor hits the spot with a glass of ouzo.

> 3 cups plain yogurt, preferably sheep's-milk
>   yogurt
> 1 fennel bulb, trimmed
> 1 hothouse (seedless) cucumber, peeled,
>   cut in half lengthwise, center scraped out
> 4 cloves garlic, coarsely chopped
> $\frac{1}{3}$ cup coarsely chopped walnuts
> $\frac{1}{2}$ cup extra-virgin olive oil
> 2 scallions, including 1 inch green, thinly sliced
> $\frac{1}{4}$ cup finely chopped fresh dill leaves
> Freshly ground black pepper, to taste

1. Line a strainer with three layers of paper towels and set it over a bowl. Pour the yogurt into the strainer and let it drain for 3 hours in the refrigerator.

2. Cut the fennel in half lengthwise and remove the outer layer. Core and very finely dice the bulb.

3. Coarsely chop half of the cucumber and finely dice the other half.

4. Place the drained yogurt, half of the fennel, the coarsely chopped cucumber, and the garlic and walnuts in a food processor. Pulse until combined but still a bit chunky.

5. Gradually drizzle the olive oil in through the feed tube, pulsing the machine on and off until combined. Transfer the mixture to a bowl and fold in the scallions, dill, and pepper. Add the remaining chopped fennel and the finely diced cucumber.

6. Chill, uncovered, in the refrigerator for up to 1 hour before serving.

MAKES 3$\frac{1}{2}$ CUPS

GIANT BUTTER BEANS AND ROASTED BEETS

Butter beans and beets is a popular dish during Lent—first because it provides a good source of protein for those who give up meat, and second because it's a combination with a beautiful texture and a nutty sweet flavor. Canned beans are available in most supermarkets, and those are preferable in this recipe. Buy the largest butter beans you can find.

FOR THE VINAIGRETTE

> $\frac{1}{4}$ cup red wine vinegar
> 2 small cloves garlic, finely minced with
> $\frac{1}{2}$ teaspoon coarse (kosher) salt
> $\frac{1}{2}$ cup extra-virgin olive oil
> Freshly ground black pepper, to taste

FOR THE BEANS AND BEETS

> 2 cans (10 ounces each) giant butter beans
>   or lima beans, drained, rinsed, and patted
>   dry with paper towels
> $\frac{1}{4}$ cup chopped fresh flat-leaf parsley
> 4 Roasted Beets (page 399), peeled and
>   cut into thick slices
> Salt and freshly ground black pepper, to taste
> 1 cup walnut halves
> 4 scallions, including 3 inches green, thinly sliced

1. Prepare the vinaigrette: Combine the vinegar, garlic, and coarse salt in a small bowl. Slowly drizzle in the olive oil, whisking constantly. Add a generous grinding of pepper.

2. Place the beans and the parsley in a bowl and toss with about ½ cup of the vinaigrette.

3. Just before serving, gently fold in the beets. Season with salt and pepper and toss lightly. Transfer the salad to a decorative plate and sprinkle the walnuts and the scallions over it.

Butter bean is another name for the lima bean. I don't know where the butter part came from, but so far as *lima* goes, food archaeologists think that this wonderful bean originally was cultivated by the Peruvians thousands of years ago and slowly made its way north.

GREEK TARAMA SLATHER

Fish roe, whether it is the silky gray eggs of ripe sturgeon that give us beluga, sevruga, and osetra caviar, or *tarama*, the pink eggs of the carp or the cod that make the basis of this fish dip, all share a briny, smooth quality that hits the palate with explosions of flavor. Combining *tarama* with cream cheese makes for an ambrosial dip that no Greek would pass up.

1 jar (10 ounces) tarama (carp roe) caviar (see Note)
16 ounces cream cheese, cut into small pieces
2 tablespoons fresh lemon juice
2 teaspoons minced garlic
3 tablespoons heavy (whipping) cream
3 tablespoons olive oil
Freshly ground black pepper, to taste

1. Combine the carp roe, cream cheese, lemon juice, and garlic in a food processor and process until smooth.

2. With the motor running, pour the cream and olive oil through the feed tube. Transfer the mixture to a bowl, add the pepper, and adjust the seasonings to taste. Serve immediately or refrigerate, covered, for up to 2 days.

MAKES 1 QUART

Note: *Tarama* (carp roe) is available in Greek and specialty food stores.

SKORDALIA

Skordalia is a nearly universal *meze* on the tables of restaurants in Greece. In the Plaka, the old area of Athens near the Acropolis, it seems that every charming taverna offers this creamy white garlic-and-potato sauce, ready to be scooped up in a small triangle of pita bread. My favorite skordalia in New York is served at Periyali, and this recipe, which also appears in *The Periyali Cookbook*, comes from that restaurant.

1 small (4 ounces) Yukon Gold or other waxy potato
5 slices stale good-quality white bread, such as Pepperidge Farm, crusts removed
3 tablespoons fresh lemon juice
3 tablespoons white wine vinegar
3 tablespoons extra-virgin olive oil
¾ teaspoon salt
½ teaspoon sugar
½ cup blanched almonds
2 cloves garlic, pressed through a garlic press
Salt and coarsely ground black pepper, to taste

1. Place the potato in a small saucepan, cover with water, and bring to a boil over high heat. Cook until tender, 12 to 15 minutes. Drain and let cool to room temperature. Then peel the potato and set it aside.

2. Fill a bowl with water. One slice at a time, drop the bread into the water and let it get saturated. Remove the bread and squeeze it out very slightly before dropping in the next slice. Place the squeezed bread in a bowl and set it aside.

3. Mix the lemon juice, vinegar, olive oil, ¾ teaspoon salt, and the sugar together in a measuring cup. Set it aside.

4. Place the almonds, garlic, and potato in a food processor. Pulse the machine on and off until the mixture is just smooth. Do not over-process.

5. With the machine running, add a little at a time, the lemon juice mixture and the bread along with any water that might have accumulated in the bowl, alternating between the two. Stop the machine occasionally to scrape down the sides of the bowl.

6. Transfer the skordalia to a bowl and season with salt and coarse pepper. Refrigerate, covered, for several hours. Serve at room temperature.

MAKES 1½ TO 2 CUPS

ROASTED BABA GHANOUSH

Whether you call it baba ghanoush or eggplant caviar, this tantalizing eggplant spread is de rigueur as part of any *meze* offering. Its flavor is enhanced here by the addition of fresh lemon juice and mint.

> 2 eggplants (about 1 pound each)
> 2 cloves garlic
> ½ teaspoon coarse (kosher) salt
> 3 tablespoons fresh lemon juice
> 2 tablespoons chopped fresh flat-leaf parsley
> 1 tablespoon tahini (sesame paste)
> 1 tablespoon extra-virgin olive oil
> 2 teaspoons coarsely chopped fresh mint
> Salt and freshly ground black pepper, to taste

From the Department of Weird Food Facts: The largest serving of baba ghanoush ever prepared was presented in Dubai on June 28, 2001. The recipe starts: "Take 5,500 pounds of eggplant . . ." Now, that must have been some celebration.

1. Preheat the oven to 350°F.

2. Prick the eggplants with the tines of a fork and wrap each one in aluminum foil. Place them on a baking sheet and roast for 1 hour.

3. Finely mince the garlic together with the ½ teaspoon salt. Set it aside.

4. Remove the eggplants from the oven and let cool. When they are cool enough to handle, carefully open the foil packets. Slit the eggplants down the center and scoop out and discard the seeds (see Note). Scoop out the flesh and place it in a food processor. Add all the remaining ingredients except the salt and pepper.

5. Pulse the mixture until it is blended but some texture remains. Use a rubber spatula to transfer it to a bowl. Season generously with salt and pepper and serve immediately, or refrigerate, covered, for up to 1 day.

MAKES 2 CUPS

Note: The seeds are discarded because they can lend a bitter flavor to the spread.

ROASTED RED PEPPER SOUP

I can never resist a great bell pepper soup—especially when some of the peppers are broiled for a subtle smoky flavor. The smooth soup has a slight tang that sets up the palate for the richness of the super-unctuous roasted lamb. As a bonus, it can be served hot or cold.

Roasted Red Pepper Soup

*6 red bell peppers, stemmed, cut in half
   lengthwise, and seeded
2 tablespoons unsalted butter
2 tablespoons extra-virgin olive oil
1 cup chopped leeks, white part only
   (see Note)
1 cup chopped onions
3 small (¾ pound) boiling potatoes,
   peeled and thinly sliced
Salt and freshly ground black pepper,
   to taste
5 cups Basic Chicken Broth (page 397)
Extra-virgin olive oil (if serving the soup hot),
   for garnish
Freshly grated Parmesan cheese
   (if serving the soup hot), for garnish
2 tablespoons snipped fresh chives, for garnish*

1. Preheat the broiler. Line a baking sheet with aluminum foil.

2. Place 6 bell pepper halves, cut side down, on the prepared baking sheet. Broil the peppers, 2 to 3 inches from the heat source, until the skins are charred, about 10 minutes. Transfer the peppers to a plastic or paper bag, seal it, and let the pepper steam for 10 minutes. Then remove them from the bag and slip off the skins. Chop the roasted peppers coarsely and set aside.

3. Melt the butter in the olive oil in a soup pot over medium-low heat. Add the leeks and onions and cook, stirring occasionally, until soft, about 10 minutes.

4. Meanwhile, chop the 6 raw bell pepper halves.

5. Add the chopped raw peppers to the pot along with the potatoes, chopped roasted peppers, salt and pepper, and broth. Bring to a boil over high heat, skimming off any foam that forms on the surface. Reduce the heat to low and simmer, partially covered, until the vegetables are tender, 30 minutes. Allow to cool slightly.

6. Puree the soup, in batches, in a food processor or blender, and then return it to the pot. Heat through and serve immediately, or cool to room

> *"To invite a person to your house is to take charge of his happiness as long as he is beneath your roof."*
>
> —JEAN ANTHELME BRILLAT-SAVARIN

temperature and refrigerate for up to 6 hours if serving cold.

7. To serve the soup hot, garnish it with a small drizzle of olive oil in the center and a sprinkling of cheese, followed by the chives. To serve it cold, simply garnish it with a sprinkling of chives.

Note: Before chopping, soak the leeks in a bowl of cold water mixed with 2 tablespoons distilled white vinegar to remove the sand. Drain, pat dry with paper towels, and chop.

CHOPPED GREEK SALAD

Back in the days when ethnic food mostly meant Chinese and Italian, this colorful mix of lettuce, salty feta cheese, garden vegetables, and briny olives seemed very authentic. I was surprised, therefore, to read a travel article in which a Greek chef said that in Greece they never included lettuce in the salad because when beautiful Adonis tried to steal Hera, Zeus's wife, the angry father of the gods turned the would-be lover boy into a wilting head of lettuce. And you never want a wilting lover. Still, I make my Greek salad with lettuce, and if Zeus ever had a taste of it, I know he would change his mind.

2 cups chopped tender romaine lettuce
 leaves
2 roasted red bell peppers (see box, page 399),
 cut into ¹/₂-inch pieces
2 ripe tomatoes, cut into ¹/₂-inch pieces
1 hothouse (seedless) cucumber,
 peeled, cut in quarters lengthwise,
 and cut into ¹/₂-inch pieces
1 cup halved pitted Kalamata olives
¹/₃ cup diced red onion (¹/₄-inch dice)
2 tablespoons chopped fresh mint or
 flat-leaf parsley
Salt and freshly ground black pepper,
 to taste
2 tablespoons extra-virgin olive oil
2 tablespoons red wine vinegar
1 cup coarsely crumbled feta cheese

1. Combine the lettuce, bell peppers, tomatoes, cucumber, olives, onion, and mint in a large bowl.

2. Just before serving, season with salt and pepper and toss with the olive oil and vinegar. Add the feta cheese and lightly toss again, trying not to break up the feta too much. Serve in a decorative salad bowl.

SAGE-ROASTED LEG OF LAMB

All through the Mediterranean countries, sage is paired with roasted meats and fowl, and this herb's perfume pulls out every savory note from the meat. When you insert it next to the bone, it infuses the leg of lamb with its tantalizing aroma. Sage is also pretty—its pale green leaves are reminiscent of the first blush of green in the spring, although it is actually one of the garden herbs that usually lasts well into the fall. The ancient Romans believed that sage increased mental powers. If that is true, there is enough sage packed next to the bone of this lamb to create a whole tableful of college professors.

¹/₂ cup whole fresh sage leaves,
 coarsely chopped
6 large cloves garlic, chopped
3 to 4 tablespoons extra-virgin olive oil
1 bone-in leg of lamb, 6¹/₂ to 7 pounds
Salt and freshly ground black pepper,
 to taste
¹/₂ cup Basic Chicken Broth (page 397)
¹/₂ cup dry white wine
3 or 4 bunches fresh sage, for garnish

1. Preheat the oven to 400°F.

2. Combine the chopped sage, half of the garlic, and 2 tablespoons of the olive oil in a small bowl. Mix well.

3. Run a boning knife around the bone at the butt end of the leg and stuff two thirds of the sage mixture down and around the bone. Make several slits on the surface of the leg with the point of a small knife and stuff the remaining mixture into the slits. Rub the remaining 1 to 2 tablespoons oil and the remaining garlic over the lamb, along with any remaining sage mixture. Sprinkle the lamb all over with salt and pepper and place it in a shallow roasting pan. Pour the broth and the wine into the pan.

4. Put the lamb in the oven and immediately reduce the oven temperature to 350°F. Roast, basting occasionally, until the temperature on a meat thermometer inserted at the thickest part of the leg registers 140°F for medium-rare meat, 1 hour and 40 minutes. If you prefer the lamb more well-done, roast it 10 minutes more. Let the lamb rest for 10 minutes before carving. (The internal temperature will rise slightly as it rests.)

5. Place the lamb on a serving platter and garnish it with the bunches of sage. To serve, carve the lamb into thin slices.

HONEY-GLAZED ALMOND CAKE

Pastry soaked in honey and laced with nuts is a traditional dessert in Greece and elsewhere around the Eastern Mediterranean. Here I opted for the same flavors in a cake. The flavor is super-intense, so a little goes a long way.

FOR THE HONEY GLAZE
1/2 cup granulated sugar
1/4 cup honey
1 cinnamon stick (3 inches long)
3 whole cloves
1 strip lemon zest (3 inches long)

FOR THE CAKE
1 cup all-purpose flour
1 teaspoon baking powder
1 teaspoon ground cinnamon
1/4 teaspoon ground cloves
1/4 teaspoon salt
12 tablespoons (1 1/2 sticks) unsalted butter,
*   at room temperature*
3/4 cup granulated sugar
1 teaspoon lemon extract
3 large eggs, separated
1/2 cup whole milk
1 cup finely ground amaretti cookies (see Note)
1 cup finely ground blanched almonds
1/4 cup confectioners' sugar

1. Preheat the oven to 350°F. Butter a 13 x 9-inch baking pan. Line the bottom with wax paper, and butter the paper.

2. Prepare the honey glaze: Combine 1 cup water, the granulated sugar, honey, cinnamon, cloves, and lemon zest in a medium-size saucepan over high heat and bring to a boil. Reduce the heat to low and simmer, uncovered, until thickened, about 10 minutes. Remove from the heat, discard the whole spices and the lemon zest, and set aside to cool.

3. Combine the flour, baking powder, cinnamon, cloves, and salt in a bowl.

4. Cream the butter, granulated sugar, and lemon extract together in a large bowl with an electric mixer on high speed until light and fluffy. Add the egg yolks, one at a time, beating well after each addition. Using a rubber spatula, stir in the flour mixture and the milk until just incorporated. Fold in the ground amaretti and the almonds.

5. Using clean beaters, beat the egg whites in a bowl until soft peaks form. Stir one quarter of the beaten whites into the batter until combined. Then fold in the remaining whites with a rubber spatula until just incorporated. The batter will be thick. Scrape the batter into the prepared pan, spreading it evenly to the edges.

6. Bake the cake until a toothpick inserted in the center comes out clean, about 40 minutes. Set the pan on a wire rack and pour the glaze evenly over the warm cake. Let the cake cool completely and the syrup be absorbed, about 1 hour. Then invert the cake onto a platter and unmold it. Remove the wax paper and cut the cake into twelve 3-inch squares. Dust the cake with confectioners' sugar just before serving. (The cake can be made a day head.)

Note: This is about 26 cookies. A 5.3-ounce bag contains 14 double cookies, two more than the recipe calls for.

> "*Here's flowers for you;*
> *Hot lavender, mints, savory, marjoram;*
> *The marigold,*
> *that goes to bed with the sun,*
> *And with him rises weeping;*
> *these are flowers*
> *Of middle summer.*"
>
> —WILLIAM SHAKESPEARE

LAVENDER-HONEY ICE CREAM

When I think of Greece, I see hillsides covered with lavender. The aroma of this fragrant shrub intermingles in my memory with the sweet essence of orange blossoms. This perfumed ice cream was created with them in mind.

> 3 cups heavy (whipping) cream
> 1 cup whole milk
> $\frac{1}{2}$ cup sugar
> 1 tablespoon dry lavender flowers
>   (see Note)
> 2 teaspoons orange-blossom honey
> 4 large egg yolks

1. Combine the cream, milk, sugar, lavender, and honey in a saucepan over medium heat. Cook until the mixture is hot but not boiling and the sugar has dissolved, about 10 minutes. Remove from the heat and allow to steep for 30 minutes. Then strain the mixture and return it to the saucepan to reheat slightly. Remove it from the heat again.

2. Place the egg yolks in a small bowl and whisk to mix. Whisking constantly, slowly pour 1 cup of the hot milk mixture into the eggs. Continue to whisk until smooth.

3. Slowly pour the egg mixture into the saucepan, whisking constantly until well combined. Place the saucepan over medium heat and stir the mixture constantly until it is thick enough to coat the back of a spoon, 6 to 8 minutes. The mixture should never boil.

4. Strain the mixture into a bowl and allow it to cool to room temperature.

5. Freeze in an ice-cream maker according to the manufacturer's instructions. Transfer the ice cream to a container, cover, and freeze.

MAKES 1 QUART

Note: This recipe can easily be doubled. The lavender used to make this ice cream should be purchased in a market that sells edible produce. Do not use lavender from the florists—most likely it has been sprayed with a pesticide. Let the lavender dry, stems tied together and the bunch hung upside down, until the flowers crumble easily when plucked. It should take a few days.

A Run for

Wherever you live, there is a first "perfect" week every year, when the spring blossoms are at their peak and the trees wear a newborn mantle of brilliant green. In Louisville, Kentucky, a beautiful old city on the Ohio River, that time comes during the

first week in May. Although you can't miss the profusion of flowers, the main attraction is America's oldest thoroughbred race, the Kentucky Derby—two minutes of thundering hooves, brilliant racing silks, and shouting crowds all hoping for victory. Kick off racing's greatest day with a spread of Southern fare: country ham, fresh salads, steaming buttermilk biscuits, and sweet bourbon-rich desserts—with, of course, mint juleps. A Derby Day buffet is a feast for the senses, celebrating spring in all its fullness.

A Run for the Roses

BUFFET FOR SIXTEEN

Spiked Kentucky Mint Juleps

Shrimp and Belgian Endive Rémoulade

Lemon-Chive Asparagus Salad

Smithfield Country Ham

Derby Slaw

Rolled Buttermilk Biscuits

Banana Bourbon Bread

Bananas Foster Ice Cream

Kentucky Bourbon Balls

An elegant lunch in Louisville with Camille Glenn, cooking teacher, columnist, cookbook writer, and the embodiment of Southern hospitality, was the inspiration for this Kentucky Derby celebration. No one in the South would ever mark Derby Day without a mint julep (mine are spiked with Louisville's hometown liqueur, Southern Comfort). After that comes Smithfield ham, with its salty, sweet flavor that marries so well with buttermilk biscuits. Present the ham on a large tray—silver if you have one. The warm biscuits can nestle in linen napkins in pretty baskets. I like to put a dish of sweet butter and a pot of bitter orange marmalade alongside the ham and biscuits, a combination I was introduced to in Savannah. Shrimp rémoulade combines with Belgian endive in a salad that offers a creamy, savory flavor and crunchy texture.

Banana Bourbon Bread is delightful in Kentucky or anywhere else. And Bananas Foster Ice Cream accompanied by the bourbon balls makes for a temptingly decadent dessert.

Like the Super Bowl party, this is a gathering where your guests will be watching the TV—although for a much briefer time. Serve mint juleps in chilled julep cups or glasses for the race itself, and then move on to the buffet table.

The Derby winner is presented a wreath of roses, so let roses be your flower of choice.

THE MUSIC

Robert Shaw Chorale,
The Stephen Foster Songbook

Patsy Cline

Dolly Parton

THE DRINKS

Spiked Kentucky Mint Juleps
A young, fruity Cru Beaujolais

THE EXTRAS

Mint julep cups
Extra-large platter
Ice-cream maker

SPIKED KENTUCKY MINT JULEPS

The word *julep* is as pleasant to say as it is to drink. In ancient Turkey, *julep* meant a sweet drink made with rose water. But in the United States it has come to be synonymous with the signature drink of the state of Kentucky, the mint julep. Mint juleps have been served at the Kentucky Derby since its first running in 1875, reportedly from mint grown in back of the clubhouse.

Although every kind of whiskey has been tried in a julep recipe, the traditional version calls for bourbon, the queen of American whiskeys. In my spin on the cocktail, the juleps are spiked with a shot of Southern Comfort, a liqueur born in New Orleans in the nineteenth century but now produced in the Kentucky Derby's hometown of Louisville.

48 sprigs fresh mint
16 ounces Southern Comfort
*   liqueur*
4 teaspoons superfine sugar
24 ounces bourbon

1. Remove several leaves from 1 mint sprig and place them in a mint julep cup or a highball glass.

2. Add 1 ounce Southern Comfort and ¼ teaspoon superfine sugar. Using a spoon, muddle the mixture to bruise or mash the mint to release the flavorful oil from the leaves.

3. Pack the glass full of crushed ice and pour in 1½ ounces bourbon. Agitate the mixture to frost the outside of the glass. Garnish with 2 mint sprigs. Serve immediately. Repeat, preparing each mint julep individually.

MAKES 16 JULEPS

SHRIMP AND BELGIAN ENDIVE REMOULADE

While rémoulade may be far from home at a Derby buffet, the gentility of this dish echoes Southern hospitality and charm. The flavor also blends beautifully with country ham and biscuits.

FOR THE REMOULADE SAUCE
2 cups prepared mayonnaise,
*   such as Hellmann's*
2 tablespoons Dijon mustard
4 teaspoons whole-grain mustard
4 dashes Tabasco sauce
4 scallions, including 3 inches green,
*   very thinly sliced*
2 tablespoons finely chopped fresh tarragon,
*   or 1 teaspoon dried*
4 teaspoons tiny capers, drained
Salt and freshly ground black pepper, to taste

FOR THE SALAD
2 pounds Belgian endive, heads rinsed and dried
4 pounds large shrimp, cooked (page 48)
¼ cup chopped fresh flat-leaf parsley
Salt and freshly ground black pepper, to taste

1. Combine all the rémoulade sauce ingredients in a large bowl and whisk well.

2. Separate the endive leaves and set aside half of them. Cut the remaining leaves into ½-inch pieces. Place the cut-up leaves, the whole leaves, the shrimp, and 2 tablespoons of the parsley in the bowl with the rémoulade sauce. Season with salt and pepper and toss gently. Chill in the refrigerator, covered, for up to 3 hours.

3. Just before serving, transfer the salad to a decorative serving bowl and sprinkle it with the remaining 2 tablespoons chopped parsley.

LEMON-CHIVE ASPARAGUS SALAD

Bright and springy, this salad offers clean, bold tastes that go with the spirit of the day. Rather than leaving the asparagus whole, here they are cut in nice-size pieces, allowing the vinaigrette to coat them evenly. And if you are serving the menu buffet-style, they are easy to eat with just a fork. When asparagus are in season, serve them as long as the season lasts—and be sure never to overcook them!

4 pounds asparagus, woody ends trimmed,
*   cut into 2-inch lengths on the diagonal*
6 to 8 tablespoons Lemon Vinaigrette
*   (page 400)*
¼ cup cut fresh chives (1-inch lengths),
*   for garnish*

Bring a large saucepan of salted water to a boil over high heat and add the asparagus. Reduce the heat to medium-low and simmer until they are just crisp-tender, 2 to 3 minutes. (You may need to do this in batches.) Remove them with tongs, rinse under cold water, and drain. Pat the asparagus dry with paper towels and place them in a serving bowl. Toss with the vinaigrette, sprinkle with the chives, and serve immediately.

SMITHFIELD COUNTRY HAM

Among the true glories of American cuisine is the country ham. Rubbed with salt and dry-cured, it is hung in a smokehouse for weeks, then aged for anywhere from six months to two years. Like other aged foods (cheese, wine), country ham develops deep, complex flavors. These hams—made from hogs fed on peanuts, apples, acorns, peaches, blueberries (it varies from place to place), smoked over smoldering hardwood, and then aged—are still made now the way they have been made for hundreds of years. Smithfield, by the way, refers to a traditional country ham made in Smithfield, Virginia. You may have local hams that are equally good, but chances are, even if you live outside the Ham Belt (the Southeast), you can easily find a Smithfield (see Sources, page 405).

Because it is salted and then dried, a country ham needs a good long soaking before it is baked, to get rid of some of the saltiness. You'll need to get it started two days in advance.

A Smithfield ham will serve a lot more than the sixteen guests at this buffet, so there will be plenty of leftovers for guests to take home and for you to nibble on long after the Derby is over.

1 genuine bone-in uncooked Smithfield ham
*   (15 to 18 pounds)*
3 tablespoons Dijon mustard
½ cup (packed) dark brown sugar
2 cups apple juice

1. Remove the ham from the cloth bag and scrub it well under cold running water to remove surface mold and excess salt and pepper. Place it in a large turkey roaster, cover it with cold water, and let it soak for 24 hours, changing the water after 12 hours.

2. Drain the ham and place it in a deep flameproof roasting pan on top of the stove. Cover it with fresh water. Bring the water to a boil over high heat, reduce the heat to medium-low, and simmer for about 3½ hours (about 15 minutes per pound), adding more hot water when necessary to keep the ham covered. While it is cooking, skim off any foam that rises to the surface. The ham is done when an instant-reading thermometer inserted in the thickest part reaches 140°F.

Smithfield Country Ham with Rolled Buttermilk Biscuits

3. Drain the ham and let it cool to room temperature. Remove all of the skin and fat and place the ham in a shallow roasting pan.

4. Preheat the oven to 350°F.

5. Brush the ham all over with the mustard. Pat the brown sugar all over the surface and pour the apple juice into the bottom of the pan.

6. Bake the ham, basting it frequently, until it is glazed, about 45 minutes.

7. Transfer the ham to a large decorative platter and carve as much as you like into tissue-paper-thin slices, using a very sharp knife.

DERBY SLAW

Crisp slaw has a little tanginess that tempers the saltiness of a Smithfield ham and cleans your palate for the next mouthful of powerhouse tastes. There are probably as many slaw recipes as there are cookbooks, or cooks. Actually, if you are like me, you have more than one. This version is somewhat traditional.

> Why is it called a Derby? Because back in the eighteenth century, when the English first began to breed the sleek, swift, elegant thoroughbreds, a British nobleman, the Earl of Derby, put up the purse for the first Derby Stakes, a race for three-year-olds, both male and female, at Epsom Downs in Surrey. The first English Derby (pronounced "Darby") was run in 1780, and the race has been held in the first week of June ever since. "Derby Day" has become the unofficial first day of summer for British horseracing fans.

2 heads green cabbage (about 4 pounds total), tough outer leaves discarded, cored and finely shredded
4 carrots, peeled and coarsely grated
2 green bell peppers, stemmed, cut in half, seeded, and coarsely grated
1 small onion, coarsely grated
4 cups prepared mayonnaise, such as Hellmann's
1 cup sugar
$\frac{1}{2}$ cup Dijon mustard
$\frac{1}{2}$ cup cider vinegar
2 tablespoons celery seeds
Salt and freshly ground black pepper, to taste
$\frac{1}{4}$ cup chopped fresh flat-leaf parsley, for garnish

1. Toss the cabbage, carrots, bell peppers, and onion together in a large bowl.

2. In another bowl, combine the mayonnaise, sugar, mustard, vinegar, and celery seeds. Stir well and fold into the vegetables with a large rubber spatula. Let the salad rest, covered, in the refrigerator for at least 3 hours. Allow it to come to room temperature before serving.

3. Season the salad with salt and pepper and serve it in a decorative bowl, sprinkled with the parsley.

Note: This can be prepared, through step 2, a day in advance.

ROLLED BUTTERMILK BISCUITS

There is a reason why you so often hear about biscuits when Smithfield ham is being discussed: There is nothing more delicious than a paper-thin slice of country ham between two halves of a warm-from-the-oven buttermilk biscuit. Once when I was in Savannah, I was served a small pot of orange marmalade along with the ham and tiny biscuits as a savory with cocktails. Ever since, I have endorsed this idea—the marmalade is the ideal foil to the salty ham. Buttermilk adds a lovely subtle tang to the biscuits and encourages a moist texture. Two tips: The less kneading, the lighter the biscuit. And the sharper the biscuit cutter, the higher the biscuits. A dull cutter seals the edges and prevents the biscuits from rising.

8 cups sifted all-purpose flour
4 teaspoons baking powder
2 teaspoons salt
1/2 cup solid vegetable shortening, chilled
8 tablespoons (1 stick) cold unsalted butter
4 cups buttermilk

1. Preheat the oven to 450°F.

2. Sift the flour, baking powder, and salt together in a large bowl. Using a pastry cutter, cut the shortening and butter into the dry ingredients until the mixture resembles coarse meal. Pour in the buttermilk and toss the ingredients with your fingertips until they can be gathered together into a ball.

3. Transfer the dough to a lightly floured surface and knead it not more than 12 to 15 times. Roll the dough out ¾ inch thick. Using a 2-inch biscuit cutter, cut it into rounds. Gather up the scraps, reroll, and cut out as many more biscuits as possible.

4. Arrange the biscuits, edges touching, on ungreased shiny (not nonstick) baking sheets and bake until lightly browned, 10 to 12 minutes. Serve hot.

MAKES 36 BISCUITS

Note: The biscuits can be reheated, loosely covered in aluminum foil, in a 350°F oven for 10 minutes.

BANANA BOURBON BREAD

If you are a baker, you probably have a banana bread in your repertoire. It is what I would call a "stealth favorite" because while we all make it, it is not the first thing that comes to mind when you think of a special meal. Yet the reason banana bread is so universal is that it is so delicious and so open to creativity. Nuts, dried fruit, and aromatic spices are used by one cook or another to add flavor and interest. But for Derby Day, what better to add than bourbon? "Run for the Bananas," anyone?

2 cups all-purpose flour
1 teaspoon baking soda
1/2 teaspoon salt
1/3 cup unsalted butter, at room temperature
1/3 cup solid vegetable shortening
1 cup (packed) dark brown sugar
2 large eggs
1 1/2 cups mashed ripe bananas (about 4 bananas)
3 tablespoons bourbon
1 teaspoon pure vanilla extract
3/4 cup chopped pecans

1. Position a rack in the center of the oven, and preheat the oven to 350°F. Grease and lightly flour a 9 x 5 x 2¾-inch loaf pan.

2. Sift the flour, baking soda, and salt together into a bowl and set it aside.

3. Using an electric mixer on high speed, cream the butter, shortening, and brown sugar in a large bowl until fluffy, about 2 minutes. Add the eggs, one at a time, beating well after each addition. Add the bananas, bourbon, and vanilla and mix well. Add the flour mixture and mix until just combined. Stir in the pecans.

4. Scrape the batter into the prepared pan and bake until a wooden toothpick inserted in the center comes out just clean, 60 to 75 minutes. Let the loaf cool in the pan on a wire rack for 10 minutes. Then run a knife around the edges of the pan to loosen the bread, and transfer it to the rack to cool completely.

MAKES 1 LOAF

BANANAS FOSTER ICE CREAM

Bananas Foster, an ineffably scrumptious dessert, was first dispatched from the kitchen of Brennan's in New Orleans in the early 1950s by chef Paul Blange. The rum-and-brown-sugar-flavored bananas were sautéed, then topped with vanilla ice cream—and named after one of the restaurant's best customers, Rich Foster. If Rich ever showed up at one of my Run for the Roses feasts, he would feel right at home with this variation on his namesake.

1/2 cup dark rum
6 tablespoons banana liqueur
8 tablespoons (1 stick) unsalted butter
1/2 cup (packed) dark brown sugar
1/4 cup fresh lime juice (from 3 limes)
12 ripe bananas, peeled and cut in half
    lengthwise
1/2 teaspoon ground cinnamon
6 cups heavy (whipping) cream
2 cups whole milk
1 cup granulated sugar
2 tablespoons pure vanilla extract
8 large egg yolks

1. Preheat the oven to 375°F.
2. Combine the rum and banana liqueur in a small bowl.

HOW TO TOAST NUTS

Preheat the oven to 350°F. Spread the nuts in a single layer on a baking sheet and toast, shaking the pan occasionally, until the nuts are golden brown and fragrant, 5 to 10 minutes, depending on their size. Check the nuts often, as they burn easily.

3. Melt the butter in a small saucepan over low heat, and stir in the brown sugar and lime juice. Stir to melt the sugar, 1 minute, then remove the pan from the heat.
4. Arrange the bananas in one or two oven-proof baking dishes that hold them in a tight single layer, and pour the butter mixture over them, dividing it evenly, if using more than one baking dish. Drizzle the rum mixture over the top and sprinkle with the cinnamon. Bake until the bananas are tender and candied, about 30 minutes.
5. Puree the mixture, in batches, in a food processor and set it aside.
6. Combine the cream, milk, granulated sugar, and vanilla in a large saucepan over medium heat. Cook until the milk is hot (but not boiling), and the sugar has dissolved, about 10 minutes. Remove the pan from the heat.
7. Whisk the egg yolks in a bowl. Whisking constantly, slowly pour in 1 cup of the hot cream mixture. Whisk until smooth.
8. Slowly pour the egg mixture into the saucepan, whisking constantly, and cook over medium-low heat until the custard is thick enough to coat the back of a spoon, 6 to 8 minutes. Do not let it boil.
9. Strain the mixture into a bowl, and stir in the banana puree. Cool to room temperature, then refrigerate until cold.

10. Freeze in an ice-cream maker, in batches if necessary, according to the manufacturer's directions (see Note). Transfer the ice cream to a container, cover, and freeze.

MAKES 3 QUARTS

Note: If you are freezing the ice cream in batches, keep the custard refrigerated until ready to freeze.

KENTUCKY BOURBON BALLS

S ave these bourbon balls for a last delicious bite after the race. You can make them several weeks in advance—they keep well in the refrigerator. Do make them at least a day ahead to allow the flavors to develop. If you want to be more festive, dust half the balls with cocoa powder and half with confectioners' sugar. I like to serve these in little paper or foil candy cups—they keep the hands clean when you pick them up.

2½ cups ground vanilla wafers
(one 12-ounce box of wafers)
½ cup pecan halves, toasted
(see box, facing page)
2 tablespoons unsweetened cocoa powder
¼ cup bourbon
½ cup golden raisins
6 tablespoons light corn syrup
About 2 cups confectioners' sugar

1. Place the ground wafers, pecans, cocoa powder, bourbon, raisins, and corn syrup in a food processor and process until the ingredients are ground and evenly blended. Scrape the mixture into a bowl.

2. Place the confectioners' sugar in a shallow bowl.

3. Roll the bourbon ball mixture between your palms to form balls the size of cherries. Then roll them around in the confectioners' sugar, coating them completely. Store in a covered container with wax paper between the layers until ready to serve. The bourbon balls will keep for several weeks.

MAKES 35 TO 40 BALLS

Mother's

Day Luncheon

Every culture reveres its mothers, setting aside special days for commemoration. Our celebration comes mid-spring, when days are long, gardens are lush with flowering bulbs, and the promise of summer is in the air. What better time to honor all Moms—the brand new ones, the proud grandmothers, and the even prouder great-grandmothers. This is a meal for very special people, created from the heart to be served with love.

MENU

Mother's Day Luncheon

FOR EIGHT

FRESH RASPBERRY LEMONADE

———

CUCUMBER SOUP WITH A CRUNCH

———

FESTIVE TUNA

———

LEMON-MINT COUSCOUS

———

LEMON-GLAZED ANGEL FOOD CAKE

———

RASPBERRY SORBET

This luncheon is elegant and light, featuring a menu of delicious warm-weather food, set off by a tall, cool glass of pink Fresh Raspberry Lemonade. Begin the meal with bowls of silky smooth cucumber soup; it's delightful and a great prelude to the Festive Tuna that follows.

Served alongside the fish, a scoop of Lemon-Mint Couscous, resplendent with carrots and fresh herbs, adds balance. Slices of Lemon-Glazed Angel Food Cake topped with Raspberry Sorbet make for a sweet, satisfying finish. If you are a mother and the host of this luncheon, you'll find that most dishes can be made in advance so that you can enjoy yourself as well.

The vibrant pastels of this menu would look gorgeous on Depression glass plates in pale pink, green, and yellow. An embroidered white tablecloth, widely available at flea markets and antiques malls, could be the backdrop for the colorful setting. For a centerpiece, try a pedestal dish full of beautiful ripe strawberries.

Flowers for mother, naturally: A bright, soft motif around the table will set the tone and complement the food. Masses of pink and yellow ranunculus and sweet peas in small vases will look beautiful. And so will pastel pink peonies and bright green viburnum leaves.

THE MUSIC

Lerner & Loewe

Jerome Kern

Lorenz Hart

THE DRINKS

Champagne or cava

Fresh raspberry lemonade

THE EXTRAS

Pretty glass pitcher

Soup tureen with a lid

White pedestal cake stand

Ice-cream maker

FRESH RASPBERRY LEMONADE

First toast Mom with something sparkling— champagne perhaps? Then bring out a pitcher of freshly made raspberry lemonade. There is nothing lovelier. The raspberries give the lemonade just the right blush!

3 cups fresh raspberries, gently rinsed
1 cup sugar
6 cups cold water
3 cups fresh lemon juice
(from about 12 large lemons)
8 large mint sprigs, for garnish

1. Puree the raspberries in a blender or food processor. Strain the puree through a fine-mesh sieve to remove the seeds. Set the strained puree aside.

2. Place the sugar and water in a saucepan over medium heat and cook, stirring occasionally, until the sugar has dissolved, about 5 minutes. Allow to cool to room temperature.

3. Combine the reserved raspberry puree and the sugar-water mixture in a large pitcher. Stir in the lemon juice.

4. Serve over ice in tall gasses, garnished with a mint sprig.

MAKES 10 CUPS

CUCUMBER SOUP WITH A CRUNCH

Cooling and aromatic, this soup is in part inspired by *raita*, the yogurt and cucumber condiment that is so popular on Indian menus for its ability to soothe a palate all fired up by curry. On this menu it is simply a sublime and smooth springtime starter.

Cucumber Soup with a Crunch

5 hothouse (seedless) cucumbers, peeled
1/4 cup minced garlic
2 cups Basic Chicken Broth (page 397)
8 cups plain nonfat yogurt
2 cups coarsely chopped fresh mint
2 tablespoons fresh lemon juice
Salt and freshly ground black pepper, to taste
8 large red radishes, cut into 1/4-inch dice,
for garnish

1. Cut 4 of the cucumbers into 1-inch pieces and place them in a food processor or blender. Add the garlic, broth, 6 cups of the yogurt, 1 1/2 cups of the mint, and the lemon juice. Process until smooth. Transfer the mixture to a large bowl. (If using a blender, prepare the puree in batches.)

2. Whisk in the remaining 2 cups yogurt and 1/2 cup mint. Season with salt and pepper. Chill, covered, for 2 to 3 hours.

3. Cut the remaining cucumber into ¼-inch dice and toss with the radishes. Divide the soup among eight bowls. Top each with the cucumber-radish mixture and serve immediately.

FESTIVE TUNA

Tuna recipes are a standby for luncheons, but I guarantee that none of them is as full of party spirit as this one using freshly seared steaks. Bonneted with a salsa made from pineapple, tomatoes, and jalapeños, the tuna looks as festive as confetti. And the varied and powerful flavors of the salsa beautifully punctuate the flavor of the tuna.

FOR THE SALSA

1 cup diced peeled hothouse (seedless)
cucumber (¼-inch dice)
1 cup diced seeded ripe tomato
(¼-inch dice)
1 cup diced fresh ripe pineapple
(¼-inch dice)
3 scallions, including 3 inches green,
very thinly sliced
1 tablespoon very finely diced red jalapeño
pepper, or other chile pepper, seeds
and ribs removed
6 tablespoons fresh lime juice
(from 3 large limes)
¼ cup olive oil
Salt and freshly ground black pepper,
to taste

FOR THE TUNA AND GARNISH

¼ cup olive oil
¼ cup fresh lemon juice (from 1 large lemon)
Salt and freshly ground black pepper,
to taste
8 tuna steaks (6 to 8 ounces each),
cut 1 inch thick
¼ cup chopped fresh cilantro, for garnish

1. Combine all the salsa ingredients in a medium-size bowl. Refrigerate, covered, for up to 1 hour.

2. To prepare the tuna, combine the olive oil, lemon juice, and salt and pepper in a large shallow bowl. Add the tuna steaks, turning to coat, and let sit for 15 minutes. Turn them once as they sit.

3. Heat a nonstick skillet over medium heat. Sear the tuna steaks for 4 to 5 minutes on the first side, adding any remaining marinade, or extra oil, if necessary, to prevent sticking. Turn the tuna, and sear it for 3 minutes on the second side for medium-rare (see Note).

4. Using a spatula, transfer the tuna steaks to eight dinner plates. Spoon the salsa, with its juices, over the tuna, and garnish with the chopped cilantro. Serve immediately.

Note: If cooking in batches, transfer the cooked steaks to a platter and loosely cover with aluminum foil to keep them warm while you cook the remaining ones.

LEMON-MINT COUSCOUS

Food for Mother's Day should be delicate, and this lovely salad is. It complements the delectable fish without overwhelming it. Lemon zest and a tiny dice of carrot brighten the flavor of the couscous, and their colors make for a pretty presentation.

1 cup couscous
2 tablespoons fresh lemon juice
1 tablespoon extra-virgin olive oil
Finely grated zest of 2 large lemons
¼ cup coarsely chopped fresh mint
1 carrot, cut into tiny dice
Salt and freshly ground black pepper,
to taste

"*Mighty is the force of motherhood!*
It transforms all things by its vital heart."
—GEORGE ELIOT

Festive Tuna

1. Bring 2 cups water to a boil over high heat in a medium-size saucepan. Remove the pan from the heat, stir in the couscous, cover, and let rest for 5 minutes. Uncover and fluff the grains with a fork. Transfer the couscous to a bowl.

2. Add the lemon juice, olive oil, and lemon zest and stir with a fork. Stir in the mint and carrots. Season with salt and pepper and serve.

LEMON-GLAZED ANGEL FOOD CAKE

Angel food cake is so called, they say, because it is light enough to be eaten by angels. Maybe so, but of this I am sure: There is no lovelier dessert for all our beloved mothers. A sweet-tart lemon accent in the cake and its glaze is a good match for the cloudlike texture of this confection (see Note).

FOR THE CAKE
1 tablespoon fresh lemon juice
1 teaspoon pure vanilla extract
1 cup cake flour
1 1/2 cups granulated sugar
1 1/2 cups large egg whites
(from about 12 eggs),
at room temperature
1/2 teaspoon salt
1 1/4 teaspoons cream of tartar
1/4 cup finely grated lemon zest
(from about 4 lemons)

FOR THE GLAZE
3 cups confectioners' sugar, sifted
1/2 cup fresh lemon juice
(from 3 large lemons)
4 tablespoons (1/2 stick) unsalted butter,
melted

1. Position a rack in the lower half of the oven, and preheat the oven to 350°F.

2. Prepare the cake: Combine the lemon juice, 1 tablespoon water, and the vanilla in a small bowl. Set it aside.

3. Sift the cake flour with 6 tablespoons of the granulated sugar into a bowl. Resift the mixture two more times. Set it aside.

4. Place the egg whites in a large bowl. Add the lemon juice mixture and the salt and beat with an electric mixer on low speed until foamy. Add the cream of tartar, increase the speed to high, and gradually add the remaining 1 cup plus 2 tablespoons sugar, 1 tablespoon at a time.

Lemon-Glazed Angel Food Cake

> *"Motherhood:*
> *All love begins and*
> *ends there."*
>
> —ROBERT BROWNING

Continue beating the whites until they are shiny and hold stiff peaks but are not dry, about 10 minutes.

5. Sift one fourth of the flour mixture over the egg whites and fold in until just mixed. Add the remaining flour mixture and the lemon zest and fold in until just mixed and smooth.

6. Scrape the batter into a 10-inch ungreased angel food cake pan with removable bottom. Run a knife through the batter to remove any air bubbles. Smooth the top.

7. Bake until the cake is brown on the top and a wooden toothpick inserted in the center comes out clean, 45 minutes to 1 hour. Do not underbake. The cake should be pulling away from the sides of the pan. Remove the pan from the oven and invert it immediately over the neck of a bottle. Allow it to cool completely in this position. (If the cake is not cooled in this manner, it will flatten.)

8. Once it is thoroughly cool, run a knife around the inner and outer sides of the pan and gently loosen the cake from the pan. Remove the bottom, gently sliding a knife between the cake and the pan if necessary. Place the cake on a wire rack set over a baking sheet.

9. Prepare the glaze: Whisk the confectioners' sugar and lemon juice together in a bowl. Add the melted butter and whisk until smooth. Immediately spoon this evenly over the cake, allowing the glaze to drip down the sides. When set, transfer the cake to a decorative plate for serving.

Note: Here are some angel cake tips: Do not grease the pan for angel food cake! And do not use a nonstick pan—use an angel food cake pan with a removable bottom. Use hands instead of a spatula to fold in the flour mixture so you can feel when the flour is *just* mixed in. Use a serrated knife for slicing the finished cake.

RASPBERRY SORBET

Bright, tart, sweet, cool—a raspberry sorbet sits elegantly next to a slice of angel food cake. It is said that Martha Custis, when she was setting the marital trap for George Washington, lived up to her reputation as the richest widow in the colonies by serving him "Preserved Raspberries," "Raspberry Syrup," and a "Quidony of Raspberries and Red Wine." The notion of a meal that begins and ends rich in raspberries is a grand idea.

2 pints fresh raspberries, or
24 ounces frozen unsweetened
raspberries, thawed
1¼ cups Simple Syrup
(page 403)
2 tablespoons fresh orange juice

1. Puree the raspberries with ¼ cup of the Simple Syrup in a food processor until smooth. If desired, this mixture can be strained into a bowl to remove the seeds, but it is not necessary.

2. Stir in the remaining 1 cup syrup and the orange juice.

3. Transfer the mixture to an ice-cream maker and freeze according to the manufacturer's instructions. Transfer the sorbet to a container, cover, and freeze until ready to serve.

MAKES 1 QUART

FIRE UP THE

T GRILL

The time-honored phrase that signals the beginning of the Indianapolis 500, the heart-stopping race held each Memorial Day in the heartland of the Midwest, is "Gentlemen, start your engines." For the rest of us, the phrase might just as well be "America, start your barbecues." Memorial Day, usually the first day we can count on for warmer weather from Maine to Minnesota, is when the lake cottages and beach houses are opened up, when the charred soot from Labor Day barbecues is wire-brushed off winter-idle grills, when foods cooked outside fill every backyard with "feed me now" aromas.

> "No man can be
> a patriot on
> an empty stomach."
> —WILLIAM COWPER BRANN

MENU

M emorial Day is the time to freshen your grilling repertoire. This menu features traditional favorites with a little spin on them. Clams and oysters cook in the blink of an eye on the grill and are then jazzed up served over zesty orzo. Chicken breasts are transformed into a tasty salad using the flavors of popular Buffalo chicken wings, and salade Niçoise is enhanced with grilled fresh (instead of canned) tuna. The sliced porterhouse—tender and running with meaty juices—should be served with a chopped salad full of colorful vegetables. And what better to finish off the meal than Blueberry Pie? You won't miss the hot dogs and burgers.

This meal is a backyard affair, whether on the lawn, patio, or deck. And because this is a patriotic day, the decorating palette begs for red, white, and blue. Carry the theme through with a red, white, and blue windowpane-check tablecloth. Generous white ceramic serving bowls and platters are all you need for the entrees, which look cheerful when garnished with bunches of parsley. I like to use a large carving board with a well for serving the steak— the well catches all the flavorful juices. On each slice of pie, a scoop of vanilla ice cream with fresh strawberry sauce would wrap up the theme.

Pitchers of red and white anemones are a perfect accent, and if you have any lilacs left, especially white ones, add them for softness. And one more thing: Fly the biggest, most flappingest flag you have!

FIRE UP THE GRILL

BACKYARD PICNIC FOR EIGHT

GRILLED CLAMS AND OYSTERS
ATOP ORZO SALAD

BUFFALO CHICKEN SALAD
WITH MY FAVORITE
BLUE CHEESE SAUCE

THE PERFECT GRILLED
PORTERHOUSE

TUNA OVER NICE

CONFETTI CHOPPED SALAD

BLUEBERRY PIE

THE MUSIC

Duane Eddy
Dick Dale & His Del-Tones
Sousa marches

THE DRINKS

California Pinot Blanc
Australian Shiraz
Lots of beer

THE EXTRAS

Barbecue grill and accessories
American flag
Steak knives

GRILLED CLAMS AND OYSTERS ATOP ORZO SALAD

My vote for the most delicious simple dish on the grill would have to go to clams and oysters. It certainly is an easy way to begin the grilling season—no need for a confab around the coals, no prodding the food and discussions among the guys to see if it's cooked. It's simple: When the shellfish open, they are done. Arrange the clams and oysters on top of the orzo salad and let the warm briny juices from the shellfish mix with the orzo.

FOR THE VINAIGRETTE
6 tablespoons red wine vinegar
1 teaspoon Dijon mustard
1 teaspoon sugar
Salt and freshly ground black pepper,
    to taste
3/4 cup olive oil

FOR THE SALAD
1 pound orzo
1 cup diced red bell pepper (1/4-inch dice)
1 cup diced yellow bell pepper (1/4-inch dice)
1 cup diced red onions (1/4-inch dice)
1 cup diced zucchini (1/4-inch dice)
1 cup coarsely chopped pitted black olives,
    such as Gaeta
1/2 cup chopped fresh flat-leaf parsley
32 cherrystone clams, well scrubbed
32 oysters, well scrubbed

1. Heat a barbecue grill to high.

2. Prepare the vinaigrette: Combine the vinegar, mustard, sugar, and salt and pepper in a small bowl. Slowly drizzle in the olive oil, whisking constantly until thickened. Set aside.

3. Bring a large pot of salted water to a boil over high heat. Reduce the heat slightly, add the orzo, stir, and cook until tender, about 8 minutes. Drain, rinse under warm water, and drain well again. Place the orzo in a bowl and toss with half of the vinaigrette. Stir in the bell peppers, onions, zucchini, olives, and 1/4 cup of the parsley. Spoon the salad onto two large serving platters.

4. When ready to grill, place the clams and the oysters on the grill rack and cook until they open. Depending on size, this will take 2 to 8 minutes. Remove the shellfish with tongs as they open, adding more as space becomes available. Discard any that don't open.

5. Arrange the opened clams and oysters attractively on top of the orzo salad. Drizzle the remaining vinaigrette over all, and sprinkle with the remaining 1/4 cup chopped parsley. Serve immediately.

Grilled Clams and Oysters

BUFFALO CHICKEN SALAD

It is not often in our lives that we see a new dish invented that spreads all over the country. In fact, I remember it happening with only one recipe, Buffalo chicken wings. According to Dom "The Rooster" Bellissimo, it was Friday night (payday) in 1964 at the Anchor Bar, which his parents owned in Buffalo, New York. The regulars were throwing down shots and beers when a carload of Dom's friends arrived and announced their hunger. Because the place was hopping, Dom's mother, Teresa, asked the guys to hang out until things quieted down. By the time she got around to them, she was pretty much out of everything except chicken wings—which she coated in hot spices, fired up, and served with celery sticks and blue cheese dip. Thus was born the Buffalo chicken wing. A great wing deserves its due respect, but I had fun reinterpreting this popular dish with its simple flavors and familiar veggies into a zesty summer salad using chicken breasts.

Buffalo Chicken Salad

8 skinless, boneless chicken breast halves
  (about 6 ounces each)
2 tablespoons unsalted butter, melted
6 tablespoons olive oil
4 teaspoons Tabasco sauce
Salt and freshly ground black pepper,
  to taste
¼ cup fresh orange juice
1 teaspoon Dijon mustard
1 teaspoon sugar
2 cups diced celery (¼-inch dice)
2 cups diced carrots (¼-inch dice)
2 cups diced red radishes (¼-inch dice)
2 cups diced cucumber (¼-inch dice)
My Favorite Blue Cheese Sauce
  (recipe follows)
¼ cup chopped fresh flat-leaf parsley,
  for garnish

1. Rinse the chicken breasts, pat them dry, and place them in a large bowl. Mix the melted butter, 2 tablespoons of the olive oil, the Tabasco sauce, and salt and pepper together in a small bowl. Pour over the chicken, turning the breasts to coat them evenly. Marinate, covered, at room temperature for 30 minutes.

2. Heat a barbecue grill to high.

3. Combine the orange juice, mustard, sugar, salt and pepper, and the remaining 4 tablespoons olive oil in a small bowl. Set this vinaigrette aside.

4. When ready to grill, place the chicken on the grill rack and cook, turning once, until nicely charred on the outside and cooked through, 4 to 5 minutes per side. Remove from the grill and slice each breast in half horizontally.

5. Place the celery, carrots, radishes, and cucumber in a bowl and toss with the vinaigrette.

Divide the salad evenly among eight dinner plates. For each serving, place the bottom half of a chicken breast on top of the vegetables, and then lay the top half at a slight angle on top of it. Dollop each with a generous tablespoon of the blue cheese sauce. Sprinkle with the parsley and serve.

MY FAVORITE BLUE CHEESE SAUCE

Smooth, yet crumbly and zesty, this blue cheese dressing is flavorful yet not overpowering. The garlic adds bite, and Tabasco adds a likable heat to the grilled chicken and vegetables. Try it on a baked potato, too.

THE BUSY GRILL

Four of the dishes in this menu call for grilling, but only two of them need to be grilled at mealtime—the clams and oysters and the steak. If you prepare the chicken for the Buffalo Chicken Salad and the tuna for the Tuna over Nice a day in advance, keep the meat and fish wrapped in plastic wrap in the refrigerator.

If you're doing a full-out grill fest on the day of your party be sure you're well fueled. Gas grillers should have an extra tank of gas on hand, and charcoalers should have plenty of briquettes or lump charcoal ready for adding to the grill. Get a chimney starter's worth of fresh coals ready before grilling the steak. A porterhouse over a cold bed of coals is a sorry sight.

¼ cup sour cream
¼ cup prepared mayonnaise,
* such as Hellmann's*
¼ cup crumbled blue cheese
½ teaspoon cider vinegar
½ teaspoon fresh lemon juice
Dash of Tabasco sauce
½ teaspoon finely minced onion
Pinch of finely chopped garlic
Salt and freshly ground black pepper,
* to taste*
1 teaspoon chopped fresh flat-leaf parsley

Combine the sour cream and mayonnaise in a bowl and blend well. Add the blue cheese and fold it in gently—do not mash the cheese. Fold in the remaining ingredients and adjust the seasonings to taste. This will keep for up to 3 days, covered and refrigerated.

MAKES ¾ CUP

THE PERFECT GRILLED PORTERHOUSE

The porterhouse—thick, huge, and flavorful—is the king of steaks. It's a tender T-bone with the added plus of a large portion of tender fillet. And that bone—it's delicious to chew on once most of the meat is finished. While you may think it needs no help to taste terrific, a dollop of mayonnaise, rich with roasted garlic, makes for a spectacular finish.

4 porterhouse steaks, cut 1½ inches thick
* (about 2 pounds each)*
Salt and freshly ground black pepper,
* to taste*
Roasted Garlic Mayonnaise (page 134),
* for serving*

1. Heat a barbecue grill to high, or preheat the broiler.

2. Grill or broil the steaks 4 inches from the heat source, over (or under) high heat, for 5 minutes on the first side. Turn, and cook for 5 to 7 minutes on the other side for medium-rare. (An instant-reading thermometer will register 130°F.) Season with salt and pepper.

3. Transfer the steaks to a carving board and let them rest for 5 minutes. Then cut away the T-bones to separate the sirloins and the fillet. Carve the steaks into ½-inch-thick slices and serve with Roasted Garlic Mayonnaise.

TUNA OVER NICE

Niçoise salad is, quite simply, a salad combining ingredients favored in Nice, on the French Riviera. Although traditionally made with canned tuna, plus eggs, fresh tomatoes, green beans, and anchovies, using fresh seared tuna brings it into the twenty-first century.

2 cloves garlic
Coarse (kosher) salt
5 tablespoons red wine vinegar
⅔ cup plus ¼ cup extra-virgin olive oil
Freshly ground black pepper, to taste
1 pound green beans, trimmed and
  halved lengthwise
8 red-skinned new potatoes, unpeeled, scrubbed
1 small red onion, thinly slivered lengthwise
1 cup diced red bell pepper (¼-inch dice)
4 ripe plum tomatoes, cut into 8 pieces each
½ cup pitted Niçoise olives
2 tablespoons tiny capers, drained
½ cup loosely packed slivered fresh basil leaves
8 tuna steaks, cut 1 inch thick
  (about 6 ounces each)
2 hard-cooked eggs (page 9), chopped

1. Heat a barbecue grill to high.

2. Finely mince the garlic together with a generous pinch of coarse salt and place it in a large serving bowl. Add the vinegar. Whisking constantly, slowly drizzle in the ⅔ cup olive oil. Season with pepper and set aside.

3. Bring a saucepan of lightly salted water to a boil over high heat. Add the beans, lower the heat to medium, and cook until crisp-tender, 3 to 4 minutes. Using a slotted spoon, transfer the beans to a colander, leaving the water in the pan, and rinse them under cold water to stop the cooking. Set them aside.

4. Cook the potatoes in the same boiling water until tender and not mushy, about 10 minutes. Drain, and allow to cool. Slice the cooled potatoes and place them in the bowl with the vinaigrette. Layer the green beans on top of the potatoes, followed by the onion, bell pepper, tomatoes, olives, capers, and slivered basil. Do not toss.

5. Brush the tuna steaks on both sides with the remaining ¼ cup olive oil and season them with salt and pepper.

6. When ready to grill, oil the grill rack well. Grill the tuna over high heat for 4 minutes per side for medium-rare. Let the tuna rest for 10 minutes, then slice it thinly on the diagonal.

7. Lightly toss the salad together from underneath. Adjust the seasonings if necessary. Divide the salad among eight dinner plates and sprinkle with the chopped eggs. Top with the sliced tuna and serve immediately.

CONFETTI CHOPPED SALAD

This chopped salad is all about crunch and color. Red and yellow bell peppers, diced zucchini, tomato, avocado: It looks like a bowl of colorful confetti. With all the big tastes in this menu, a big bunch of vegetables is just right for the salad course—powerful but light.

1 red bell pepper, stemmed, seeded, and
cut into ¹/₂-inch dice
1 orange bell pepper (or 1 more red
bell pepper), stemmed, seeded,
and cut into ¹/₂-inch dice
1 yellow bell pepper, stemmed, seeded,
and cut into ¹/₂-inch dice
1 green bell pepper, stemmed, seeded,
and cut into ¹/₂-inch dice
2 ripe tomatoes, seeded and cut into
¹/₂-inch dice
1 medium zucchini, cut into ¹/₂-inch dice
1 hothouse (seedless) cucumber, unpeeled,
cut into ¹/₂-inch dice
3 scallions, including 3 inches green,
thinly sliced on the diagonal
2 tablespoons chopped fresh flat-leaf parsley
2 tablespoons olive oil
1 tablespoon red wine vinegar
¹/₂ teaspoon sugar
Salt and freshly ground black pepper, to taste
1 ripe avocado
1 tablespoon fresh lemon juice

1. Combine the peppers, tomatoes, zucchini, cucumber, scallions, and parsley in a bowl.

2. Whisk the olive oil, vinegar, sugar, and salt and pepper together in a small bowl. Pour this over the salad and toss well. Correct the seasonings, if necessary.

3. Peel and pit the avocado. Cut it into ¼-inch dice and toss it with the lemon juice in a small bowl.

4. Sprinkle the avocado over the salad and serve.

BLUEBERRY PIE

For delicacy of texture, deepness of flavor, and the funny purple smile that kids like to horrify their parents with, a great blueberry pie has no competition.

Basic Pie Crust for a 9-inch double-crust pie
(page 401)
5 cups fresh blueberries, picked over
Juice of ¹/₂ lemon
2 teaspoons pure maple syrup
¹/₂ cup granulated sugar
2 tablespoons light brown sugar
5 tablespoons all-purpose flour
1 large egg white
Double Vanilla-Bean Ice Cream (page 53),
for serving (optional)
Fresh Strawberry Sauce (page 32),
for serving (optional)

1. Prepare the pie dough as directed, rolling out the bottom crust to fit a 9-inch pie plate. Roll out the top crust and place it on a plate (it will eventually be cut into lattice strips). Cover both crusts with plastic wrap and refrigerate until ready to use.

2. Lightly rinse the blueberries, using the spray attachment at your kitchen sink if you have one. Drain and pat dry with paper towels. Place the blueberries in a large bowl and toss with the lemon juice and maple syrup.

3. Add both sugars and the flour and mix well.

4. Position a rack in the center of the oven, and preheat the oven to 350°F.

5. Combine the egg white and 2 teaspoons water in a small bowl. Remove the bottom crust from the refrigerator and brush the bottom and sides with some of the egg white mixture. (This prevents the crust from becoming soggy.) Fill the crust with the blueberry mixture.

6. Cut the top crust into ¹/₂-inch-wide lattice strips. Weave the lattice strips over the top, fold the ends over the edge, and trim away any excess pastry. Crimp the edge decoratively. Carefully brush the lattice with the remaining egg white mixture.

7. Bake the pie on a baking sheet until the crust is golden brown and the juices are bubbling, about 60 minutes. Let the pie cool on a wire rack before serving it slightly warm or at room temperature with scoops of ice cream and drizzles of strawberry sauce, if desired.

Father's

Legend has it that the observance of Father's Day came about through the efforts of a devoted daughter. Sonora Louise Dodd's father, William Jackson Smart, was a Civil War veteran and widower who singlehandedly raised his six children. When Sonora Louise heard a Mother's Day sermon in 1909, she thought

Dads deserved their own day as well. Her efforts were successful, and although she didn't plan for it, the day designated—the third Sunday in June—is perfect grilling weather. That works out well for both cooks and Dads.

MENU

Father's Day
DINNER FOR SIX

LU'S OLD-FASHIONEDS

———

LEMON GRILLED SHRIMP COCKTAIL

———

ANDREW'S ICEBERG SALAD
WITH ROQUEFORT

———

GRILLED RIB-EYE STEAKS

———

SMASHED POTATOES

———

LUSCIOUS
STRAWBERRY SHORTCAKE

On his special day, treat dad to a meal of straight-forward favorites, beginning with an old-fashioned. Make double use of the grill, first for a great starter—Lemon Grilled Shrimp Cocktail—then for those thick rib-eye steaks. Iceberg with creamy Roquefort dressing is a hearty, crunchy salad, the perfect accompaniment to the steaks. And there isn't a dad in the world who can resist the chuck-wagon feel of Smashed Potatoes. The Luscious Strawberry Shortcake with fresh berries is just the right finale for this no-fuss dinner.

Father's Day should be fun and casual and, if possible, outdoors. Have tongs, forks, a cutting board, and mitts at hand near the grill. Scatter buckets of early-summer flowers about—nothing fancy, whatever's in season and easy.

Dad will prefer the every-day dishes (or more likely, won't notice), so heavy white restaurant-style dishes bordered in blue or red and good steak knives are all you really need. Pressed wood salad bowls are just the thing for the retro iceberg salad. Sit the strawberry shortcake on color-ful plates. Late June is the time strawberry lovers wait for all year—local berries are in and are plentiful. So don't just use them in the cake. Pile up heaps of berries in bowls or baskets for easy nibbling.

THE MUSIC

Beach Boys' *Pet Sounds*

Elvis Presley's
All Time Greatest Hits

THE DRINKS

Lu's Old-Fashioneds

Sonoma Chardonnay

Napa Cabernet Sauvignon

THE EXTRAS

Barbecue grill and accessories

Steak knives

LU'S OLD-FASHIONEDS

My friend Lu Fletcher is an old-fashioned kind of guy—debonair, well traveled, a lover of good food, and a connoisseur of the cocktail. His drink of choice is the old-fashioned, a sweet powerhouse first invented in Louisville, Kentucky, in the late 1880s for James E. Pepper, an early bourbon maker.

3 oranges, each cut into 8 wedges,
* seeds removed*
6 pieces (each 2 inches long) lemon zest
Bitters, such as Angostura bitters, to taste
6 maraschino cherries
3 tablespoons sugar, or to taste
12 ounces bourbon
Ice cubes
Sparkling or tap water

1. Combine 4 orange wedges, 1 piece of lemon zest twisted to release the oils, several generous dashes of bitters, a cherry, and 1½ teaspoons sugar in each of six old-fashioned glasses. Muddle the ingredients thoroughly by crushing them with the back of a spoon.

2. Add about 2 ounces bourbon to each glass, and mix well again. Add ice cubes to reach almost to the top of each glass. Top with sparkling or tap water. Mix again and serve.

LEMON GRILLED SHRIMP COCKTAIL

Have you ever noticed that there is no such thing as leftover shrimp cocktail? No matter how many you put out, the last shrimp gets eaten. Their sweet buttery flesh, heightened by a lemon marinade and a few minutes on the grill, is the definition of a satisfying mouthful. Serve this ultimate shrimp cocktail in wineglasses, accompanied by a lemony, garlicky dip.

48 large shrimp, peeled and deveined,
* tails left on*
3 tablespoons extra-virgin olive oil
3 tablespoons fresh lemon juice
3 cloves garlic, finely minced with
* ½ teaspoon coarse (kosher) salt*
* (see box, page 127)*
1 tablespoon finely minced fresh
* rosemary*
Finely ground black pepper, to taste
3 lemons, cut in half crosswise, for serving
6 large fresh sprigs rosemary, for garnish
Lemon-Garlic Aïoli (page 6), for serving

1. Soak eighteen 10-inch wooden skewers in water to cover for 1 hour.

2. Rinse the shrimp under cold water. Drain and pat dry. Place them in a bowl.

3. Combine the olive oil, lemon juice, garlic and salt, rosemary, and pepper in a bowl, whisk well, and then toss with the shrimp. Let rest for 30 minutes.

4. Heat a barbecue grill to high or preheat the broiler.

5. Remove the shrimp from the marinade and drain them, reserving the marinade.

6. Thread twelve skewers with 3 shrimp each, and six skewers with 2 shrimp each. Grill or broil the shrimp, 4 inches from the heat source, brushing once on each side with extra marinade, for 3 minutes per side.

7. Place a lemon half, cut side down, in the bottom of each of six wineglasses. Stick two skewers with 3 shrimp each, and one skewer with 2 shrimp, into each lemon, balancing them. Make a hole with the tip of another skewer and insert a rosemary sprig. Serve in the center of small plates, with a bowl of Lemon-Garlic Aïoli for dipping.

ANDREW'S ICEBERG SALAD WITH ROQUEFORT

This is the best Roquefort dressing I've ever tasted. It is the invention of Andrew Engle, one of my favorite young American chefs, currently at a restaurant called The Laundry in East Hampton, New York. Robust and powerful, it delivers one strong flavor after another. Where many modern salads rely on lettuces as light as flower petals, a wedge of good old-fashioned iceberg lettuce takes center stage here. Its crunchy leaves stand up to the fragrant, sharp, salty, creamy queen of cheeses. Andrew serves this salad with sliced red onion, ripe beefsteak tomatoes, crisp bacon, and fresh chives.

FOR THE ROQUEFORT DRESSING

3/4 cup crumbled Roquefort cheese
1 3/4 cups heavy (whipping) cream
3/4 cup prepared mayonnaise,
*   such as Hellmann's*
2 shallots, chopped
2 tablespoons fresh lemon juice
2 teaspoons Worcestershire sauce
1/2 teaspoon coarsely ground
*   black pepper*

FOR THE SALAD

12 slices bacon
1 1/2 heads iceberg lettuce, trimmed,
*   rinsed, drained, and dried*
1 to 2 red onions, thinly sliced
6 slices ripe beefsteak tomato
2 tablespoons snipped fresh chives,
*   for garnish*

1. Combine all the dressing ingredients in a bowl and mash with a fork. Do not puree the Roquefort—leave it crumbly (see Note).

2. Place the bacon in a large skillet over medium heat and fry, turning once, until crisp, 10 to 12 minutes. Remove to paper towels to drain.

3. Cut the iceberg into 6 wedges and place on individual salad plates, or bowls, and dollop with the dressing. Surround each wedge with some of the onions, a slice of tomato, and 2 slices of bacon, crumbled or left whole. Sprinkle with the chives and serve.

Note: This dressing can be prepared 2 days in advance. Store it, covered, in the refrigerator. Let it come to room temperature before serving.

GRILLED RIB-EYE STEAKS

Since Dads are being celebrated, full flavor is the theme of this meal, and steak makes for just the right choice of entree. Rib-eye comes from the most flavorful part of the steer, the same part that gives us prime rib. The olive oil, balsamic vinegar, and tomato in this recipe are inspired by the famous steakhouses of Tuscany: The kick of the tomatoes and chives gets a boost from the vinegar, all of which enhances the flavor of the meat.

6 rib-eye steaks, cut 1 to 1 1/4 inches thick
*   (about 12 ounces each; see Note)*
Coarsely ground black pepper, to taste
6 large ripe tomatoes, thinly sliced
4 tablespoons extra-virgin olive oil
4 tablespoons balsamic vinegar
Salt, to taste
2 tablespoons snipped fresh chives
Mustard, for serving

1. Heat a barbecue grill to high.

2. Sprinkle the steaks with pepper on both sides, pressing it into the meat. Grill the steaks over high heat, about 3 to 4 minutes per side for rare, 4 to 5 minutes per side for medium-rare, and 5 to 6 minutes per side for medium. Let the steaks rest for 3 minutes before serving.

3. To serve, arrange the tomato slices so they cover the center of each of six plates. Drizzle lightly with the olive oil and vinegar, and season with salt and pepper. Sprinkle with the chives.

4. Transfer the steaks to a cutting board and slice them ½ inch thick. Arrange the steak slices on top of the tomatoes. Serve the mustard alongside.

Note: A good butcher will usually cut a standard rib-eye steak 1 inch thick; if your meat is cut with an extra ¼ inch thickness, it doesn't affect the cooking time.

SMASHED POTATOES

P otatoes smashed with their skins on and creamed with lots of garlic have real dad appeal.

2 tablespoons olive oil
1 onion, halved and slivered lengthwise
2 tablespoons minced garlic
2 pounds red-skinned new potatoes, unpeeled, scrubbed
6 tablespoons (¾ stick) unsalted butter, at room temperature
½ cup heavy (whipping) cream
1½ teaspoons salt
½ teaspoon coarsely ground black pepper
2 tablespoons chopped fresh flat-leaf parsley

1. Heat the olive oil in a skillet over medium heat. Add the onion and cook, stirring, until nicely browned, 20 minutes. Add the garlic and cook 5 minutes more. Set aside.

2. Place the potatoes in a large heavy saucepan and cover with cold water. Bring the

CHOPPING GARLIC

W hen I chop garlic, I often sprinkle it with coarse salt first. This acts as an abrasive and aids in the process, letting me chop the garlic very fine. Just be aware that when you add the garlic to your dish, you are including salt. So taste the dish for seasoning before adding more salt.

water to a boil over high heat, reduce the heat to medium, and cook until the potatoes are tender, 25 to 30 minutes. Drain well and return the potatoes to the pot. Place the pot over very low heat for about 30 seconds to dry the potatoes well. Transfer them to a large bowl.

3. Smash the potatoes with a fork to retain some texture. Add the butter and cream and mix well. Season with the salt and pepper. Stir in the onion mixture and the parsley and combine. Serve immediately.

LUSCIOUS STRAWBERRY SHORTCAKE

I n the Northeast, June is the season of strawberries—lush red and juicy ripe. A walk through a farmer's market, when the plump berries are displayed in their green cardboard cartons, heralds the bounty of summer. There are many legends about where the strawberry shortcake originated, and the combination of sweet cake, berries, and fresh whipped cream is such a natural that probably many of them are true. My

Luscious Strawberry Shortcake

favorite credits the Native Americans, who called the strawberry "the heart-seed berry," and who made a kind of bread of crushed strawberries mixed with cornmeal. The colonists knew a good thing when they saw it and adapted this original American treat.

FOR THE BISCUITS

2 cups all-purpose flour
1/4 cup sugar, plus extra for sprinkling
1 tablespoon baking powder
1/2 teaspoon salt
8 tablespoons (1 stick) cold unsalted butter, cut into cubes
1 cup heavy (whipping) cream, plus extra for brushing

FOR THE STRAWBERRIES AND TOPPING

2 pints ripe strawberries, very gently rinsed and patted dry
5 tablespoons sugar
1 cup heavy (whipping) cream
1 teaspoon pure vanilla extract

1. Preheat the oven to 375°F. Butter a baking sheet.

2. Prepare the biscuits: Combine the flour, 1/4 cup sugar, the baking powder, and the salt in a bowl. Using a pastry blender or your fingertips, rub the butter into the dry ingredients until you have a crumbly, coarse meal with some pieces of butter still visible. Add the 1 cup cream in a slow, steady stream while continuing to blend (you may not need all the cream). The dough should be moistened but still have a few loose crumbs.

3. On a lightly floured board, press the dough out to form a 1½-inch-thick round. Using a 2½-inch biscuit cutter, cut out 6 rounds and place them on the prepared baking sheet. Brush the tops with cream and sprinkle with sugar. Bake until the biscuits are golden brown, about 20 minutes. Transfer them to a wire rack to cool (see Note).

4. Hull the strawberries and cut them into quarters. Place them in a bowl and toss with 4 tablespoons of the sugar. If desired, transfer half of the berries to another bowl and mash them with a fork or a potato masher. Then return the mashed berries to the bowl with the unmashed ones and stir. Set aside.

5. Combine the cream, vanilla, and remaining 1 tablespoon sugar in a bowl. Using an electric mixer, whip the cream on low speed until the mixture is foamy, about 3 minutes. Then mix on high speed until soft peaks form, 2 to 3 minutes more.

6. To assemble the shortcake: Split each biscuit in half with a fork, as you would an English muffin. Place the bottoms of the biscuits on dessert plates. Top each biscuit with some of the whipped cream and 2 generous tablespoons of the strawberry mixture (including the juices). Cover with the top half of the biscuit. Dollop generously with the remaining whipped cream, then divide the remaining strawberries among the biscuits. Serve immediately.

Note: If you like, bake the biscuits a day ahead. Let them cool completely, and then store them in a covered container.

BANG-UP FOURTH

Fireworks, parades, summer's heat, baseball doubleheaders, politicos making the same long speeches they made last year, firecrackers, the Top 100 (or 500, or 1,000) hits of all time on the oldies station, beach parties, canoe races, kayaking around the lake, barbecues, cold beer, lemonade.

OF JULY

Every facet of the Fourth of July calls up a festive image. To be sure, the glorious Fourth celebrates a day of national independence, but it is also a day when the national capacity for fun is on display—at table, on the ball field, on the dance floor, and at the grand fireworks display that lights up skies and spirits at the end of a festive day.

MENU

BANG-UP FOURTH OF JULY

LATE-AFTERNOON PICNIC FOR EIGHT

GLORIOUS GAZPACHO

DAZZLING GRILLED VEAL CHOPS

OUTRAGEOUS LOBSTER SALAD ROLLS

A DECORATIVE
CUCUMBER SALAD

GARDEN SQUASH SALAD

FRESH PEACH COBBLER

BUTTERMILK ICE CREAM

This red, white, and blue day coincides with delicious vegetables at the farm stands, so begin the celebration with fresh gazpacho, a favorite summer soup. Along with the Dazzling Grilled Veal Chops and the Outrageous Lobster Salad Rolls you'll find highly flavored seasonal salads of summer squash, zucchini, tomatoes, and cucumbers. To top it all off, what could be more American than a ripe juicy peach cobbler served with Buttermilk Ice Cream. Start the fireworks!

A great thing about this delicious outdoor meal is that almost all of it can be made ahead of time.

For the table, use large white serving platters for the lobster rolls and the veal chops. Or nestle the lobster rolls in individual plastic baskets clam shack–style. Gazpacho is even more brilliant when served in brightly colored mugs. Carafes of red and white wine or sparkling water go right on the table, as do big arrangements of blue cornflowers, lots of red carnations, and daisies (there's your red, white, and blue) in painted tin buckets. Baskets filled with strawberries and raspberries would be pretty.

Now, bring out the flags, lots and lots of them in all different shapes and sizes. Hang a huge one on the front of your house. Stick small ones in a watermelon placed in a big basket. Stack up some colorful blankets or quilts for those who want to lie on the lawn. And don't forget to light sparklers as the sun sets.

THE MUSIC

Tchaikovsky's *1812 Overture*

Johnny Cash

Soundtrack from
Yankee Doodle Dandy

THE WINE

California Sauvignon Blanc

Oregon Pinot Noir

THE EXTRAS

Barbecue grill and accessories

American flags

Ice-cream maker

GLORIOUS GAZPACHO

Short of putting your whole vegetable garden into a bowl, no dish so totally delivers the cool, crunchy, thirst-quenching pleasure of salad vegetables as gazpacho. Chilled mugfuls of this refreshing starter can be enjoyed at the table, under a tree, sitting on the porch steps, or anywhere friends gather for the start of the meal.

2 cups diced peeled hothouse (seedless)
*   cucumber (1/4-inch dice)*
2 cups diced red bell pepper (1/4-inch dice)
2 cups diced ripe tomato (1/4-inch dice)
1/2 cup diced red onion (1/4-inch dice)
2 cups tomato juice
1/2 cup red wine vinegar
1/3 cup extra-virgin olive oil
2 dashes Tabasco sauce
Salt and freshly ground black pepper, to taste
1 ripe avocado, preferably Hass

1. Place the cucumber, bell peppers, tomatoes, and onion in a large bowl.

2. Add the tomato juice, vinegar, olive oil, and Tabasco sauce. Season with salt and pepper and toss.

3. Transfer half of the mixture to a blender or food processor and pulse the machine on and off to coarsely puree the contents. Return the pureed mixture to the bowl and stir to combine. Refrigerate for up to 6 hours before serving. Right before serving, halve the avocado and remove the pit. Dice the flesh and top each serving with a garnish of avocado. Serve.

DAZZLING GRILLED VEAL CHOPS

A thick veal chop—caramelized and crisp on the outside, nicely moist on the inside—is luxurious and easy to make, as are the roasted garlic and béarnaise mayonnaises.

8 veal chops (12 ounces each),
*   bones frenched (see box, page 72)*
About 1/3 cup olive oil
Salt and freshly ground black pepper, to taste
1/2 cup Roasted Garlic Mayonnaise
*   (recipe follows) or Béarnaise Mayonnaise*
*   (page 401)*

1. Heat a barbecue grill to high.

2. Brush the chops lightly with olive oil and sprinkle them generously with salt and pepper. Grill the chops over high heat, 3 inches from the heat source, until cooked through, 8 to 10 minutes per side. Do not overcook them; you don't want them to dry out.

3. Dollop each chop with a tablespoon of the Roasted Garlic Mayonnaise and serve immediately.

ROASTED GARLIC MAYONNAISE

Roasted garlic is nutty, sweet, and fragrant. It is in no danger of getting lost in the strong flavors in this meal. This recipe makes a generous amount—try the leftovers with steak, fish, and chicken, or dolloped on sliced tomatoes.

4 large heads garlic
2 cups prepared mayonnaise,
*   such as Hellmann's*
2 dashes Tabasco sauce
Salt and freshly ground black pepper,
*   to taste*

1. Preheat the oven to 350°F.

2. Remove the outer papery layer of the heads of garlic, leaving the heads intact. Cut off the top ¼ inch of the cloves, and wrap each head in aluminum foil. Bake until soft, 1¼ hours. Unwrap the garlic heads and allow them to cool.

3. When the garlic is cool enough to handle, squeeze the pulp out of the skins into a small bowl. Mash the garlic to form a smooth paste. Add the mayonnaise, Tabasco sauce, and salt and pepper and stir to combine. Refrigerate, covered, for up to 5 days.

MAKES ABOUT 2 CUPS

OUTRAGEOUS LOBSTER SALAD ROLLS

A harbor in Maine, sailboats on a sun-dappled sea. Granite cliffs, fir trees, and daisies. Little rowboats bobbing at anchor. Giant steaming rigs at the local lobster pound. You pay your few dollars, they give you fresh lobster in big chunks on a hot dog bun, slathered with mayonnaise. You sit at one of the tables in the little picnic grove overlooking the harbor and bless all summer afternoons. I can't bring Maine to you, but I can give you a recipe that is inspired by those Maine days. The secret is big pieces of lobster, a real lobster commitment.

4 live lobsters (about 1¼ pounds each)
8 hot dog rolls
½ cup prepared mayonnaise,
*   such as Hellmann's*
2 cups mâche leaves or other baby
*   salad greens*
8 yellow cherry or pear tomatoes,
*   cut in half*
8 red cherry or pear tomatoes, cut in half
Salt and freshly ground black pepper, to taste

1. Bring a large kettle of water to a rolling boil over high heat. Drop in the lobsters (you'll probably have to cook 2 at a time) head first, cover, and return the water to a boil. Cook until the shells turn bright red, 10 minutes. Remove the lobsters from the water with tongs and allow them to cool.

2. Twist the tails off and push out the meat (or use kitchen scissors to cut down the center of the underside of the tail and remove the meat in one piece). Cut each piece of lobster tail meat in half lengthwise. Set the rest of the lobster aside. (Luscious claw meat is the post-party treat for the hosts. Crack open the claws using a lobster cracker

Luscious claw meat is the post-party treat for the hosts. Crack open the claws using a lobster cracker and extract as much claw meat as possible. Place it in a bowl, cover with plastic wrap, and refrigerate until after the party. Eight lobster claws should yield enough for a hearty midnight snack for two, tossed with tomatoes and mâche and a generous dollop of mayonnaise. When your guests are gone, the dishes are put away, and the temperature has cooled down, enjoy!

Outrageous Lobster Salad Rolls

and extract as much claw meat as possible. Place it in a bowl, cover with plastic wrap, and refrigerate until after the party, see previous page).

3. Spread both sides of each hot dog roll with 1 tablespoon of the mayonnaise. Lay a halved lobster tail on the bottom half of each roll, and top with some of the mâche and tomatoes. Close, and serve immediately, passing the salt and pepper.

A DECORATIVE CUCUMBER SALAD

In this crunchy and colorful summer salad, with all the spirit of a fine Greek salad minus the feta cheese, the first impression makes a difference. Herbs are usually chopped so fine that all you can tell is that there is something green in the dish. In this recipe, though, the dill leaves are an inch long: beautiful and delicious, and definitely present.

2 hothouse (seedless) cucumbers
6 ripe tomatoes, cut into quarters
1 small red onion
½ cup halved pitted Kalamata or other
*   imported black olives*
½ cup cut fresh dill leaves (1-inch lengths)
¼ cup extra-virgin olive oil
2 tablespoons red wine vinegar
Salt and freshly ground black pepper,
*   to taste*

1. Peel the cucumbers, then halve them lengthwise, scoop out the center, and cut them crosswise into ¼-inch pieces. Place them in a bowl and add the tomatoes.

2. Halve the onion lengthwise and then slice it crosswise. Add the onion to the cucumbers, along with the olives and dill.

3. Whisk the olive oil and vinegar together in a small bowl, and season with salt and pepper.

Just before serving, toss the dressing with the salad. Serve immediately.

GARDEN SQUASH SALAD

Summer squash, both zucchini and yellow, are crisp and delicious when served raw and very thinly sliced in a salad. Dressed with plenty of lemon juice and Parmesan cheese (look for the finest Parmigiano-Reggiano), it matches up well with peppery arugula and some fine ripe tomatoes.

4 small zucchini, ends trimmed
4 small yellow squash, ends trimmed
½ cup fresh lemon juice
¼ cup extra-virgin olive oil
Salt and freshly ground black pepper,
*   to taste*
8 ounces Parmesan cheese, shaved or
*   cut into thin slivers*
2 large bunches arugula (12 ounces total),
*   stems trimmed, leaves washed and*
*   patted dry*
2 large ripe tomatoes, cored
¼ cup chopped fresh flat-leaf parsley

1. Cut the zucchini and squash into very thin slices on the diagonal and place them in a bowl.

2. Whisk the lemon juice, olive oil, and salt and pepper together in a small bowl and toss with the squash. Let the squash rest for 10 to 15 minutes. Then add the cheese.

3. Place the arugula in a salad bowl. Cut the tomatoes in half lengthwise, and then into very thin wedges, and scatter them over the greens.

4. Just before serving, spoon the squash and dressing over the arugula and tomatoes. Sprinkle with the parsley and season with salt and pepper to taste. Serve immediately, tossing the salad at the table.

FRESH PEACH COBBLER

A cobbler is a fruit pie without the fuss of pastry—just sweet ripe fruit and a sweet biscuit crust. Serve a scoop of Buttermilk Ice Cream alongside.

FOR THE PEACHES

$7^1/_2$ cups quartered pitted ripe peaches
    (about 12 peaches)
$^1/_2$ cup sugar
1 tablespoon fresh lemon juice
2 teaspoons finely grated lemon zest
2 teaspoons pure vanilla extract

FOR THE TOPPING

$1^1/_2$ cups cake flour or all-purpose flour
    (see Note)
4 tablespoons sugar
2 teaspoons baking powder
Pinch of salt
5 tablespoons cold unsalted butter,
    cut into small pieces
$^2/_3$ cup light cream or half-and-half

1. Position a rack in the center of the oven, and preheat the oven to 400°F. Butter a 9-inch square baking dish. Set it aside.

2. Prepare the peaches: Toss the peaches in a bowl with the sugar, lemon juice, lemon zest, and vanilla. Set aside.

3. Prepare the topping: Sift the cake flour, 3 tablespoons of the sugar, the baking powder, and the salt together into a bowl. Using an electric mixer, add the butter and combine until it is evenly distributed, 1 minute. Add the cream and mix until the dough just comes together, 30 seconds.

4. Spoon the peach mixture into the prepared baking dish. Crumble on the topping mixture and sprinkle with the remaining 1 tablespoon sugar.

5. Bake for 15 minutes, then reduce the temperature to 350°F and continue baking until the topping is golden brown and the filling is bubbly, 30 to 40 minutes more.

6. Serve warm or at room temperature.

Note: When made with cake flour, the topping will be a bit more tender than it is when it's made with regular all-purpose flour.

BUTTERMILK ICE CREAM

Buttermilk produces a creamy, textured ice cream with a very light tang. Scoop it onto the Fresh Peach Cobbler for a luscious dessert with an old-fashioned feel.

2 cups heavy (whipping) cream
2 cups buttermilk
$^1/_2$ cup sugar
1 tablespoon pure vanilla extract
4 large egg yolks

1. Combine the cream, buttermilk, sugar, and vanilla in a heavy saucepan over medium heat. Cook until the mixture is hot but not boiling and the sugar has dissolved, about 10 minutes. Remove the pan from the heat.

2. Place the egg yolks in a small bowl and whisk to mix them. Whisking constantly, slowly pour 1 cup of the hot milk mixture into the eggs. Continue to whisk until smooth.

3. Slowly pour the egg mixture into the saucepan, whisking constantly until well combined. Place the saucepan over medium heat and stir the mixture constantly until it is thick enough to coat the back of a spoon, 6 to 8 minutes. The mixture should never boil.

4. Strain the mixture into a bowl and allow it to cool to room temperature.

5. Freeze in an ice-cream maker according to the manufacturer's instructions. Transfer to a container, cover, and freeze until serving time.

MAKES 1 QUART

Glorious

rom every grill in the neighborhood come the seductive smells of burgers, steaks, chicken, salmon, and kebabs of every description. In one yard the sound of Sarah Vaughan on the stereo is punctuated by the splash of a pool party. Cars in the streets, their tops down, pull over for us to have quick chats with friends. The kids run in and out,

Summertime

slamming screen doors. Cheers and groans arise from the group watching baseball. The crickets chirp. There's a slight whisper of a breeze. . . . The sounds of summer are a symphony. So are the tastes and textures: crisp, crunchy, juicy, sweet. The foods are so good that the best advice is, don't do too much to them. The flavor is all there to begin with.

MENU

Summer food dazzles. Easy seafood salads or sandwiches; bowls filled with farmstand-fresh vegetables—corn, green and wax beans, tomatoes and bell peppers—it's hard to know when to stop chopping! Don't—instead try them all. Corn salads, bread salads, Gazpacho Salad . . .

What do you need to show off summer food to its best advantage? Well, short of a lobster trap, a farm stand, or a basket, almost nothing: brightly checked place mats, brightly colored dishes, generously sized plates and bowls, and maybe linens trimmed with contrasting rickrack.

Summertime color schemes echo the colors of the food. Pretty much anything in shades of yellow, crisp light greens, white, pink, peach, lavender, orange, and watermelon will be great. Turquoise is the color of the summer sea and July skies and is so right for the season.

There are so many ways to be playful with flowers in the summertime. Since they are all around in such profusion, choose an array. From small to huge sunflowers, to large bouquets of cosmos, to the saturated reds, yellows, peaches, and pinks of zinnias. Outdoors or in, place vases all around.

Glorious Summertime
A CELEBRATION FOR EIGHT

SUMMER CHICKEN SALAD

———

LOBSTER, TOMATO, AND SWEET CORN SALAD
WITH GARLIC VINAIGRETTE

———

SCALLOP ROLLS WITH BLUSHING TARTAR SAUCE

———

GAZPACHO SALAD

———

MINTY GARDEN BREAD SALAD

———

SUMMER CORN SALAD

———

MINTED GREEN AND WAX BEANS

———

GRILLED CORN SALSA

———

WATERMELON SORBET

THE MUSIC

The Essential Sarah Vaughan

THE WINE

Red Sancerre

Bandol rosé

Riesling

THE EXTRAS

Barbecue grill and accessories

Ice-cream maker

Summer Chicken Salad

1. Combine the chicken, celery, tomatoes, and grapes in a bowl. Season with salt and pepper. Toss in the parsley leaves.

2. Stir the mayonnaise and yogurt together in a small bowl. Add enough dressing to the salad to make it moist. Refrigerate, covered, for 2 to 6 hours before serving. Remove the salad from the refrigerator 30 minutes before serving.

Note: A take-out roasted chicken makes it super-easy to put this salad together.

SUMMER CHICKEN SALAD

I like to make this chicken salad with both white and dark meat, so begin by roasting a whole chicken. If you prefer an all-white-meat salad, then use breast meat that's been poached or baked. Either way, plump cherry tomatoes and sweet grapes add color, sweetness, and zest. Serve this over arugula, hearts of romaine, or even dandelion greens.

> 4 cups coarsely shredded cooked chicken (see Note)
> 3 ribs celery, cut into 1/4-inch dice
> 1 1/4 cups ripe grape or cherry tomatoes, halved crosswise
> 1 1/4 cups seedless red grapes, halved crosswise
> Salt and freshly ground black pepper, to taste
> 1/2 cup whole fresh flat-leaf parsley leaves
> Generous 1/2 cup prepared mayonnaise, such as Hellmann's
> Generous 1/2 cup nonfat plain yogurt

LOBSTER, TOMATO, AND SWEET CORN SALAD

This started out as a vision: a rustic glazed green plate, holding a salad that I see as a summer vacation on a plate. Where is the vacation? Doesn't matter. It's just summer: high puffy clouds in a hot blue sky. It could be the coast of Maine or the coast of France. The simplicity of the ingredients is a testament to the elegant rich flavors. Wait—the vision continues. Serve this with ripe figs, a good chèvre, and a cool Bandol rosé from Provence.

> 1 1/2 cups fresh corn kernels (from 3 ears corn)
> 4 cups cut-up cooked lobster (see Note)
> 2 cups diced seeded ripe tomatoes (1/4-inch dice)
> Salt and freshly ground black pepper, to taste
> 6 to 8 tablespoons Garlic Vinaigrette (recipe follows)
> 2 bunches arugula (about 12 ounces), trimmed, rinsed, and patted dry
> 1/2 cup thinly slivered fresh basil leaves, for garnish
> 8 fresh nasturtium blossoms, for garnish (optional)

"*To make a good salad is to be a brilliant diplomatist—
the problem is entirely the same in both cases.
To know how much oil one must mix with one's vinegar.*"

—OSCAR WILDE

Lobster, Tomato, and Sweet Corn Salad

1. Bring a saucepan of water to a boil. Add the corn kernels and cook until just tender, 1 minute. Drain into a colander and run under cold water to stop the cooking. Drain again and pat dry.

2. Using a rubber spatula, gently combine the corn, lobster, and tomatoes in a bowl.

3. Just before serving, season the salad with salt and pepper. Dress it lightly with the vinaigrette.

4. Arrange the arugula in the center of a large platter and top with the lobster salad. Garnish the salad with the slivered basil, and nasturtium blossoms, if desired, before serving.

Note: You'll get 4 cups lobster meat from four 1½-pound lobsters.

GARLIC VINAIGRETTE

When preparing this dressing it is important to crush—almost mash—the garlic. Sprinkling it with coarse salt makes the crushed garlic easier to mince.

> *¼ teaspoon coarse (kosher) salt*
> *2 cloves garlic, crushed*
> *¼ cup red wine vinegar*
> *2 tablespoons Dijon mustard*
> *½ cup extra-virgin olive oil*
> *Freshly ground black pepper,*
> *to taste*

Sprinkle the salt over the garlic on a chopping board and finely mince the garlic. Combine this with the vinegar and the mustard in a small bowl. Whisking constantly, slowly drizzle in the olive oil. Continue whisking until the vinaigrette thickens. Season with pepper. Refrigerate, covered, until ready to use.

MAKES ¾ CUP

SCALLOP ROLLS

I have eaten lobster rolls since my hands were big enough to hold a bun, but for some inexplicable reason scallop rolls are not as common. I first came across them when my associate, Laurie, and I went to a clam festival in Massachusetts and came upon a vendor cooking up scallops on an electric griddle, then tucking them into hot dog rolls. No offense to "Monsieur Homard," but sweet sautéed scallops, slightly caramelized, are as summery as a breeze off the ocean. With Blushing Tartar Sauce, they are just a little dressier than with plain old white (though still delicious) tartar sauce.

> *1 pound sea scallops, rinsed and*
> *patted dry*
> *1 tablespoon unsalted butter*
> *1 tablespoon vegetable oil*
> *Salt and freshly ground black pepper,*
> *to taste*
> *Pinch of paprika*
> *8 hot dog rolls*
> *½ cup Blushing Tartar Sauce*
> *(recipe follows), for serving*

1. Heat a barbecue grill to high.

2. Place the scallops in a bowl.

3. Melt the butter in the oil in a small saucepan over low heat. Let it cool slightly, and then toss with the scallops. Season with salt and pepper and paprika.

4. Thread the scallops on two or three metal skewers, leaving about 1 inch between them. Grill the scallops, 3 to 4 inches from the heat source, for 2 minutes per side (4 minutes total). Transfer them to a plate and let them rest for 5 minutes.

5. Split open the hot dog rolls and grill the insides and outsides, if desired, 30 seconds per side. Divide the scallops among the rolls, garnish each with about 1½ tablespoons of the Blushing Tartar Sauce, and serve.

BLUSHING TARTAR SAUCE

I love tartar sauce on many things. Many folks, on the other hand, are ketchup people. This sauce makes everyone happy. It is satiny and piquant—dressier than regular tartar sauce—but with all of its bite and savor.

½ cup prepared mayonnaise,
  such as Hellmann's
1 tablespoon ketchup
½ teaspoon Dijon mustard
½ teaspoon finely grated lemon zest
1 teaspoon fresh lemon juice
Dash of Tabasco sauce
1 tablespoon sweet pickle relish,
  drained
1 tablespoon chopped fresh
  flat-leaf parsley
1 tablespoon finely minced shallot
1 teaspoon tiny capers, drained
Salt and freshly ground black pepper,
  to taste

Combine the mayonnaise, ketchup, mustard, lemon zest, lemon juice, Tabasco sauce, and relish in a bowl. Mix well. Stir in the parsley, shallot, capers, and salt and pepper. Refrigerate, covered, for at least 1 hour. This will keep for up to 3 days.

MAKES A GENEROUS ¾ CUP

GAZPACHO SALAD

This height-of-summer salad offers you all the crunch and color of gazpacho without the pureeing. The dressing includes a healthy dose of tomato juice—a perfect moistener for the salad—and a few drops of Tabasco for some heat.

FOR THE DRESSING
½ cup tomato juice
¼ cup red wine vinegar
¼ cup extra-virgin olive oil
Dash of Tabasco sauce
1 shallot, minced

FOR THE SALAD
2 hothouse (seedless) cucumbers,
  peeled and cut into ¼-inch dice
2 red bell peppers, stemmed, seeded,
  and cut into ¼-inch dice
1 small red onion, cut into ¼-inch dice
6 to 8 ripe plum tomatoes, cut into
  8 pieces each
1 cup finely slivered fresh basil leaves

1. Prepare the dressing: Whisk the tomato juice, vinegar, and olive oil together in a small bowl until well combined. Stir in the Tabasco

Gazpacho Salad

sauce and the shallot. Refrigerate, covered, until ready to use. Rewhisk before serving.

2. Shortly before serving, combine all the vegetables and the basil in a large bowl and toss gently with the dressing. Transfer to a decorative bowl and serve.

MINTY GARDEN BREAD SALAD

A lthough Webster's does not list "mint" as a synonym for "cool," most people would agree that that is the case. The inspiration here is the cooking of the Middle East: mint, pita, feta. With a cold ale in a frosted mug, or a chilled riesling, this dish is a light meal for a hot night.

4 pita breads
4 large ripe tomatoes, cut into ¹/₂-inch pieces
2 hothouse (seedless) cucumbers, peeled,
*   cut in half lengthwise, and cut into*
*   ¹/₂-inch pieces*
4 scallions, including 2 inches green,
*   thinly sliced on the diagonal*
1 cup imported black olives, such as Gaeta
2 cups coarsely crumbled feta cheese
1 cup chopped fresh mint
6 tablespoons extra-virgin olive oil
¹/₄ cup red wine vinegar
Salt and freshly ground black pepper,
*   to taste*

1. If the grill or the broiler is hot, place the pitas about 3 inches from the heat and grill until crisp and golden, about 1 minute per side. Or you can simply toast them in a toaster. Set aside.

2. Combine the tomatoes, cucumbers, scallions, olives, feta, and mint in a large bowl. Toss to combine.

3. Whisk the olive oil and vinegar together in a small bowl and set it aside.

> *"A s for the garden of mint, the very smell of it alone recovers and refreshes our spirits, as the taste stirs up our appetite."*
>
> —PLINY

4. Shortly before serving, tear the pita breads into 1¹/₂-inch pieces and add them to the salad. Season the salad with salt and pepper, rewhisk the vinaigrette, and then drizzle it over the salad. Toss well and serve immediately.

SUMMER CORN SALAD

K ernels of summer's finest, freshest corn, combined with zucchini and tomatoes, make for a salad you can enjoy by the bowlful. All it needs is a light, slightly sweet dressing, and the Cumin-Honey Vinaigrette adds that touch.

4 cups fresh corn kernels (from about 8 ears)
1 small zucchini, quartered lengthwise,
*   seeded, and diced*
8 cherry tomatoes, cut into quarters
¹/₂ cup diced hothouse (seedless) cucumber
*   (¹/₄-inch dice)*
4 red radishes, cut into small dice
¹/₄ cup chopped fresh flat-leaf parsley
Freshly ground black pepper, to taste
¹/₄ cup Cumin-Honey Vinaigrette (page 400)

1. Bring a saucepan of water to a boil over high heat. Add the corn kernels and cook until just tender, 1 minute. Drain into a colander, then run under cold water to stop the cooking. Drain again and pat dry.

2. Combine the corn, zucchini, tomatoes, cucumber, radishes, and parsley in a bowl and toss to combine. Season with pepper.

3. Just before serving, toss the salad with the vinaigrette, transfer to a decorative bowl, and serve.

MINTED GREEN AND WAX BEANS

You can never say it enough: Ingredients in their season are like a different species from those that are out of season. Case in point: beans. A fresh-picked green or wax bean fairly crackles with sugar and juiciness. And in season, they are abundant. Shallots have always been a wonderful partner for green beans, and mint gives a cool snap to this salad. Serve it at room temperature.

1 pound tender green beans, trimmed
1 pound tender wax beans, trimmed
¼ cup extra-virgin olive oil
2 tablespoons finely minced shallot
6 purple or regular scallions, including
*   3 inches green, thinly sliced on the*
*   diagonal*
2 cups mixed red and yellow pear
*   tomatoes, halved lengthwise*
½ cup chopped fresh mint
Coarse (kosher) salt and coarsely
*   ground black pepper, to taste*
¼ cup fresh lemon juice
*   (from 2 lemons)*

1. Bring a large pot of water to a boil over high heat. Add the green and wax beans and cook until tender, 4 to 5 minutes. Drain into a colander and run under cold water to stop the cooking, drain again, and pat dry. Place the beans in a large bowl.

2. Add the olive oil, shallot, and scallions to the beans and toss. Add the tomatoes and mint and season generously with salt and coarse pepper. Just before serving, toss the beans with the lemon juice.

Note: The beans will discolor if you toss them with the lemon juice too far in advance.

GRILLED CORN SALSA

A salsa, by definition, goes with something. This salsa, made with fresh corn that's been grilled for a light smoky flavor, goes with just about everything. Here, it is part of a midsummer celebratory feast, but you can serve it alongside grilled fish, steaks, burgers, and ribs, too. When grilled, the kernels become golden brown and slightly crunchy, and their succulent sugars caramelize to perfection.

4 ears fresh corn, shucked
About 5 tablespoons extra-virgin olive oil
Salt and freshly ground black pepper,
*   to taste*
½ teaspoon finely minced garlic
½ cup diced red onion (¼-inch dice)
2 ripe plum tomatoes, seeded and
*   cut into ¼-inch dice*
½ ripe avocado (preferably Hass),
*   cut into ¼-inch dice*
2 tablespoons fresh lime juice
1 teaspoon finely chopped green
*   jalapeño pepper*
1 tablespoon chopped fresh flat-leaf parsley

1. Heat a barbecue grill to high.

2. Brush the ears of corn with 2 to 4 tablespoons of the olive oil. Grill the corn over high heat, turning occasionally, until all sides are well grilled, about 10 minutes. Transfer the corn to a plate and sprinkle with salt and pepper.

3. When the corn is cool enough to handle, cut the kernels off the ears and place them in a large bowl.

4. Stir in the remaining ingredients, along with the remaining 1 tablespoon olive oil. Refrigerate, covered, for up to 1 day. Serve at room temperature.

MAKES 4 CUPS

CORN EVERY WHICH WAY

Sure, ears of farmstand-fresh corn, boiled for a couple of minutes and buttered and salted, are hard to beat, but the kernels, scraped from the cob, add sweet flavor and lovely texture to salads and soups. Buy enough, and always prepare the corn on the day you buy it.

WATERMELON SORBET

The juice of the watermelon says "Cool off" in a large stage whisper. And no watermelon dish cools one off more gently than this tangy pink ice, invoking memories of summers past.

8 cups cubed watermelon
(1-inch cubes), seeds and
rind discarded
1 cup Simple Syrup (page 403)
2 tablespoons fresh lemon juice

Puree the watermelon cubes in a food processor in batches and transfer to a large bowl. Measure out 4 cups of the puree (you may have a little left over) and place it in another bowl. Add the Simple Syrup and the lemon juice and stir well. Freeze in an ice-cream maker according to the manufacturer's instructions. Transfer the sorbet to a container, cover, and freeze.

MAKES 1½ QUARTS

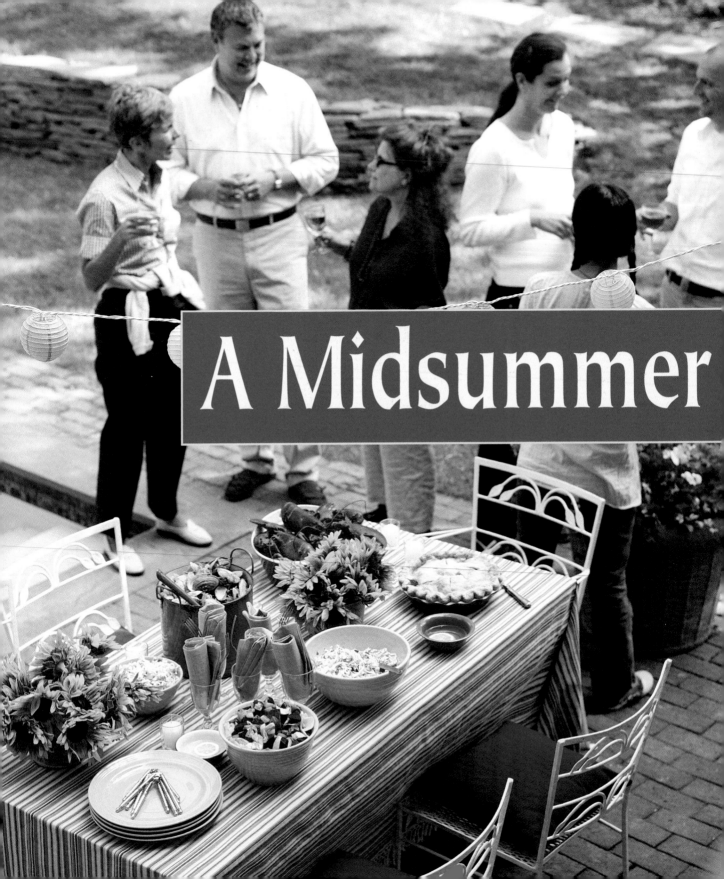

A Midsummer

Night's Feast

William Shakespeare celebrated midsummer night with a play about the magical goings-on in the forest on that night filled with fairies and wood spirits looking for mortals to love. Just a dream, perhaps, but at one time in Ireland beautiful daughters were locked in on midsummer night so that the fairies couldn't take them as brides. The height of the summer definitely calls for a celebration: The best food of the year combines with the best weather—and those flowers! Everything good is happening at the same time.

MENU

A Midsummer Night's Feast

DINNER FOR EIGHT

Summer Corn Soup

White-Wine Steamed Clams

Steamed Lobsters

Nice and Peachy Beet Salad

Roasted Red New Potato and Fennel Salad

Creamy Island Slaw

Peach and Blackberry Pie

THE MUSIC

Mendelssohn's
Midsummer Night's Dream

Renaissance or Baroque Recorder Music

THE WINE

California Viognier or Rhône Condrieu

THE EXTRAS

Lobster pot
Lobster crackers
Small forks
Demitasse or espresso cups

When the corn is high and the ears are ripe, you want to cook them in every way possible—and for this feast that means chilled corn soup. Steamer clams are another summer wow—especially when served with a wine-laced broth and a small bowl of melted butter. Keep the butter on the table for the boiled lobsters—so simple, so right for the warm weather. For sides, coleslaw and potato salad are the natural choices. But here the slaw takes on tropical flavors and the potatoes pop with the sweet bite of fennel. The audacious combination of beets and peaches adds a splash of color, not to mention an unexpected blending of flavors. When it comes to dessert, there's nothing like a fresh fruit pie, this one filled with some more of those great peaches and a handful of blackberries. Make up some lemonade or minty iced tea,

and you're in business for a summertime feast.

Cotton napkins in watermelon-pink and white stripes and turquoise and white stripes are bright and happy, and complement the food. Fill enamel buckets with ice to chill everything from sparkling water to champagne to beer to wine. If you can find some cobalt blue bottles of fancy water, mix a couple in for a color highlight that calls up the Mediterranean and the summer sun. Serve the corn soup in tiny bright green or turquoise Fiestaware

demitasse cups. Find an extra-large white platter for the lobsters. Place bowls of lemon halves nearby for squeezing onto the lobsters, and for cleaning your hands (lemon juice gets rid of the briny lobster juices and any lingering fish odor). The colorful beet salad looks inviting in a ceramic bowl, and the clams say "open me and eat" when served in a colorful bucket or steamer pot.

For flowers, my choice is a riot of zinnias, black-eyed Susans, and cosmos—gay, frivolous, and summery.

SUMMER CORN SOUP

Smooth as velvet, the combination of corn, lemongrass, and basil here melds delicacy with strength of flavor. It is simple but eccentric and elegant. If they're available, float a red or orange nasturtium blossom in each serving.

10 to 12 ears fresh corn, shucked (see step 1)
2 quarts Basic Chicken Broth (page 397)
    or Vegetable Broth (page 398)
4 stalks fresh lemongrass, trimmed and
    cut into ½-inch pieces (see box, page 290)
¼ cup fresh lemon juice (from 2 lemons)
Salt, to taste
⅓ cup unsweetened coconut milk
2 tablespoons finely slivered fresh basil leaves
    or chopped fresh cilantro

1. Strip the kernels off the corn cobs, cutting as close to the cobs as possible. You should have about 6 cups of kernels. Place both the corn kernels and the cobs in a large heavy pot and add the broth, making sure it covers the corn. Add the lemongrass. Bring to a boil over high heat, reduce the heat to medium-low, and simmer, partially covered, until the corn is tender and the broth is flavored, 30 minutes. Set aside to cool. Remove and discard the cobs and lemongrass.

> Corn must be picked at the peak of its ripeness to achieve really full flavor, and then it should be eaten right away, for it can turn starchy in a few hours. If you must store it, place it in the fridge. Scientists have shown that ears that are left at room temperature lose sugar six times faster than ears that are stored cold.

2. Puree the soup, in batches, in a food processor or blender.

3. Pour the soup through a fine-mesh strainer back into the pot, pressing down on the puree to extract as much liquid as possible. Add the lemon juice and season with salt. Heat over very low heat until the soup is heated through and the flavors are blended, 10 minutes. Allow the soup to cool to room temperature.

4. Stir in the coconut milk. Cover with plastic wrap and chill in the refrigerator for at least 2 hours and as long as 6 before serving.

5. Taste and adjust the salt, if necessary. Serve the soup cold, garnished with the basil.

WHITE-WINE STEAMED CLAMS

Summer is vacation, summer is fun, and summer, or at least a lot of it, is eating with your fingers—a hot dog in a bun, a lobster claw, a slice of watermelon, an ear of corn, and steamer clams swirled in butter. When I was growing up, my family used to love to go to The Pier, a restaurant in East Norwalk, Connecticut, where the feast always started with pots of steamers before we moved on to the lobster. We would remove the steamers from their shells, clean off the chewy necks, dip the clam meat in a little bowl of broth to wash off any remaining sand, and finally swirl them in melted butter before devouring them.

8 pounds steamer clams, scrubbed clean
1 fennel bulb, trimmed, cored, and slivered
1 large onion, halved lengthwise
    and slivered
½ teaspoon cracked black peppercorns
1 bottle dry white wine
1 cup (2 sticks) unsalted butter, melted
    (or drawn; see Note), for serving (optional)

1. Place the cleaned clams in a large pot and add the fennel, onion, peppercorns, wine, and a splash of water. Bring to a boil over high heat. Then reduce the heat to medium-high and cook, shaking the pot once or twice, until the clams open, 5 to 7 minutes.

2. Remove the clams to shallow bowls, discarding any that haven't opened. Strain the clam broth through a fine-mesh sieve. Serve each diner a small bowl of broth and a little dish of melted butter for dipping the clams.

Note: Drawn, or clarified, butter is simply melted butter with the milk solids removed. Melt the butter, and then let it sit off the heat for a few minutes. When the solids have settled to the bottom of the pan, carefully pour off the clarified butter, leaving the solids behind.

> *All the ingenious men, and all the scientific men, and all the imaginative men in the world could never invent, if all their wits were boiled into one, anything so curious and so ridiculous as the lobster.*
>
> —**CHARLES KINGSLEY**

STEAMED LOBSTERS

As curious and ridiculous as they are to look at, that's how delicious lobsters are to eat. When cooked, the shells will be bright red and the meat should be opaque and firm to the touch. The coral, if there is any, will be coral-colored. Wait for the water to reach a rolling boil before putting the lobsters in it. Serve them with some of the drawn butter you prepared for the clams.

8 live lobsters, about 1 1/2 pounds each
Lemon wedges, for serving

1. Bring a large kettle of salted water to a rolling boil over high heat.

2. Plunge the lobsters, two at a time, into the boiling water head first. Return to a boil and cook the lobsters until they are bright red and cooked through, 10 minutes. Using long tongs, carefully transfer the lobsters from the water to a colander. Repeat with the remaining lobsters.

3. Serve each lobster with lemon wedges, a shell cracker, a small fork for digging out the meat (for anyone too dainty to use their fingers), and plenty of napkins.

NICE AND PEACHY BEET SALAD

The colors of this salad are midsummer magic indeed: magenta roasted beets and juicy yellow peaches. Belgian endive and red bell pepper add more color while contributing a bit of sharpness and some crunch. The red onion counteracts the sweetness of the fruit. It is a salad of complex, luscious flavors.

*6 Roasted Beets (page 399),
    cut into 1/2-inch pieces
4 ripe peaches, halved, pitted, peeled,
    and cut into 1/2-inch pieces
1 red bell pepper, stemmed, seeded,
    and cut into 1/4-inch dice
1/4 cup diced red onion (1/4-inch dice)
1/4 cup fresh lemon juice
    (from 2 large lemons)
1/4 cup extra-virgin olive oil
Salt and freshly ground black pepper,
    to taste
2 heads Belgian endive*

1. Combine the beets, peaches, bell pepper, onion, lemon juice, and olive oil in a large bowl. Season with salt and pepper.

2. Trim off and discard the bottom of the endives, then cut them in half lengthwise. Discard the outer leaves and rinse the remaining ones. Pat dry and cut them into 1/2-inch slices on the diagonal.

3. Shortly before serving, gently toss the endive with the beets and peaches. Transfer the salad to a serving bowl and serve immediately.

ROASTED RED NEW POTATO AND FENNEL SALAD

Roasting potatoes for salad, rather than boiling them, intensifies their earthy flavor. This allows the potato to play a more active role in the combination of flavors and textures in this semi-traditional potato salad. I say "semi" because instead of getting crunch from the more typical celery, I went with the fresh garden crunch of fennel. Likewise, rather than topping the salad with dill, a time-honored northern European garnish, I use fennel fronds. The

result—a salad that will have the taste of familiarity and the surprise of the new.

*16 to 18 red-skinned new potatoes
    (about 2 pounds), unpeeled, scrubbed,
    and patted dry
3/4 cup diced fennel bulb (1/4-inch dice)
4 scallions, including 3 inches green,
    thinly sliced on the diagonal
1/3 cup plus 1 tablespoon chopped
    fennel fronds
1/2 cup prepared mayonnaise,
    such as Hellmann's
1/2 cup low-fat sour cream or plain nonfat
    yogurt
Salt and coarsely ground black pepper, to taste*

1. Preheat the oven to 400°F.

2. Prick the potatoes with the tines of a fork and place them on a baking sheet in a single layer. Bake until tender inside and crisp on the outside, about 1 hour. Allow them to cool. When they are cool enough to handle, quarter the potatoes and place them in a bowl.

3. Add the fennel, scallions, and the 1/3 cup fennel fronds to the potatoes.

4. In a small bowl, combine the mayonnaise and sour cream. Fold it into the potato salad. Season well with salt and coarse pepper and garnish with the remaining 1 tablespoon fennel fronds. Chill, covered, in the refrigerator for at least 2 hours and as long as 4 before serving.

CREAMY ISLAND SLAW

Here's a coleslaw of a different kind: creamy, yes, but with a tropical flair. The cabbage blends beautifully with the ginger, fresh papaya, and succulent beefsteak tomatoes. In this salad, the cabbage is cut into 1/2-inch pieces rather

Peach and Blackberry Pie

than shredded; so are the tomatoes and papaya. It doesn't take long to do the chopping, and the result is a whole new texture for a coleslaw.

*1 head green cabbage, tough outer leaves
   removed, cored
1/2 cup prepared mayonnaise,
   such as Hellmann's
1/2 cup low-fat sour cream
2 tablespoons Dijon mustard
1 tablespoon grated fresh ginger
Salt and coarsely ground black pepper,
   to taste
4 ripe tomatoes, cut into 1/2-inch pieces
1 ripe papaya, seeded, peeled, and
   cut into 1/2-inch pieces
3 tablespoons coarsely chopped
   fresh flat-leaf parsley*

1. Separate the cabbage leaves and cut them into rough 1/2-inch pieces. Place them in a large bowl.

2. Combine the mayonnaise, sour cream, mustard, and ginger in a small bowl and fold into the cabbage. Season with salt and coarse pepper. Refrigerate, covered, for 1 to 2 hours.

3. Just before serving, gently fold in the tomatoes, papaya, and parsley.

PEACH AND BLACKBERRY PIE

Summer fruit pies are some of the best eating there is. Peaches and blackberries work beautifully together—they are picked at the same time of the year and they look and taste great in a pie.

*Basic Pie Crust for a 9-inch double-crust pie
   (page 401)
5 cups sliced peeled ripe peaches (1/2-inch slices)
1/4 cup fresh blackberries, rinsed and
   patted dry
3 tablespoons fresh lemon juice
Pinch of salt
5 tablespoons all-purpose flour
1/4 cup plus 2 teaspoons (packed)
   light brown sugar
2 tablespoons crystallized ginger,
   finely chopped
1 large egg white
2 tablespoons granulated sugar*

1. Prepare the pie dough as directed, rolling out the bottom crust to fit a 9-inch pie plate. Roll out the top crust and place it on a plate. Cover both crusts with plastic wrap and refrigerate until ready to use.

2. In a large bowl, toss the peaches with the blackberries, lemon juice, and salt.

3. Combine the flour, brown sugar, and ginger in another bowl and add the mixture to the peaches. Combine well and let rest, uncovered, for 1 hour.

4. Position a rack in the center of the oven, and preheat the oven to 350°F.

5. Combine the egg white with 2 teaspoons water in a small bowl. Remove the pie crusts from the refrigerator. Brush some of the egg white mixture over the bottom and sides of the bottom pie crust (to prevent sogginess). Add the peach mixture, mounding it in the center.

6. Cover the filling with the top crust. Trim the overhang to 1 inch. Moisten the edges of the crusts where they meet with a little water, then press them together lightly and turn them under. Crimp the edges decoratively. Cut six decorative steam slits in the top crust. Brush the top crust lightly all over with the remaining egg white mixture. Sprinkle with the granulated sugar.

7. Place the pie in the oven and bake until the crust is golden and the juices are bubbling, 60 to 70 minutes. Let the pie cool on a wire rack before serving it just slightly warm or at room temperature.

LABOR DAY

As summer's last bash, a Labor Day party has a nostalgic feel to it, invoking brand-new memories of the long warm days that are coming

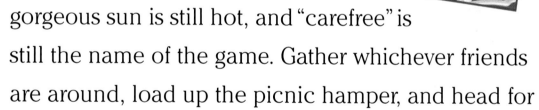

to an end. Whatever your age, the notion that school is about to start sits a little heavy in the heart—but that gorgeous sun is still hot, and "carefree" is still the name of the game. Gather whichever friends are around, load up the picnic hamper, and head for the closest beach or park—or simply your own backyard.

PICNIC

MENU

LABOR DAY PICNIC
FOR EIGHT

SAVORY LENTIL SALAD

SKIRT STEAK WITH NUEVO SALSA

PICNIC CHICKEN SALAD

ROASTED REDS

LUSTROUS LEEKS

PLUM CRISP

Summer holds its breath for just one more weekend and one more picnic. Pack a light chicken salad and a lime-marinated skirt steak topped with a lively salsa. Both can be made in advance, if your picnic is far from home and your time will be spent in traveling. The vegetables and the savory lentils hint at the cooler days to come. And no one can ever resist the plum crisp—summer's harvest still at its best.

Set up your picnic in a park, on a porch in your backyard, or at the beach. Seating is informal and depends on location. At home, pull benches or painted chairs up to the table. Place opened bottles of red wine on the table and chilled white wine and water in wine buckets so everybody can help themselves.

If you have some old picnic hampers, stack them alongside the table. Drape them with a colorful cloth, place a flat, lined basket on top, and fill it with farmstead cheeses. Scatter an array of smaller baskets filled with berries, peaches, and early apples and pears and plums around the table. Try to set the food out on one big table; but if there's too much, set up a second table nearby.

Go through your flower garden and pick heaps of vibrant-colored zinnias, dahlias, white cosmos, and mums. Viburnums and other flowering shrubs are showing their fruit. Arrange branches in enamel pitchers, glass jugs, ceramic crocks, or colorful buckets.

Brightly colored plastic plates travel well and make cheery away-from-home picnic ware. At home, stack your everyday plates on the table in a few piles with silverware on top. Soft fabric napkins add elegance to the rustic setting.

Party with panache, and you will float gently into the next good season.

THE MUSIC
Muddy Waters
The Weavers' *Wasn't That A Time*

THE WINE
Fino or Palo Cortado Sherry
Chilean Carmenère

THE EXTRAS
Picnic hamper (if traveling)
Picnic table
Ice bucket
Barbecue grill and accessories

SAVORY LENTIL SALAD

The starchy, earthy texture of the lentils picks up all the flavors of the pungent onions and garlic and the Lemon-Mint Dressing in this hearty salad.

FOR THE LENTILS

2 cups (8 ounces) dried lentils
2 ribs celery, with leaves, cut in half
1 small onion, quartered
2 cloves garlic, lightly crushed
6 cups Vegetable Broth (page 398) or
    Basic Chicken Broth (page 397)

FOR THE SALAD

$1/3$ cup red wine vinegar
$1/3$ cup extra-virgin olive oil
2 carrots, cut into $1/4$-inch dice
2 ribs celery, cut into $1/4$-inch dice
2 scallions, including 3 inches green, thinly sliced
$1/3$ cup chopped fresh mint leaves,
    plus 3 tablespoons for garnish
Salt and coarsely ground black pepper, to taste
$1/2$ cup Lemon-Mint Dressing (page 400)

1. Prepare the lentils: Pick over the lentils and rinse them in a fine-mesh strainer under cold water. Place them in a heavy pot.

2. Add the celery, onion, garlic, and broth and bring to a boil over high heat. Reduce the heat to medium and simmer, skimming off any foam that rises to the surface, until the lentils are just tender, about 20 minutes. Do not overcook or they will become mushy. Drain the lentils and place them in a large bowl. Discard the flavoring vegetables.

3. Combine the vinegar, olive oil, carrots, and diced celery in a small skillet over low heat. Cook, shaking the skillet, for 5 to 7 minutes to blend the flavors. Toss with the lentils. Add the scallions, the $1/3$ cup chopped mint, and generous amounts of salt and coarse pepper.

4. Place the lentils on a big platter and spoon the dressing over it. Sprinkle with the remaining chopped mint and serve.

SKIRT STEAK WITH NUEVO SALSA

Chewy and flavorful skirt steak, thanks to the popularity of Mexican fajitas, has gained well-deserved respect. The onions, Tabasco, lime, vinegar, and herbs in the salsa add some heat and piquancy. If you're traveling to the picnic site, the steaks can marinate in a cooler on the way. But even if you have to grill the steaks before you hit the road, they'll taste delicious cold with the salsa.

FOR THE SKIRT STEAK

2 skirt steaks (about $1\frac{1}{4}$ pounds each)
$1/4$ cup fresh lime juice (from 2 large limes)
$1/4$ cup extra-virgin olive oil
4 dashes Tabasco sauce
4 cloves garlic, finely minced
$1/2$ cup coarsely chopped fresh cilantro leaves
Salt and freshly ground black pepper, to taste

FOR THE SALSA

10 ripe plum tomatoes, seeded and
    cut into $1/4$-inch dice
$3/4$ cup diced red onion ($1/4$-inch dice)
6 scallions, including 2 inches green,
    thinly sliced
2 tablespoons finely minced garlic
$1/2$ cup extra-virgin olive oil
6 tablespoons fresh lime juice
    (from 3 large limes)
2 tablespoons red wine vinegar
8 dashes Tabasco sauce
Coarse (kosher) salt and freshly ground
    black pepper, to taste
$3/4$ cup coarsely chopped fresh cilantro

1. Prepare the skirt steak: Place the steaks in a large nonreactive bowl or a shallow baking dish.

2. Combine the lime juice, olive oil, Tabasco sauce, garlic, cilantro, and salt and pepper in a small bowl, mix well, and rub the mixture all over the steaks. Cover and set aside to marinate in the refrigerator for 4 hours.

3. Meanwhile, prepare the salsa: Combine the tomatoes, onion, scallions, and garlic in a bowl. Add the olive oil, lime juice, vinegar, Tabasco sauce, and salt and coarse pepper. Using a fork, stir in the cilantro. Refrigerate, covered.

4. Heat a barbecue grill to high.

5. Grill the steaks over high heat, 3 inches from the heat source, for 2 to 3 minutes per side for rare (125°F on an instant-reading thermometer), or to desired doneness. Transfer them to a cutting board and let them rest for 5 minutes. Then cut them into thin slices on the diagonal and serve topped with the salsa.

Note: The salsa can be prepared up to 6 hours ahead; cover and refrigerate. Remove it from the refrigerator 1 hour before serving to allow it to come to room temperature.

PICNIC CHICKEN SALAD

One wise, and anonymous, writer of the eighteenth century wrote, "Picnics are the happy occasions when people try to forget that they are being civilized." Whether yours is wild and wacky or calm and laid back, foodwise, it should include a chicken salad. This one, showered with cherry tomatoes, tender lettuce, pungent Roquefort cheese, and sweet aromatic olive oil, definitely suits all moods. Served in a pretty bowl on a checkered tablecloth, it is as summery as a sun-drenched scene by Van Gogh.

4 whole skinless, boneless chicken breasts (about 4 pounds total)
¾ cup Basic Chicken Broth (page 397)
Salt and freshly ground black pepper, to taste
1 hothouse (seedless) cucumber
2 tablespoons fresh lemon juice
¼ cup extra-virgin olive oil
2 heads Boston lettuce, separated into leaves (damaged outer leaves discarded), rinsed and patted dry
1 pint cherry or grape tomatoes, cut in half
⅓ cup imported black olives, preferably Gaeta
4 ounces Roquefort cheese, cut into chunks
½ cup whole fresh flat-leaf parsley leaves

1. Preheat the oven to 350°F.

2. Place the chicken in a shallow baking pan in one layer, pour the broth over it, and season with salt and pepper. Bake, basting once or twice, until cooked through, about 25 minutes. Let the chicken cool to room temperature.

3. Cut the two halves of the chicken breasts apart, removing any gristle, then cut each half diagonally into thirds. Set them aside.

4. Using a vegetable peeler, cut off 4 stripes of peel evenly spaced along the length of the cucumber. Halve the cucumber lengthwise, and then slice it crosswise into ¼-inch slices.

5. Just before serving, whisk together the lemon juice, olive oil, and salt and pepper to taste in a large bowl. Tear the lettuce leaves into medium-size pieces and place them in the bowl. Add the tomatoes, cucumber, chicken, and olives. Gently fold together from underneath, coating the ingredients with the dressing.

6. Add the cheese and parsley and toss carefully.

7. Adjust the seasonings, if necessary, and serve.

Unlike other holidays, Labor Day, said Samuel Gompers, founder of the AFL, "is devoted to no man, living or dead, to no sect, race, or nation." It was, in fact, created by the labor movement to pay tribute to the achievements of the American worker. First observed in New York City on September 5, 1882, by 1884 it was being officially celebrated in that city on the first Monday of that month. Throughout the next decade, more and more states adopted the holiday, and in June 1894, Congress passed an act making it a legal holiday in the District of Columbia and the territories.

Picnic Chicken Salad and *Roasted Reds*

ROASTED REDS

Red is happy. Red is joyous. Red is roasted sweet beets, succulent smoky ripe tomatoes, crunchy onions, and smooth peppers. Add summer corn and scallions (for a touch of yellow and green).

> 4 red bell peppers, stemmed, cut in half, and
>   seeded
> 8 beets, trimmed
> 8 large ripe tomatoes, cored and quartered
> 4 red onions, cut in quarters
> 4 tablespoons olive oil
> $\frac{1}{2}$ cup fresh corn kernels (from 1 ear)
> 2 tablespoons fresh lemon juice
> Salt and freshly ground black pepper, to taste
> 3 scallions, including 3 inches green,
>   thinly sliced on the diagonal

1. Preheat the broiler.

2. Flatten the bell pepper halves slightly with the palm of your hand. Lay the halves, skin side up, in a single layer on a small baking sheet. Broil about 3 inches from the heat until the skins are charred, 12 to 15 minutes. Remove the peppers from the broiler and place them in a paper or plastic bag. Close it tight and let the peppers steam for about 15 minutes. Then slip off the charred skin and set the peppers aside.

3. Preheat the oven to 350°F.

4. Wrap the beets individually in aluminum foil and place them on a baking sheet. Arrange the tomatoes and onions on a second baking sheet and brush them with 2 tablespoons of the olive oil. Place both baking sheets in the oven and roast until the vegetables are tender, about 1 hour. Much of the liquid from the tomatoes will have evaporated and the onions will be lightly browned.

5. Meanwhile, bring a saucepan of water to a boil over high heat. Add the corn and cook for 1 minute. Drain into a colander, rinse under cold water to stop the cooking, and set the colander aside to drain.

6. Remove the vegetables from the oven and set them aside to cool. When the beets are cool enough to handle, unwrap them and slip off the skins. Cut them into quarters.

7. To serve, arrange the peppers, beets, tomatoes, and onions on a large platter. Drizzle with the remaining 2 tablespoons olive oil and the lemon juice, and sprinkle with salt and pepper. Sprinkle the corn and scallions over the top.

LUSTROUS LEEKS

Leeks, like onions, are sharp when raw (so sharp, in fact, that I have never come across a recipe for raw leeks). However, when cooked, like onions or garlic, they have a sweetness and a bouquet that combines beautifully with brawny steak and subtler chicken.

> 8 large leeks
> $2\frac{1}{2}$ tablespoons distilled white vinegar
> 5 tablespoons extra-virgin olive oil
> 2 large ripe tomatoes, each cut into
>   8 wedges
> $\frac{1}{4}$ cup imported back olives, preferably
>   Niçoise or Gaeta, pitted
> $\frac{1}{4}$ cup chopped fresh flat-leaf parsley
> Freshly ground black pepper, to taste

1. Trim the greens of the leeks to within 3 inches of the white bulb. Trim off the roots just at the bulb, leaving the bulb intact. Without splitting the leek entirely, cut a slit from the top of the green to within 3 inches of the bottom of the bulb. Place the leeks in a large bowl, cover with cold water, and add the vinegar. Set aside for 1 hour to remove the sand. Rinse the leeks well under cold running water.

2. Bring a large pot of salted water to a boil over high heat and add the leeks. Cook until the bulbs are tender, about 8 minutes. Drain well, cut off the base of the bulbs, and pat dry.

3. Heat the olive oil in a large nonstick skillet over medium heat. Add the leeks and cook, turning the leeks and shaking the pan, until golden, about 5 minutes.

4. Stir in the tomatoes, olives, and parsley, shaking the pan. Season with pepper, cover, and heat through, 3 to 5 minutes.

5. Transfer the leeks to a serving platter and spoon the sauce over them. Allow to cool to room temperature before serving.

Plum Crisp

PLUM CRISP

The lazy, late-summer warmth around Labor Day brings out the best in plums. A crisp is more like a substantial compote than a pie. Sprinkled with a topping made from crustlike ingredients, the crisp gives you all the flavor of buttery pastry without the worries of rolling it out. And a crisp is easy to take with you to a picnic. Plum crisp is scrumptious paired with vanilla ice cream, but with some crème fraîche it really jazzes up a picnic.

FOR THE TOPPING
1 cup all-purpose flour
½ cup quick-cooking oats
1 cup (packed) light brown sugar
Pinch of salt
¼ teaspoon ground cinnamon
10 tablespoons (1¼ sticks) cold unsalted
*   butter, cut into tablespoon-size pieces*

FOR THE CRISP
12 large ripe black plums, each
*   pitted and cut into 8 wedges*
1 cup granulated sugar
1 tablespoon fresh lemon juice
1 teaspoon pure vanilla extract
2 cups fresh raspberries, gently rinsed and
*   drained, or thawed frozen raspberries*

Crème fraîche, Double Vanilla-Bean
*   Ice Cream (page 53), or Sweetened*
*   Whipped Cream (page 403),*
*   for serving*

1. Position a rack in the center of the oven, and preheat the oven to 400°F. Butter a 9-inch square baking dish and set it aside.

2. Prepare the topping: Place the flour, oats, brown sugar, salt, and cinnamon in a food processor and process until completely smooth. Add the butter and pulse until it is incorporated and the mixture is crumbly and starting to clump together. Set the topping aside.

3. Toss the plums with the granulated sugar, lemon juice, and vanilla in a large bowl. Add the raspberries and toss lightly. Transfer the fruit to the prepared baking dish. Crumble the topping evenly over the fruit.

4. Bake for 10 minutes, then reduce the temperature to 350°F and continue to bake until the fruit is soft and bubbly and the topping is golden, 30 to 40 minutes more. (If the topping is browning too quickly, cover loosely with aluminum foil.) Serve warm, with crème fraîche, Double Vanilla-Bean Ice Cream, or Sweetened Whipped Cream.

AN OLD-FASHIONED

HALLOWEEN

Halloween is a day to set inhibitions aside and give the imagination free rein. Normally conservative co-workers show up at the office in outrageous costumes. Frankensteins, fairies, Glindas, and godfathers walk down the street in broad daylight. Shopkeepers arrange jars of candy for the local trick-or-treaters—young and old—and cities like New York and San Francisco host huge, joyous, wacky ghost and goblin parades.

> From ghoulies and ghosties, and long-leggedy beasties
> And things that go bump in the night,
> Lord God protect us!
>
> — IRISH PRAYER

The giddy revelry of Halloween in Manhattan makes me want to cook up some devilishly hot dishes for friends—as long as they show up in costume.

MENU

This is just about the most fun menu of the year. Think of the spookiest, scariest, hottest, most brilliantly orange food, and you're set to go. Devilish Deviled Chicken Wings set the tone. Then, for a fun, easy-eating, spicy entree, Red-Hot Short Ribs of Beef fit the bill perfectly. Sunny Sweet Potatoes are intensely orange, with just the right amount of sweetness to beat the heat of the ribs. Horseradish Cream Mashed Potatoes offer a piquant partner to the sweets. Jicama Slaw, in a tangle of white, orange, and red swirls, adds a pleasing crunch. And who could resist the moist and luscious Devil's Food Cake, bejeweled with a scoop of bright orange Tangerine Sorbet? Don't forget the cinnamon red-hots! They burn the devil out of your tongue.

It's okay to be a little hokey, or at least kitschy, for Halloween. No matter how sophisticated you are, black and orange crepe-paper streamers are a must. To please the more design-oriented crowd, go with a dramatic black and white décor and place carved jack-o'-lanterns, lit by candles, along the table. A few small paper black cats and bats hanging from the ceiling are appropriately spooky, and don't forget a skeleton on the door. The entrees will look great on large white platters, but use orange Fiestaware-type bowls for the side dishes.

Place a mess of bottled hot sauces near the Deviled Chicken Wings and the Red-Hot Short Ribs. Use a large wooden, tin, or pottery bowl filled with shiny apples in place of a floral arrangement. And set bowls of cinnamon red-hot candies near the cake for an after-dinner bite.

AN OLD-FASHIONED HALLOWEEN
PARTY FOR EIGHT

Deviled Chicken Wings

Red-Hot Short Ribs of Beef

Horseradish Cream Mashed Potatoes

Jicama Slaw

Sunny Sweet Potatoes

Devil's Food Cake with Old-Fashioned Chocolate Buttercream

Tangerine Sorbet

THE MUSIC

Stephen Sondheim's
Sweeney Todd and *Into the Woods*
Edvard Grieg's *Peer Gynt Suite*

THE WINE

Dry Creek Zinfandel
California Sauvignon Blanc

THE EXTRAS

Pedestal cake stand
Crepe paper and jack-o'-lanterns
Ice-cream maker

DEVILED CHICKEN WINGS

Chicken wings are great for picking up, sucking all the meat off the bones, and licking the sauce off your fingers. And these have a great spicy kick to them. Sweet, sour, salty, hot—every basic taste is present . . . in force!

5 pounds chicken wings, wing tips snipped off,
    rinsed and patted dry
1 tablespoon finely minced garlic
2 tablespoons unsalted butter
2 tablespoons olive oil
2 tablespoons Dijon mustard
2 tablespoons fresh lemon juice
2 teaspoons Worcestershire sauce
1 to 2 teaspoons Tabasco sauce, to taste
1 teaspoon chili powder
$1/2$ teaspoon paprika, plus more for dusting
Coarse (kosher) salt, to taste
1 small red onion, cut into $1/4$-inch dice,
    or 4 scallions, including 3 inches green,
    thinly sliced on the diagonal, for garnish

1. Preheat the oven to 375°F.

2. Place the chicken wings in a large bowl, scatter the garlic over them, and toss.

The idea of "trick or treat" seems to have originated in Europe in connection with All Hallows Eve (the origin of the word *Halloween*). Believing that spirits were abroad on that night, villagers went from house to house begging for "soul cakes." The more cakes they received, the more prayers they would say for the deceased relatives of the homeowners, thus ensuring them a place in heaven.

3. Melt the butter in the olive oil in a small saucepan over low heat. Allow to cool slightly, and then whisk in the mustard, lemon juice, Worcestershire sauce, Tabasco sauce, chili powder, the $1/2$ teaspoon paprika, and salt to taste. Pour the mixture over the chicken wings and toss, coating the wings well.

4. Divide the wings between two shallow baking dishes and bake for 30 minutes. Reduce the heat to 350°F and continue to bake until the wings are deep golden brown and cooked through, about 30 minutes more. Arrange them on a decorative platter, sprinkle with salt, and lightly dust with paprika. Garnish with the onion and serve.

RED-HOT SHORT RIBS OF BEEF

The short rib, a humble cut of beef, has come into favor in fancy restaurants because you can braise the dickens out of it and it just develops more and more flavor. It seems there is no sauce that it can't stand up to. Equally popular in recent years is good old-fashioned peppery heat. The two are combined in this Halloween entree. The hot sauce is the trick, and the ribs are the treat.

6 pounds meaty beef short ribs,
    cut into 6-inch-long pieces
Salt and freshly ground black pepper, to taste
2 tablespoons olive oil
2 onions, slivered lengthwise
2 tablespoons finely minced garlic
2 tablespoons Dijon mustard
3 tablespoons fresh lemon juice
2 teaspoons Tabasco sauce
1 teaspoon chili powder
1 teaspoon light or dark brown sugar
1 cup Beef Broth (page 397)
Tabasco, or another hot sauce, for serving

1. Preheat the oven to 425°F.

2. Season the ribs well with salt and pepper.

3. Heat the olive oil in a flameproof casserole over medium-high heat. Add the ribs (you'll have to do this in batches) and brown them well, about 8 minutes per batch. Transfer the ribs to a plate.

4. Remove all but 1 to 2 tablespoons of the fat from the casserole. Add the onions and cook over low heat, stirring occasionally, for 7 minutes. Add the garlic and cook until the onions and garlic are well softened, about 3 minutes more.

5. Return the ribs to the casserole, arranging them on top of the onions.

6. Combine the mustard, lemon juice, 2 teaspoons Tabasco sauce, the chili powder, brown sugar, and broth in a small bowl and pour over the ribs and onions. Reduce the oven temperature to 350°F and immediately place the casserole, covered, in the oven. Bake the ribs, basting and stirring them around occasionally, until they are tender, about 2½ hours.

7. Remove the casserole from the oven and transfer the ribs to a plate. Strain the gravy through a sieve, discarding the onions and garlic. Then pour the gravy through a gravy separator to remove the fat (or skim off as much as possible with a spoon). Return the ribs to the casserole, cover with the defatted gravy, and reheat before serving. (If you like, remove the meat from the bones and discard the bones before reheating.) Serve the ribs with plenty of gravy, and pass the Tabasco sauce for spicing up if desired.

Note: You can prepare the ribs up to 1 day in advance. Cover the ribs with aluminum foil and pour the gravy into a covered container. Refrigerate both until ready to reheat. Before reheating, remove the solidified fat from the gravy. Then combine the gravy with the ribs in a large pot and cook over medium-low heat until heated through, 20 to 25 minutes.

Sixty percent of the world's supply of horseradish is grown in the American Bottoms—a glacially formed basin in southern Illinois, on the east bank of the Mississippi River across from St. Louis. Horseradish thrives in its potassium-rich soil, cold winters, and long, hot summers. German immigrants began growing horseradish there at the end of the nineteenth century, passing their methods down to succeeding generations. Today, the pungent root is celebrated each May at the International Horseradish Festival in Collinsville, Illinois. Events include a root toss, a horseradish-eating contest, and a horseradish recipe contest.

HORSERADISH CREAM MASHED POTATOES

There is a proverb that goes "To a worm in a horseradish, the whole world is a horseradish." I think you could extend that to "To a person with horseradish in the mouth, the whole world is horseradish." There is nothing shy about the horseradish: Its heat enhances flavor, and its sharpness helps to slow down your palate so that rich meaty dishes don't overwhelm it. Mashed together with heavy cream into smooth and subtle potatoes, it is a flavor package that announces itself with authority.

2½ pounds russet potatoes,
  peeled and cut in quarters
½ cup heavy (whipping) cream, warmed

4 tablespoons (¹/₂ stick) unsalted butter,
at room temperature
3 tablespoons prepared horseradish,
well drained
1 teaspoon salt
¹/₂ teaspoon freshly ground black pepper

1. Place the potatoes in a large heavy saucepan and cover with cold water. Bring to a boil over high heat. Reduce the heat to medium-low and simmer until the potatoes are tender, 25 to 30 minutes. Drain well and return the potatoes to the pot. Place the pot over very low heat for about 30 seconds to dry the potatoes well.

2. Using a ricer, a potato masher, or a large fork, mash the potatoes in a large bowl with the cream, butter, and horseradish. Season with the salt and pepper and fluff with a fork. Serve immediately.

JICAMA SLAW

If a vegetable is crunchy, it has good slaw potential. The centerpiece here is jicama, a vegetable that has recently come into wider use with the growing popularity of Latin American food. Once available only in Latino markets, this fruity, crunchy, apple-ish, water-chestnutty vegetable is now available in many supermarkets. Tossed with a rainbow collection of bell peppers and accented with a lemon vinaigrette, it lives up to its slaw potential.

2 jicama (about 1 pound total),
peeled and julienned
2 red bell peppers, stemmed, seeded,
and julienned
2 orange bell peppers, stemmed, seeded,
and julienned
2 yellow bell peppers, stemmed, seeded,
and julienned
¹/₄ cup chopped fresh cilantro
¹/₂ cup Lemon Vinaigrette (page 400)

Combine all the julienned vegetables and the cilantro in a bowl. Toss with the vinaigrette and serve (see Note).

Note: You can combine all the vegetables and cilantro up to 4 hours in advance, but don't dress the slaw more than 1 hour before serving.

SUNNY SWEET POTATOES

Their orange color makes sweet potatoes a must at Halloween. And what could be more devilish than the additions of lemon and ginger? Sweets are so deliciously soft that a simple fork is all you need to mash them.

8 sweet potatoes (about 6 ounces each),
peeled and cut in quarters
²/₃ cup (packed) light brown sugar
6 tablespoons (³/₄ stick) unsalted butter,
at room temperature
1 tablespoon finely grated lemon zest
2 tablespoons fresh lemon juice
2 teaspoons ground ginger
Salt, to taste

1. Place the sweet potatoes in a large heavy saucepan and cover with cold water. Bring to a boil over high heat. Reduce the heat to medium-low and simmer until the potatoes are tender, 20 minutes. Drain well and return the potatoes to the pot. Place the pot over very low heat for about 30 seconds to dry the potatoes well.

2. Using a fork or a potato masher, mash the potatoes in a large bowl with all the remaining ingredients. Adjust the seasonings, if necessary, and serve immediately.

Note: These potatoes can be prepared up to 4 hours ahead of time and reheated, covered, in a 350°F oven. If you make them in advance, transfer them to an ovenproof casserole before reheating.

DEVIL'S FOOD CAKE

Perfectly in keeping with our devilish theme, this wickedly, sinfully rich cake is made with unsweetened chocolate and brown sugar. The drops of red food coloring pay homage to you-know-who. Sour cream, by the way, always enhances the texture of baked goods. A scoop of Tangerine Sorbet alongside a slice of this cake looks suitably Halloweenish, and the citrus and chocolate flavors make a perfect combination.

Unsweetened cocoa powder,
  for dusting the pans
4 ounces unsweetened chocolate,
  coarsely chopped
$1/2$ cup (1 stick) unsalted butter,
  at room temperature
$2 1/2$ cups (packed) light brown sugar
3 large eggs
$1 1/4$ cups cake flour, sifted
2 teaspoons baking soda
$1/2$ teaspoon salt
1 cup sour cream
3 drops red food coloring
1 teaspoon pure vanilla extract
1 cup boiling water
Old-Fashioned Chocolate Buttercream
  (recipe follows)

1. Position a rack in the center of the oven, and preheat the oven to 350°F. Butter the bottom and sides of two 9-inch round cake pans. Line the bottoms with circles of wax or parchment paper and butter the paper. Dust the bottom and sides of the pans with cocoa powder, tapping out any excess. Set the pans aside.

2. Melt the chocolate in the top of a double boiler over simmering water. Set it aside.

3. Cream the butter and brown sugar together in a large bowl, using an electric mixer, until light and fluffy, about 5 minutes. With the mixer on low speed, add the eggs, one at a time, beating well after each addition. Stir in the melted chocolate.

4. Sift the flour, baking soda, and salt into another bowl. With the mixer on low speed, and alternating between the two, add the flour mixture (one third at a time) and the sour cream ($1/2$ cup at a time) to the chocolate mixture, starting and ending with flour. Scrape down the sides of the bowl and beat on medium speed for 2 minutes. Add the food coloring and vanilla to the boiling water, then slowly add it to the batter. Continue mixing until combined, 1 minute more.

5. Divide the batter between the prepared pans and bake until a wooden toothpick inserted in the center of the layers comes out clean, 25 to 30 minutes. Let the layers cool in the pans on wire racks for 10 minutes, then remove the layers from the pans and let them cool completely on the rack. Carefully peel off the paper.

6. To assemble the cake, place one cake layer, top side up, on a serving plate. Spread it with one third of the buttercream. Top with the

Devil's Food Cake

remaining layer, top side up. Frost the sides and top of the cake with the remaining buttercream. This cake is best served at room temperature.

Note: If you want your layers level instead of rounded, use a serrated knife to remove a thin slice from each top. Turn the layers bottom side up to frost and stack.

OLD-FASHIONED CHOCOLATE BUTTERCREAM

This thick buttercream really is the "icing on the cake." Rich, sweet, and creamy, it's so good it's a wonder that any of it makes it to the cake at all.

8 ounces semisweet chocolate,
  coarsely chopped
3 ounces unsweetened chocolate,
  coarsely chopped
4 large egg yolks
2 cups sifted confectioners' sugar
1/3 cup strong brewed coffee, boiling hot
1 1/2 cups (3 sticks) unsalted butter,
  at room temperature
2 teaspoons pure vanilla extract

1. Melt the chocolates together in the top of a double boiler over simmering water. Set it aside to cool.

2. Place the egg yolks and confectioners' sugar in a bowl. Beat with an electric mixer on low speed until combined. Increase the speed to high and continue mixing until the mixture is fluffy and lemon-colored, about 5 minutes.

3. Reduce the speed to low and add the cooled chocolate, mixing until well combined, 1 minute. Add the hot coffee in a steady stream. Continue beating until incorporated, 30 seconds. Add the butter, a tablespoon at a time, until incorporated. Increase the speed to high and whip until light and fluffy, about 5 minutes. Mix in the vanilla.

4. Use the buttercream immediately, or store, covered, in the refrigerator for up to 2 days.

MAKES 4 CUPS, ENOUGH TO FROST 1 9-INCH 2-LAYER CAKE

Note: The boiling hot coffee should cook the egg yolks, but to be safe, use very fresh eggs that have been kept refrigerated.

TANGERINE SORBET

Make a list of the reasons why we serve sorbet, and this fruity cooler hits every point: It's zippy, refreshing, clean-tasting, sweet, and a palate waker upper. People always take a second or two to place the flavor, and then they pucker and smile.

2 cups fresh tangerine juice
  (from about 8 tangerines)
2 cups Simple Syrup (page 403)

Place the tangerine juice and the Simple Syrup in an ice-cream maker and freeze according to the manufacturer's instructions. Transfer to a container, cover, and freeze until serving.

MAKES ABOUT 1 QUART

Thanksgiving

Dinner

Throughout history, every society has celebrated the end of the harvest. Likewise, most have set aside a day of thanks. George Washington sought to combine them, but it wasn't until Abraham Lincoln was in office that the event became an annual one, and it wasn't until 1941, under F.D.R., that it became a national holiday celebrated on the fourth Thursday in November with an abundance of food consumed without a second thought about calories. Laden tables, well-fed uncles snoozing happily in front of a TV—a Norman Rockwell image perhaps, but one we're happy to relive in the twenty-first century.

MENU

This Thanksgiving menu is fairly traditional, with a little modern twist or two. Chowders are so American, and a Lobster and Corn Chowder makes a lovely fanfare for the star of the Thanksgiving show, the turkey—here glazed with a maple-ginger sauce and stuffed with cornbread and spicy sausage. Winter Squash and Sweet Potato Mash is a seasonal tweak and slightly lighter than plain mashed sweets. Mixed Vegetables U.S.A. evokes those frozen vegetable combos, but these are fresh—and what a difference fresh makes! A fresh Chunky Pear Apple Sauce and Orange-Ginger Cranberries are the condiments of choice for this meal, and the finale is a Thanksgiving tradition: Pumpkin Pie dolloped with sweetened whipped cream.

To accommodate sixteen people, you may need two tables. Use matching linens on both to pull things together—blue-and-white gingham creates a festive country scene. Arrange an assortment of brass candlesticks down the centers of both tables, with ivory-colored candles.

On the sideboard, pedestal cake stands are perfect for cascading arrangements of red and green grapes. An additional stand can hold an artfully arranged pyramid of the season's first clementine oranges.

Decorate the tables with large fragrant bunches of herbs in small pitchers and soft yellow roses, cut low and full. (Always arrange your flowers a day in advance so that they have a chance to open in time for your meal.)

Thanksgiving Dinner

FOR SIXTEEN

Lobster and Corn Chowder

Maple-Ginger Roast Turkey with
Cornbread Chorizo Stuffing

Mixed Vegetables U.S.A.

Winter Squash and Sweet Potato Mash

Orange-Ginger Cranberries

Chunky Pear Apple Sauce

Pumpkin Pie

THE MUSIC

Aaron Copland
James Taylor

THE WINE

Australian Chardonnay
Sonoma Pinot Noir

THE EXTRAS

Extra linens
Extra candlesticks
Soup tureen
Large turkey platter
Carving knife and fork

Lobster and Corn Chowder

LOBSTER AND CORN CHOWDER

The word *chowder* calls to mind the rocky New England coast, where cornfields go down to the sea, the seaweed lies in mats above the high-tide mark, and the lobster traps are full of fat lobsters. Although *chowder* derives from the kettle in which French fishermen cooked up their seafood stew (*chaudière,* or "cauldron"), it is a classic American dish, never more so than when made with corn and lobster.

8 ounces slab bacon, rind removed,
    cut into small dice
2 tablespoons unsalted butter
4 cups diced onions (¼-inch dice)
8 cups Basic Chicken Broth
    (page 397)
4 bay leaves
2 teaspoons sweet paprika
¼ cup all-purpose flour
4 russet potatoes, peeled and cut into
    ¼-inch dice
6 sprigs fresh thyme
2 cups half-and-half or heavy
    (whipping) cream
6 cups frozen corn kernels, thawed
2 red or yellow bell peppers, stemmed,
    seeded, and cut into ¼-inch dice
8 scallions, including 3 inches green,
    very thinly sliced on the diagonal
Salt and freshly ground black pepper,
    to taste
About 4 cups diced cooked lobster meat
    (½-inch dice; see Note)
½ cup chopped fresh flat-leaf parsley

1. Place the bacon in a large pot over low heat. Cook, stirring, to render the fat, 5 to 7 minutes. Add the butter to the pot and when it melts, add the onions and cook, stirring occasionally, until softened, about 10 minutes.

2. Meanwhile, combine the broth, bay leaves, and paprika in a small pot and bring to a boil over high heat. Reduce the heat to medium and simmer for 5 minutes to give the broth a rich flavor. Keep hot.

3. Add the flour to the bacon and onions and cook, stirring, for 1 minute.

4. Add the hot broth, the potatoes, and the thyme to the onions and cook, stirring occasionally, until the potatoes are just tender, about 15 minutes.

5. Add the half-and-half, corn, bell peppers, and scallions and cook until the peppers and scallions are softened, about 10 minutes more. Season with salt and pepper.

6. Remove the bay leaves, and add the lobster and parsley just before serving. Heat over medium-low heat for 5 minutes, and serve immediately.

Note: This requires four 1½-pound lobsters. See page 152 for cooking instructions.

MAPLE-GINGER ROAST TURKEY

There is something both tantalizing and comforting about stuffed turkey, and the glaze makes this one so beautiful it must be seen by all before it's sliced. The ginger in it is a perfect foil for the sweet maple syrup, a New World gift to cuisine. Because the turkey is also a New World culinary gift, why not use another American original, corn, for the stuffing? And because corn came from Mexico, why not spice the cornbread with Mexican chorizo sausage? No more bland birds on your Thanksgiving table.

There are a number of steps to this recipe, but you can make it easier on yourself by making the glaze two days ahead and the cornbread stuffing and the broth one day ahead.

FOR THE GIBLET BROTH

Turkey giblets and neck
1 cup (about 12 ounces) extra giblets
4 chicken backs (about 1¾ pounds total;
*   optional)*
2 ribs celery, with leaves
2 medium onions, unpeeled
2 cloves garlic, lightly crushed
4 sprigs fresh flat-leaf parsley
4 whole cloves
3 whole black peppercorns
1 bay leaf
Salt, to taste

FOR THE TURKEY

1 fresh turkey (18 pounds, with giblets
*   and neck)*
1 orange, cut in half
Paprika, to taste
Salt and freshly ground black pepper, to taste
10 to 12 cups Cornbread Chorizo Stuffing
*   (recipe follows)*
6 tablespoons (¾ stick) unsalted butter,
*   at room temperature*
Maple-Ginger Glaze (recipe follows)

FOR THE GIBLET GRAVY

4 tablespoons (½ stick) unsalted butter
¼ cup all-purpose flour
1 teaspoon dried thyme
Salt and freshly ground black pepper, to taste
1 tablespoon chopped fresh flat-leaf parsley
Giblet broth, if needed

2 to 3 large bunches fresh sage, for garnish
Red grapes, for garnish

1. Prepare the giblet broth 1 day ahead: Set aside the liver for another use and wash the giblets well. Place all the broth ingredients in a large heavy saucepan, add water just to cover (about 6 cups), and bring to a boil over high heat, then reduce the heat to medium-low and simmer, skimming off any foam that rises to the surface, until the giblets are tender, about 1 hour. Strain the broth into a bowl, reserving the giblets, turkey neck, and chicken backs (if used); discard the vegetables. Cover and refrigerate the strained broth.

2. When they are cool enough to handle, shred the meat from the neck and the chicken backs, discarding any skin. Finely chop the giblets. Mix the meat and giblets together. Cover and refrigerate.

3. On Thanksgiving day, preheat the oven to 325°F.

4. Prepare the turkey: Rinse the turkey well inside and out, removing any excess fat. Pat the turkey dry with paper towels.

5. Squeeze the orange halves inside the body and neck cavities. Sprinkle the cavities with paprika, salt, and pepper. Stuff the cavities loosely with the stuffing, using about 3 cups for the neck and 8 cups for the body. Close with turkey lacers, or sew closed with a large needle and heavy thread. Tie the legs together with kitchen string.

6. Rub the turkey generously with the butter and sprinkle with paprika, salt, and pepper.

7. Place the turkey, breast side up, on a rack in a large flameproof roasting pan. Pour 2 cups of the giblet broth into the bottom of the pan, and cover the turkey loosely with aluminum foil. Place it in the oven and roast for 1½ hours.

8. Remove the foil and roast the turkey, basting it with the pan juices every 30 minutes, for 2½ hours more.

9. Raise the oven temperature to 350°F and cook the turkey for another 45 minutes. Brush the glaze liberally over the turkey and cook it for 30 minutes longer. The turkey is done when an instant-reading thermometer inserted into the thickest part of the thigh reads 180°F.

10. Transfer the turkey to a platter. Remove the stuffing from the body and neck cavities, place it in a serving dish, and cover it with aluminum foil to keep warm. Let the turkey rest, loosely covered with foil, for 20 minutes before carving.

11. While the turkey is resting, prepare the giblet gravy: Place the roasting pan on the stove and heat the pan juices over medium-low heat, scraping up all the brown bits on the bottom of the pan. Pour the pan juices through a gravy separator to remove the fat (or skim the fat off with a metal spoon). Pour the defatted juices into a measuring cup and add any remaining glaze. You should have at least 2 cups. If you don't, add enough of the remaining giblet broth to make 2 cups. Stir well.

12. Melt the butter in a heavy saucepan over medium-low heat. Gradually whisk in the flour and continue whisking until it browns slightly, 2 to 3 minutes. Whisking constantly, slowly pour in the 2 cups defatted pan juices and continue whisking until smooth. Bring the gravy to a boil, reduce the heat to medium-low, and add the thyme, salt and pepper, parsley, and giblet mixture. Simmer, stirring, until the gravy has thickened, about 10 minutes. If you prefer a thinner gravy, add some of the remaining broth until the desired consistency is achieved. Adjust the seasonings to taste.

13. Present the turkey to your guests before carving it. Arrange the carved meat on a large decorative platter. Garnish the platter with bunches of fresh sage and grapes and serve with the stuffing and the hot gravy.

CORNBREAD CHORIZO STUFFING

The bite of chorizo sausage breathes new life into a cornbread stuffing, and while I usually prefer fresh herbs to dry, the dried thyme adds a deeper, more intense flavor when combined with the sweetness of apricots and cherries. Cornbread falls apart easily, so go light on the broth—the stuffing will moisten as it cooks.

1 recipe Jalapeño Corn Muffins, without the
   jalapeños (page 331), made 1 day ahead
   (see Notes) and left loosely wrapped
   at room temperature
4 tablespoons olive oil
1 tablespoon dried thyme
Salt and freshly ground black pepper, to taste
1½ pounds chorizo or andouille sausage,
   cut in half lengthwise and then cut into
   ½-inch pieces
2 tablespoons unsalted butter
3 cups chopped red or yellow onions
6 ribs celery, chopped
1 cup dried apricots, cut in half
1 cup dried cherries
1 cup coarsely chopped pecan halves
½ cup turkey giblet broth (step 1, page 177)
   or Basic Chicken Broth (page 397)

1. Preheat the oven to 350°F.

2. Cut the corn muffins into rough 1-inch cubes; you should have about 12 cups. Place the muffin cubes in a large bowl and toss with 2 tablespoons of the olive oil and the thyme. Season to taste with salt and pepper. Spread the muffin cubes on two baking sheets and bake, shaking the pans occasionally, until lightly toasted, 15 to 20 minutes. Return the bread cubes to the bowl.

3. Meanwhile, cook the chorizo in two batches in a nonstick skillet over medium-high heat until browned, about 10 minutes per batch. Using a slotted spoon, transfer the chorizo to the bowl of cornbread, discarding any fat.

4. Melt the butter in the remaining 2 tablespoons olive oil in a heavy saucepan over medium-low heat. Add the onions and celery and cook, stirring occasionally, until wilted, 15 to 20 minutes. Then add the apricots and cherries and cook to soften them, 5 to 10 minutes more. Using a rubber spatula, carefully fold this into the cornbread, along with the pecans.

5. Slowly drizzle in the broth until the stuffing is moist but not soaking wet. Season with salt and pepper. Allow to cool to room temperature before stuffing the turkey. Do not stuff the turkey until right before cooking it.

MAKES 16 CUPS, ENOUGH STUFFING FOR A 20- TO 24-POUND TURKEY

Notes: You can bake the cornbread as muffins and cut them into cubes for the stuffing. But it may be easier to divide the batter between two 8-inch square baking pans and bake it as cornbread, in a preheated 400°F oven, until a wooden toothpick inserted in the center comes out clean, 45 minutes. Cool, following the muffin baking instructions, before loosely wrapping in plastic wrap.

Cook the stuffing in the turkey cavity and neck. Any extra can be cooked in an ovenproof dish, covered, at 350°F for 20 to 25 minutes.

MAPLE-GINGER GLAZE

Glazes serve dual purposes. First, they give a beautiful sheen to roasts and vegetables. Second, they deliver powerful flavor without overwhelming the delicate succulence of the main ingredient, in this case turkey.

2 tablespoons olive oil
2 tablespoons minced onion
1 tablespoon finely minced fresh ginger
1/2 teaspoon finely minced garlic
1/2 cup fresh orange juice
1/4 cup molasses
2 tablespoons ketchup
1 tablespoon pure maple syrup
1 tablespoon honey
1 tablespoon finely grated orange zest
Salt and freshly ground black pepper, to taste

1. Heat the olive oil in a small heavy saucepan over low heat. Add the onion, ginger, and garlic and cook, stirring once or twice, until wilted, 5 to 7 minutes.

2. Add all the remaining ingredients and bring to a boil over medium-high heat. Cook, stirring, for 3 to 5 minutes. Then reduce the heat to

medium and simmer, stirring occasionally, until thickened, 10 minutes. Strain the sauce through a fine-mesh strainer, reserving the solids. Finely mince the solids again and return them to the sauce. Allow to cool to room temperature. Refrigerate, covered, until ready to use.

MAKES 1 CUP

MIXED VEGETABLES U.S.A.

I don't think there is one of us who didn't grow up with bags of mixed carrots and peas in the freezer. "Mixed vegetables" meant something not very exciting that often required parental encouragement to finish. But when fresh (or individually frozen) and given a little tender loving care in the form of butter, parsley, garlic, and shallots, that combination makes a delicious, multicolored garden offering at the Thanksgiving table.

2 cups diced carrots (1/4-inch dice)
2 cups cut green beans (1/4-inch pieces)
2 cups frozen corn kernels, thawed (see Note)
2 cups frozen peas, thawed (see Note)
4 tablespoons (1/2 stick) unsalted butter,
   at room temperature
1 tablespoon finely chopped shallot
1 1/2 teaspoons finely chopped garlic
2 teaspoons chopped fresh flat-leaf parsley
Salt and freshly ground black pepper, to taste

1. Bring a large saucepan of lightly salted water to a boil over high heat. Add the carrots and cook until crisp tender, 2 minutes. Using a slotted spoon, transfer them to a colander and place under cold running water to stop the cooking. Drain and set aside in a bowl. Repeat the process with the green beans, cooking them for 1 minute. Add the green beans to the bowl with the carrots when cooled and drained. Add the corn and peas to the vegetables in the bowl.

2. Melt 1 teaspoon of the butter in a skillet over low heat. Add the shallot and garlic and cook, stirring, for 3 to 4 minutes. Set aside.

3. Place the remaining butter in a small bowl and cream it well. Add the shallot mixture and the parsley and stir well.

4. Place the carrots, green beans, peas, corn, and the butter mixture in a large skillet, and cook until the butter has melted and the vegetables are heated through, about 5 minutes. Season with salt and pepper and serve immediately.

Note: This vegetable mix goes well with almost any menu. If you make it for a summer party, be sure to use fresh corn; in spring use fresh peas. Both the corn and peas will cook in the boiling water in 1 minute. Drain and cool as you do the other vegetables.

WINTER SQUASH AND SWEET POTATO MASH

Two tastes of autumn, married in the mixing bowl. The color: like maple leaves when they start to turn. Both the squash and the potatoes absorb the fragrant nutmeg and the sweet nectar of the maple syrup. A little finely grated orange zest, with the same autumnal color, accentuates the flavor.

2 butternut squash (about 5 pounds total)
8 sweet potatoes (about 4 pounds total)
1 tablespoon salt
½ cup pure maple syrup
4 tablespoons (½ stick) unsalted butter,
 at room temperature
1 teaspoon freshly grated nutmeg
1½ tablespoons finely grated orange zest
Salt and freshly ground black pepper, to taste

1. Halve the squash lengthwise and discard the seeds. Peel and cut them into large chunks.

2. Peel the sweet potatoes and cut them into large chunks.

3. Place the squash and sweet potatoes in a large pot and cover with water. Add the salt and bring to a boil over high heat. Reduce the heat to medium-low and simmer, uncovered, until the vegetables are tender, 15 to 20 minutes. Drain well and transfer to a bowl.

4. While the squash and potatoes are hot, add the remaining ingredients and mash well with a potato masher (the mixture will not be ultrasmooth).

5. Keep warm until serving in an oven-to-table dish, covered with aluminum foil. If reheating is necessary, place in a 350°F oven until warmed through, about 15 minutes.

Note: This can be prepared 1 day ahead. Allow the mash to cool completely; then cover and refrigerate. Bring it to room temperature before reheating in a 350°F oven.

Cranberries are sometimes called "bounce berries" by growers in the Northeast. Though the origin of this term is lost to legend, most tales seem to agree on part of the story: A nineteenth-century New Jersey farmer, John Webb, had lost one of his legs. Rather than lug all of his berries down from the hayloft where he kept them, he would pour them down the stairs. The mushy, overripe berries stuck to the stairs, but the perfectly ripe, hard berries bounced down the stairs to the floor below. To this day, major companies such as Ocean Spray separate their berries by bouncing them over a 4-inch barrier.

ORANGE-GINGER CRANBERRIES

There are only three commonly eaten fruits that are native to North America: the blueberry, the Concord grape, and the cranberry. By far the tartest and sharpest is the cranberry. Known as *ibimi* to the Wampanoag Indians, it was an important ingredient of pemmican, the dried venison staple of the Native Americans. Because the blossom recalled the shape of a crane's head, the colonists called it "craneberry," later shortened to "cranberry." Combined with tangy oranges and a healthy dose of fresh ginger, they are a Thanksgiving must.

2 pounds fresh cranberries, picked over and rinsed
4 cups sugar
2 cups fresh orange juice
2 tablespoons finely minced fresh ginger

1. Divide the ingredients evenly between two heavy saucepans and stir well. Cook over medium heat until the berries pop open, about 10 minutes.
2. Skim the foam off the surface with a metal spoon. Cool to room temperature. Then refrigerate, covered, for as long as 2 months. Serve chilled or at room temperature.
Note: I prefer to cook the cranberries in small batches for better texture.

CHUNKY PEAR APPLE SAUCE

During autumn holidays, the aromas of slow-cooking fruit and sugar evoke a real feeling of nostalgia. At Thanksgiving I make a point of serving a crisp-tasting apple compote, and with the addition of succulent, fragrant pears, I find that the smooth flavor combination marries well with the savory herbs and spices used in the stuffing, gravy, and—of course—the turkey.

6 Anjou or Comice pears, slightly underripe
4 apples (preferably a mixture of Granny Smith, McIntosh, and Golden Delicious)
2 tablespoons fresh lemon juice, or more to taste
1 cup apple juice
1/2 cup sugar, or more to taste
1 teaspoon finely grated lemon zest

1. Core, peel, and cut the pears and apples into large chunks. Toss them with the 2 tablespoons lemon juice in a large heavy pot.
2. Add the apple juice, 1/2 cup sugar, and the lemon zest. Stir and bring to a boil over high heat. Reduce the heat to medium-low and simmer, partially covered, until the fruit is tender but not mushy, about 15 minutes.
3. Uncover the pot, stir, and continue cooking to thicken the juices, 5 minutes more. Taste

and add more sugar or lemon juice if desired, stirring carefully so as not to break up the fruit too much. Remove from the heat and allow to cool to room temperature. Then transfer to a container, cover, and refrigerate for as long as 4 days. Bring to room temperature before serving.

MAKES 8 CUPS

PUMPKIN PIE

Pumpkin pie, or something like it, has been part of Thanksgiving for just about as long as there has been a Thanksgiving. It was so popular among early colonists that in 1705 one town in Connecticut delayed their day of thanks while the colonists awaited a shipment of molasses, their preferred sweetener. Puddinglike in consistency, with a nice crisp crust, this pie will compel your guests to squeeze in an extra helping.

This recipe makes two pies. Just cut it in half if you need only one.

*Basic Pie Crust (page 401), for two
    single-crust pies
4 cups canned or fresh pumpkin puree
2 tablespoons crystallized ginger,
    very finely minced
2¹/₂ cups half-and-half
1 teaspoon ground cinnamon
¹/₂ teaspoon freshly grated nutmeg
¹/₂ teaspoon ground cloves
1 teaspoon salt
1¹/₃ cups (packed) light brown sugar
6 large eggs, lightly beaten
4 large egg yolks, lightly beaten
¹/₄ teaspoon freshly ground white pepper
2 recipes Sweetened Whipped Cream
    (page 403), for serving*

1. Position a rack in the lower half of the oven, and preheat the oven to 425°F.

2. Place 2 sheets of heavy-duty aluminum foil, one on top of the other, directly on the surface of each pie crust to weight it down. Bake the crusts until they turn golden brown, about 10 minutes. Remove the foil and bake 5 minutes more to crisp the crust slightly, then set them aside.

3. Reduce the oven temperature to 350°F.

4. Place the pumpkin puree, ginger, and half-and-half in a blender (in batches), and puree until the mixture is smooth, about 4 minutes. Transfer the puree to a large bowl and whisk in the remaining ingredients (except the whipped cream) until well blended.

5. Pour the filling into the pie shells, dividing it evenly, and smooth the tops. Bake until a knife inserted into the center of the pie comes out clean, 45 minutes to 1 hour. Let cool on a wire rack to room temperature. Serve dolloped with Sweetened Whipped Cream.

Pumpkin Pie

Chanukah,

According to tradition, Chanukah started shortly after the Syrian-Greek king Antiochus Epiphanes made the huge mistake of installing a statue of Zeus on the altar in the holy temple at Jerusalem. The Jewish populace rose up in revolt under the leadership of Judah Maccabee and drove the profaners from the temple. When they sought to reconsecrate their place of worship, however, there was very little oil for the eternal lamp. Miraculously, the scant supply lasted eight days and nights, a sign of divine pleasure with the courage of the Jews. Ever since, Jews have lit candles during the eight days of Chanukah, the Festival of Lights, a time of great joy, great food, and, for the children, great presents.

Festival of Lights

MENU

S ometimes the Chanukah meal is formal and sometimes it is just a potato *latkes* (pancake) party. The flavors and taste sensations—sweet, sour, spicy, salty—of this meal meld together in an unusual, but seasonally appropriate way.

Begin with lacy potato latkes accompanied by a slightly chunky, translucent applesauce. The apples also complement the other entrees. Blazing Beet Soup is pure beets cooked in a rich chicken broth, quite different from its creamy summer sister. Short ribs of beef cooked in the style of sauerbraten strike the right balance between Old World and New World. To gild the lily, why not include a goose? Red cabbage is a natural with either entree. The sweet Honey-Roasted Carrots complement the ribs, and the silky smooth Celery Root Puree melts on the tongue. Parsnip mash adds wonderful creaminess. Dessert brings tradition back home with a Rustic Apple

Spice Cake laden with chunks of apples and heady spices.

Religious holidays evoke respect, tradition, and lots of memories. For Chanukah, first and foremost is the menorah. Put it in a place of honor, ready to be lit on each of the eight nights of the holiday. Search the linen closet to find a white damask tablecloth.

Next for this Festival of Lights are the candles. If you have

Chanukah, Festival of Lights
DINNER FOR EIGHT

Chanukah Latkes with Golden Applesauce

Blazing Beet Soup

Short Rib Sauerbraten

Roasted Goose

Celery Root Puree

Honey-Roasted Carrots

Savory Braised Red Cabbage

Creamy Parsnip Mash

Rustic Apple Spice Cake

more than one set of candlesticks, mix them up—brass, ceramic, glass—and use matching candles in them all.

This is the time to pull out your very best dishes. Cranberry-toned wineglasses or water glasses add a festive touch and enhance formal linens. Since beet soup and braised red cabbage are on the menu—both shades of vibrant fuchsia—create tight bunches of fuchsia roses and fuchsia carnations to decorate the table. A holiday that is joyous and also religious should retain a certain refinement, so don't overdo the decorations for this one.

THE MUSIC

Benny Goodman's *Sing, Sing, Sing*

Klezmer music

THE WINE

Vouvray Sec (kosher or not)

Crozes Hermitage or Saint-Joseph

THE EXTRAS

Menorah and candles
Candlesticks and candles
Soup tureen
Bundt cake pan

Chanukah Latkes

CHANUKAH LATKES

Tradition has it that we eat potato pancakes on Chanukah because they are fried in oil, and oil—of course—is at the base of the Chanukah legend. *Latke* is simply the Yiddish word for potato pancakes, and latke parties—featuring platters of crisp, fried, salty, super-crunchy, slightly peppery, sweetly onionish potato pancakes—are fun. Serve them with Golden Applesauce, sour cream, and even jam.

4 russet potatoes, peeled (about 2 pounds total)
1 large onion, peeled
3 tablespoons snipped fresh chives
Coarse (kosher) salt and freshly ground
  black pepper, to taste
1/4 to 1/2 cup vegetable oil, or more if necessary
Golden Applesauce (recipe follows),
  for serving
Pareve sour cream substitute
  (see box, page 193), for serving

1. Coarsely grate the potatoes and onion into a large bowl. (Work quickly so the potatoes don't discolor. The potatoes will give off a starchy liquid, but do not drain.) Then add the chives, season with salt and pepper, and mix well.

2. Working with two large nonstick skillets, heat 2 to 4 tablespoons of the oil in each skillet over medium heat. Add about 2 tablespoons of the potato mixture for each latke and cook, pressing down with a spatula, until golden brown, 3 to 4 minutes per side. Drain on paper towels. As you continue to cook latkes, add more oil as necessary. Serve hot, with Golden Applesauce and pareve sour cream.

MAKES 30 LATKES

Note: If you are not serving them immediately, reheat the latkes in a 400°F oven for about 7 minutes. Remove and drain on paper towels, then serve immediately.

GOLDEN APPLESAUCE

By the time Chanukah rolls around, all the apples should be out of the orchard. Turn them into a sauce, sweetened and spiced and cooked to a rich gold. Your latkes will love this. So will your guests.

8 assorted apples (Golden Delicious, Rome,
  McIntosh, Royal Gala, Granny Smith,
  Red Delicious)
1 tablespoon fresh lemon juice
1 cup fresh apple cider
1/2 cup sugar
1 cinnamon stick (3 inches long)

1. Core, peel, and cut the apples into large chunks, tossing them with the lemon juice in a large heavy pot.

2. Add the cider, sugar, and cinnamon stick and bring to a boil over high heat. Reduce the heat to medium-low and simmer, partially covered, until the apples are very tender, 15 minutes.

3. Uncover the pot and cook for 5 minutes more to evaporate some of the liquid.

4. Remove the pot from the heat and discard the cinnamon stick. Use a potato masher to coarsely mash the apples with the juices. Allow to cool to room temperature and then refrigerate, covered, for up to 5 days.

MAKES 5 CUPS

BLAZING BEET SOUP

Borscht, which is nothing more than beet soup, served cold is a great summer treat. Serving it hot with a dollop of sour cream (in this case, pareve sour cream substitute) intensifies the flavors and helps clean the palate after the equally intense and much richer potato pancakes.

Blazing Beet Soup

8 beets, scrubbed
8 cups Vegetable Broth (page 398) or
    Basic Chicken Broth (page 397)
2 cups water
3 tablespoons fresh lemon juice, or
    to taste
Salt, to taste
1/2 cup pareve sour cream substitute
    (optional; see box, page 193)

1. Place the beets in a large heavy pot and cover with the broth. Bring to a boil, partially covered, over high heat. Reduce the heat to medium and simmer until the beets are tender, about 45 minutes. Using a slotted spoon, transfer the beets to a bowl. Pour the broth through a fine-mesh strainer into another pot.

2. When the beets are cool enough to handle, slip off the skins and cut them into pieces.

3. Puree the beets, in batches, in a food processor, adding the broth and 2 cups water through the feed tube. Return the soup to the pot and add lemon juice until the right balance of sweet and sour is achieved. Season with salt. Reheat over medium-low heat to a simmer.

4. Serve small portions of the soup, dolloped with pareve sour cream substitute, if desired.

SHORT RIB SAUERBRATEN

Combine flavorful beef with a spicy, sweet-and-sour marinade and you have the beguiling flavors of *sauerbraten*. Folklorists say that it was invented by Charlemagne, in ninth-century France, but history records few conquerors who had the spare time to stand around the stove inventing a slow-cooked dish. Here short ribs substitute for the more predictable chuck or rump roast.

6 to 8 meaty short ribs of beef, cut lengthwise
    between the bones, trimmed of excess fat
2 1/4 cups cider vinegar
2 large cloves garlic, lightly crushed
1 cup sliced onions
2 bay leaves
6 black peppercorns
5 whole cloves
1/4 cup (packed) light brown sugar
1 1/2 cups Beef Broth (page 397)
2 cups good-quality chili sauce, such as Heinz
1 cup dry red wine
Zest from 1 lemon removed in 1 long strip
    with a paring knife
1/2 teaspoon ground ginger
1/2 teaspoon ground cinnamon
Salt and freshly ground black pepper, to taste
1/4 cup all-purpose flour
2 tablespoons olive oil
2 tablespoons chopped fresh dill leaves
8 small sprigs fresh dill, for garnish

1. Place the short ribs in a large bowl.

2. Combine 2 cups of the vinegar with 2 cups water, the garlic, onions, bay leaves, peppercorns, and cloves in a heavy saucepan. Bring to a boil over high heat, reduce the heat to medium, and simmer to blend the flavors, 5 minutes. Pour this over the ribs. Allow to cool to room temperature; stir to redistribute the ribs, cover, and refrigerate overnight.

3. Prepare the sauce: Combine the remaining ¼ cup vinegar and the brown sugar in a small heavy saucepan and bring it to a slow boil over medium heat. Cook until thick and bubbling, 2 to 3 minutes. Stir in the broth. Add the chili sauce, wine, lemon zest, ginger, and cinnamon. Season with salt and pepper. Simmer over medium-low heat to blend the flavors, 10 minutes. Allow to cool to room temperature, then transfer to a container and refrigerate, covered, overnight.

4. The following day, remove the short ribs from the marinade and pat them dry. Season them with salt and pepper and then dust them with the flour (shake it through a fine-mesh strainer), shaking off any excess. Set the ribs aside. Strain the marinade and set it aside, covered, in the refrigerator.

5. Preheat the oven to 350°F.

6. Heat the olive oil in a large heavy flameproof casserole over medium heat. Brown the ribs well on all sides, in batches if necessary, 4 to 5 minutes per side. Transfer them to a plate. Discard the oil in the casserole and return the ribs to it. Cover the ribs with the sauce you made the day before. Bring the ribs and sauce to a boil over medium heat. Cover the pot and place it in the oven. Bake for 2 hours, occasionally skimming off any excess fat that accumulates on the surface with a metal spoon. Uncover and bake until the meat is falling off the bones, about 30 minutes more.

7. Remove the ribs from the sauce and, when cool enough to handle, remove and discard the bones and any excess gristle or fat. Pour the sauce through a gravy separator to remove the fat and return the defatted sauce to the pot (see Note). If the sauce seems too thick, add some of the reserved marinade to thin it.

8. Return the ribs to the pot and cover them with the sauce. Reheat over medium-low heat and, just before serving, stir in the chopped dill. Garnish each serving with a dill sprig.

Note: You can make the sauerbraten to this point up to a day in advance. Store, covered, in the refrigerator and reheat in a preheated 350°F

oven for 25 minutes, thinning the sauce with some of the reserved marinade if it's too thick. Stir in the chopped dill right before serving.

ROASTED GOOSE

D omestic goose is deeply flavored but not gamy. Although most of the fat dissolves away in the cooking process, enough remains to pull out the meaty depth of flavor. Accompany the goose with a bottle of Rhône wine, such as one of two reds suggested in the menu.

FOR THE STUFFING
1 cup pitted prunes, cut in half
1 cup dried apricots, cut in half
2 Granny Smith apples, cored and
  coarsely chopped
2 cups coarsely chopped red onions
2 tablespoons finely grated orange zest
2 tablespoons fresh orange juice

FOR THE GOOSE
1 goose (10 to 12 pounds)
Juice of 1 orange
Coarse (kosher) salt and coarsely
  ground black pepper, to taste
8 slices turkey pastrami
1 cup Basic Chicken Broth (page 397)
½ cup tawny port
1 tablespoon red currant jelly
1 tablespoon unsalted pareve margarine
  (see box, page 193)

1. Prepare the stuffing: Toss the prunes, apricots, apples, onions, and orange zest and juice together in a bowl. Set it aside.

2. Preheat the oven to 325°F.

3. Rinse the goose well inside and out, and pat dry with paper towels. Prick the skin all over with the tines of a fork. Rub the goose inside with the orange juice; then sprinkle it inside and out with coarse salt and pepper.

4. Fill the neck and body cavities with the stuffing and close them with poultry lacers.

5. Place the goose, breast side up, on a rack in a large roasting pan. Lay the turkey pastrami slices across the breast. Roast the goose for 1½ hours, removing any accumulated fat in the pan every 30 minutes.

6. Remove the turkey pastrami and continue to roast the goose, occasionally removing the excess fat, until an instant-reading thermometer inserted into the thigh reads between 175° and 180°F, about 3 hours more. Transfer the goose to a platter, cover it loosely with aluminum foil, and let it rest for 20 minutes.

7. Pour off any remaining fat in the roasting pan. Add the broth and port to the pan and bring to a boil, scraping up any browned bits on the bottom of the pan. Simmer over low heat for 5 minutes. Add the red currant jelly and simmer, stirring, for 2 minutes longer. Set the sauce aside.

8. Just before serving, warm the sauce in a saucepan over low heat. Add the pareve margarine and whisk until it is just mixed in. Serve the stuffing and sauce alongside the goose.

CELERY ROOT PUREE

Beauty is important when it comes to food, but there are exceptions. Take the celery root. It is knobby, kind of ungainly in shape, and usually covered with dark spots—like potato eyes. But step into the kitchen of any great French restaurant and you will see an abundance of this homely vegetable being used. When caramelized and roasted it has a delicate taste, a subtle crunch, and an even more subtle bitter note that helps to tame strong meat and game flavors. As a puree, there is nothing better with a roast.

2 celery roots (about 1¾ pounds each)
Juice of 1 lemon
Salt, to taste
8 tablespoons (1 stick) unsalted pareve
    margarine (see box, page 193),
    at room temperature
¾ cup pareve heavy (whipping)
    cream substitute
Freshly ground black pepper, to taste

1. Peel the celery root and cut it into chunks. Place it in a saucepan, cover with water, and add the lemon juice and salt to taste. Bring to a boil over high heat, reduce the heat to medium, and simmer until the celery root is tender, about 20 minutes. Drain the celery root, return it to the pot, and cook over very low heat, shaking the pot, for 1 minute to remove all moisture.

2. Combine the celery root and the pareve margarine in a food processor and puree. With the motor running, add the cream through the food tube. Season with salt and pepper.

3. Serve immediately, or transfer to a container, cover, and refrigerate up to 4 hours in advance. Reheat in a double boiler over simmering water or in the microwave.

HONEY-ROASTED CARROTS

Carrots are rich in natural sugars. Caramelizing them at high heat coaxes out even more sweetness, and the floral sugars in honey create a rich bouquet for this exceedingly simple but consistently pleasing combination.

2½ pounds carrots, peeled
2 tablespoons extra-virgin olive oil
2 tablespoons honey
Salt and freshly ground black pepper,
    to taste

1. Preheat the oven to 450°F.

2. Cut the carrots into thirds crosswise on a sharp diagonal.

3. Bring water to a boil in a large pot fitted with a steamer basket. (The water level should be below the bottom of the basket.) Add the carrots to the basket, reduce the heat to medium, and steam until just tender, 5 minutes.

4. Combine the oil and honey in a large bowl. Drain the carrots and transfer them to the bowl. Toss with the oil and honey and season well with salt and pepper.

5. Place the carrots in a single layer on a baking sheet and roast in the oven for 25 minutes. Loosen them from the baking sheet with a spatula and correct the seasonings if necessary.

SAVORY BRAISED RED CABBAGE

Sweet-and-sour is such a classic combination that it is hard to think of red cabbage made any other way. On the East End of Long Island, where the buffering influence of the surrounding waters delays the coming of frost, cabbages are harvested until late in the season. It is a great pleasure to have a fresh-picked garden vegetable that goes so well with the hearty dishes of fall.

1 head red cabbage (about 3 pounds),
   tough outer leaves discarded
2 tablespoons olive oil
2 large red onions, slivered
1/4-pound piece turkey pastrami, cut into
   1/4-inch pieces
4 beets, peeled and coarsely grated
1/2 cup (packed) dark brown sugar
1/4 cup orange marmalade
1/2 cup dry red wine
1/2 cup red wine vinegar
Salt and freshly ground black pepper, to taste

1. Preheat the oven to 400°F.

2. Quarter the cabbage, remove the core, and finely shred the leaves.

3. Heat the olive oil in a flameproof casserole over low heat. Add the turkey pastrami and cook to release some of the smoke flavor, 2 minutes more. Add the onions and cook, stirring, until wilted, about 10 minutes. Add the shredded cabbage, the beets, and all the remaining ingredients and stir well. Cover the casserole, transfer it to the oven, and bake, stirring occasionally, for 2 1/2 hours. Adjust the seasoning if necessary before serving.

CREAMY PARSNIP MASH

Roasted, caramelized, and pureed, parsnips do everything that mashed potatoes do, but they are easier to mash, fluffier, sweeter, creamier, and a good change of pace.

2 1/2 pounds parsnips, peeled
3 cups Basic Chicken Broth
   (page 397), or more if necessary
1 tablespoon fresh lemon juice
4 tablespoons (1/2 stick) unsalted pareve
   margarine (see box, facing page)
1/2 cup pareve heavy (whipping) cream
   substitute
Salt and freshly ground black pepper, to taste
2 tablespoons snipped fresh chives, for garnish

1. Cut the parsnips in half lengthwise and then again crosswise. Place them in a heavy saucepan and add the broth and lemon juice. If the liquid doesn't cover the parsnips, add more broth. Bring to a boil over high heat, then reduce the heat to medium-high and cook at a slow boil until very tender, 20 minutes.

2. Meanwhile, melt the pareve margarine in the cream substitute in a small saucepan over low heat.

3. Drain the parsnips well and place them in a large bowl. Add the margarine-cream mixture and mash until smooth (if you like, you can do this in a food processor). Season with salt and pepper, sprinkle with the chives, and serve immediately.

Note: This can be prepared ahead and then reheated, covered, in a 350°F oven for 15 to 20 minutes.

RUSTIC APPLE SPICE CAKE

The oil in this cake represents the oil in the story of Chanukah. At holiday time, spice cake and spiced cookies are equally traditional. And apples, at their best in fall, are a must in this moist, richly flavored cake.

FOR THE CAKE

> 4 tablespoons (¹/₂ stick) unsalted pareve
>   margarine (see box, right)
> 3 Golden Delicious apples, peeled and
>   cut into 1-inch cubes (about 3¹/₂ cups)
> 1 cup (packed) light brown sugar
> 3 cups all-purpose flour
> 1 tablespoon baking powder
> 2 teaspoons ground cinnamon
> ³/₄ teaspoon salt
> ¹/₂ teaspoon ground ginger
> ¹/₄ teaspoon ground cloves
> ¹/₄ teaspoon ground nutmeg
> ³/₄ cup granulated sugar
> 1 cup vegetable oil
> 3 large eggs
> 1 teaspoon pure vanilla extract
> ¹/₂ cup pareve milk substitute
> 1 cup finely chopped walnuts

FOR THE CITRUS GLAZE

> 1 cup confectioners' sugar
> 1 teaspoon finely grated lemon zest
> 4 teaspoons fresh lemon juice

According to traditional Jewish practice, mixing dairy and meat products is forbidden. Nowadays we have many delicious dairy substitutes, such as non-dairy margarine, milk, and cream. All are identified with the word *pareve.* Rich's is one popular brand that's distributed nationally, but others are available as well.

1. Melt the pareve margarine in a nonstick skillet over medium heat. Add the apples and ¹/₄ cup of the brown sugar, stirring to coat. Cook over medium heat, stirring often, until the apples begin to soften and brown lightly, 10 to 12 minutes. Remove the skillet from the heat and allow to cool slightly. Set aside.

2. Preheat the oven to 350°F. Oil and lightly flour a 10-inch bundt pan.

3. Combine the flour, baking powder, cinnamon, salt, ginger, cloves, and nutmeg in a medium-size bowl.

4. Blend the remaining ³/₄ cup brown sugar, the granulated sugar, and the oil, eggs, and vanilla in a large bowl with an electric mixer on medium speed. With the mixer on low speed, alternately add the flour mixture and the milk substitute, beating until just blended. Using a rubber spatula, fold in the apple mixture and the walnuts.

5. Scrape the batter into the prepared pan. Bake until a toothpick inserted in the center comes out clean, 1 hour and 10 minutes. Allow the cake to cool in the pan on a wire rack for 15 minutes. Then remove it from the pan to the wire rack, and let it cool completely, for 2 hours.

6. Prepare the citrus glaze: Combine the confectioners' sugar, lemon zest, and lemon juice in a bowl, stirring until blended and smooth. Place the cake on a serving plate and pour the glaze over the top, letting it drip down the sides. Let the glaze set, then serve.

Celebrate the

Winter Hearth

Hearty, warming, stick-to-your-ribs . . . these are the words I think of for cold-weather food. A bracing cocktail, a steamy bowl of thick soup, meltingly moist meat, old favorites on the stereo. The room is candlelit, bright vases of bright flowers play against the backdrop of trees bare of leaves or a silvery winter moon. There isn't much you can do about the cold, but you certainly can create an atmosphere of warmth and conviviality indoors.

> "*T*he art of dining well is no slight art, the pleasure no slight pleasure."
>
> —MICHEL EYQUEM DE MONTAIGNE

MENU

C old weather inspires cozy comfort. This is not the time for fancy or formal place settings. It is the time for a homey feel, so go ahead and put those craft-fair ceramic bowls to use.

An antique soup tureen filled with Winter Vegetable Pea Soup is just the right starter. Alongside, serve an oven-warmed sourdough baguette wrapped in a napkin. Serve "Rough" Braised Lamb Shanks straight from the oven in an oven-to-table casserole dish, or a delectable Savory Oxtail Stew in the same way. This is what cold-weather food is all about: easy, hearty, and warm.

Old linens found in antique stores and flea markets tend to be slightly oversize, somewhere between a napkin and a dish towel, which is ideal if you plan to eat on your lap in front of a glowing fire.

Fill ceramic jugs with small dark-red or flame-orange calla lilies for a cozy look— especially when mixed with some full bunches of sage. As another choice, orange roses also suggest the warmth of the fire. Fruit arrangements are colorful, decorative, and edible. Tangerines and shelled nuts are especially appealing. Even though informality is the key, definitely light the candles for this one.

Celebrate the Winter Hearth

DINNER FOR FOUR

WINTER VEGETABLE PEA SOUP

FROSTY WEATHER SALAD

"ROUGH" BRAISED LAMB SHANKS WITH STEWED WHITE BEANS

OR

SAVORY OXTAIL STEW

COZY BAKED APPLES

THE MUSIC

Patti Page's *Golden Greats*

Jo Stafford's
Capitol Collections Series

Frank Sinatra's *Classic Sinatra*

THE WINE

Barolo
Côte du Rhône

THE EXTRAS

Soup tureen
Oven-to-table casserole dish
Ceramic cream jug

WINTER VEGETABLE PEA SOUP

In some other book this might be called Split Pea Soup, but truthfully the peas, though they provide protein and texture, are not the stars here. The ham and the deeply cooked vegetables are. Long, slow cooking will fill the house with a savory scent that hits the spot when you come in from outdoors with rosy cheeks and tingling fingers.

1 large smoked ham hock
3 tablespoons olive oil
1 large onion, cut into 1/4-inch dice
2 leeks, including 3 inches green,
  well rinsed and cut into 1/4-inch dice
2 carrots, peeled and cut into 1/4-inch dice
1 tablespoon minced garlic
3/4 cup yellow or green dried split peas
6 cups Basic Chicken Broth (page 397),
  or more if needed
1 bay leaf
1 teaspoon dried tarragon
2 zucchini, trimmed and cut into 1/4-inch dice
Salt and freshly ground black pepper, to taste
3 ripe plum tomatoes, seeded and cut
  into 1/2-inch dice
2 tablespoons chopped fresh flat-leaf parsley

1. Place the ham hock in a small saucepan and add water to cover. Bring to a boil over high heat, then reduce the heat to medium-low and simmer to remove the excess salt, 10 minutes. Drain, rinse, and set aside.

2. Heat the olive oil in a large heavy pot over low heat. Add the onion, leeks, carrots, and garlic. Cook, stirring occasionally, until the vegetables are softened, 10 to 15 minutes.

3. Add the split peas and cook, stirring, to coat the peas, 2 minutes.

4. Add the broth, the ham hock, the bay leaf, and tarragon. Raise the heat to high and bring the stock to a boil. Reduce the heat to medium-low and simmer, partially covered, until the split peas are very soft, 30 minutes.

5. Remove the soup from the heat and remove the ham hock from the soup. When it is cool enough to handle, cut the meat from the bone, dice it, and return it to the pot, along with the zucchini. Heat the soup over medium-low heat and simmer, covered, until the zucchini is cooked through, 15 minutes. Remove the bay leaf and season the soup with salt and pepper.

6. Just before serving, warm the soup through and stir in the tomatoes and parsley. Add a bit more broth if the soup seems too thick. Serve immediately.

FROSTY WEATHER SALAD

Lead into winter's slow-cooked stews with a salad of deep wine-red beets, on a slightly biting mix of frisée and green beans, sprinkled with creamy Roquefort and walnuts. It definitely helps to soothe the effects of the harsh winds.

1/2 pound thin green beans, trimmed
  and cut in half crosswise
6 cups frisée, white ends removed,
  rinsed and patted dry
4 tablespoons snipped fresh chives
4 medium-size roasted beets (page 399),
  cut into 1/2-inch dice
Salt and freshly ground black pepper, to taste
2/3 cup Red Wine Vinaigrette (page 312)
1/2 cup walnut halves
4 ounces Roquefort cheese, coarsely crumbled

1. Bring a saucepan of salted water to a boil over high heat. Add the green beans and cook until just crisp-tender, about 3 minutes. Drain the beans in a colander and run under cold water to stop the cooking. Drain and pat dry. Toss the green beans in a large bowl, along with the frisée and 2 tablespoons of the chives.

2. In another bowl, toss the beets with salt and pepper and 2 tablespoons of the vinaigrette. Set aside.

3. Just before serving, season the frisée and green beans with salt and pepper and toss with the remaining vinaigrette.

4. Divide the frisée and green beans among four large salad plates. Spoon the beets evenly over the frisée mixture and scatter with walnuts. Sprinkle the salads with the cheese, garnish with the remaining 2 tablespoons chives, and serve.

"ROUGH" BRAISED LAMB SHANKS

B raising—the word itself is as warm as a favorite old cardigan. Nothing is quite so silky smooth and broadly flavorful as a lamb shank braised until it is falling off the bone. It is a rustic, country kind of dish, so no teeny tiny dicing for these vegetables—big chunks of everything. These lamb shanks are delectable when served in bowls over Stewed White Beans.

4 lamb shanks (about 1 pound each)
1 teaspoon coarse (kosher) salt
1 teaspoon freshly ground black pepper
3 tablespoons olive oil
1 onion, cut in half lengthwise and slivered
4 large cloves garlic, lightly crushed
1 sprig fresh rosemary
1 cup Beef Broth (page 397)
1 cup dry red wine
3 red bell peppers, roasted (page 399)
   and cut into 1-inch squares
2 bay leaves
2 tablespoons tomato paste
1 cup coarsely chopped ripe plum tomatoes
1/2 cup chopped fresh flat-leaf parsley
Stewed White Beans (recipe follows), for serving

1. Preheat the oven to 350°F.

2. Rinse the lamb shanks and pat dry. Sprinkle them all over with the salt and pepper. Heat 2 tablespoons of the olive oil in a large heavy flameproof casserole over medium heat. Add the lamb shanks, in batches, and cook until well browned, about 8 minutes per batch. Transfer them to a plate. Discard any fat in the casserole.

3. Add the remaining 1 tablespoon olive oil to the casserole. Add the onion and cook over low heat until it is almost softened, 10 minutes. Add the garlic and rosemary and cook for 5 minutes more.

4. Add the broth, wine, roasted peppers, and bay leaves. Raise the heat to medium-high and bring to a boil. Return the lamb shanks to the casserole, cover, and transfer to the oven. Bake 1 hour, then stir in the tomato paste and the chopped tomatoes. Adjust the seasonings, if necessary, and bake, until the lamb shanks are tender, uncovered, 45 minutes more.

5. Before serving, remove the rosemary sprigs and bay leaves and stir in the chopped parsley. Spoon some Stewed White Beans into each of four shallow bowls. Carefully transfer a lamb shank to each bowls, spoon some of the sauce over each, and serve.

STEWED WHITE BEANS

B eans are hearty, beans are healthy, beans are warming and rib-sticking. The trick is to cook the flavor in without cooking the texture out. Once they've been properly soaked, white kidney beans don't need more than 40 minutes of cooking time. Though beans work so well in winter, there is no reason not to include them in warm-weather menus as well. In spring, lightly toss them with dandelion greens in a simple vinaigrette. In summer, serve them as a cold salad with thinly sliced onions and crunchy celery.

12 ounces dried white kidney beans
4 ounces slab bacon, rind discarded,
cut into ¼-inch pieces
4 tablespoons extra-virgin olive oil
1 onion, cut into ¼-inch dice
2 carrots, peeled and cut into
¼-inch dice
1 tablespoon finely minced garlic
3 sprigs fresh thyme
3 whole cloves
2 bay leaves
Coarse (kosher) salt and freshly ground
black pepper, to taste
2 to 3 tablespoons chopped fresh
flat-leaf parsley

1. Pick over the beans, discarding any debris. Place them in a bowl, add cold water to cover by 2 inches, and soak overnight (see Note).

2. Drain and rise the beans and place them in a large pot. Set them aside.

3. Place the bacon and 2 tablespoons of the olive oil in a skillet over low heat and cook to render the fat, 6 to 7 minutes. Add the onion, carrots, and garlic. Cook, stirring occasionally, until the vegetables are slightly softened, about 10 minutes.

4. Using a slotted spoon, transfer the bacon and vegetables to the pot with the beans. Add the thyme, cloves, bay leaves, and 8 cups water. Bring to a boil over high heat, skimming off any foam that rises to the top. Reduce the heat to medium-low and simmer, uncovered, stirring once or twice, until the beans are just tender (not mushy), 35 to 40 minutes.

5. Drain the beans in a colander and return them to the pot. Discard the thyme sprigs, cloves, and bay leaves. Stir in the remaining 2 tablespoons olive oil. Season with salt and pepper. Stir in the parsley and serve hot.

Note: For a quick bean-soaking method, see page 10.

SAVORY OXTAIL STEW

Oxtail is a rich, silky meat, and with the surge in popularity of classic bistro food, it has gone from a novelty cut to a standby for many home cooks. Its richness fairly cries out "winter meal," and it's perfect to prepare when there's time in the kitchen on a stormy afternoon. The result is a luxurious one-pot meal. The red currant jelly might seem out of place, but it cuts the acidity of the tomatoes and wine. The Black Forest ham adds a slight smokiness, and the nutmeg provides an aromatic accent. Serve this with lightly buttered egg noodles.

½ cup all-purpose flour
1 teaspoon salt
¼ teaspoon paprika
Freshly ground black pepper, to taste
2 oxtails (about 5 pounds total),
cut into 2-inch lengths
5 tablespoons olive oil, or more as needed
1 cup diced onion (¼-inch dice)
1 cup diced carrots (¼-inch dice)
1 cup diced celery (¼-inch dice)
6 large cloves garlic, finely minced
1 piece (4 ounces) Black Forest ham,
cut into ¼-inch dice
1 bay leaf
1 teaspoon dried thyme
½ teaspoon ground nutmeg
2 cups diced seeded tomatoes
2 tablespoons tomato paste
2½ cups Basic Chicken Broth (page 397)
1 cup dry red wine
1 tablespoon red currant jelly
Zest of 1 orange, removed in 1 long strip
with a paring knife
¼ cup chopped fresh flat-leaf parsley
Lightly buttered egg noodles, for serving
(optional; see box, page 274)

Savory Oxtail Stew

> *"I know the look of an apple that is roasting and sizzling on the hearth on a winter's evening, and I know the comfort that comes of eating it hot, along with some sugar and a drench of cream. . . . I know how the nuts taken in conjunction with winter apples, cider, and doughnuts, make old people's tales and old jokes sound fresh and crisp and enchanting."*
>
> —MARK TWAIN

1. Combine the flour, salt, paprika, and pepper in a plastic bag. Add the oxtail pieces and shake them in the seasoned flour to dredge them. Remove, shaking off any excess flour.

2. Heat 3 tablespoons of the olive oil in a heavy flameproof casserole over medium-high heat. Add the meat, in batches, and cook until well browned, about 10 minutes per batch. Add more oil if necessary as the meat cooks. Set the meat aside.

3. Wipe the casserole clean and add the remaining 2 tablespoons olive oil. Add the onion, carrots, and celery and cook, stirring occasionally, over medium-low heat until softened, 10 minutes. Then stir in the garlic, ham, bay leaf, thyme, and nutmeg and cook to blend the flavors, 2 minutes more.

4. Add the tomatoes, tomato paste, broth, wine, currant jelly, and orange zest. Return the meat to the casserole and bring to a boil over medium-high heat. Reduce the heat to medium and simmer, partially covered and stirring occasionally, until the meat is very tender, 1¾ to 2 hours. Remove the bay leaf, stir in the parsley, season to taste, and serve, with the noodles if desired.

COZY BAKED APPLES

Apples—the season's finest—are sweet comfort baked and served warm with thick cream. Apples may seem like a distant memory of grandma's kitchen, but there is nothing better for dessert when the chill of winter is here. If you bake extra, they are great the next day. Cream, whipped or not, is a must.

4 large Pippin, Granny Smith, or other tart apples
⅓ cup sugar
¼ teaspoon ground cinnamon
Pinch of salt
1 long strip lemon zest, removed with a paring knife
1 cup heavy cream or Sweetened Whipped Cream (page 403), for serving

1. Preheat the oven to 350°F.

2. Core the apples and remove the peel from around the top third of each fruit. Place the apples in a baking pan large enough to just hold them.

3. Place the sugar, cinnamon, salt, and ¾ cup water in a small saucepan and stir to combine. Add the lemon zest and bring to a simmer over medium heat. Simmer for 1 minute, stirring until the sugar and salt are dissolved, then spoon the sugar syrup over the apples.

4. Cover the pan with the apples tightly with aluminum foil. Bake for 1 hour, basting once after 30 minutes. Re-cover tightly with the foil before returning the pan to the oven to finish baking. When done, the apples will be very tender when pierced with the tip of a knife and the sauce will have thickened during cooking to a syrupy consistency. Spoon the syrup over the apples several times to coat them well.

5. Serve the apples warm in bowls with a bit of the syrup spooned over them. Serve with the cream in a small pitcher alongside.

The Night

I don't know which came first, Santa Claus or insomnia, but I do know that many of us experienced our first night of tossing and turning on

Before Christmas

Christmas Eve. Even as adults, our anticipation levels are high and need the taming that comes from the company of good friends and good food. Families gather for a big meal, perhaps as a prelude to Midnight Mass; outside, carolers go from house to house spreading cheer. You can't walk or drive a block without hearing bells ringing or music playing. It's hard to be out of sorts on Christmas Eve.

MENU

The Night Before Christmas
DINNER FOR EIGHT

Christmas Eve Champagne Cocktail	Roast Salmon with Lemon-Caviar Potatoes
Celeriac Brandade	Savory Cassoulet
Foie Gras and Thinly Sliced Fig Log	Herbed Boston Lettuce Salad with Shallot Vinaigrette
	Tangerine Tart

Christmas Eve's meal is flavorful and as full of color as a Christmas tree ornament.

It's always lovely to begin a holiday eve (or any eve, for that matter) with a champagne cocktail—its effervescence sets the tone. Sliced very thin, the foie gras, with a touch of sweetness in the form of a little fig log, is easy to prepare and is rich to the point of deca-dence. Another special begin-ning is Celeriac Brandade, served with delicate slices of toast. An alternative choice is the small roast salmon fillet atop Lemon-Caviar Potatoes—extremely elegant. The cassoulet entree is a much lighter, newer version of an old standby, appropriate for today's taste. A fresh salad and a spectacular Tangerine Tart will certainly send you to bed dreaming of Santa. Be sure to save a slice for him!

Christmas Eve: The shop-ping is complete, the gifts are wrapped, the tree is decorated and a-twinkle. This is a time to show off your very best, starting with elegant flutes for the champagne cocktail. For the table, bring out the candle-sticks and the ivory candles. Tie your napkins with wide velvet ribbons to add even more festivity.

Fill a couple of interesting glass bowls with old-fashioned glass Christmas balls—a dra-matic touch for the table setting. A fireplace mantel or decorative molding looks more "of the season" when festooned with pine garlands, so drape away. A few pomander balls—small oranges stuck all over with whole cloves—lend a delicious perfume to the room. Allow yourself plenty of time to set the scene, because it's so much fun.

THE MUSIC

Carols: Norman Luboff Choir and the Mormon Tabernacle Choir

Handel's *Messiah*

THE DRINKS

Christmas Eve Champagne Cocktail

Chilled Bual Madeira with the foie gras

Puligny-Montrachet with the salmon

Bandol with the cassoulet

THE EXTRAS

Champagne flutes

Salad bowl with servers

Oven-to-table casserole dish

Tart pan

CHRISTMAS EVE CHAMPAGNE COCKTAIL

A s Bette Davis said in *Old Acquaintance,* "There comes a time in every woman's life when the only thing that helps is a glass of champagne." I'll drink to that. Here, that champagne is mixed with Pineau des Charentes, the delicious sweet aperitif. Just before serving, drop a sugar cube into each glass and then top with the Pineau and champagne. Watch the bubbles rise in a steady stream. This is truly a cocktail in the holiday spirit.

> *8 small Demerara (raw) sugar cubes*
>   *(such as Sugar-in-the-Raw brand)*
> *16 ounces Pineau des Charentes*
> *32 ounces chilled champagne*
>   *(about 1 1/2 bottles)*

Place a sugar cube in each of eight champagne flutes. Pour 2 ounces of Pineau des Charentes into each glass over the sugar cube. Just before serving, top each glass with champagne.

CELERIAC BRANDADE

T wo hundred-dollar words for an exceedingly down-home dish—if your home happens to be in Provence. Celeriac is just another name for celery root, and brandade is a mixture of salt cod, olive oil, and milk, usually with mashed potatoes thrown in for good measure. The result is salty, creamy, and luxurious; perfect for a first course. The celeriac, while not typical in brandade, works well in this powerful concerto of tastes. Serve it with a loaf of crusty peasant bread.

FOIE GRAS AND THINLY SLICED FIG LOG

D elicious and luxurious, foie gras has a deep affinity for fruit, especially dried fruit. For Christmas Eve, a pairing of foie gras with thin slices of fig log makes for a lovely seasonal starter.

Fig logs are small cylinders of compressed dried figs, sometimes enriched with liquors and nuts and wrapped in fig leaves. They range in size from 4 to 10 ounces. These fig mixtures are also sold by the pound in wedges from larger fig cakes.

For eight people, you will need 8 ounces of foie gras terrine and about 10 ounces of fig log or cake. Both are available in gourmet stores. Place thin slices of each on small plates with toast points. It is a rich and sweet combination that's hard to beat.

> *1 cup dry white wine*
> *6 whole black peppercorns*
> *1 bay leaf*
> *1 1/2 pounds salt cod, soaked overnight*
>   *(see Note)*
> *1 1/2 pounds Yukon Gold or other waxy*
>   *potatoes, peeled and cut in half*
> *12 ounces celery root, peeled and*
>   *cut into 1-inch cubes*
> *3/4 cup extra-virgin olive oil*
> *3/4 cup minced onion*
> *1 1/2 tablespoons coarsely chopped garlic*
> *1 1/2 cups crème fraîche*
> *1 1/2 tablespoons fresh thyme leaves*
> *Coarsely ground black pepper, to taste*

Roast Salmon with Lemon-Caviar Potatoes

1. Place the wine, 1 cup water, the peppercorns, and bay leaf in a large saucepan. Bring to a boil over high heat, then reduce the heat to medium-low, add the salt cod, and simmer until the fish is cooked through, about 10 minutes. Remove the fish from the cooking liquid and allow it to cool to room temperature. Remove any bones, and flake the fish into medium-size pieces. Set it aside.

2. Place the potatoes and celery root in a saucepan and add cold water to cover. Bring to a boil over high heat and cook, uncovered, until tender, about 20 minutes. Drain. While the potatoes and celery root are still warm, press them through a ricer or mash them with a fork.

3. Heat the olive oil in a large nonstick skillet over medium heat. Add the onion and cook until softened, 10 minutes. Remove the skillet from the heat and add the garlic, crème fraîche, thyme, and pepper. Fold this mixture into the mashed potatoes and celery root. The mixture should be moist and fluffy.

4. Stir in the flaked fish. Adjust the seasonings, if necessary, transfer to a decorative bowl, and serve immediately.

Note: Salt cod can be found in ethnic markets or ordered from your local fish shop. It is sold dried, and the typical piece weighs about 1½ pounds. To prepare the salt cod for use in recipes, it needs to be rehydrated: Cut it into large pieces and place them in a large bowl. Cover with cold water and soak overnight, changing the water two or three times. The next day, drain the fish, rinse it under cold water, and drain again.

ROAST SALMON WITH LEMON-CAVIAR POTATOES

A most extravagant appetizer—but, hey—it's Christmas Eve! Very few members of the fish world could stand up to the briny flavor in osetra caviar. But roast salmon, rich with its own delicious and healthful oils, has the texture and flavor of a true lead player in this delightful starter.

FOR THE LEMON-CAVIAR MAYONNAISE
¾ cup prepared mayonnaise,
  such as Hellmann's
¾ cup sour cream
1½ tablespoons finely grated lemon zest
1½ tablespoons fresh lemon juice
1½ tablespoons (½ ounce) osetra caviar
  (or red salmon or American sturgeon caviar)
Salt and freshly ground black pepper, to taste

FOR THE SALAD AND FISH
12 Yukon Gold potatoes (about 4 pounds)
Salt and freshly ground black pepper, to taste
4 center-cut salmon fillets (about 8 ounces each)
¼ cup fresh lemon juice
2 tablespoons extra-virgin olive oil
8 heaping teaspoons (about 3 ounces)
  osetra caviar (or red salmon or
  American sturgeon caviar), for garnish

1. Prepare the lemon-caviar mayonnaise: Combine the mayonnaise, sour cream, lemon zest, and lemon juice in a bowl. Blend thoroughly. Then carefully fold in the caviar, using a rubber spatula. Season with salt and pepper and set aside.

2. Place the potatoes in a saucepan and cover with cold water. Add 1 teaspoon salt and bring to a boil. Reduce the heat and simmer until tender, 25 to 30 minutes.

3. Drain the potatoes. When they are cool enough to handle, peel and quarter them; then cut the quarters into ¼-inch slices. Place them in a bowl and gently fold in the lemon-caviar mayonnaise. Season with salt and pepper. Refrigerate, covered, until ready to use.

4. Preheat the oven to 450°F.

5. Cut the salmon fillets in half crosswise, into 8 pieces, each about 3 inches square. Place the salmon fillets, skin side down, in a baking dish.

6. Combine the lemon juice, olive oil, and salt and pepper to taste in a small bowl and pour this over the salmon. Let it rest for 15 to 20 minutes.

7. Roast the salmon until it is medium-rare, 7 to 9 minutes. Let it rest for about 5 minutes, then carefully transfer the pieces to large salad plates. Place a generous scoop of the potato salad alongside the salmon. Dollop each piece of salmon with a heaping teaspoon of caviar and serve.

SAVORY CASSOULET

In southwestern France, the cassoulet is the down-home dish par excellence—a stunning ragoût of meats and beans, slow-cooked until it is one savory mass of flavor. This version is somewhat lighter but still retains that deep old-time flavor. (Note that you need to start it a day ahead.) Legend has it that cassoulet in its modern form comes to us from the Hundred Years' War (1337 to 1453). When the citizens of Castelnaudary were besieged by the English, they threw all the meat and beans and vegetables they had into one big pot, and the result was history's first cassoulet. Thus invigorated, the French sallied forth and put the English to rout. I have my doubts about that legend. Still, after eating cassoulet, I can very much understand wanting to do anything to defend the homeland.

12 ounces dried Great Northern beans
4 tablespoons olive oil
8 chicken thighs (3 to 3½ pounds)
2 pounds lamb shoulder with bones,
*   cut into 2-inch pieces*
Salt and freshly ground black pepper, to taste
1 pound andouille sausage
1 pound spiced turkey sausage
3 cups coarsely chopped carrots
2 cups coarsely chopped onions
6 cloves garlic, chopped
1 can (28 ounces) peeled Italian plum
*   tomatoes, chopped, with juices*
3 cups Basic Chicken Broth (page 397)
1 teaspoon dried thyme
1 teaspoon dried sage leaves, crumbled
2 bay leaves
½ teaspoon ground allspice
6 tablespoons chopped fresh flat-leaf parsley

1. Pick over the beans, discarding any debris. Soak the beans overnight in cold water to cover. Drain, rinse once or twice, and set aside.

2. Heat 2 tablespoons of the olive oil in a large nonstick skillet over medium heat. Add the chicken and sauté until golden on all sides, 10 minutes. Remove the chicken and set it aside.

3. Place the lamb in the same skillet over medium-high heat and sauté until well browned on all sides, about 8 minutes total. Remove the lamb and set it aside. Season the chicken and the lamb well with salt and pepper.

4. Pour off all but 2 to 3 tablespoons of the fat in the skillet. Place the skillet over medium-high heat, add the andouille and turkey sausages, and brown them well, about 10 minutes. Remove the sausages, and after they have cooled slightly, cut them into ½-inch pieces. Set the sausage aside.

5. Heat the remaining 2 tablespoons olive oil in a large flameproof casserole over medium-low heat. Add the carrots and onions and cook until they start to soften, 7 minutes. Add the garlic and cook, stirring occasionally, to blend the flavors, 3 minutes more. Then add the tomatoes, 1½ cups

Savory Cassoulet

of the broth, and the thyme, sage, bay leaves, and allspice. Stir the beans into the mixture. Bring to a boil over high heat, reduce the heat to medium-low, cover, and simmer for 1 hour.

6. Preheat the oven to 350°F.

7. Stir the remaining 1½ cups broth into the casserole. Arrange the lamb among the beans. Cover, transfer the casserole to the oven, and bake, stirring once, for 45 minutes.

8. Add the chicken and sausage and bake for 50 minutes more. Stir in 4 tablespoons of the parsley and cook for another 10 minutes. Just before serving, sprinkle the remaining 2 tablespoons parsley over the cassoulet.

Note: You can make the cassoulet in the morning and keep it, covered, in the refrigerator. Let it come to room temperature and then reheat it in a preheated 350°F oven for 25 to 30 minutes, sprinkling in the 4 tablespoons of parsley after the cassoulet has been reheating for 20 minutes. Sprinkle the remaining parsley over the cassoulet just before serving it.

HERBED BOSTON LETTUCE SALAD

W<!---->hen the occasion is special, each course deserves tender loving care. The night before Christmas calls for a light salad of soft lettuce leaves dressed in a slightly sweet vinaigrette. It complements the holiday dinner and gently leads into dessert.

2 large heads Boston lettuce,
  damaged outer leaves discarded
2 large shallots, finely diced
¾ cup small fresh flat-leaf parsley leaves
Coarse (kosher) salt and freshly ground
  black pepper, to taste
¼ cup Shallot Vinaigrette (recipe follows)

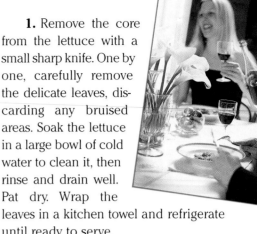

1. Remove the core from the lettuce with a small sharp knife. One by one, carefully remove the delicate leaves, discarding any bruised areas. Soak the lettuce in a large bowl of cold water to clean it, then rinse and drain well. Pat dry. Wrap the leaves in a kitchen towel and refrigerate until ready to serve.

2. Place the lettuce leaves in a large salad bowl and toss with the shallots and parsley. Season with salt and pepper. Lightly toss with the Shallot Vinaigrette.

3. Serve from the bowl, or divide among eight salad plates.

SHALLOT VINAIGRETTE

T<!---->his vinaigrette comes to life with the addition of shallots. What is most important is to find a shallot that is firm and crisp. The sugar mellows the flavors and adds just the right balance to the vinaigrette.

½ cup cider vinegar
1 tablespoon finely chopped shallot
1 teaspoon Dijon mustard
1 teaspoon sugar
Salt and freshly ground black pepper, to taste
½ cup extra-virgin olive oil

Whisk the vinegar, shallot, mustard, sugar, and salt and pepper together in a small bowl. Slowly drizzle in the olive oil, whisking constantly until thickened. Adjust the seasonings to taste. Store, covered, in the refrigerator for up to 2 days. Bring to room temperature before using.

MAKES ABOUT ¾ CUP

TANGERINE TART

In 1880, Louis Alexandre Marnier-Lapostolle gave the world a new liqueur that combined cognac (which is made from champagne grapes) and the essence of bitter oranges from the West Indies: Grand Marnier. Its exquisite and refined taste is an ambrosial enhancement to the sweet yet tart tangerine filling here. If you make the tart a day ahead, the flavors will mix and deepen.

FOR THE TART DOUGH
1 cup all-purpose flour
6 tablespoons confectioners' sugar
¼ cup ground blanched almonds
1 tablespoon finely grated orange zest
6 tablespoons (¾ stick) cold unsalted butter, cut into 6 pieces
1 large egg, beaten

FOR THE TANGERINE FILLING
6 tangerines, unpeeled
¾ cup fresh tangerine juice (from about 4 tangerines)
¼ cup Grand Marnier
6 tablespoons granulated sugar

FOR THE CHOCOLATE FILLING
8 ounces bittersweet chocolate
8 tablespoons (1 stick) unsalted butter
¼ cup whole milk

1. Prepare the dough: Place the flour, confectioners' sugar, almonds, and orange zest in a food processor. Process until the flour and almonds are powdery smooth. Add the butter and process until uniformly crumbly. Add half the egg and process until the dough just forms a ball. (Discard the rest of the egg or reserve it for another use.) Flatten the ball slightly, wrap it in plastic wrap, and refrigerate for at least 1 hour, or as long as overnight.

2. Press the tart dough evenly into a 9-inch tart pan with removable bottom. Refrigerate, covered with plastic wrap, for 1 hour.

3. Preheat the oven to 350°F. Line a rimmed baking sheet with parchment paper.

4. Prepare the tangerine filling: Slice the unpeeled tangerines into very thin rounds. Discard the top and bottom slices of each and the seeds. Place the tangerine slices in a small layer on the prepared baking sheet. Combine the tangerine juice and Grand Marnier in a small bowl, and pour this evenly over the tangerine slices. Sprinkle evenly with 2 tablespoons of the sugar. Cover lightly with aluminum foil and bake until the tangerines are tender, 1 hour. Uncover the tangerines and sprinkle with the remaining 4 tablespoons sugar. Bake until there is barely any syrup remaining in the baking sheet, about 20 minutes. Set aside to cool. Raise the oven temperature to 400°F.

5. Line the tart shell with a piece of aluminum foil, pressing it evenly onto the surface. Bake for 10 minutes. Carefully remove the foil, reduce the temperature to 350°F, and continue to bake the shell until it is golden brown, 20 to 30 minutes. Set it aside.

6. Prepare the chocolate filling: Melt the chocolate and butter together in a heavy saucepan over low heat. Remove from the heat.

7. In a separate small saucepan, bring the milk to a simmer. Then whisk the milk into the chocolate mixture until it is smooth. Allow to cool to room temperature.

8. Scrape the cooled chocolate mixture into the prebaked pie shell and spread it evenly over the bottom.

9. Arrange the tangerine slices on top of the chocolate in concentric circles, ending with one in the center. Cover loosely with aluminum foil, and let sit on the kitchen counter until ready to serve.

An Extremely

Christmas is meant to be shared. Family, friends, friends of friends, and friends of family—everyone is welcome at the table. The perfect fantasy: outside, bright sun shining down on a layer of freshly fallen

Merry Christmas

snow (warmer climes included—this is, after all, a fantasy), inside, warm hearth, warm hearts, and enough food to go around, no matter how many people show up. Cliché it may be, but it is great to be home for this holiday.

MENU

An Extremely Merry Christmas

DINNER FOR EIGHT

Spirited Eggnog

Elegant Butternut Truffle Soup

Endive Salad
with Creamy Roquefort Vinaigrette

A Majestic Rib Roast

Corn and Chanterelle Risotto

Haricots Verts with Shallot Herb Butter

Apple Brown Betty

Peanut Brittle

There's no better way to begin the Christmas festivities than with a cup of Spirited Eggnog. Elegant Butternut Truffle Soup, drizzled with truffle oil, plants the idea of luxury. But it is the grand centerpiece, a standing rib roast, that makes the greatest impression, especially when served with a fluffy Horseradish Cream sauce. Haricots verts and Corn and Chanterelle Risotto accompany the roast. The bold-tasting Endive Salad can be served either after the soup or before dessert, which is the yummiest Apple Brown Betty, all warm and cozy. Peanut Brittle is the perfect final treat to enjoy while you watch *It's a Wonderful Life* or *A Christmas Carol* on television.

For the table, choose linens in a fairly pale color such as ivory, celadon, or light blue, because all the vibrant Christmas decorations around the house will be enough to capture the eye. With ivory or white linens, use moss green or burgundy velvet ribbon to tie the napkins in generous bows. Soft and lush-looking white amaryllis are my choice of flowers for the table.

Bring out the best dishes for Christmas—and best silver, too. It is definitely the time to get down the punch bowl for the Spirited Eggnog—and all those little cups. Punch, especially eggnog, is sweetly nostalgic.

THE MUSIC

Leroy Anderson's *White Christmas*
Soundtrack from
White Christmas

THE DRINKS

Spirited Eggnog
Grand Cru Chablis
Pessac-Leognan

THE EXTRAS

Punch bowl and cups
Carving knife and fork

There are as many legends about Christmas as there are twinkling lights on the giant tree in Rockefeller Center, but the story of mistletoe is one that is particularly appealing (you have to like something that says it's all right to go ahead and kiss). According to Scandinavian legend, Baldur was the favorite of the gods. Loki, the god of destruction, was jealous and had set his evil heart on doing away with Baldur. But Baldur's mother, Frigga, made everything that was "begotten of earth, air, fire, or water" swear that they would never harm her son. The one thing she overlooked was mistletoe. Loki made an arrow out of mistletoe and shot it through Baldur's heart. When Frigga was given the fatal mistletoe, she hung it from a rafter, saying it would never touch the earth, and, wise goddess that she was, she also said that anyone who passed under it would be given a kiss. This was her way of saying that the symbol of Loki's hatred and jealousy would become one of love and forgiveness.

SPIRITED EGGNOG

Years ago, when Rabelaisian feasts were no problem, my spirited friends Donaldo and Louise Soviero used to whip up this luxurious eggnog at holiday time. There was always a fire roaring in the living room to welcome guests, and you just slipped into a cocoon of good feeling as you sipped this sumptuous brew. This nog packs a punch, so use small punch cups.

6 large eggs, separated
¾ cup sugar
2 cups heavy (whipping) cream
2 cups whole milk
1¾ cups bourbon
1 cup cognac
3 tablespoons dark rum
Freshly grated nutmeg, for dusting

1. Beat the egg yolks in a large bowl with an electric mixer, gradually adding the sugar until the mixture is pale yellow. Set it aside.

2. Place the cream in another bowl and beat it with clean mixer beaters until it holds soft peaks.

3. Stir the milk into the egg yolk mixture. Then, using a large rubber spatula, fold in the whipped cream.

4. Shortly before serving, gently stir in the bourbon and cognac. Transfer the mixture to a punch bowl.

5. Beat the egg whites in a bowl with an electric mixer until they hold soft peaks. Carefully fold them into the eggnog. Drizzle the top with the rum, and sprinkle with the nutmeg. Surround the bowl with punch cups, and serve immediately.

ELEGANT BUTTERNUT TRUFFLE SOUP

Flavored with mace, ginger, and brown sugar, this tangerine-hued nectar, laced with truffle oil, is a beautifully rich beginning to a meal. It definitely sets up the palate for the tastes to come, but it is so powerful in its own right that my advice is to make the servings small—shallow bowls are ideal.

2 butternut squash (about 4 pounds)
8 cups Basic Chicken Broth (page 397)
2 tablespoons unsalted butter
4 teaspoons olive oil
1 onion, chopped
½ teaspoon ground mace
½ teaspoon ground ginger
4 teaspoons light brown sugar
Salt and freshly ground black pepper,
    to taste
Truffle oil, for garnish
About ½ cup freshly grated Parmesan
    cheese

1. Halve the squash lengthwise and discard the seeds. Peel it and cut it into chunks.

2. Place the squash in a heavy soup pot and add the broth. Bring to a boil over high heat, reduce the heat to medium, and simmer, partially covered, until tender, 20 to 25 minutes. Using a slotted spoon, transfer the squash to a bowl. Reserve the broth.

3. Melt the butter in the olive oil in a non-stick skillet over very low heat. Add the onion and cook, stirring, until softened, 15 minutes. Sprinkle with the mace and ginger and cook, stirring, for 1 minute more. Add the onion and the brown sugar to the squash and stir well. Season with salt and pepper.

4. Puree the squash mixture, in batches if necessary, in a food processor or blender, gradually adding the reserved broth. Return the soup to the pot and adjust the seasonings if necessary. Heat through over low heat.

5. Serve small portions of the soup in shallow bowls. Drizzle a small swirl of truffle oil over each portion, and scatter a generous pinch of Parmesan in the center of the swirl.

Elegant Butternut Truffle Soup

ENDIVE SALAD

Bitter and sweet—in life the combination makes me wistful, but on the plate, it gets my attention. There is no better example than this salad, with the creamy underlying sweetness and richness of Roquefort cheese and the bracing crunchiness of endive.

12 Belgian endives, any bruised outer leaves
    discarded, leaves separated, rinsed, and
    patted dry
Coarse (kosher) salt and freshly ground
    black pepper, to taste
¼ cup snipped fresh chives or chopped
    fresh flat-leaf parsley
Creamy Roquefort Vinaigrette (recipe follows)
1½ cups walnut halves, for garnish

1. Cut the endive leaves crosswise into ¼-inch-wide strips and place in a large bowl. Cover with a damp towel and refrigerate.

2. Before serving, season the endive with salt and pepper, and toss with the chives. Toss lightly with the vinaigrette, beginning with about ⅔ cup. Divide the salad among eight plates, and garnish with the walnut halves.

CREAMY ROQUEFORT VINAIGRETTE

If you're lucky enough to have any extra dressing, spoon it over halved grape tomatoes sprinkled with chopped red onion.

¼ *cup red wine vinegar*
4 teaspoons Dijon mustard
Salt and freshly ground black pepper, to taste
½ *cup extra-virgin olive oil*
⅔ *cup crumbled Roquefort cheese*
2 teaspoons finely grated lemon zest
6 tablespoons heavy (whipping) cream

Whisk together the vinegar, mustard, and salt and pepper in a small bowl. Whisking constantly, slowly drizzle in the olive oil. Continue whisking until the dressing thickens. Carefully add the Roquefort cheese. Once it is evenly blended, add the lemon zest and heavy cream, whisking gently.

MAKES A GENEROUS 1 CUP

Note: This vinaigrette can be prepared up to 2 days in advance. Rewhisk before tossing it with the endive.

A MAJESTIC RIB ROAST

The great French chef Marie-Antoine Carême said, "Beef is the soul of cooking." Truly, nothing is heartier or more fortifying. The standing roast is handsome to behold, easy to prepare, just as easy to serve—and when you

Belgian endive—a delicacy in the United States but an important winter vegetable in northern Europe—is the result of an accident. In 1830, a Belgian farmer was growing chicory for its root, which was used then as a coffee substitute. He threw some of his chicory roots into soft soil in a dark shed and forgot them. Three weeks later, he found that tight blanched heads had grown from the roots. When he tasted them, he discovered that they had a delicious, distinctive, delicate, slightly bitter flavor and crisp texture.

Belgian endive, also known as Witloof chicory, is grown in two stages. Seeds are planted in the spring. In the late summer and fall, carrotlike roots are dug up and the leaves are trimmed back. After a period of cold storage, these roots are planted in dark forcing chambers. The first delicate blanched heads, called chicons, can be harvested about four weeks later.

are finished with the knife and fork part, the bone is positively a Neanderthal delight to pick up with your fingers and gnaw at. Ah, what a way to celebrate Christmas Day!

1 standing rib roast of beef (6½ pounds, 3 ribs)
3 to 4 cloves garlic, thinly sliced
Coarse (kosher) salt and freshly ground black pepper, to taste
Horseradish Cream (page 39), for serving

1. Preheat the oven to 450°F.
2. Pat the roast dry, then make small slits all over the top with the tip of a small paring knife

A Majestic Rib Roast

and insert the garlic slivers in them. Rub the roast all over with salt and pepper. Place it on a rack in a shallow roasting pan and roast for 25 minutes.

3. Reduce the oven temperature to 350°F and roast until an instant-reading thermometer registers 135° to 140°F for medium-rare, 1¾ hours. Let the meat rest for 15 minutes before carving. Serve with the Horseradish Cream.

CORN AND CHANTERELLE RISOTTO

Inventive risottos have appeared in many guises on restaurant menus and in cookbooks. Here golden corn and fresh chanterelles add further luxury to the creamy rice, making it an ideal opener or an elegant side dish. I prefer my risotto creamy in texture, and therefore add a bit of cream just toward the end.

1 pound fresh chanterelle, cremini,
  or shiitake mushrooms
½ cup extra-virgin olive oil
6 leeks, including 2 inches green,
  well washed (see Notes), chopped
8 cups Basic Chicken Broth (page 397)
2 cups frozen corn kernels
2 cups arborio rice
1 cup dry white wine
½ cup heavy (whipping) cream, warmed
2 tablespoons unsalted butter,
  at room temperature
Salt and freshly ground black pepper,
  to taste
¼ cup snipped fresh chives (1-inch pieces)

1. Trim the ends off the mushroom stems. Wipe the caps clean with damp paper towels, and then cut the mushrooms in half lengthwise.

2. Heat ¼ cup of the olive oil in a heavy saucepan over medium heat. Add the mushrooms and cook, stirring, for 5 minutes. Transfer them to a bowl and cover to keep warm.

3. Add the remaining ¼ cup olive oil to the saucepan, add the leeks, and cook over low heat, stirring occasionally, until wilted, 10 minutes.

4. While the leeks are cooking, bring the broth to a boil in a saucepan over high heat. Reduce the heat to medium-low to keep the broth at a simmer. Add the corn and cook for 1 minute to heat through. Use a slotted spoon to remove the corn to a bowl. Cover to keep warm. Keep the broth at a gentle simmer.

5. Add the rice to the leeks and stir well with a wooden spoon for 1 minute, so that the grains of rice are all well coated with oil. Add the wine and cook, stirring, over medium heat until it has been absorbed by the rice, 3 to 4 minutes.

6. Add ¾ cup of the hot broth to the rice mixture and cook, stirring, until it has been absorbed by the rice, about 5 minutes. Repeat, letting each ¾ cup of broth be absorbed before adding the next (see Notes).

7. When the rice is tender and nearly all the broth has been absorbed, after about 45 minutes, fold in the corn and the mushrooms.

8. Stir in the cream and the butter. Season with salt and pepper. Stir in the chives and serve.

Notes: Cut the trimmed leeks in half lengthwise. Stir 2 tablespoons distilled white vinegar into a large bowl of water and soak the leeks for 30 minutes. Rinse and drain the leeks before chopping them.

You can make the risotto up to 2 hours in advance to just before adding the last ¾ cup broth. Cover the rice and the broth to keep warm on the stovetop. When ready to finish the dish, reheat the rice over medium heat for 1 minute, stirring to prevent it from sticking. Heat the remaining broth to a simmer, about 1 minute. Add the broth to the rice and cook, stirring, until it is almost absorbed, about 5 minutes, then continue with steps 7 and 8.

HARICOTS VERTS WITH SHALLOT HERB BUTTER

A lavish Christmas dinner calls for a delicate vegetable to round out the meal. Haricots verts are an excellent winter choice, making a statement of good taste without overpowering the meat or the equally delicate chanterelles in the risotto. A dab of Shallot Herb Butter adds a special flavor without screaming "I'm here!"

2 pounds haricots verts (thin green beans),
*   stem ends trimmed*
4 to 6 tablespoons Shallot Herb Butter
*   (page 401), or to taste*
Salt and freshly ground black pepper, to taste

1. Bring a large pot of salted water to a boil over high heat. Add the haricots verts and cook until they are just tender, about 4 minutes. Drain, rinse under cold water, and drain again.

2. Return the haricots verts to the pot and add 4 tablespoons of the butter. Season with salt and pepper and cook over medium heat, tossing the beans often, until they are warmed through and coated with butter, 3 to 4 minutes. Add more butter if they seem too dry, and toss to melt. Serve immediately.

APPLE BROWN BETTY

This is actually two traditional dishes combined into one irresistible dessert. A brown betty is an American dessert that the early colonists made. (I had hoped to find in my research that since desserts are sweet, Betty was somebody's sweetheart. It seems, though, that

> *On the table spread the cloth,*
>
> *Let the knives be sharp and clean,*
>
> *Pickles get and salad both,*
>
> *Let them each be fresh and green;*
>
> *With small beer, good ale, and wine,*
>
> *O ye gods! how I shall dine!*
>
> —*FROM AN ENGLISH FOLK SONG*

George Washington's contemporaries called many puddings betties.) I have added some mincemeat, the central ingredient in the famed mincemeat pie, without which an English Christmas spread can never be complete. In the old days, mincemeat was a combination of fruit, meat, suet, and alcohol; today's commercially made mincemeat omits the meat and contains instead plenty of dried fruits, spices, cider, and other good things.

FOR THE FRUIT
2 Granny Smith apples
2 McIntosh apples
2 tablespoons granulated sugar
2 tablespoons kirsch
Pinch of salt
1/2 cup mincemeat (see Note)

FOR THE TOPPING
4 slices slightly stale white bread, chopped into
*   rough crumbs (no need to remove crusts)*
1/4 cup (packed) light brown sugar
2 tablespoons granulated sugar
1/4 teaspoon ground cinnamon
1/4 cup chopped pecans
3 tablespoons unsalted butter, melted

Sweetened Whipped Cream (page 403),
*   for serving*

1. Preheat the oven to 375°F. Butter a 9-inch square baking pan.

2. Peel and core the apples. Cut them into 1-inch chunks and place them in a large bowl. Toss the apples with the sugar, kirsch, salt, and mincemeat. Spoon the mixture into the prepared baking pan.

3. Prepare the topping: Place the bread crumbs, brown sugar, granulated sugar, cinnamon, and pecans in a bowl and toss well. Add the butter and mix it in thoroughly with your fingertips. Sprinkle the topping evenly over the apple mixture.

4. Bake until the top is browned and crunchy, 40 to 45 minutes. Serve warm, topped with Sweetened Whipped Cream.

Note: Mincemeat is sold in cans or jars and is available in the baking section of most supermarkets and in specialty food shops.

PEANUT
BRITTLE

B less the peanut! It is so versatile and delicious, and has a wonderful affinity for both sweetness and saltiness.

Making brittle requires some caution—it's not a bad idea to wear long sleeves (and definitely mitts) when you are handling the hot sugar.

Corn oil, for oiling the baking sheet
3 cups salted dry-roasted peanuts
4 cups sugar
1/8 teaspoon cream of tartar
2 tablespoons unsalted butter,
 cut into small pieces

1. Lightly oil a 17 x 12 x 1-inch rimmed baking sheet with corn oil. Oil a spatula, and set it aside.

2. Scatter the peanuts evenly over the prepared baking sheet and set it aside.

3. Combine the sugar, ½ cup cold water, and cream of tartar in a heavy saucepan over low heat. Cook, stirring to combine, for 5 minutes. Raise the heat to medium-high and bring the mixture to a boil. Cook without stirring until the mixture reaches about 310°F on a candy thermometer, or until it is between a butterscotch and a caramel color, about 10 minutes. While it is cooking, use a pastry brush dipped in warm water to periodically wash down the sugar crystals on the sides of the pan.

4. Remove the pan from the heat and immediately stir in the butter. *Be careful:* The sugar is *very hot,* and the mixture will foam up a bit and can spatter.

5. Immediately pour the mixture over the peanuts, using the oiled spatula to smooth the mixture. Let it cool completely, about 1 hour. Then remove the hardened candy from the pan and break it into irregular pieces. The brittle will keep, stored in an airtight container, for up to 1 week.

A TOAST TO THE

NEW YEAR

A romantic dinner for two, a blowout for a hundred, a dinner party for twenty at a Chinese restaurant, a subzero barbecue on the shores of Lake Michigan—the inventiveness that people use in dreaming up ways to celebrate New Year's Eve exceeds every other holiday. There is something universal about the feeling of excitement at the prospect of a new year beginning. Maybe it is because, deep down inside, everyone thinks, "This could be my year!" And you know what? It very well should be.

MENU

A TOAST TO THE NEW YEAR

FOR EIGHT

CELEBRATION COCKTAIL

SPARKLING CRAB SALAD

FRISEE FOLIE
WITH TANGERINE VINAIGRETTE

MAHOGANY SQUABS

FANCY NEW YEAR'S PILAF

CARROT-GINGER WHIP

BEET AND APPLE WHIP

FROZEN LIME SOUFFLE

CHOCOLATE TRUFFLES

The more glamorous it is, the more successful the New Year's Eve party. This menu has a stylish Oriental flair—the colors evoking a North African bazaar or a caliph's pleasure garden. Toast the old year out with champagne cocktails, then move onto a gorgeous Sparkling Crab Salad followed by a Frisée Folie studded with ruby pomegranate seeds and cool green pistachios. The centerpiece, a platter of mahogany lacquered squabs, is surrounded by smooth vegetable purees in tones of orange and magenta. Cinnamon and currants enhance a traditional pilaf—it's one luscious flavor after another. Top off this sophisticated dinner by ringing in the new year with a cool Frozen Lime Soufflé and sweet Chocolate Truffles.

Continue the sumptuous color in the décor. Scour the flea markets for old painted hookahs to use as vases for full-blown apricot-hued roses. Beg, borrow, or steal (well, not really) turquoise glass vases or small pitchers to hold the flowers. Use anything trimmed with gold.

A Milky Way of votive candles suits the evening, creating an aura that is sexy and passionate. Float white orchids in clear glass bowls. Drape your tables in paisley fabric, and use pink linen napkins tied with gold wire-ribbon bows. If you are lucky enough to have an ornamental set of china, this is the time to bring it out. Begin the New Year on an exotic luscious note.

THE MUSIC

Rimsky-Korsakov's *Scheherazade*
John Coltrane's *My Favorite Things*

THE DRINKS

Celebration Cocktail
Tête de Cuvée Champagne
Chambertin Clos de Bèze

THE EXTRAS

Champagne flutes
Paper candy cups
Soufflé dish

Sparkling Crab Salad

CELEBRATION COCKTAIL

A romatic, sweet, fragrant, bubbly, tangy—this dazzling sparkler is a holiday gift in a glass of champagne. Now that's festive.

8 cubes Demerara (raw) sugar
  (such as Sugar-in-the-Raw brand)
16 dashes Angostura bitters
8 ounces Grand Marnier
40 ounces (1¾ bottles) chilled champagne
8 twists of orange peel

Place a sugar cube in each of eight champagne flutes. Sprinkle each with 2 dashes of bitters and add 1 ounce of Grand Marnier. Just before serving, top with champagne and add a twist.

SPARKLING CRAB SALAD

L obster may somehow have gotten the reputation of being the gourmet crustacean, but for versatility and inherent nobility, the crab is the aristocrat. Here the restrained accents of basil and mint work in tandem to bring out the character of the crab.

2 pounds fresh lump crabmeat, picked over to
  remove all cartilage (see Note)
2 cups diced peeled hothouse (seedless)
  cucumber (¼-inch dice)
¼ cup fresh lime juice (from 3 limes)
2 tablespoons olive oil
½ cup finely slivered fresh basil leaves
Salt and freshly ground black pepper, to taste
2 cups Mango and Mint Salsa (page 291),
  for serving
¼ cup chopped fresh mint, for garnish
8 sprigs fresh mint or basil, for garnish

1. Combine the crabmeat and cucumber in a bowl. Add the lime juice and olive oil and carefully toss together. Add the slivered basil and salt and pepper and combine gently, trying not to break up the crabmeat.

2. Mound the crabmeat mixture on eight plates. Top each serving with ¼ cup of the Mango and Mint Salsa. Sprinkle with the chopped mint and place a sprig mint alongside each salad.

Note: When buying crab, splurge for jumbo lump crabmeat. These are very generous portions, and the more delicate among us might choose to serve twelve instead of eight.

FRISEE FOLIE

F olly is related to the French word *folie*, which means a kind of happy madness. My Frisée Folie is a blend of the exotic—curly frisée, pomegranate seeds, persimmon slices, and a salad dressing made with tangerine juice instead of vinegar. Not so much madness as a reminiscence of romantic adventure in some far-off place.

2 heads frisée lettuce, tough outer
  leaves discarded
3 ripe persimmons, cut in half lengthwise
Salt and freshly ground black pepper,
  to taste
¼ cup snipped fresh chives
½ cup Tangerine Vinaigrette
  (recipe follows)
½ cup shelled pistachio nuts,
  preferably unsalted
Seeds of 1 pomegranate (see Note)

1. Separate the frisée leaves and rinse them in cold water. Drain and pat dry. Wrap the leaves in kitchen towels and refrigerate until ready to use.

2. Core the persimmons and carefully peel them with a very sharp knife. Cut them into very thin lengthwise slices. Cover with plastic wrap and refrigerate.

3. Shortly before serving, place the frisée in a large bowl. Season it with salt and pepper and toss with the chives. Dress the greens lightly with the vinaigrette, then divide them among eight large salad plates.

4. Lay about 4 persimmon slices over each salad. Sprinkle the pistachios and pomegranate seeds over them and serve immediately.

Note: To free the pomegranate seeds, cut or break the fruit open and use your fingers to push the seeds out of the surrounding membranes. Then wash your hands—the translucent red pulp may stain them slightly.

TANGERINE VINAIGRETTE

An exotic New Year's Eve salad calls for something out of the ordinary in a vinaigrette—something tangy, sweet, and taste-popping. Tangerine juice made velvety with the addition of Dijon mustard adds just the right accent, coating the frisée (or whatever your choice of green) with a distinctive, but not too heavy, flavor.

¼ cup fresh tangerine juice
2 teaspoons Dijon mustard
Salt and freshly ground black pepper,
*   to taste*
¼ cup olive oil

In a small bowl, whisk together the tangerine juice, mustard, and salt and pepper. Slowly drizzle in the olive oil, whisking constantly until thickened.

MAKES ½ CUP

Note: This vinaigrette can be prepared 2 to 3 days in advance. Store, covered, in the refrigerator. Bring to room temperature before dressing the salad.

MAHOGANY SQUABS

One of the virtues of squab is that it is mostly luscious-tasting breast. The flesh of these farm-raised pigeons has a strength of flavor approaching that of a wild bird that has feasted on berries and spruce buds. Here the squabs are marinated and then roasted to perfection. The only trick is the timing. There is a moment when a squab goes from succulent to dry, and you want to get it off the heat just before that happens. Just follow the directions and you will have a memorable party dish.

Mahogany Squabs

8 squabs (12 to 16 ounces each), quartered
3 large cloves garlic, chopped
1 piece (1 inch) peeled fresh ginger, chopped
1/2 cup soy sauce
1/2 cup honey
2 tablespoons corn oil
2 tablespoons fresh orange juice
1 tablespoon finely grated orange zest
2 tablespoons unsalted butter
4 tablespoons olive oil
Salt and freshly ground black pepper,
  to taste
3 to 4 bunches watercress, for garnish

1. Rinse the squabs quarters well and pat them dry. Trim off and discard the wing tips. Place the squab pieces in a large bowl.

2. Combine the garlic, ginger, soy sauce, honey, corn oil, orange juice, and orange zest in a food processor and process until smooth. Pour this mixture over the squabs. Marinate, covered, in the refrigerator for 2 hours or as long as overnight, turning them once or twice.

3. Drain the squabs, reserving the marinade. Pat the pieces dry with paper towels.

4. Preheat the oven to 375°F.

5. In each of two skillets, melt 1 tablespoon of the butter in 2 tablespoons of the olive oil over medium-high heat. Add the squab breasts, skin side down, and sauté until golden brown, 3 to 4 minutes. Turn and cook for 1 minute on the other side. Transfer the breast to a baking sheet. Add the legs to the skillets and sauté until golden brown, about 2 minutes per side. Place them in the baking dish. Season the squab with salt and pepper.

6. Roast the squab in the oven until the legs are cooked through (medium-rare), about 7 minutes. Remove the legs and keep warm, loosely covered with aluminum foil. Continue to roast the breasts until medium-rare, another 5 minutes.

7. Meanwhile, pour the reserved marinade into a small saucepan and bring to a boil. Reduce the heat to a simmer and cook until slightly thickened, about 15 minutes.

8. Arrange the squabs on a decorative platter, and spoon the thickened sauce over them. Surround the squab with the watercress and serve immediately.

FANCY NEW YEAR'S PILAF

It seems that every country that cultivates rice has come up with a one-pot rice dish with a variety of sweet or savory ingredients, or both. The Indians have *pullao* and the Spanish have *paella*. The Turks are masters at delicate rice dishes, none more delicious than pilaf. I would be happy to offer this intoxicating variation up to Ali Baba himself if he came to my party.

1 1/2 tablespoons unsalted butter
1 1/2 tablespoons olive oil
1 1/2 onions, cut into 1/4-inch dice
5 carrots, peeled and cut into 1/4-inch dice
1 1/2 tablespoons finely minced garlic
3/4 teaspoon ground cumin
1/4 teaspoon ground allspice
1/2 teaspoon crumbled saffron threads
1 1/2 cups long-grain rice
4 1/2 cups Basic Chicken Broth (page 397)
1/2 cup dried currants
1/3 cup golden raisins
1 cinnamon stick (3 inches long)
Salt and freshly ground black pepper,
  to taste
2 tablespoons chopped fresh flat-leaf parsley

1. Melt the butter in the olive oil in a heavy saucepan over low heat. Add the onions and carrots and cook, stirring occasionally, until softened, about 10 minutes. Add the garlic and cook 5 minutes longer. Add the cumin, allspice, and saffron and cook, stirring, for 1 minute more.

2. Add the rice and cook, stirring, for 1 minute.

3. Stir in the broth, currants, raisins, and cinnamon stick. Raise the heat to high, bring to a boil, then reduce the heat to medium-low and simmer, covered, until cooked through, about 20 minutes. Fluff with a fork, remove the cinnamon stick, season with salt and pepper, and stir in the parsley. Transfer to a pretty bowl and serve.

CARROT-GINGER WHIP

Color counts, and the deep orange of this whip complements the purple of the beet and apple whip beautifully. Using both crystallized and ground ginger adds sweetness, bite, and fruity floral notes. It tames the wildness of the squab and accents its underlying meaty succulence.

> 12 carrots, peeled and cut into 1-inch
> lengths
> 6 tablespoons ($^3/_4$ stick) unsalted butter,
> at room temperature
> $^1/_2$ cup (packed) light brown sugar
> 1 tablespoon ground ginger
> $1^1/_2$ teaspoons chopped crystallized ginger
> Salt, to taste

1. Place the carrots in a large saucepan, cover with salted water, and bring to a boil over high heat. Reduce the heat to medium and simmer until the carrots are very tender, about 25 minutes.

2. Meanwhile, place the remaining ingredients in a large bowl. When the carrots are cooked, drain them, reserving 1 cup of the cooking liquid, and add them to the bowl. Toss to coat well.

3. Transfer the carrots to a food processor and puree them, adding some of the reserved liquid if the puree seems too thick. Transfer the puree to a

bowl, correct the seasonings if necessary, and serve immediately (see Note).

Note: If you prepare this ahead, reheat it, loosely covered with aluminum foil, in a 350°F oven for 15 minutes. Bring to room temperature before reheating.

BEET AND APPLE WHIP

Sweet and tangy are classic tastes to accompany game. The luminescent ruby color and the beguiling flavor of beets and apples embrace the roasted squab. This puree can also be served cold.

> 6 Roasted Beets (page 399)
> 3 tablespoons unsalted butter
> 2 tablespoons olive oil
> 1 cup chopped red onions
> 3 Granny Smith apples, peeled, cored,
> and chopped
> 2 tablespoons sugar
> Salt, to taste
> $^1/_4$ cup cider vinegar

1. Coarsely chop the peeled beets and place them in a food processor. Puree the beets, stopping the machine once or twice to scrape down the sides of the bowl. Leave the puree in the food processor.

2. Melt 2 tablespoons of the butter in the olive oil in a heavy saucepan over low heat. Add the onions and cook, stirring occasionally, until wilted, about 15 minutes. Add the apples and cook, covered, for 20 minutes. Stir in the sugar, salt, and vinegar and cook for 2 minutes more. Add this mixture to the beets in the food processor and puree everything together.

3. Meanwhile, preheat the oven to 350°F.

4. Transfer the puree to a baking dish, dot it with the remaining 1 tablespoon butter, and cover the dish loosely with aluminum foil. Bake until heated through, 10 to 15 minutes. Serve immediately.

Note: To serve the puree cold, simply transfer the mixture from the food processor to a container, cover, and refrigerate for as long as 2 days. Serve chilled or at room temperature.

FROZEN LIME SOUFFLE

Light, airy, and accented with candied roses, this elegant lime dessert is unforgettable in appearance and taste. And you make it a day ahead, which takes the pressure off!

12 large egg yolks (see Notes)
1¾ cups plus 2 teaspoons sugar
¾ cup fresh lime juice (from about 8 limes)
Finely grated zest of 1 lime
½ cup heavy (whipping) cream
6 large egg whites
Candied rose petals, candied violets, or fresh
   mint leaves, for garnish (see Notes)
Sweetened Whipped Cream (page 403),
   for garnish

Frozen Lime Soufflé

1. Select a saucepan that a 2-quart bowl can fit in comfortably, with room for a water bath around it. Fill the saucepan about halfway with water and bring the water to a gentle simmer over medium-low heat.

2. Meanwhile, place the egg yolks and 1½ cups of the sugar in a 2-quart bowl and beat with an electric mixer until light and lemon-colored, 4 to 5 minutes. Beat in the lime juice and zest to just combine. When the water is simmering gently, place the bowl in the water and continue to beat until the temperature of the mixture is between 120°F and 140°F on a candy thermometer, about 10 minutes. It will be thick and creamy.

3. Scrape the mixture into another bowl and refrigerate it, covered, until completely chilled, 1½ to 2 hours.

4. Prepare a 5-cup soufflé dish: Tear off a length of wax paper to fit around the dish, adding an inch or two for overlap. Fold the wax paper lengthwise into thirds. Wrap it around the outside of the dish so it extends about 2 inches above the rim, making sure that it overlaps at the ends by at least 1 inch. Secure it with string or paper clips.

5. Beat the heavy cream in a bowl with an electric mixer. When it starts to thicken (after about 1 minute), add the 2 teaspoons sugar. Continue beating until it forms soft peaks. Fold this gently into the chilled lime mixture.

6. Beat the egg whites in a separate bowl with clean beaters. As they start to mound, add the remaining ¼ cup sugar, beating constantly. Continue beating until the eggs whites are stiff but not dry. Using a rubber spatula, fold them gently into the soufflé mixture.

7. Pour the mixture into the prepared soufflé dish and carefully place it in the freezer. Freeze overnight.

8. Carefully remove the wax paper. Decorate the top of the soufflé with candied roses, and serve with Sweetened Whipped Cream alongside.

Notes: This recipe uses raw egg whites, so buy only the best-quality farm-fresh eggs that have been kept refrigerated for its preparation.

Candied rose petals are available in specialty stores and by mail order (see Sources, page 405).

CHOCOLATE TRUFFLES

There is only one thing in the world that looks as deep, dark, and sinful, and smells as sexy (according to scientists), as the truffle that grows on the roots of oak trees, and that is the dense, deep, dark, odorous, intense Chocolate Truffle. Gild the lily by serving them in decorative candy cups, which come in floral designs as well as gold.

¼ cup heavy (whipping) cream
2 tablespoons Grand Marnier or other liqueur (see Note)
6 ounces best-quality semisweet chocolate, in pieces
4 tablespoons (½ stick) unsalted butter, at room temperature
½ cup unsweetened cocoa powder, or more if necessary

1. Pour the cream into a small heavy saucepan and bring it to a boil over medium-high heat. Boil until reduced by half, about 4 minutes. Remove the pan from the heat, stir in the Grand Marnier and the chocolate, and return the pan to low heat. Stir until the chocolate melts, 3 to 4 minutes.

2. Remove the pan from the heat and whisk in the butter. When the mixture is smooth, transfer it to a shallow bowl and refrigerate until firm but moldable, about 40 minutes.

3. Spread the cocoa powder on a plate. Scoop the chocolate up with a small spoon and form it into 1-inch balls by rolling it between the palms of your hands. Roll the truffle balls in the cocoa, adding more if necessary. Place on a baking sheet, cover lightly with wax paper, and refrigerate. Remove from the refrigerator 20 minutes before serving.

MAKES ABOUT 24 TRUFFLES
Note: Variations include Chambord, crème de menthe, Kahlúa, cognac, and amaretto.

Celebrating

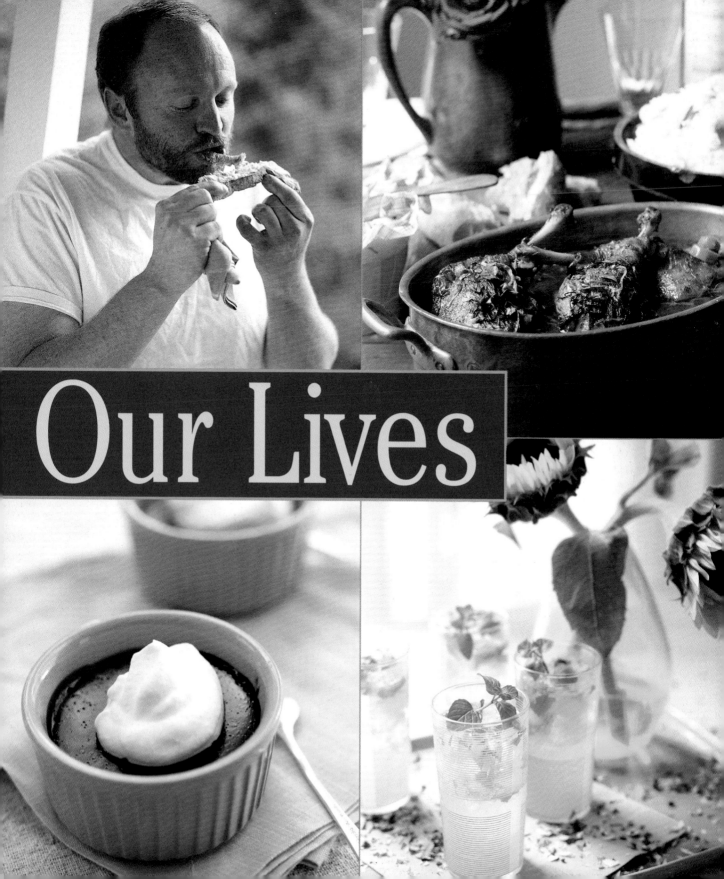

Our Lives

Congratulations

on a New Job

A new job represents a new beginning. It can mean good riddance to a grumpy boss, good-bye to the same old office gossip, and new places to get coffee or have lunch. It often means a bigger paycheck, or at least the possibility of one. No matter what the job, it always calls for a celebration—who knows where it can lead, especially if you start it off with a wonderful meal, sort of a vocational housewarming.

> "*Laughter is brightest where food is best.*"
> —IRISH PROVERB

MENU

Congratulations on a New Job

DINNER FOR SIX

Roasted Carrot and Beet Soup

Cha-Cha Pork Chops

Garden Vegetable Stew

Crisp Fennel Salad

Key Lime Pie

Roasted Carrot and Beet Soup is rich in flavor and glistens with color—it's a soothing and festive way to begin the meal. Grilling the spicy pork chops gives the outside a nice crust—and impressive grill marks—while keeping the interior moist and juicy. The stew of squash and peppers picks up some of the spicy flavors in the pork, and the fennel salad—with radishes and arugula—adds a sweet-and-tangy accent. The luscious Key Lime Pie rounds out the meal and prepares you for a fine first day on the new job.

Keep this occasion special but informal. Lay the table with a cloth that will complement the upbeat mood of the meal—a vintage 1940s tablecloth with a flower print in soft greens, blues, and reds definitely says "happy meal happening here." With all that color, go with white cloth napkins. If you have Jadite dishes and Bakelite-handled flatware, this is the night to use them. Depression glass for the water and wine glasses works with the color scheme.

For the flowers, if it's spring, look to lilacs—from lavender to white and dark purple—arranged in a green glass pitcher. If it's autumn, arrange bouquets of pink, blue-green, or lavender hydrangeas. Since dinner is casual, dispense with the candles.

THE MUSIC

Dr. John's *The Very Best of Dr. John*
The Pointer Sisters' *Greatest Hits*
The Beatles' *White Album*

THE WINE

Rosé Champagne
Oregon Pinot Noir
Washington State Riesling

THE EXTRAS

Barbecue grill and accessories

ROASTED CARROT AND BEET SOUP

The bold and brassy flavors of caramelized vegetables and the heady bouquet of aromatic spices combine during roasting to create a soup that is both calming and assertive. These are two qualities that will serve you well in your new job, provided you keep them in the right balance. A tiny dollop of crème fraîche would suggest perfection.

5 large carrots, peeled and cut in half
2 ribs celery, with leaves, cut in half
1 large onion, sliced
4 tablespoons (¹/₂ stick) unsalted butter
2 tablespoons light brown sugar
³/₄ teaspoon ground ginger
³/₄ teaspoon ground mace
6 to 7 cups Basic Chicken Broth (page 397)
¹/₃ cup diced Roasted Beets (page 399)
Crème fraîche, for garnish
Snipped fresh chives, for garnish

1. Preheat the oven to 350°F.

2. Place the carrots, celery, and onion in a shallow baking pan. Dot with the butter and sprinkle with the brown sugar, ginger, and mace. Pour 2 cups of the broth into the bottom of the dish. Cover tightly with aluminum foil and bake until the vegetables are meltingly soft and the broth is absorbed, 2 hours.

3. Remove the dish from the oven and transfer the vegetables, along with any liquid in the dish, to a large heavy pot. Add 4 cups of the remaining broth and bring to a boil over high heat. Cover partially, reduce the heat to medium, and simmer for 10 minutes to blend the flavors. Allow to cool slightly.

4. Puree the soup, along with the beets, in batches, in a blender or food processor until smooth. Return the soup to the pot and season with salt and pepper. Heat over medium-low heat until heated through, adding the remaining 1 cup broth for a thinner soup, if desired. Serve in pretty bowls with a dollop of crème fraîche and a sprinkling of chives.

CHA-CHA PORK CHOPS

Infused with citrus, garlic, and aromatic spices, these succulent, meaty pork chops perfume the air as they cook. Why "cha-cha"? Just taste and see.

³/₄ cup fresh orange juice
¹/₂ cup extra-virgin olive oil
1¹/₂ tablespoons finely minced garlic
1 tablespoon ground cumin
³/₄ teaspoon ground cinnamon
Coarse (kosher) salt and freshly ground
  black pepper, to taste
6 center-cut pork chops (about 12 ounces
  each), bones frenched (see box, page 72)
Mango and Mint Salsa (page 291)

1. Combine the orange juice, olive oil, garlic, cumin, cinnamon, and salt and pepper in a large

"Soup puts the heart at ease, calms down the violence of hunger, eliminates the tension of the day, and awakens and refines the appetite."

—*AUGUSTE ESCOFFIER*

bowl. Add the pork chops and coat them well in the marinade. Set aside, covered, for 2 to 4 hours in the refrigerator, turning them once or twice.

2. Heat a barbecue grill to high, or preheat a broiler.

3. Grill the chops, 3 inches from the heat source, over (or under) high heat until cooked through, about 6 minutes per side. Do not overcook them. Serve immediately, with the salsa on the side.

GARDEN VEGETABLE STEW

It says right on the dollar bill (and dollars are an important element of the new job experience) *E pluribus unum*—"out of many, one." That is certainly true of any vegetable mélange, whether it's a Provençal ratatouille or this combination of squashes, bell peppers, and aromatic seasonings. Picking up some of the flavors in the pork chop marinade, it adds to the meal the sublime texture of stewed garden vegetables.

> 3 tablespoons extra-virgin olive oil
> 6 cups diced butternut squash ($1/2$-inch dice, from about a 2-pound squash)
> $1^1/2$ red bell peppers, stemmed, seeded, and cut into $1/4$-inch dice
> $1^1/2$ yellow bell peppers, stemmed, seeded, and cut into $1/4$-inch dice
> $1^1/2$ cups diced onions ($1/4$-inch dice)
> 3 tablespoons finely minced garlic
> $2^1/4$ cups Vegetable Broth (page 398) or Basic Chicken Broth (page 397)
> $2^1/2$ cups diced zucchini ($1/2$-inch dice)
> $1^1/2$ teaspoons sugar
> $1^1/2$ teaspoons salt
> $3/4$ teaspoon ground cumin
> $1/4$ teaspoon ground cinnamon
> $1/4$ teaspoon freshly ground black pepper
> 3 tablespoons chopped fresh flat-leaf parsley

1. Heat the olive oil in a large heavy pot over medium-low heat. Add the squash, bell peppers, onions, and garlic. Cook, stirring occasionally, until the vegetables begin to soften, about 15 minutes.

2. Add all the remaining ingredients except the parsley. Reduce the heat to low and cook, covered, stirring occasionally, until the vegetables are soft but still hold their shape, 20 minutes (see Note). Stir in the parsley and serve.

Note: The stew can be made as long as a day ahead to this point. Store, covered, in the refrigerator, and reheat over medium-low heat.

CRISP FENNEL SALAD

Aromatic fennel and orange have a great affinity for each other, and the licorice flavor of the fennel and the peppery bite of arugula make an interesting partnership too.

> 2 tablespoons fresh orange juice
> 1 teaspoon red wine vinegar
> 1 tablespoon honey
> 1 tablespoon Dijon mustard
> $1/4$ cup extra-virgin olive oil
> Salt and freshly ground black pepper, to taste
> 2 cloves garlic, crushed
> 2 fennel bulbs, trimmed, fronds chopped and reserved
> 4 large red radishes
> 8 fresh basil leaves, finely slivered
> 2 large bunches arugula (12 ounces total), rinsed and dried

1. Whisk the orange juice, vinegar, honey, and mustard together in a small bowl until smooth. Whisking constantly, drizzle in the olive oil. Continue whisking until the dressing is slightly thickened. Season with salt and pepper, add the

Key Lime Pie

KEY LIME PIE

K ey lime pie is a true American dessert. Although tiny key limes are found mostly in South Florida and in California (they are also known as Mexican limes), key lime juice is conveniently sold in bottles and should be available in your supermarket. Use it to make this easy, tart-sweet pie; it tastes luscious as is, but a dollop of Sweetened Whipped Cream (page 403) alongside would not be out of place. After all, you are celebrating a new job!

> *³⁄₄ cup graham cracker crumbs*
> *(9 to 10 graham crackers)*
> *¹⁄₄ cup finely chopped blanched almonds*
> *4 tablespoons (¹⁄₂ stick) unsalted butter,*
> *at room temperature*
> *3 tablespoons sugar*
> *³⁄₄ teaspoon ground cinnamon*
> *2 cans (14 ounces each) sweetened*
> *condensed milk*
> *1 cup fresh or bottled key lime juice*
> *5 egg yolks*
> *1 tablespoon grated lime zest*
> *³⁄₄ teaspoon grated fresh ginger*

1. Preheat the oven to 350°F.

2. Prepare the crust: Combine the graham cracker crumbs, almonds, butter, sugar, and cinnamon in a mixing bowl, tossing the ingredients with a fork until the mixture holds together. Press the mixture evenly into the bottom and sides of a 9-inch pie plate. Bake until the crust is golden, about 8 minutes. Set the crust on a wire rack to cool for about 15 minutes. Keep the oven on.

3. Meanwhile, prepare the filling: Whisk the condensed milk, lime juice, egg yolks, lime zest, and ginger together in a bowl until blended. Pour the filling into the cooled crust. Bake until the filling is just set in the center, about 20 minutes. Cool the pie slightly on a wire rack, then refrigerate for at least 4 hours or as long as overnight before serving.

garlic cloves, and let rest at room temperature for at least 1 hour.

2. Cut the fennel bulbs in half lengthwise and remove the cores and any tough outer pieces. Cut the fennel into julienne strips. Place in a large bowl. Trim and discard the ends from the radishes and thinly slice. Toss the radish slices with the fennel in the bowl.

3. Remove the garlic cloves from the dressing, whisk again, and pour the dressing over the fennel and radishes. (You can dress the salad up to 2 hours before serving.)

4. Shortly before serving, toss the fennel fronds and the basil with the salad.

5. Divide the arugula among six salad plates, top with the fennel salad, and serve immediately.

Saturday Night

with Friends

For many of us, Saturday is a day off followed by another day off. Even if you do have to take the kids to Little League and dance class, get a haircut, do the laundry, mow the lawn, there is no boss and no job and no school to deal with. It is great to plan a Saturday-night dinner party weeks in advance, but sometimes spontaneity is the best of all. It's especially nice when a friend calls and you make a last-minute date to get together. If there are two or three couples pitching in, this menu comes together in a hurry. The only question left is: Your place or theirs?

MENU

A meal featuring elegant ingredients shows care. Sea scallops make a delicious appetizer, with the chile sauce and crème fraîche. Thick loin lamb chops infused with Asian seasonings say, "special entree," especially when accompanied by pineapple-tinged rice and spicy broccolini. The orange salad is a refreshing note, and the lemon sorbet is a nice, light finisher. Next thing you know, your friends will be inviting *you* over.

Make this a relaxing and congenial evening. The menu has Asian overtones, but it's not too esoteric. Keep things comfortable but not simply thrown together. Everyday dishes and flatware are fine. Use place mats and cloth napkins, and definitely bring out the wineglasses and a nice bottle (or two) of wine. Because there are only six at this dinner, arrange the sea scallops in the kitchen and have the plates on the table when you call your guests in.

For the table, create an artistic arrangement of flowers, such as a casual assortment of yellow, red, and orange ranunculus. For an Asian-influenced arrangement, use a ceramic crock. Then light the candles and you're set to go.

Saturday Night with Friends

DINNER FOR SIX

Sea Scallops à la Sweet Chile Sauce

———

Grilled Lamb Chops with Asian Flavors

———

Pineapple Rice

———

Spiced Broccolini with New Asian Vinaigrette

———

Minty Orange Salad

———

Party Lemon Sorbet

THE MUSIC

Sade
Sarah Vaughan

THE DRINKS

Alsace Gewürztraminer
Rioja Gran Reserva
India Pale Ale

THE EXTRAS

Barbecue grill and accessories
Ice-cream maker

SEA SCALLOPS A LA SWEET CHILE SAUCE

Sea scallops have gained hugely in popularity over the past few years due to the delicacy with which they have been prepared by many fine chefs, and to their availability—harvested year-round in the North Atlantic, they can always be bought fresh. The rich flavor and meaty consistency of sea scallops make them an ideal canvas for this fruity, piquant, Asian-inspired sauce, as well as more robust Italian sauces.

12 large sea scallops
3 tablespoons fresh lime juice
4½ tablespoons extra-virgin olive oil, or more as needed
Salt and freshly ground black pepper, to taste
¾ cup Sweet Chile Sauce (page 47)
6 tablespoons crème fraîche
Fresh cilantro sprigs, for garnish
Fresh nasturtium blossoms, for garnish (optional)

1. Place the scallops in a bowl. Toss with the lime juice and 1½ tablespoons of the olive oil. Season with salt and pepper and set aside to marinate for 15 to 20 minutes.

2. Drain the scallops and pat them dry. Heat the remaining 3 tablespoons olive oil in a non-stick skillet over medium-high heat and sear the scallops in small batches until just barely cooked through, 2 minutes per side (4 minutes total), adding more oil if necessary.

3. Place 2 scallops in the center of each of six plates. Drizzle 2 tablespoons of the Sweet Chile Sauce around each serving. Dollop each portion with 1 tablespoon crème fraîche and sprinkle with cilantro. Place a nasturtium blossom, if using, decoratively alongside and serve immediately.

Sea Scallops à la Sweet Chile Sauce

GRILLED LAMB CHOPS WITH ASIAN FLAVORS

I'll be honest with you: I have no idea if they make lamb chops like these anywhere in Asia. However, lamb has such complex flavors and silky texture that it is a perfect carrier of contrasting strong tastes. So the garlic, ginger, sesame oil, and chiles that work so well with other assertive Asian ingredients couldn't miss with a tender grilled lamb chop.

> "*Rice is a beautiful food.*
> *It is beautiful when it grows,*
> *precision rows of sparkling green stalk*
> *shooting up to reach the hot summer sun.*
> *It is beautiful when harvested,*
> *autumn gold sheaves piled on diked,*
> *patchwork paddies. It is beautiful when,*
> *once threshed, it enters granary bins*
> *like a (flood) of tiny seed-pearls.*
> *It is beautiful when cooked by a practiced*
> *hand, pure white and sweetly fragrant.*"
> **—SHIZUO TSUJI**

3 small fresh red serrano chiles, finely minced
3 tablespoons minced garlic
1 piece (3 inches) fresh ginger,
   finely minced
1/2 cup Asian sesame oil
1/4 cup corn oil
3/4 cup chopped fresh cilantro
Salt and freshly ground black pepper,
   to taste
12 loin lamb chops, cut 1 1/2 inches thick

1. Combine all the ingredients except the lamb chops in a large bowl or other container. Add the lamb chops and turn to coat them well with the marinade.

2. Refrigerate, covered, for 8 hours or overnight, turning the chops once or twice.

3. Heat a barbecue grill to high, or preheat the broiler.

4. Remove the chops from the marinade and carefully scrape the excess marinade off them. Grill the chops over (or under) high heat, 3 inches from the heat source, for 4 to 5 minutes per side for medium-rare. Serve immediately.

PINEAPPLE RICE

Fried rice, with chicken, pork, or vegetables, is still a favorite of Chinese take-out food fans. This is a fruity, lighter version: steamed rice all dressed up with pineapple and a delicate flurry of vegetables and smoky ham.

1 tablespoon extra-virgin olive oil
1 teaspoon salt
2 cups long-grain rice
8 ounces (in 1 piece) Virginia or
   Black Forest ham
1 can (20 ounces) crushed pineapple,
   drained, juices reserved
3 scallions, including 3 inches green,
   thinly sliced on the diagonal
1 carrot, peeled and cut into tiny dice
2 tablespoons soy sauce
1/2 cup frozen peas, thawed
2 tablespoons snipped fresh chives
Salt and freshly ground black pepper,
   to taste

1. Combine 4 cups water with the olive oil and salt in a saucepan and bring to a boil over high heat. Add the rice, stir, reduce the heat to medium, and cover the pan. Cook until all the liquid has been absorbed, 20 minutes.

2. Meanwhile, cut the ham into 1/4-inch dice.

3. Fluff the rice with a fork. Add the pineapple and toss to combine. Then add the ham, scallions, carrot, soy sauce, and 2 tablespoons of the reserved pineapple juice and transfer it to a serving bowl.

4. Shortly before serving, add the peas and the chives and season with salt and pepper. Serve immediately.

Note: If you make the rice ahead and want to reheat it, do not add the peas and chives. Place the rice in a microwave-safe container, cover with a paper towel, and reheat on high power for 3 to 4 minutes. Then stir in the peas and chives, taste for seasoning, and serve.

SPICED BROCCOLINI

Broccolini—a cross between Chinese broccoli (*gai lan*) and our broccoli—has been showing up more and more in American markets. A drizzle of New Asian Vinaigrette complements the bitterness of the green, whose taste and crunch help to punctuate the big bold flavors in this menu.

> 3 tablespoons vegetable oil
> 1/4 cup Asian sesame oil
> 2 1/4 pounds broccolini, 1 inch trimmed off
>   stems on the diagonal
> 1/2 cup Basic Chicken Broth (page 397)
>   or Vegetable Broth (page 398)
> 6 tablespoons New Asian Vinaigrette
>   (recipe follows)
> 4 scallions, including 3 inches green,
>   thinly sliced on the diagonal,
>   for garnish

1. Heat the vegetable and sesame oils in a nonstick skillet over medium heat. Add the broccolini and sauté, in two batches, turning it with tongs and shaking the skillet, for 8 minutes per batch. As each batch is done, transfer it to a plate and set aside.

2. Return all the broccolini to the skillet, add the broth, cover, and bring to a boil. Reduce the heat to low and simmer, occasionally shaking the skillet to lightly toss, for 5 minutes. Drain off the broth and gently toss the broccolini with the New Asian Vinaigrette. Transfer it to a decorative bowl, sprinkle it with the scallions, and serve immediately.

Note: You can cook the broccolini in the broth, drain it, reserving 3 tablespoons liquid, and set it aside in the covered skillet for up to 2 hours. Then gently reheat the broccolini in the reserved liquid before tossing it with the vinaigrette.

NEW ASIAN VINAIGRETTE

Some vegetables call for the ideal blending of sesame oil and the slight salty bite of light soy sauce along with the delicate sweetness of rice vinegar. Broccolini marries well with this dressing, as does asparagus or a mixture of tart and mild garden greens. Just stay with a delicate olive oil, to avoid overpowering the sesame and soy flavors.

> 1/4 cup light soy sauce
> Juice of 1/2 lemon
> 2 tablespoons honey
> 1/3 cup corn oil
> 1/3 cup olive oil
> 3 tablespoons Asian sesame oil
> 1/4 teaspoon finely minced garlic
> Salt and freshly ground black pepper,
>   to taste

Whisk the soy sauce, lemon juice, and honey together in a small bowl. Whisking constantly, drizzle in the corn oil, olive oil, and finally the sesame oil. Continue whisking until the dressing is slightly thickened. Stir in the garlic and season with salt and pepper. Store in a covered container in the refrigerator for as long as 8 hours. Before using, bring the vinaigrette to room temperature, strain out the garlic, and rewhisk as necessary.

MAKES A SCANT 1 CUP

> *"It isn't so much what's on the table that matters, as what's on the chairs."*
> —*W. S. GILBERT*

Party Lemon Sorbet

MINTY ORANGE SALAD

Serving citrus-based salads to refresh the palate is a right-headed culinary idea that works with food from Sicily to Szechuan. This variation can be served comfortably at two places during dinner: as a side dish along with the rice and broccolini, or as a dessert along with the Party Lemon Sorbet.

> *9 large navel oranges*
> *6 tablespoons fresh orange juice*
> *2 tablespoons sugar*
> *1/3 cup small whole fresh mint leaves*

1. Using a sharp knife, carefully remove the peel and all the white pith from the oranges. (It's easiest to begin by cutting a slice off the top and bottom of the fruit.)

2. Thinly slice the oranges crosswise. Remove any pits. Place the orange slices in a bowl.

3. Combine the orange juice and sugar and pour it over the oranges. Be sure all the slices are covered.

4. Toss the oranges with the mint leaves. Chill for 1 to 4 hours before serving.

PARTY LEMON SORBET

An ultra-light dessert, puckeringly tangy with sweet floral fruitiness. You could finish off your meal with this simple sorbet and feel that you've made a deal with your waistline. Or, what the heck—it's Saturday night, after all. Pass a plateful of Molasses Cookies (page 23), Chocolate Chunk Brownies (page 25), or whatever else strikes your fancy and your sweet tooth. (By the way, if you're not in the mood to bake, store-bought tuiles partner up nicely.)

> *2 tablespoons finely grated*
> *lemon zest*
> *1 1/2 cups fresh lemon juice*
> *(from 6 to 8 lemons)*
> *3 cups Simple Syrup (page 403)*

Combine all the ingredients in a bowl and stir well. Transfer the mixture to an ice-cream maker and freeze according to the manufacturer's instructions. Place the sorbet in a covered container and freeze.

MAKES 5 CUPS

Plump Chicken

for Two

Is there any restaurant that would dare not have a roast chicken entree as part of its menu? As one of the country's most beloved dishes—the nutty, rich flavor of the dark meat, the juiciness of the white, the perfect crispness of the skin, set off with a generous sprinkling of coarse sea salt and freshly ground black pepper—nothing is more delicious or more elegantly simple. A roast chicken, well made, is the measure of a good chef. And definitely worthy of a celebration.

When Herbert Hoover ran for president in 1928, he coined the famous phrase "A chicken in every pot and a car in every garage." Actually, he almost coined it. The car and garage part were his, but back in the sixteenth century Henri of Navarre, who became Henri IV of France, said, "I want there to be no peasant so poor in my realm that he cannot have a chicken in his pot every Sunday."

MENU

Plump Chicken for Two

MUSSELS STEAMED IN WINE

A PLUMP ROAST CHICKEN

CANDIED BUTTERNUT MASH

PARSLEY SALAD
WITH MUSTARD VINAIGRETTE

LAURIE'S LEMON LOAF SUNDAE

NEXT-DAY CREAMY
CHICKEN POTPIE

A roast chicken may be the queen of the evening, but like all royalty, a strong "court" really points up just what a standout it is. A heaping bowl of succulent mussels starts the meal off. Steamed in a luscious broth, they are deliciously drippy, so to enjoy them without concern, be sure you have plenty of napkins on hand and provide bowls for the empty shells. The roast chicken, fragrant with rosemary and garlic, is the splendid centerpiece, accompanied by two unusual and enjoyable side dishes: Candied Butternut Mash and pungent Parsley Salad. Laurie's Lemon Loaf Sundae is the evening's final tribute to the beautiful bird.

As a bonus, I've also included a recipe for a favorite homey pot pie that includes already-cooked chicken. Not that I expect you to have leftovers, but in case you do, this potpie extends the celebration to yet another meal.

Set the table bistro-style—big red-and-white-checked napkins and tablecloth, large hotel-style plates, everyday glasses—maybe even small tumblers for the wine—and silverware with Bakelite handles, if you own any. A milk glass vase full of daisies would be just right for the occasion.

THE MUSIC

Ry Cooder's
Buena Vista Social Club
The Best of the Gipsy Kings

THE WINE

Australian Chardonnay
New Zealand Pinot Noir

THE EXTRAS

Small poultry roaster
Ice-cream maker

MUSSELS STEAMED IN WINE

A big bowlful of fresh mussels steamed in a pungent wine broth is a fragrant, light, yet satisfying lead-in to the beautiful roast chicken that follows. Serve the mussels with slices of toasted crusty bread rubbed with a cut garlic clove and a little olive oil for sopping up some of the broth, but don't overdo it. There's plenty of good food on this menu and you want to be sure to leave room. You don't really need special forks for this dish—just use the top shell as a spoon to detach the mussel and savor it.

1 tablespoon distilled white vinegar
1 small leek
2 pounds mussels
1 tablespoon unsalted butter
1 tablespoon extra-virgin olive oil
¼ cup diced celery (¼ inch)
¼ cup chopped onion
¼ cup chopped fresh flat-leaf parsley,
*   plus 1 tablespoon for garnish*
2 teaspoons finely minced garlic
Salt and freshly ground black pepper, to taste
1 cup dry white wine

1. Trim the roots and tough outer leaves off the leeks and discard them. Trim the remaining leaves to about 3 inches. Cut the leek in half lengthwise. Stir the vinegar into a bowl of water, add the leek, and soak for 30 minutes. Then rinse and drain.

2. Scrub the mussels well and rinse them in several changes of cold water to remove any sand. If they have beards, pull them off as described in the box on this page just before cooking.

3. Melt the butter in the oil in a large heavy pot over medium-low heat. Add the leek, celery, and onion and cook, stirring, until the vegetables are softened, 5 minutes. Add the ¼ cup parsley and the garlic and cook, stirring, for 3 minutes more. Season with salt and pepper.

Most mussels available today are farm-raised and require much less cleaning than those collected in the wild. But it is still a good idea to scrub the mussel shells under running water, using a stiff brush if they are very dirty or encrusted with barnacles. Remove the "beard," the clump of fibers also known as byssal threads that are attached to the mussel meat and stick out of the shell, by grasping the fibers with a dry paper towel or tweezers and giving a sharp yank. Remove the beards right before cooking the mussels.

4. Add the mussels, wine, and ½ cup water to the pot and raise the heat to high. Cover and cook, shaking the pan occasionally, until the mussels have opened, 6 to 8 minutes.

5. Divide the mussels between two shallow bowls, discarding any that haven't opened. Spoon plenty of broth over each serving, sprinkle with black pepper and the remaining tablespoon of chopped parsley, and serve.

A PLUMP ROAST CHICKEN

It is a known fact that grandmothers make the best roast chicken. They know—without measuring—how much seasoning is just right; they know how to test the oven for the spot-on degree of roasting hotness; they know just how to time the chicken so that the dark meat is cooked to a succulent turn and the white meat is juicy, not dry. And as for the skin, grandmas present it cracklingly crisp, irresistible to even the most conscientious dieter. This recipe is the one to serve your grandmother. She will be so proud!

CELEBRATE! PLUMP CHICKEN FOR TWO

1 chicken (about 3¹/₂ pounds)
4 sprigs fresh rosemary
4 small cloves garlic, lightly crushed
Salt and freshly ground black pepper,
  to taste
1 cup Basic Chicken Broth (page 397)
2 tablespoons fresh lemon juice
2 tablespoons unsalted butter

1. Rinse the chicken, inside and out, and pat it dry. Remove and discard any excess fat. Carefully slide your fingers between the skin and the meat on the breast and thighs and tuck in the rosemary sprigs and the garlic. Season the chicken well with salt and pepper inside the neck and body cavities and all over the skin. Tie the ends of the chicken legs together with kitchen string and place the chicken, breast side up, in a shallow flameproof roasting pan. Cover it loosely with aluminum foil and refrigerate overnight.

2. Remove the chicken from the refrigerator, uncover it, and let it sit for 1 hour to come to room temperature. Meanwhile, preheat the oven to 450°F.

3. Roast the chicken until a leg moves easily in its socket and the juices run clear when a thigh is pricked with a small knife, 45 to 50 minutes.

4. Remove the chicken from the pan and let it rest in a warm place for 10 minutes.

5. Meanwhile, remove and discard the excess fat from the pan and add the broth and lemon juice to the juices remaining in the pan. Place over medium-high heat and boil, scraping up any brown bits on the bottom, until the juices are reduced, about 2 minutes. Swirl in the butter, adjust the seasonings, if necessary, and strain the sauce into a small saucepan. Keep warm.

6. Remove the kitchen string and the rosemary sprigs and garlic from the chicken. Cut the chicken into serving pieces and place on a pretty platter. Pour the juices into a gravy boat for spooning over each serving, and serve.

CANDIED BUTTERNUT MASH

Mashed potatoes may be traditional with roast chicken, but just wait until you try this squash. A sweet butternut, baked and blended with a little brown sugar and lemon, makes a terrific change of pace. Prepare it in advance (see Note) so there are no oven conflicts with the chicken.

1 butternut squash (about 1 pound),
  cut in half lengthwise, seeds removed
3 tablespoons dark brown sugar
2 tablespoons unsalted butter
3 tablespoons Basic Chicken Broth (page 397)
  or Vegetable Broth (page 398)
2 teaspoons finely grated lemon zest
2 teaspoons fresh lemon juice
³/₄ teaspoon ground ginger
Salt, to taste

1. Preheat the oven to 350°F.

2. Place the squash, skin side down, in a shallow baking pan just large enough to hold it. Divide the brown sugar and butter evenly between the squash cavities. Pour the broth into the bottom of the pan, cover it tightly with aluminum foil, and bake until the squash is very tender, about 1 hour.

3. Remove the foil from the pan, and when cool enough to handle, carefully scrape the squash from the skin into a bowl, making sure to get all the candied sugar and butter.

4. Add the lemon zest, lemon juice, ginger, and salt and combine with the squash using a potato masher or fork. (You can also use a food processor.) Adjust the seasoning and serve.

Note: The squash can be prepared up to 4 hours in advance. Reheat, covered, in a 350°F oven until heated through, 15 to 20 minutes.

PARSLEY SALAD WITH MUSTARD VINAIGRETTE

What an unexpected salad this is. Parsley, so long relegated to garnish status, takes on a starring role—and handles it beautifully. Assisted by cornichons, capers, and slices of radish, it's quite a pungent plateful. Serve the salad after the chicken and squash. It need only be accompanied by thick slices of toasted crusty bread and a crock of unsalted butter.

FOR THE VINAIGRETTE
1 teaspoon Dijon mustard
2 teaspoons red wine vinegar
Salt and freshly ground black pepper,
  to taste
2 tablespoons extra-virgin olive oil

FOR THE SALAD
2 cups fresh flat-leaf parsley leaves,
  all stems removed
2 large radishes, trimmed and
  very thinly sliced lengthwise
2 large cornichons, thinly sliced on
  the diagonal
1 shallot, peeled and very thinly
  sliced
1 tablespoon drained tiny capers

1. Prepare the vinaigrette: Whisk the mustard, vinegar, and salt and pepper together in a small bowl. Continue whisking and slowly drizzle in the olive oil; whisk until the vinaigrette is well combined and thick. Set it aside.

2. Rinse the parsley leaves and pat dry. Place them and all the remaining salad ingredients in a decorative bowl. Just before serving, toss with the vinaigrette and serve immediately.

LAURIE'S LEMON LOAF SUNDAE

Laurie, my associate, originally created her wonderful Sweet Lemon Loaf to serve with morning or afternoon tea, but when dressed up with a scoop of Winter Lemon Ice Cream and a drizzle of chocolate sauce, you couldn't ask for a tastier dessert on a menu honoring the noble roast chicken.

2 slices (1 inch thick) Laurie's Sweet Lemon
  Loaf (recipe follows)
2 scoops Laurie's Winter Lemon Ice Cream
  (recipe follows)
1/4 cup Silky Chocolate Sauce (page 42)
Sweetened Whipped Cream (page 403)

Place a slice of the lemon loaf on each of two dessert plates. Top each with a scoop of ice cream, 2 tablespoons of the chocolate sauce, and a dollop of whipped cream.

LAURIE'S WINTER LEMON ICE CREAM

Laurie created this recipe several years ago for my *USA Cookbook*. It's been a favorite ever since and is delicious on its own or scooped onto a favorite loaf cake or sweet bread.

3 lemons, well scrubbed
1 cup Simple Syrup (page 403)
3 cups heavy (whipping) cream
1 cup milk
1/2 cup sugar
4 large egg yolks

1. Remove the zest from 2 of the lemons in long strips, using a sharp paring knife. Place the strips in a small saucepan with the Simple Syrup and bring to a boil over high heat. Cook for 5 minutes, then remove the pan from the heat. Remove the zest from the syrup with a slotted spoon and set it aside. Cool the syrup to room temperature.

2. Meanwhile, remove the zest from the remaining lemon and finely chop it. Set it aside. Squeeze the lemons to obtain ½ cup of juice and set it aside.

3. Combine the cream, milk, and sugar in a heavy saucepan. Cook over medium heat, stirring frequently, until the milk is hot but not boiling, and the sugar is dissolved, about 10 minutes. Remove the pan from the heat.

4. Place the egg yolks in a small bowl and whisk to mix. Whisking constantly, slowly pour 1 cup of the hot milk mixture into the eggs and continue whisking until smooth.

5. Slowly pour the egg mixture into the hot mixture in the saucepan, whisking constantly until well combined. Place the saucepan over medium heat and stir the mixture constantly until it is thick enough to coat the back of a spoon, 6 to 8 minutes. The mixture should never boil.

6. Strain the mixture into a bowl and cool to room temperature.

7. Stir in the cooled syrup, the lemon juice, and chopped lemon zest. Freeze the mixture in an ice-cream maker according to the manufacturer's instructions. Just before the mixture has finished freezing, with the motor off, add the reserved lemon zest strips, then turn on the motor again briefly to combine.

MAKES ABOUT 1½ QUARTS

LAURIE'S SWEET LEMON LOAF

Cut in thick slices, this easy-to-make moist lemon sweet bread is delicious when freshly baked, but it also freezes well and can be served at any meal, including breakfast. Here it helps make an elegant sundae.

FOR THE LOAF
1½ cups all-purpose flour
1½ teaspoons baking powder
½ teaspoon baking soda
½ teaspoon salt
8 tablespoons (1 stick) unsalted butter, at room temperature
1 cup granulated sugar
2 large eggs
½ cup sour cream
1 teaspoon pure vanilla extract
2 tablespoons finely grated lemon zest
2 tablespoons fresh lemon juice

FOR THE GLAZE
1½ cups confectioners' sugar
2 tablespoons fresh lemon juice

1. Position a rack in the center of the oven, and preheat the oven to 350°F. Lightly butter and flour a 9 x 5 x 2¾-inch loaf pan.

2. Prepare the batter: Sift the flour, baking powder, baking soda, and salt together into a medium-size bowl.

3. Cream the butter and sugar together in a large bowl with an electric mixer until light and fluffy, about 5 minutes. Add the eggs, one at a time, beating well after each addition. Add the sour cream, vanilla, lemon zest, and lemon juice and mix well. Add the flour mixture and mix until just combined.

4. Scrape the batter into the prepared pan and bake until a wooden toothpick inserted in the center comes out clean, 55 to 60 minutes. Let the loaf cool in the pan on a wire rack for 10 minutes. Then a run a knife around the edges of the pan to loosen the bread, remove it from the pan, and place it on a wire rack.

5. While the bread is still warm, prepare the glaze: Place the confectioners' sugar and the lemon juice in a small saucepan and bring to a boil, stirring occasionally. Boil for 2 minutes, stirring, then remove from the heat. Use a skewer or a long pick to poke holes about 1 inch apart all over the surface of the warm bread. Brush the glaze all over the warm loaf, and then let it cool completely.

Note: If you plan to freeze the loaf, let it cool completely, wrap it tightly in plastic wrap, and freeze it unglazed. It will keep for 1 month. When you are ready to serve it, let it defrost fully in the refrigerator (it's not necessary to warm it). Then continue with step 5.

NEXT-DAY CREAMY CHICKEN POTPIE

Chicken potpie is one of the pillars of comfort food, and eating one often brings up nostalgic memories of childhood. The pleasure and anticipation you felt when you broke into the crust to release a tower of steam and a fountain of wonderful aromas will come flooding back with this updated version. Filled with hearty vegetables, savory herbs, and—of course—big pieces of chicken all bound together in a creamy sauce, it is worth roasting a chicken for, or keeping in mind when you have leftovers.

1 tablespoon unsalted butter
1 tablespoon olive oil
1 large onion, chopped
1 tablespoon finely minced garlic
2 tablespoons all-purpose flour
2 teaspoons dried tarragon
3 carrots, peeled, halved lengthwise, and cut into $1/2$-inch slices (1 cup)
2 parsnips, peeled and cut into $1/2$-inch pieces (1 cup)

1 fennel bulb, trimmed, cored, and cut into $1/2$-inch pieces
$2 1/2$ cups Basic Chicken Broth (page 397)
$1/2$ cup fresh or (thawed) frozen peas
1 ripe tomato, seeded and cut into $1/2$-inch dice
$1/4$ cup chopped fresh dill
$2 1/2$ cups diced cooked chicken ($1/2$-inch pieces)
Salt and freshly ground black pepper, to taste
1 sheet prepared puff pastry ($1/2$ pound), thawed if frozen
1 large egg, beaten with 1 tablespoon water

1. Melt the butter with the olive oil in a large heavy pot over low heat. Add the onion and cook, stirring occasionally, until softened, about 10 minutes. Add the garlic and cook to soften, 2 minutes. Sprinkle in the flour and tarragon and cook, stirring constantly, 1 to 2 minutes longer. The flour will have absorbed the butter and oil.

2. Add the carrots, parsnips, fennel, and broth. Raise the heat to high and bring to a boil. Then reduce the heat to medium-low and simmer, partially covered, until the vegetables are tender, about 20 minutes. Add the peas, tomato, dill, and chicken and cook 5 minutes more.

3. Preheat the oven to 350°F.

4. Spoon the mixture into a 2-quart round ovenproof casserole. On a lightly floured surface, roll the puff pastry out to form a circle 2 inches larger than the casserole. Brush the egg wash around the inside and outside rim of the casserole. Lay the pastry over the top, trim the overhang to 1 inch, and crimp the edges around the rim to seal. Cut several slits in the pastry to release the steam, and brush it with the remaining egg wash. Bake, on a baking sheet, until the crust is golden, 40 to 45 minutes. Serve immediately.

A Springtime

Bridal Shower

There is no one happier than the bride-to-be at her shower, with the possible exception of the mother of the bride-to-be. That day is filled with joy and possibility and love.

It used to be that brides came to a marriage with a full hope chest and the other makings of a proper dowry. In these high-tech days, the dowry has gone the way of the Model T and the typewriter. But the couple still needs to start a household and to catch up on that trousseau that young women used to keep in their hope chest. For that reason, and as an excuse for friends to get together to prepare for an important event, the shower is still one of the nicest ways to say "Good luck in your marriage," as gifts, gab, and good food make for a very special day.

MENU

A Springtime Bridal Shower

FOR SIXTEEN

Sweetheart Champagne Cocktail

Pink Lemonade

Sweet Pea and Fennel Soup

Orange-Mint Chicken Breasts *or*
Lustrous Lobster Salad

Primavera Salad with
Sherry Vinaigrette

Coconut Trousseau Cake

Greet your guests with a delicate pink Sweetheart Champagne Cocktail in a slender flute. For a nonalcoholic drink, offer Pink Lemonade. To dress it up, set a tiny wedge of watermelon on the rim and spear it with a little pink paper umbrella. The light green Sweet Pea and Fennel Soup is smooth, with an air of spring about it—the perfect lead-in for the Orange-Mint Chicken Breasts or, if you choose, the Lustrous Lobster Salad, studded with mango and tomato. The refreshing vegetable-laced green salad goes well with either entree. Wrap lots of pink and white tulle around the base of the coconut cake's stand for a diaphanous effect.

Think pink for the decorations. That doesn't mean everything has to be pink—yellow, mint green, lavender, and peach work well, too. Just stay away from navy, red, and black—nice colors but not for this occasion.

A sit-down luncheon makes for easy, comfortable conversation. This may mean renting an extra table or two. Rental companies carry white or clear glass plates, and soft pink tablecloths, too. Or use your own pretty, flowered pastel tablecloths with white napkins. In the center of the tables, set large bunches of springtime's lily of the valley, with their beautiful leaves intact.

Designate an area of the room for the presents, and while they are being opened, pass around a candy dish of pretty pink-coated mints, and everyone will be seeing hearts and flowers.

THE MUSIC

Soundtrack from *My Fair Lady*
Soundtrack from *The Fantasticks*
Henry Mancini

THE DRINKS

Sweetheart Champagne Cocktail
Pink lemonade
Pinot Bianco

THE EXTRAS

Champagne flutes
Pedestal cake stand
Espresso cups

SWEETHEART CHAMPAGNE COCKTAIL

The Chambord bottle, black raspberry liqueur in an orb surmounted by a gold cross, reminds me of the Crown Jewels, which is the least a bride-to-be deserves. Then rose water, the sweet essence of the flower and most suited for this day, and champagne, because if you are going to celebrate, it's always right.

1 cup Chambord or raspberry syrup
4 teaspoons rose water
4 bottles chilled champagne
Fresh raspberries, for garnish

Place 1 tablespoon of the Chambord and ¼ teaspoon of the rose water in each champagne flute. Just before serving, fill each flute with champagne and add 1 or 2 raspberries.

PINK LEMONADE

There is nothing more perfect at a shower than pink lemonade. It's the grenadine syrup, with its exotic color of pomegranates, that gives the lemonade just the right blush.

8 cups fresh lemon juice
(from about 32 lemons)
2 cups sugar
16 cups cold water
2 tablespoons grenadine syrup
Ice cubes

Strain the lemon juice into a large pitcher and stir in the sugar, water, and grenadine. Serve over ice in tall glasses.

SWEET PEA AND FENNEL SOUP

You probably have heard it a million times from chefs and food writers: Always use fresh ingredients. Proving that every rule was made to be broken, I recommend frozen peas for this silky smooth soup. They give it a consistently bright and sweet flavor, and they retain their excellent green color. And also, they allow you to make sweet pea soup any time of the year. The fennel plays on the peas' sweetness, reinforcing it in a soup that has the lightness of a puffy cloud in an April sky.

3 tablespoons unsalted butter
1 tablespoon olive oil
2 cups chopped onions
1 cup chopped fennel bulb
(fronds reserved for garnish)
8 cups Basic Chicken Broth (page 397) or
Vegetable Broth (page 398)
4 packages (10 ounces each) frozen peas,
defrosted
1 cup heavy (whipping) cream
Salt and freshly ground black pepper,
to taste
1 ripe tomato, seeded and cut into tiny dice,
for garnish
2 tablespoons chopped fennel fronds,
for garnish
Fresh pea shoots (optional), for garnish

1. Melt the butter in the olive oil in a heavy pot over low heat. Add the onions and fennel and cook, stirring occasionally, until softened, about 15 minutes.

2. Add the broth and peas. Raise the heat to medium-high, bring to a boil, then reduce the heat to a medium-low and simmer, partially covered, until the fennel is soft, 15 minutes.

3. Puree the soup, in batches, in a food processor or blender until completely smooth.

After you puree each batch, pour it through a strainer into a bowl to remove the skins of the peas. Using the back of a large spoon, mash the solids in the strainer to extract as much liquid as possible. Add the cream to the strained puree and season with salt and pepper.

4. If you are serving the soup cold, cover and chill it well in the refrigerator until serving time, at least 6 hours. If you are serving it hot, return the soup to the pot and heat it through, stirring, over low heat, but do not allow it to boil.

5. To serve, ladle the soup into demitasse cups and garnish each one with a small spoonful of diced tomatoes, a scattering of fennel fronds, and, if desired, a fresh pea shoot.

Sweet Pea and Fennel Soup

ORANGE-MINT CHICKEN BREASTS

A tall frosted glass of pink lemonade, and an excited bride-to-be surrounded by best friends and family. The order of the day is the lightest of chicken salads.

FOR THE DRESSING
1 cup prepared mayonnaise,
  such as Hellmann's
¼ cup finely grated orange zest
2 tablespoons fresh orange juice
1 tablespoon chopped fresh mint
Salt and freshly ground black pepper,
  to taste

FOR THE CHICKEN
12 cooked boneless, skinless chicken
  breast halves (see Note)
16 leaves Boston lettuce, rinsed and
  patted dry
¾ cup shelled pistachio nuts,
  preferably unsalted
¼ cup chopped fresh mint,
  for garnish
2 large bunches fresh mint, for garnish

1. Combine the dressing ingredients in a small bowl, mix well, and set it aside.

2. Holding a knife sideways, slice each chicken breast horizontally through its thickness into 3 thin slices, about ⅓ inch thick.

3. Line a platter with the lettuce leaves. Overlap 2 slices of chicken in each leaf (you'll have a few extra slices of chicken; use the neatest ones), and dollop with a teaspoon of the dressing. Sprinkle with a few pistachios and some chopped mint. Garnish the platter with the bunches of mint and serve.

Note: Although this dish will taste delicious if you use poached chicken breasts, it tastes even better if you take the time to bake the breasts.

Simply brush each breast with a little olive oil and sprinkle with salt and freshly ground black pepper to taste, then place them in one layer in a baking pan. Bake in a preheated 350°F oven until cooked through, about 40 minutes. Allow the breasts to cool completely, then refrigerate them for at least an hour before cutting. They are easier to cut into thin horizontal slices when chilled.

LUSTROUS LOBSTER SALAD

If the party budget has the room, serve this special salad. The sweet, buttery, almost nutty meat of the lobster matches up well with the red onions, tangy and fruity tangerine vinaigrette, and, because every bride needs a bouquet, a shower of sweet nasturtium blossoms.

4 pounds cooked lobster meat
  (from about eleven 1 1/2-pound lobsters;
  see page 152), cut into 3/4-inch pieces
4 ripe mangos, peeled, pitted, and cut into
  3/4-inch pieces (see box, page 291)
12 ripe plum tomatoes, seeded and cut into
  16 pieces each
3/4 cup finely diced red onion
2 tablespoons finely grated orange zest
2 cups coarsely torn fresh basil leaves
Salt and freshly ground black pepper,
  to taste
About 1/2 cup Tangerine Vinaigrette
  (page 227), or more to taste
Radicchio leaves, for serving
Nasturtium blossoms, for garnish
  (see Note)

1. Combine the lobster meat, mangos, tomatoes, onion, orange zest, and basil in a bowl. Just before serving, season with salt and pepper and toss lightly with the vinaigrette.

The origins of the bridal shower are lost in the mists of history. One legend has it that in Holland the beautiful daughter of wealthy parents had fallen in love with a man who didn't measure up to her family's hopes—a poor miller who had spent his life helping those less fortunate than himself. Rather than bless this marriage, which was one purely of love, her mother and father decided not to give their daughter any of her substantial dowry. But the couple was so much in love and so right for each other that friends and neighbors collected their own "dowry," all kinds of gifts with which they "showered" the young lovers.

2. Arrange each salad in the center of a radicchio leaf on a dinner plate and garnish with a nasturtium blossom.

Note: Buy only untreated edible flowers to use as garnish. They are available in gourmet and other specialty food markets and at some larger supermarkets.

PRIMAVERA SALAD

Today's salads feature a wide assortment of spectacular, readily available greens and vegetables. The combination in this one includes an attractive mix of the thinnest green beans and asparagus and slices of avocado. It's a sweep of green that involves minimal cooking for maximum taste.

"*A woman should never be seen
eating or drinking,
unless it be lobster salad and
Champagne….*"

—LORD BYRON

Lustrous Lobster Salad

As the shower gifts are being opened, it's fun to have the maid or matron of honor construct a ribbon bouquet for the bride-to-be to carry at her rehearsal dinner.

To make a bouquet, cover a round piece of cardboard with a pretty doily. Be sure to have on hand a sharp knife for poking holes through the cardboard and also some double-sided tape.

As each package is opened, the pretty bows and novelty items used to make the gift wrap special should be attached decoratively to the cardboard or box lid. The finished bouquet will make a wonderful bridal shower keepsake.

8 ounces haricots verts (very thin green beans), trimmed
8 ounces asparagus (about 20 spears), trimmed to 3 inches long
2 ripe avocados, preferably Hass
1/4 cup fresh lemon juice
8 cups torn tender radicchio leaves (1-inch pieces)
8 cups torn frisée lettuce leaves (1-inch pieces)
4 red radishes, very thinly sliced
Salt and freshly ground black pepper, to taste
2/3 cup Sherry Vinaigrette (recipe follows)

1. Bring a saucepan of lightly salted water to a boil over high heat. Add the haricots verts and cook until just tender, 1 minute. Using a skimmer, remove them from the pot to a colander. Run under cold water to stop the cooking. Drain, pat dry, cut them in half crosswise, and set them aside in a large bowl.

2. Add the asparagus spears to the boiling water and cook until just tender, 1 minute. Drain in the colander and repeat the cooling, draining, and drying process. Then cut the spears in half lengthwise and add them to the haricots verts in the bowl.

3. Cut the avocados in half and remove and discard the pits. Peel the avocados and place the halves, pitted side down, on a cutting board and cut them into coarse slices. Place the avocado slices in a small bowl, add the lemon juice, and toss gently.

4. Add the radicchio, frisée, radishes, and avocado slices to the large bowl and toss gently to combine. Right before serving, season the salad with salt and pepper, then toss it gently with the vinaigrette.

SHERRY VINAIGRETTE

Different foods define different time periods. Vinegar-wise, the nineties were defined by dark, sweet-tangy balsamic, but ever since the turn of the millennium, it's been tawny-colored sherry. Its luxurious flavor complements game birds, pork dishes, vegetables, and fish. Sherry vinegar blends well with Spain's extra-virgin olive oils.

6 tablespoons sherry vinegar
3 tablespoons honey
1 1/2 teaspoons Dijon mustard
Salt and freshly ground black pepper, to taste
3/4 cup extra-virgin olive oil

Whisk the vinegar, honey, mustard, and salt and pepper together in a small bowl. Whisking constantly, drizzle in the olive oil. Continue whisking until the dressing is slightly thickened. Store in a covered container in the refrigerator. Bring to room temperature before use, rewhisking as necessary.

MAKES A GENEROUS 1 CUP

COCONUT TROUSSEAU CAKE

A homemade layer cake is *the* definitive dessert, the one that diners leave room for and dieters cheat for. And this one makes a particularly special ending to a special meal, enveloping you in coconut from the first bite to the last finger lick. There is coconut extract in the batter and coconut milk in the buttercream between the layers, all of which guarantees a cake no one will pass up. Be sure to tuck a calligraphed copy of the recipe into the bride-to-be's shower gifts. Something this luscious is as important to that hope chest as a lovely piece of lingerie.

FOR THE CAKE

1 cup (2 sticks) unsalted butter,
   at room temperature
2 cups sugar
1 teaspoon coconut extract
2 large egg yolks
3 cups sifted cake flour
4 teaspoons baking powder
1 teaspoon salt
1 cup unsweetened coconut milk
4 large egg whites

FOR THE BUTTERCREAM

4 large egg yolks, at room temperature
   (see Note)
1 cup (2 sticks) unsalted butter,
   at room temperature
1¾ cups confectioners' sugar, sifted
Pinch of salt
6 tablespoons unsweetened
   coconut milk

FOR THE FROSTING

1 cup granulated sugar
4 large egg whites
½ teaspoon cream of tartar
1 tablespoon pure vanilla extract

1. Position a rack in the center of the oven, and preheat the oven to 350°F. Butter the bottom and sides of two 9-inch round cake pans. Line the bottoms with wax or parchment paper, and butter the paper. Dust the bottom and sides of the pans with flour, tapping out any excess.

2. Prepare the cake: Cream the butter and 1 cup of the sugar in a large bowl with an electric mixer on medium speed until it is light and fluffy, 3 to 4 minutes. Add the coconut extract. Then add the egg yolks, one at a time, beating well after each addition and scraping the bowl often.

3. Sift the cake flour, baking powder, and salt together into another bowl. Add one third of the flour mixture to the butter mixture, beating on low speed until it is incorporated. Add half of the coconut milk and beat until incorporated, scrap-

Coconut Trousseau Cake

ing down the sides of the bowl. Repeat with another third of the flour, followed by the remaining coconut milk. Add the remaining flour, scrape down the sides of the bowl, and beat on medium speed until well incorporated, 2 minutes.

4. In another bowl, with clean beaters, beat the egg whites on low speed until they are foamy, 1 minute. Add the remaining 1 cup sugar, increase the speed to high, and whip the whites until soft peaks form, 3 to 4 minutes more. Fold half of the whites gently into the cake batter, using a large rubber spatula. Then gently fold in the remaining whites until the batter is just combined.

5. Scrape the batter evenly into the prepared pans. Bake until a wooden toothpick inserted in the center of the layers comes out clean, 20 to 30 minutes. Let the layers cool in the pans on a wire rack for 10 minutes. Then remove the layers from the pans and place on the rack to cool completely, at least 2 hours. Carefully peel off the paper. Then split each layer in half horizontally with a serrated knife. Wrap the layers in plastic wrap and chill in the refrigerator for 2 hours or overnight.

6. Prepare the buttercream: Place the egg yolks and butter in a bowl and beat with an electric mixer on high speed until the mixture is pale yellow, 2 minutes. Add the confectioners' sugar and salt and beat on low speed until combined.

Increase the speed to high and beat until the mixture is creamy, 2 minutes more. Add the coconut milk and beat again until well combined and creamy, 1 minute. Refrigerate, covered, while you prepare the frosting.

7. Prepare the frosting: Place the sugar, the egg whites, ¼ cup water, and cream of tartar in the top of a double boiler over simmering water. (If you don't have a double boiler, set a mixing bowl over a pan of simmering water; do not let the bowl touch the water.) Beat with an electric mixer on high speed until very firm, 7 minutes. Remove from the heat, add the vanilla, and beat until the frosting is cooled and holds a stiff peak.

8. As soon as the frosting is made, assemble the cake: Place 1 cake layer, cut side down, on a serving plate. Spread it with one third of the buttercream. Repeat with 2 more layers (always spread on the smooth side, not the cut side) and the remaining buttercream. Top with the remaining cake layer, smooth side up.

9. Immediately frost the sides and top of the cake with the frosting. Swirl it on attractively with a frosting knife. This cake is best served on the day it is frosted. Keep at room temperature in a cake server until serving.

Note: This buttercream uses raw egg yolks, which can cause health problems. Be sure to use very fresh eggs that have been kept refrigerated.

Celebrate

I have heard it said that it is impossible to get a bad meal in Italy. Even though nothing is absolutely impossible, that saying is pretty near the truth. The Italian kitchen, with its reliance on fresh herbs and seasonal ingredients,

is a magnificent source of inventive and delicious meals. In fact, even the French, who believe that theirs is the only "real" cuisine, credit the Italian chefs who accompanied Catherine de Medici to her home in France (she married Henri II) with elevating the traditional food of the Gallic nobles to real haute cuisine. Let the critics battle it out. Crusty breads, hearty wines, lots of oregano, rosemary, and garlic, blood-red tomatoes, pungent cheeses, and plenty of pasta are enough to keep us coming back to Italy for ten lifetimes of eating.

MENU

This is a menu with choices and is perfect for early autumn, when fresh basil is still available yet there's enough of a chill to enjoy osso buco. The refreshing Campari-based Cardinale is a *molto Italiano* way to begin an Italian celebration. An antipasto of multi-hued grilled peppers follows (don't forget the bread), along with Cotechino Sausage and Crisp Celery Salad. The Pasta Carbonara is silky and luxurious, and the basil linguine is robustly textured. Choose one or the other as the pasta course, although if you're making the polenta, you may want to serve the lighter linguine. As an entree, serve osso buco atop egg noodles or creamy polenta. If blue Italian plums are in season, you'll surely want the plum tart for dessert. *Cin cin!*

Pasta bowls have a distinct advantage over plates: You can place the linguine or penne and a piece of bread in one bowl, with no worry that the pasta and sauce will wind up on the table or your lap instead of on your fork. Beige cloth napkins, with a small fringe or delicate fagoting around the border, and simple flatware, preferably modern, will keep the look smart. For an attractive touch, snuggle a small vase of mixed flowers—small roses, pretty berries, greens, and small lilies—by a lamp or a candle on an intimate table.

Fill tall glasses with bread sticks and small bowls with Italian olives for nibbling.

Celebrate Italy

DINNER FOR SIX

LESLIE RUSSO'S CARDINALE

A RAINBOW OF GRILLED PEPPERS

COTECHINO SAUSAGE
AND CRISP CELERY SALAD

PASTA CARBONARA
OR
BASIL VEGETABLE LINGUINE

VOLUPTUOUS OSSO BUCO WITH GREMOLATA

EGG NOODLES
OR
CREAMY POLENTA WITH MASCARPONE

ITALIAN PLUM TART

THE MUSIC

Puccini

Verdi

THE DRINKS

Leslie Russo's Cardinale

Barbera or Nebbiolo d'Alba

THE EXTRAS

Highball glasses

Marrow spoons

Double boiler

LESLIE RUSSO'S CARDINALE

The Negroni, they say, was named after a dedicated Florentine cocktail drinker of the 1920s, Camillo Negroni. This is a lighter version of that drink, using dry rather than sweet vermouth. The dry vermouth accents the bitter herbs in the Campari. For an extra little something, my dear friend Leslie Russo adds a splash of Meyer lemon juice from a tree in her California backyard. Lime juice makes a good substitute.

2 Meyer lemons or regular limes, cut in quarters
Ice cubes
12 ounces gin, preferably Tanqueray or Bombay
3 ounces extra-dry vermouth
3 ounces Campari

1. Squeeze a lemon quarter into each of six 8-ounce glasses, then drop the wedge into the glass. Fill each glass with ice cubes.

2. Combine the gin, vermouth, and Campari in a pitcher filled with ice cubes and strain into the glasses. Stir and serve.

A RAINBOW OF GRILLED PEPPERS

Sweet, slightly tart, smooth—roasted peppers go with any meat, any fish. As a display of pure color, they are a party decoration in themselves. With their happy hues and deep, clean flavor, they match up beautifully with the Cotechino Sausage and Crisp Celery Salad for an appealing antipasto. Cleaning the skins from the roasted peppers is not difficult—a little time spent steaming and they slip right off.

2 red bell peppers
2 yellow bell peppers
2 orange bell peppers
2 tablespoons extra-virgin olive oil
Salt and freshly ground black pepper, to taste
3 large cloves garlic, thinly sliced
1 tablespoon large capers, drained
1 tablespoon whole fresh oregano leaves
8 slices peasant bread, toasted, for serving

1. Preheat the broiler.

2. Stem the peppers and cut them in half lengthwise. Remove the core and seeds and carefully trim off all the inner white membrane. Lay the pepper halves, skin side up, in a single layer on a baking sheet. Broil, 3 to 5 inches from the heat source, until the skins are charred black, 12 to 15 minutes.

3. Remove the peppers from the broiler and place them in a paper or plastic bag. Close it tight and let the peppers steam for about 15 minutes. Then use your fingers to slip off the charred skins.

4. Arrange the peeled peppers in arcs (like a rainbow), one color to each arc, on a platter. Drizzle with the olive oil and sprinkle generously with salt and pepper. Place the garlic slivers attractively around the peppers. Scatter the capers and the oregano over the peppers. Serve with peasant bread.

COTECHINO SAUSAGE

These plump, mild fresh pork sausages are a traditional New Year's dish all over Italy, served up with lentils. The richness of the fatty sausages is believed to help bring good fortune in the coming year. If you respect tradition, match them up with the Savory Lentil Salad (page 159) next New Year's Day. Here, enjoy them as part of an antipasto.

1 uncooked cotechino sausage
(about 1¹/₂ pounds)
Dijon mustard, for serving
Pickled wild cherries, for serving (see Note)

1. Pierce the sausage in a few places with the tines of a fork.

2. Bring a saucepan of water to a slow boil. Reduce the heat to medium-low, add the sausage, and simmer until it is cooked through, 30 minutes. Drain and allow to cool to room temperature. Then gently remove the skin from the sausage by slitting it with the tip of a sharp knife and peeling it off.

3. To serve, cut the sausage into ¹/₂-inch-thick slices, and serve with the mustard and pickled wild cherries.

Note: Pickled wild cherries are available at specialty food stores. Most often you'll find them jarred, but some stores carry them loose, in large tubs, much the same way they sell olives.

CRISP
CELERY SALAD

C elery has that crisp snap that you get from pickles, but it is more subtle and acts as a counterpoint to the stronger flavors in this menu. Here celery is dressed with a simple vinaigrette and fresh herbs and it remains crunchy even the next day. Try serving it atop thinly sliced roasted beets.

12 outer ribs celery, trimmed and
thinly sliced on the diagonal
6 to 8 inner ribs celery, including the leaves,
chopped
¹/₄ cup extra-virgin olive oil
2 tablespoons red wine vinegar
Salt and freshly ground black pepper, to taste
¹/₂ cup small flat-leaf parsley leaves
¹/₄ cup coarsely chopped fresh mint

Place all the celery in a bowl. Add the olive oil and vinegar and toss. Season with salt and pepper. Just before serving, toss with the parsley leaves and chopped mint.

PASTA
CARBONARA

P asta Carbonara may be named for the charcoal makers of Umbria, but no one really knows. Made with pancetta, which is salt-cured pork belly (similar to bacon, but not smoked), and served up liberally with cheese and black pepper, this sauce was hugely popular with American GIs in Italy after World War II. It's delicious as a basic recipe, but you can also doll it up with fresh peas, asparagus tips, or sautéed baby artichokes.

2 tablespoons olive oil
12 ounces pancetta, cut into ¹/₂-inch pieces
4 large egg yolks
²/₃ cup heavy (whipping) cream
Salt and freshly ground black pepper, to taste
1 cup freshly grated Parmesan cheese
1 pound dried penne

1. Heat the olive oil in a large skillet over medium-low heat. Add the pancetta and sauté until it is crisp, about 15 minutes. Transfer the pancetta to paper towels to drain.

2. While the pancetta is cooking, bring a large pot of salted water to a boil over high heat.

3. Beat the egg yolks and cream together in a bowl and season well with salt and pepper. Whisk in ¹/₂ cup of the cheese.

4. Add the penne to the boiling water and cook until just tender, 10 to 12 minutes. Transfer it to a colander to drain thoroughly, then return it at once to the pot. Add the pancetta and the egg mixture and toss to combine well. The heat of the pasta will cook the eggs. Stir in the remaining ¹/₂ cup cheese and serve immediately.

Pasta Carbonara

BASIL VEGETABLE LINGUINE

On the rocky hills of Liguria, on the northwest coast of Italy, fragrant olives, plump pine nuts, aromatic garlic, and green herbs grow lush in the hot sun and sea air. Although rosemary, thyme, sage, and parsley grow in abundance there and are used in hundreds of recipes, perhaps no herb is as prized and as delicately delicious as sweet basil. It is, quite literally, the king of herbs (*basil* from the Greek *basileus,* meaning "king"). Pesto, which is traditionally made by crushing basil, olive oil, and garlic with a mortar and pestle, is one of the best ways to feature the herb front and center. When fresh young potatoes and string beans are tossed with pasta and pesto, you have a fine vegetarian dish.

> 8 ounces green beans, cut into
> ¼-inch pieces
> 8 ounces red-skinned new potatoes,
> peeled and cut into ¼-inch pieces
> 12 ounces dried linguine
> Garden Pesto (recipe follows)
> Freshly ground black pepper, to taste
> 6 ripe plum tomatoes, cut into
> ¼-inch dice
> ½ cup slivered fresh basil leaves

1. Bring a saucepan of lightly salted water to a boil over high heat. Add the green beans and cook until just tender, 1 minute. Using a skimmer, remove them from the pot to a colander. Rinse under cold water to stop the cooking. Drain, pat dry, and set them aside.

2. Add the potatoes to the boiling water and cook until just tender, 2 minutes. Drain the potatoes in a colander and run under cold water to stop the cooking. Drain, pat dry, and set them aside.

3. Shortly before serving, bring a large pot of salted water to a boil over high heat. Add the linguine and cook until just tender, about 8 minutes. Drain the pasta well and place it in a serving bowl. Add the Garden Pesto and toss well. Season with pepper.

4. Sprinkle the green beans, potatoes, and tomatoes over the linguine and top with the slivered basil. Serve immediately, tossing the pasta at the table.

GARDEN PESTO

Thanks to the food processor, it takes little time to prepare a fresh pesto. When basil is in season, keep pesto on hand to toss with pasta, stir into mashed potatoes, or drizzle over tomatoes, crusty bread, grilled chicken—almost anything. Add it judiciously; a little can go a long way. It's delicious as a dip with raw vegetables, too.

> 2 cups fresh basil leaves
> 4 teaspoons minced garlic
> 2 tablespoons pine nuts
> ⅓ cup extra-virgin olive oil,
> or more as needed
> 2 tablespoons freshly grated
> Parmesan cheese
> Salt and freshly ground black pepper,
> to taste

Combine the basil, garlic, and pine nuts in a food processor and pulse until chopped. With the motor running, slowly drizzle the olive oil in through the feed tube. Add the cheese and process until combined. Season with salt and pepper. Add a bit more oil if the sauce seems too thick. Refrigerate, covered, for up to 3 days. Let the pesto come to room temperature before serving.

MAKES ABOUT 1 CUP

VOLUPTUOUS OSSO BUCO

Succulent, falling-off-the-bone veal in a thick, full-flavored sauce is a quintessential Italian dish. Besides the lush meat, osso buco offers up a serving of rich marrow from the center of its bone. If little spoons are unavailable, use the tip of a sharp knife to ease it out. Riding above the symphony of tastes, like the clear notes of a trumpet, is the herbaceous, fruity, and pungent garnish known as *gremolata*.

³/₄ cup all-purpose flour
Salt and freshly ground black pepper, to taste
6 center-cut veal shanks, cut 2¹/₂ inches
*   thick (about 6 pounds total)*
¹/₃ cup extra-virgin olive oil, or
*   more as needed*
8 ounces pancetta, cut into ¹/₄-inch dice
1 onion, cut into ¹/₄-inch dice
1 carrot, peeled and cut into ¹/₄-inch dice
1 rib celery, cut into ¹/₄-inch dice
1 tablespoon finely minced garlic
¹/₂ teaspoon dried oregano
¹/₂ teaspoon dried basil
Pinch of crushed red pepper flakes
2 cups Marinara Sauce (page 399)
2 tablespoons tomato paste
2 teaspoons finely grated orange zest
2 teaspoons finely grated lemon zest
1¹/₂ cups dry white wine
1¹/₂ cups Basic Chicken Broth (page 397)
Cooked egg noodles (see box, page 274) or
*   Creamy Polenta with Mascarpone*
*   (recipe follows), for serving*
Gremolata (recipe follows), for serving

1. Place the flour in a shallow bowl and season it generously with salt and pepper. Dredge the veal shanks in the flour, shaking off any excess.

2. Heat the olive oil in a large flameproof casserole over medium-high heat. Add the veal and brown on all sides, about 10 minutes. Remove the veal from the casserole and set it aside.

3. Reduce the heat to medium and add the pancetta. Cook, stirring, until it starts to crisp, 5 minutes. Add the onion, carrot, celery, and garlic and cook, stirring and scraping up any brown bits on the bottom of the casserole, until the vegetables are softened, 8 to 10 minutes.

4. Add the oregano, basil, and pepper flakes. Stir in the marinara sauce, tomato paste, and orange and lemon zests. Cook, stirring, over medium heat for the flavors to blend, about 8 minutes.

Voluptuous Osso Buco

5. Add the wine and broth and bring to a boil. Reduce the heat to medium-low and simmer for 10 minutes.

6. Meanwhile, preheat the oven to 350°F.

7. Return the veal shanks to the casserole, cover, and transfer it to the oven. Bake for 2 hours. Then remove the cover and bake until the veal is very tender, about 30 minutes more. Remove the casserole from the oven and let cool slightly. With a metal spoon, carefully skim off any accumulated fat on the surface and discard it. Adjust the seasonings if necessary. Heat through over medium-low heat if necessary. Serve over egg noodles or Creamy Polenta with Mascarpone, and sprinkle with the Gremolata.

GREMOLATA

The traditional garnish for osso buco, gremolata adds a zesty spark of freshness to the deep, melded flavors of the veal and sauce.

¼ cup coarsely chopped fresh flat-leaf
  parsley
Finely grated zest of 1 large lemon
1 tablespoon finely minced garlic

Combine all of the ingredients, and use immediately for the freshest texture and flavor.

MAKES 5 TABLESPOONS

CREAMY POLENTA WITH MASCARPONE

Every cuisine has its comfort food. In the north of Italy, warm, filling, creamy polenta is *comfortissimo*. Really cornmeal mush

with an Italian accent, when combined with abundantly creamy and sweet mascarpone cheese, it inspires sighs of pleasure. It is sinfully rich, but with Voluptuous Osso Buco, there is nothing more delectable. This version is based on one I ate at Katharine Kagel's restaurant, Cafe Pasqual's, in Santa Fe, New Mexico.

¾ teaspoon saffron threads
2 teaspoons salt
2 cups polenta (stone-ground cornmeal)
8 ounces mascarpone cheese
1 cup freshly grated Asiago or
  Parmesan cheese

Combine 8 cups water, the saffron, and salt in a heavy saucepan and bring to a boil over high heat. Slowly add the polenta, stirring constantly. When all the polenta has been added, lower the heat to medium-high and cook, stirring, until the raw taste disappears and the polenta begins to come away from the sides of the pan, 10 to 15 minutes. Add the mascarpone and the grated cheese and stir well. Serve immediately, or transfer to a double boiler, cover, and keep warm for up to 30 minutes over the lowest possible heat.

COOKING EGG NOODLES

If you decide to prepare egg noodles as a bed for the osso buco, here's how:

• Bring a large pot of lightly salted water to a boil. Add 1 pound dried egg noodles, reduce the heat to medium-high, and cook until the noodles are just tender, 10 to 12 minutes. Drain well, fluff with a fork to separate the noodles, transfer to a serving platter, and spoon the osso buco over the top.

ITALIAN PLUM TART

If autumn is the most bountiful season, then in Italy it is both the most bountiful and the most beautiful: golden poplars on the hillsides, the smell of roasting meat on bonfires of cut grapevi nes, and sensuous, deep purple plums. Packed in a free-form pastry crust, this impossibly delicious dessert speaks unforgettably of the Italian countryside.

FOR THE PASTRY

2 cups all-purpose flour
8 tablespoons (1 stick) cold unsalted
   butter, cut into small pieces
1 tablespoon sugar
1/2 teaspoon salt
1 large egg yolk
1/3 cup cold water

FOR THE TART

1/2 cup shelled almonds
   (not blanched)
1/4 cup plus 2 tablespoons sugar
1/4 cup all-purpose flour
1 1/2 pounds small Italian plums,
   halved and pitted
4 tablespoons (1/2 stick) unsalted
   butter, cut into small pieces
1/2 cup red currant jelly
1 tablespoon Grand Marnier
Crème fraîche, for serving
   (optional)

1. Prepare the pastry: Combine the flour, butter, sugar, and salt in a food processor and process until the mixture resembles coarse meal. Add the egg yolk and cold water and process until the dough just comes together in the bowl. Wrap the dough in plastic wrap and refrigerate it for 1 hour. Clean out the processor bowl.

2. Preheat the oven to 400°F.

3. Combine the almonds, the ¼ cup sugar, and the flour in the food processor and process until the mixture is a powder. Set it aside.

4. On a lightly floured surface, roll the dough out to form a large rectangle, ⅛ inch thick. Transfer the dough to a baking sheet. Sprinkle the almond mixture over the pastry, leaving a 1-inch border all around.

5. Arrange the plum halves, cut side down, over the almond mixture. Fold the border of the dough up, pressing and pinching it together to make a nice rim. Dot the plums with the butter and sprinkle the remaining 2 tablespoons sugar over them.

6. Bake until the filling is bubbly and the crust is golden, 1 hour.

7. Meanwhile, whisk the red currant jelly and the Grand Marnier together in a small bowl. Brush the mixture over the entire tart just after it comes out of the oven. Let the tart cool slightly. Serve warm or at room temperature, with crème fraîche if desired (see Note).

Note: You can make this tart up to 1 day in advance. Cover with aluminum foil and keep at room temperature. If you wish to reheat it before serving, remove the wrap and place in a low oven for 15 minutes.

Graduation

Honors

Every culture has its rites of passage marking the coming of age of young men and women. Although we have no defined rituals to note the move from high school to college (when so many kids leave the nest) or from college to "grown-up" life (which, hopefully, means a job), the graduation celebration—whether a picnic, buffet, or sit-down dinner—surely is in order, complete with Mom and Dad's slightly teary testimonials. A new watch, a new fountain pen, maybe even a new laptop or a plane ticket for a trip to some must-see place, all underscore the promise that lies ahead.

MENU

Each dish on this menu should be a favorite of the graduate. This selection is both classic and contemporary. What could be more celebratory than a salsa-spiked shrimp cocktail, a succulent strip steak and fries—or for the non–meat eater thin, thin pasta with garden-fresh vegetables—the freshest of salads, and Peach Melba Cream Cake! Simple foods with uncommon flavor for your uncommon graduate.

Keep the look simple yet special. Serve the Straight-"A" Shrimp Cocktail in stemmed glasses, with some cocktail sauce and mint crowning the top. Plain white dishes will work fine, and oval ones are ideal for the strip steak—you can serve the fries on the same plate. Green- or red-and-white windowpane-checked napkins have a crisp, fresh feel and so does red, green, or blue plastic-handled flatware.

Since the steak is served sliced, heavy-duty steak knives are not really necessary. The Peach Melba Cream Cake looks particularly yummy presented on a stand. Once you've got everybody's mouth watering, slice it up and serve.

Write the menu on a small piece of parchment paper (don't forget the date!), roll it up to look like a diploma, tie it with a red satin bow, and set one above each place setting—a little corny, but nice.

Graduation Honors

DINNER FOR EIGHT

FRESH LIME AND STRAWBERRY PUNCH

———

STRAIGHT-"A" SHRIMP COCKTAIL

———

NEW YORK STRIP STEAK LAVISHED
WITH TOMATOES AND OLIVES
AND OVEN-BAKED FRIES

O R

DREAMY GARDEN-FRESH SPAGHETTINI

———

GREENMARKET SALAD

———

PEACH MELBA CREAM CAKE
WITH RASPBERRY SAUCE

THE MUSIC

The Four Freshman
Soundtrack from
The Graduate
The Goo Goo Dolls

THE DRINKS

Fresh Lime and Strawberry Punch
Chianti Classico

THE EXTRAS

Classic oval chop plates
Pedestal cake stand

FRESH LIME AND STRAWBERRY PUNCH

Graduation time turns one's thoughts to bright clear ideas and excitement for the future. For both refreshment and celebration, a fresh lime punch dappled with ripe strawberries definitely makes the grade.

4 cups fresh lime juice
    (from about 24 limes; see Note)
1 cup sugar
3 to 4 limes, very thinly sliced
Plenty of ice cubes
2 pints ripe strawberries, rinsed,
    hulled, and quartered

1. Pour the lime juice into a large pitcher or punch bowl. Add 8 cups water and the sugar, and stir until the sugar has dissolved. Add the sliced limes.

2. Just before serving, add ice to the pitcher or punch bowl. Stir in the strawberries. Serve in small glasses or punch cups.

Note: Freshly squeezed lime juice is sometimes available in the refrigerator case at specialty food stores.

STRAIGHT-"A" SHRIMP COCKTAIL

Shrimp cocktail is always a favorite, and enlivening it with a fresh salsa that packs a little heat is "icing on the cake," with the silky texture and flavors complementing each other. Top it off with Knockout Cocktail Sauce and POW! another winner for our graduate. Strike up the "Pomp and Circumstance."

$1/2$ cup dry white wine
2 ribs celery with leaves, coarsely chopped
4 sprigs fresh flat-leaf parsley
6 whole black peppercorns
$1 1/2$ pounds large shrimp, peeled, deveined,
    and well rinsed
3 ripe papayas, halved lengthwise, seeded,
    peeled, and cut into $1/2$-inch pieces
4 ripe plum tomatoes, seeded and cut into
    $1/2$-inch pieces
$1/4$ cup finely diced red onion
1 teaspoon finely diced green jalapeño
    pepper
3 tablespoons fresh lime juice
2 tablespoons extra-virgin olive oil
2 teaspoons red wine vinegar
Salt and freshly ground black pepper,
    to taste
6 tablespoons coarsely chopped fresh mint
8 tablespoons Knockout Cocktail Sauce
    (page 19)
8 large sprigs fresh mint, for garnish

1. Fill a medium-size saucepan half full with water, add the wine, celery, parsley, and peppercorns, and bring to a boil over high heat. Reduce the heat to medium-low, add the shrimp, and simmer until just done (the shrimp turn opaque pink), about 2 minutes. Drain, discarding the celery, parsley, and peppercorns. Run the shrimp under cold water, and drain well again.

2. Using a rubber spatula, toss together the papayas, tomatoes, onion, and jalapeño in a large bowl. Add the shrimp and toss with the lime juice, olive oil, and vinegar. Season generously with salt and pepper and toss in 4 tablespoons of the chopped mint.

3. Divide the shrimp mixture equally among eight martini glasses, wineglasses, or other stemmed glasses. Top each serving with a tablespoon of cocktail sauce and sprinkle with the remaining 2 tablespoons chopped mint. Garnish each glass with a mint sprig and serve.

NEW YORK STRIP STEAK
LAVISHED WITH TOMATOES AND OLIVES

The New York, or Kansas City, strip is a cut of beef that hardly needs to have its flavor embellished, but this robust topping is hard to resist because it complements the juicy texture of the meat so beautifully. The fresh taste of the tomatoes, the saltiness of the olives, and the tang of the balsamic vinegar are a simply unbeatable combination that stands up to the power of the classic steak.

*8 ripe plum tomatoes, seeded and cut into
  $1/4$-inch dice
$1^1/4$ cups coarsely chopped pitted Niçoise or
  Gaeta olives
Freshly ground black pepper, to taste
3 tablespoons balsamic vinegar
$1/4$ cup extra-virgin olive oil
$1/2$ cup coarsely chopped fresh flat-leaf parsley
4 prime aged New York strip steaks, cut
  $1^1/2$ inches thick (about 1 pound each)*

1. Preheat the broiler.

2. Combine the tomatoes and olives in a small bowl and season with pepper. Add the vinegar, olive oil, and $1/4$ cup of the parsley and toss to mix. Set the mixture aside.

3. Arrange the steaks on the rack of a large broiling pan. Broil the steaks, 4 inches from the heat source, until browned on the first side, about 4 minutes. Turn and cook for 3 minutes on the other side for medium-rare, or 4 minutes for medium.

4. Let the meat rest for 5 minutes before carving. Slice the steaks into $1/4$-inch-thick slices and arrange them on a serving platter. Spoon the tomato and olive mixture over and beside the steak, sprinkle with the remaining $1/4$ cup parsley, and serve immediately.

OVEN-BAKED FRIES

Steak and potatoes are one of the great marriages—better still if the potatoes are browned and crunchy crisp. We all love french fries, but they are usually messy to make at home, and, anyway, who needs all that fat? Oven fries satisfy the urge with fewer calories.

*8 russet potatoes (about 4 pounds total),
  unpeeled, scrubbed well
$1/2$ cup extra-virgin olive oil
2 teaspoons sweet paprika
Coarse (kosher) salt and freshly ground
  black pepper, to taste
2 cups Lemon-Garlic Aïoli (page 6),
  for serving*

1. Preheat the oven to 400°F.

2. Cut the potatoes into lengthwise quarters, and then cut each piece in half crosswise. Place them in a bowl and toss with the olive oil, paprika, and salt and pepper.

3. Arrange the potatoes in a single layer on a baking sheet and bake until tender in the center and brown and crisp on the outside, about 30 minutes, shaking them once while they are cooking. Carefully remove the fries from the baking sheet with a metal spatula and pile them on a platter. Sprinkle with a little extra coarse salt, if desired, and serve immediately. Pass the aïoli.

DREAMY GARDEN-FRESH SPAGHETTINI

If you were looking for just one word to describe this recipe, it would be "sprightly." The lemon zest, capers, and caramelized tomatoes will wake up the most jaded palate, but with a concerto rather than a full-blown symphony. Each taste is distinct, and the combination is light and lovely.

16 ripe plum tomatoes, halved lengthwise
About ¹/₂ cup extra-virgin olive oil
2 tablespoons sugar
Freshly ground black pepper
¹/₂ cup (loosely packed) small fresh flat-leaf
* parsley leaves*
2 tablespoons tiny capers, drained
2 teaspoons freshly grated lemon zest
¹/₂ cup fresh lemon juice (from 3 to 4 lemons)
1¹/₂ pounds dried spaghettini
8 ounces snow peas
2 bunches arugula, trimmed, rinsed, and
* patted dry, for garnish*

1. Preheat the oven to 250°F. Line a baking sheet with aluminum foil.

2. Place the tomatoes, cut side up, on the prepared baking sheet. Drizzle with the olive oil and sprinkle with the sugar and pepper. Bake until the tomatoes are roasted-looking and less watery, 1¹/₂ hours. Remove the baking sheet from the oven and place the tomatoes and their juices in a large bowl.

3. Add the parsley, capers, lemon zest, and lemon juice to the tomatoes and toss gently.

4. Bring a large pot of salted water to a boil over high heat and add the spaghettini. Cook until just tender, about 6 minutes. Drain and add it to the tomato mixture. Toss well.

Once salad greens have been rinsed to remove all sand and dirt, and then well drained and dried, wrap them in kitchen or paper towels and place them in a plastic bag. Store the bag in the crisper drawer of the refrigerator to keep the greens crisp.

5. Meanwhile, bring a small saucepan of water to a boil over high heat. Add the snow peas and cook until crisp-tender, 1 minute. Drain and add to the pasta and tomatoes. Toss everything together gently and serve immediately in shallow bowls. Place a small handful of arugula at the side of each bowl.

GREENMARKET SALAD

There is nothing more appealing than a green salad when you have access to a good selection of fresh greens. When putting a salad together, it's important to keep color and texture in mind by being conscious of the proportion of the various lettuces that are included. When you have finished composing the salad, it should resemble a field of wild greens. Before you season and dress it, be sure the greens are dry and crisp. Then you'll have the perfect salad. Add any of your favorites—a perfectly ripe tomato, edible flowers, a crisp cucumber—if desired. But here the greens are the stars!

2 cups small arugula leaves, tough stems
* trimmed*
2 cups baby spinach leaves
1 small head tender radicchio, leaves slivered
2 cups torn tender inner leaves of red or
* green Boston lettuce, ribs removed*
2 cups red oak-leaf lettuce, preferably
* baby leaves*
2 cups mâche (see Note)
1¹/₂ cups fresh flat-leaf parsley leaves
Salt and freshly ground black pepper, to taste
About ¹/₂ cup Sherry Vinaigrette (page 263)
* or other vinaigrette*

1. Fill a large bowl or the sink with cold water and add all greens. Swirl them around to clean. Drain them well and pat dry. Wrap them in kitchen or paper towels, then in a plastic bag, and store in the vegetable bin in the refrigerator until ready to use.

2. Place the greens in a salad bowl. Season with salt and pepper and toss lightly with the dressing just before serving.

Note: Also called lamb's lettuce (see box, page 32), mâche is a small oval-leaved green often found in fancy salad mixes. It's also sold on its own in bags or small boxes. Mâche sometimes has some of the soil-covered roots attached. Remove them and wash the greens well to remove all sand.

Peach Melba Cream Cake

PEACH MELBA CREAM CAKE

When Helen Mitchell was just beginning her operatic career, she took the stage name "Nellie Melba" in honor of her hometown, Melbourne, Australia. The greatest French chef of the era, August Escoffier, created a classic peach and raspberry dessert that he named for her in honor of the diva's dazzling talent. This variation combines the classic flavors of a well-spiced pumpkin bread with fresh peaches and vanilla-laced whipped cream—a perfect finale for your own star graduate.

FOR THE CAKE

2 1/2 cups all-purpose flour
1 1/2 teaspoons baking powder
1 teaspoon baking soda
2 cups canned pumpkin puree
1/2 teaspoon salt
1 teaspoon ground ginger
1 teaspoon ground cinnamon
1 teaspoon freshly grated nutmeg
1/2 teaspoon ground cloves
1 cup (2 sticks) unsalted butter,
    at room temperature
1 1/2 cups (packed) light brown sugar
1 cup granulated sugar
2 large eggs, lightly beaten
2 tablespoons bourbon
2 teaspoons pure vanilla extract

FOR THE FILLING

4 pounds ripe peaches
1 tablespoon fresh lemon juice
2 1/2 tablespoons granulated sugar
2 cups heavy (whipping) cream
1 1/2 teaspoons pure vanilla extract

Raspberry Sauce (recipe follows),
    for serving
1 sprig fresh mint, for garnish

1. Position a rack in the center of the oven, and preheat the oven to 350°F. Butter the bottom and sides of two 9-inch round cake pans. Line the bottoms with rounds of wax or parchment paper, and butter the paper. Dust the bottom and sides of the pans with flour, tapping out any excess.

2. Prepare the cake: Sift the flour, baking powder, and baking soda together into a bowl and set aside.

3. Combine the pumpkin with the salt and all the spices in a small bowl. Set it aside.

4. Cream the butter in a bowl with an electric mixer until light. Add both sugars and continue to beat on medium speed until light and creamy, about 5 minutes. Add the eggs and beat until fluffy, scraping down the sides of the bowl once or twice.

5. With the mixer on low speed, add one third of the flour mixture to the butter mixture and beat until smooth. Add half of the pumpkin mixture and beat until smooth. Continue with another third of the flour, the remaining pumpkin mixture, and the remaining flour mixture, beating after each addition until well mixed. Add the bourbon and vanilla and mix on medium speed for 2 minutes.

6. Scrape the batter evenly into the prepared cake pans. Bake until a wooden toothpick inserted in the center comes out clean, 30 to 35 minutes. Allow the layers to cool in the pans on a wire rack for about 1 hour. Then remove the layers from the pans and let them cool completely on a wire rack. Carefully peel off the paper.

7. Shortly before serving, prepare the filling: Pit and slice the peaches (see Notes). Toss them in a bowl with the lemon juice and 1 tablespoon of the sugar. Set this aside for 15 minutes.

8. Combine the cream, vanilla, and remaining 1½ tablespoons sugar in a bowl and whip until it holds soft peaks.

9. Place a cake layer, top side up, on a pedestal cake stand (see Notes). Spread it with

half of the whipped cream and then top the cream with half of the peaches. Cover with the remaining layer, top side up. Spread most of the remaining whipped cream over the top, and top with most of the remaining peaches. Dollop the center with the remaining cream, then the peaches. Drizzle some of the Raspberry Sauce over the top and sides, and garnish with a mint sprig. Serve immediately, with the remaining Raspberry Sauce alongside.

Notes: If you prefer, peel the peaches before slicing them.

If the smooth side of the cake layer (the bottom as it came out of the cake pan) is uneven, level it out by cutting off a thin slice with a serrated knife.

RASPBERRY SAUCE

This sweet-tart combination of raspberries, kirsch, and lemon juice will elevate an ice-cream sundae, festoon a chocolate cake, and shine when spooned over a Peach Melba Cream Cake.

2 cups fresh raspberries
1 cup confectioners' sugar
3 tablespoons fresh lemon juice
¼ cup kirsch or raspberry syrup

1. Combine the berries, confectioners' sugar, lemon juice, and liqueur in a food processor. Process until very smooth. Adjust the flavor, if necessary, by adding a bit more lemon juice or liqueur.

2. Pass the sauce through a fine-mesh strainer to remove the seeds, tapping the strainer to extract all the liquid. Store the sauce in a covered container in the refrigerator for up to 2 days. (It can also be frozen for up to 1 month. Thaw overnight in the refrigerator.)

MAKES 1 CUP

CELEBRATE

2. Add the carrots, potatoes, squash, cauliflower, fennel, and green beans. Stir in the broth, honey, cloves, and cinnamon stick, raise the heat to high, and bring to a boil. Reduce the heat to medium-low and simmer, uncovered, until the vegetables are tender, about 20 minutes. Then add the chickpeas and simmer, stirring once or twice, to blend the flavors, another 10 minutes.

3. Shortly before serving, stir in the cilantro and remove the cinnamon stick and cloves. Sprinkle with the chopped mint and serve.

FAVORITE CHICKEN CURRY

Although complexity should never be confused with worth, it is true of many great dishes from a variety of cuisines that they build layer upon layer of flavor and that the whole adds up to a deep flavor experience. A French lobster sauce, a Mexican mole, and an Indian curry all carry this hallmark. Of course, if you are going to go to the trouble, the recipe had better be worth it, and this one is, because it has a luxurious flavor—rich and silky—that you don't want to end. You cannot make a true Indian dish without a lot of ingredients. For a very special occasion, pass small bowls of dried currants, shredded coconut, and some coarsely chopped peanuts to enhance each serving.

> 24 chicken thighs, skin removed,
>   thighs rinsed and patted dry
> Salt and freshly ground black pepper,
>   to taste
> 1/4 cup clarified butter (see box, this page)
> 2 teaspoons ground cumin
> 2 teaspoons ground turmeric
> Pinch of saffron threads
> 4 teaspoons curry powder
> 1 cinnamon stick (3 inches long)
> 3 bay leaves
> 2 teaspoons sweet paprika
> 4 whole cloves
> 1 teaspoon mustard seeds
> 3 onions, finely chopped
> 6 cloves garlic, minced
> 1/4 cup finely chopped fresh ginger
> 1 teaspoon finely minced serrano chile
> 1 cup peeled and finely diced eggplant
> 2 teaspoons tomato paste
> 4 cups Basic Chicken Broth (page 397)
> 2 tablespoons fresh lemon juice
> 3/4 cup unsweetened coconut milk
> 2 tablespoons chopped fresh cilantro
> Mango chutney, for serving

1. Season the chicken thighs well with salt and pepper. Set them aside.

2. Heat the clarified butter in a large flameproof casserole over medium-low heat and add all the spices, the onions, garlic, ginger, and chile. Cook, stirring, to develop the flavors, 3 to 5 minutes.

3. Add the chicken, eggplant, and tomato paste and cook, stirring constantly, until the chicken is browned and the eggplant has softened, 5 minutes. Then add the broth and lemon juice and simmer over medium heat until the chicken is cooked through, 45 minutes. Transfer the chicken to a bowl and let it cool slightly. Discard the cinnamon stick, bay leaves, and cloves and return the casserole to medium-high heat.

HOW TO CLARIFY BUTTER

Melt 1 pound of butter in a small saucepan over low heat and let cook about 10 minutes. Let it cool slightly. Then carefully pour the clear melted butter into a container, leaving the milky solids behind. Keep in a clean jar in the refrigerator for up to 1 month.

4. Adjust the seasonings if necessary and boil the sauce until thickened, 20 minutes. Meanwhile, shred the chicken meat from the bones in large pieces. Set the meat aside.

5. Stir the coconut milk into the sauce, reduce the heat to medium-low, and cook to blend, 10 minutes more. Stir in the chicken meat and cook for 5 minutes to warm it through. Just before serving, stir in the cilantro. Serve with mango chutney (and any of the condiments mentioned in the headnote, if desired) alongside.

RED SNAPPER IN AN AROMATIC BROTH

While ginger is a familiar ingredient in Indian cuisine, lemongrass is not. I've added it to the broth in this dish because it mates so well with the ginger and the delicate red snapper. It is also at home with the other spices that are laced throughout this menu.

4 cups Basic Chicken Broth (page 397)
2 stalks fresh lemongrass, trimmed
*   and thinly sliced crosswise (see box)*
1 piece (1 inch) fresh ginger, thinly sliced
8 red snapper fillets, ¾ inch thick
*   (6 to 8 ounces each)*
Salt and freshly ground black pepper, to taste
About 4 tablespoons olive oil
2 carrots, peeled and cut into julienne
8 scallions, including 2 inches green,
*   thinly sliced on the diagonal*
56 whole fresh cilantro leaves

1. Combine the broth, lemongrass, and ginger in a heavy saucepan and bring to a boil over high heat. Reduce the heat to low and simmer, partially covered, for 15 minutes to intensify the

HOW TO PREPARE LEMONGRASS

Lemongrass is a green plant with a long, pale, woody stalk and slender leaves. Prized for its subtle citrus fragrance, it is most often used in Thai and Vietnamese cooking. The flavor is in the bottom 6 inches of the stalk. To prepare the lemongrass, cut the stalk to a 6-inch length and remove the very tough outer layer. Slice the tender inside crosswise on the diagonal into ½-inch pieces and use in the recipe as directed. Discard it after it has flavored the dish. Fresh lemongrass imparts the strongest flavor; most dried or frozen lemongrass has very little flavor.

flavors. Remove the pan from the heat and let steep for 5 minutes. Then strain the broth into another saucepan and set it aside.

2. Season the fish well on the skin side with salt and pepper.

3. Heat 1 to 2 tablespoons of the olive oil in a large nonstick skillet over medium heat. Add as many snapper fillets as will fit, skin side down, and cook, gently pressing on the fish with a spatula, until the skin is crisp and golden brown, 5 minutes.

4. Turn the fish and cook for 3 minutes on the flesh side. Place the fillets in individual shallow bowls and keep warm. Repeat with the remaining fillets, adding oil as necessary.

5. Heat the broth over medium heat. Divide the carrots equally among the bowls. Pour ½ cup of the hot broth over each portion of fish. Sprinkle with the scallions and float 7 cilantro leaves in each bowl. Serve immediately.

PERFUMED BASMATI RICE

What's in a name? In the case of basmati, a lot. In Hindi, *basmati* means "the queen of rice" or "the perfumed one." Extra-long-grained, lightly fragrant, it soaks up enough liquid to swell to three times its size. Its light bouquet and toothiness pair up beautifully with the whole larder of Indian spices—and with each of the dishes in this menu.

2 cups basmati rice
3 cups Basic Chicken Broth (page 397) or
Vegetable Broth (page 398)
1/4 teaspoon crumbled saffron threads
2 tablespoons extra-virgin olive oil
1 cup finely diced carrots
1/2 cup frozen petite peas, thawed
Salt and freshly ground black pepper,
to taste

1. Place the rice in a large saucepan. Add the broth and saffron and bring to a boil over high heat. Stir, cover, reduce the heat to low, and simmer until tender, about 15 minutes. Remove from the heat and let rest, covered, for 5 minutes. Fluff with a fork.

2. Meanwhile, heat the olive oil in a skillet over low heat. Add the carrots and cook to soften slightly, 5 minutes. Add the peas and cook until the carrots are tender, another 3 minutes. Using a slotted spoon, transfer the vegetables to the rice. Season with salt and pepper and fluff with a fork. Serve immediately.

MANGO AND MINT SALSA

I know that salsa is Mexican and this is an Indian dinner, but I have always been struck by the similarities between Indian and Mexican cuisines. Octavio Paz, the great Mexican writer, once theorized that *moles* were actually a Mexican reworking of the *molas*, or curries, that Indian nuns brought with them to convents and missions in colonial Mexico. Both rely on a spectrum of spices and herbs, especially cilantro. Neither shies away from a little *picante* heat. So besides chutney, which often includes cooked fruit, I like to serve a fresh fruit salsa with curries. It sparks the flavors of an Indian banquet and leaves a little tingle on your tongue.

HOW TO PEEL AND SEED A MANGO

If the recipe calls for peeled mango, remove the peel with a sharp paring knife. There is a large flat seed in the center of the fruit, so cut the fruit lengthwise, leaving about 1/2 inch of flesh still attached to the seed. Discard the seed and prepare the fruit as needed for the recipe.

If you just want to eat the delicious flesh, cut the unpeeled fruit from each side of the seed as described, then make evenly spaced crisscross slashes through the flesh without piercing the skin. Using both hands, gently bend back the edges of the fruit and push out the center, which will separate the cut sections. Scrape them from the skin and serve on a small plate with a spoon.

More mango is eaten than any other fruit in the world. In India, nearly 2 million acres are devoted exclusively to growing mangoes. In Hindu folk belief, the mango is a symbol of love and wishes fulfilled, which is why mango leaves figure prominently in wedding decorations. Having them around ensures a successful marriage and the birth of children.

2 ripe mangoes, peeled, pitted, and cut into
  1/4-inch dice (see box, previous page)
1/2 cup diced red onion (1/4-inch dice)
2 teaspoons finely minced garlic
1 teaspoon finely minced jalapeño pepper,
  seeds removed
2 tablespoons coarsely chopped fresh mint
2 tablespoons fresh lime juice
2 tablespoons olive oil
Salt and freshly ground black pepper,
  to taste

Place the mangoes in a bowl. Add all the remaining ingredients and fold together with a rubber spatula. Refrigerate, covered, for up to 3 hours before serving.

MAKES ABOUT 2 CUPS

A BOWL OF BERRIES

This dessert of mixed berries reminds me of a maharajah's jeweled crown, resplendent with sapphires, rubies, and amethysts. Once reserved for summer, flavorful fresh berries are available year-round in most markets these days. Although they may not be local, they are worth the price for this eye-catching dessert. A little sugar and some cinnamon-dazzled red wine coax out extra sweetness, and a few drops of orange-flower water in the whipped cream topping add an ethereal Indian accent.

1 cup dry red wine
1 cinnamon stick (3 inches long)
Zest of 1 orange, removed in long strips
  with a paring knife
2 pints fresh strawberries
1 pint fresh blueberries
1 pint fresh raspberries
1/2 pint fresh blackberries
2 tablespoons sugar
Sweetened Whipped Cream
  (page 403, substituting several
  drops orange-flower water, see Note,
  for the vanilla), for serving
6 sprigs fresh mint, for garnish

1. Combine the wine, cinnamon stick, and orange zest in a small saucepan and bring to a simmer over medium heat. Reduce the heat to medium-low and continue simmering, partially covered, until the wine has reduced slightly, 10 minutes. Set aside to cool to room temperature.

2. Rinse the berries in a strainer very gently under cold water and pat them dry with paper towels. Hull the strawberries and cut them into quarters. Place all the berries in a large bowl, sprinkle the sugar over them, and toss gently.

3. Discard the cinnamon stick and orange zest from the cooled wine and pour it over the berries. Stir to combine. Set aside to macerate for 1 hour.

4. Stir the orange-flower water into the whipped cream to flavor it lightly.

5. Spoon the berries, along with some of the juices, into a decorative bowl and garnish with the mint sprigs. Serve in small bowls or wineglasses, topped with a dollop of the whipped cream.

Note: Orange-flower water is available at specialty food stores.

RASPBERRY-ROSE WATER SORBET

To end your meal on a romantic note, put a few bud vases filled with roses on the table when you serve this, along with A Bowl of Berries, for a truly magical dessert.

2 pints fresh raspberries, or 24 ounces frozen unsweetened raspberries, thawed
1¼ cups Simple Syrup (page 403)
½ teaspoon rose water (see Note)

1. Combine the raspberries and ¼ cup of the Simple Syrup in a food processor or blender and puree until smooth. If desired, strain the puree into a bowl to remove the seeds.

2. Stir the remaining 1 cup syrup and the rose water into the puree. Transfer it to an ice-cream maker and freeze according to the manufacturer's instructions. Place the sorbet in a container, cover, and freeze.

MAKES 4 CUPS

Note: Rose water is available at some larger supermarkets and at specialty food stores.

PISTACHIO BRITTLE

I don't know if they have pistachio brittle in India, but pistachios certainly are a popular ingredient in many of that country's cuisines. Brittles—salty, nutty, crunchy, and sweet—are an old-time favorite in America. I have made them with peanuts, pecans, walnuts, and now, in honor of this menu, the small but delectable pistachio. *Namaste*—my humble salutation to you.

Corn oil, for oiling the pan
3 cups shelled pistachios, preferably salted
4 cups sugar
⅛ teaspoon cream of tartar
2 tablespoons unsalted butter, cut into small pieces

1. Lightly oil a 17 x 12 x 1-inch rimmed baking sheet with corn oil. Oil a spatula and set it aside.

2. Scatter the pistachios evenly over the prepared baking sheet and set it aside.

3. Combine the sugar, ½ cup cold water, and the cream of tartar in a heavy saucepan over low heat. Cook, stirring to combine, for 5 minutes. Raise the heat to medium-high and bring the mixture to a boil. Cook without stirring until the mixture reaches 310°F on a candy thermometer, or until it is between a butterscotch and a caramel color, about 10 minutes. While it is cooking, periodically use a pastry brush dipped in warm water to wash down the sugar crystals on the sides of the pan.

4. Remove the pan from the heat and immediately stir in the butter. *Be careful:* The sugar is *very hot* and the mixture will foam up a bit and can spatter (it's always wise to wear long sleeves when cooking hot sugar).

5. Immediately pour this mixture over the pistachios and use the oiled spatula to smooth it. Let it cool completely, about 1 hour. Then transfer the hardened candy to a work surface and break it into irregular pieces. The brittle will keep, stored in an airtight container, for up to 1 week.

Sunday Brunch

Sunday brunch always starts at the "ish" hour, as in "elevenish," or "twelveish," or "oneish." There's no desire to rush; everyone just wants to relax, socialize, hang out. Not so long ago, brunch meant smoked salmon and all the trimmings, or maybe waffles or even eggs benedict. But our repertoire has expanded deliciously to include quiches, frittatas, mimosas, huevos rancheros, crab cakes, and dim sum. Although you can't go wrong with a chewy bagel with scallion cream cheese and some glistening smoked fish, this menu betters your options.

MENU

It's easy to fall into a Sunday brunch rut. But it's also easy to get out of it. Consider the frittata, a perfect brunch food, since it can be made ahead, cut into attractive wedges, and served at room temperature. In fact, most of the dishes on this menu can be prepped ahead of time. Riad's Roasted Tomatoes and Onions are soft and subtle; the Tomatoes à la Tapenade are fuller flavored. Both are delicious accompaniments to a chicken salad that has Niçoise overtones and a crunchy texture. A sweet ending is what's called for, and Blackberry Sorbet and Rich Pecan Squares certainly fill that role beautifully.

This meal calls for a rustic wooden table or a cheerful, colorful tablecloth, perhaps in a Provençal-style fabric in blue, green, yellow, and red paisley. Pale blue or yellow plates and cobalt-colored glasses for wine or water would be perfect. Just keep it lively, pretty, and comfortable.

A casual bunch of seasonal flowers is all that's needed for the table. Look to your table-cloth for color inspiration: forsythia in the spring, or lilacs, or Oriental poppies. Just don't go in for any stiff arrangements. Have some good coffee brewing in the kitchen so that the aroma wafts across the table halfway through your luscious brunch.

Anytime Sunday Brunch

FOR EIGHT

Luscious Leek Frittata

———

Riad's Roasted Tomatoes and Onions

———

Rustic Chicken Salad

———

Tomatoes à la Tapenade

———

Blackberry Sorbet

———

Rich Pecan Squares

THE MUSIC

Claude Bolling's *Suite for Flute*
Mozart's *Concerto for Clarinet in A*
Kiri Te Kanawa's
Chants d'Auvergne

THE DRINKS

Freshly squeezed orange juice
Valpolicella
Freshly brewed coffee and tea

THE EXTRAS

Ovenproof skillet
Several baking sheets
Ice-cream maker

LUSCIOUS LEEK FRITTATA

Whereas the French have their omelets, with all the ingredients folded inside the eggs, the Italians have their frittatas, where everything is mixed up with the eggs. A superb omelet is a wonder, but a frittata can be made ahead of time, doesn't require a lot of fuss, and can be served, if you like, at room temperature. The leek adds a mellow, subtly sweet flavor to the frittata.

> 12 small leeks
> 1/4 cup distilled white vinegar
> 2 tablespoons unsalted butter
> 2 tablespoons extra-virgin olive oil
> 8 large eggs
> 5 tablespoons half-and-half
> 2 tablespoons chopped fresh tarragon
> 2 tablespoons chopped fresh flat-leaf parsley
> Salt and freshly ground black pepper, to taste

1. Remove the tough outer leaves from the leeks. Trim off all but 2 inches of the green. Remove the roots without slicing the bottoms off the leeks (this helps to keep them intact). Halve the leeks lengthwise. Place them in a large bowl, add water to cover and the vinegar, and soak for 30 minutes to remove the dirt. Carefully lift the leeks out of the water without disturbing any sediment that has settled on the bottom of the bowl. Rinse and pat dry.

2. Make frittatas in two 10-inch ovenproof skillets: Melt 1 tablespoon of the butter in 1 tablespoon of the olive oil in each skillet over medium-low heat. Divide the leeks between the two skillets, arranging them evenly. Cover the skillets and cook, shaking them occasionally, for 15 minutes.

3. Turn the leeks carefully and cook, uncovered, shaking the skillets occasionally, for another 15 minutes. The leeks should be meltingly soft.

4. Meanwhile, preheat the broiler.

5. Beat the eggs in a bowl and stir in the half-and-half, tarragon, 1 tablespoon of the parsley, and salt and pepper. Divide the egg mixture evenly between the two skillets, pouring it over the leeks. Cook, uncovered, over medium-low heat until the bottom is just set and the top is slightly wet.

6. Place the skillets under the broiler, 4 to 6 inches from the heat source, and cook until the top of each frittata is just puffed and set, about 2 minutes. Sprinkle 1½ teaspoons of the remaining tablespoon chopped parsley over each frittata. Cut each frittata into 4 wedges and serve hot or at room temperature.

RIAD'S ROASTED TOMATOES AND ONIONS

Riad Aamar, a Middle Eastern chef for whom I have great admiration, makes this intensely flavorful mélange at his restaurant, Oliva, in northwestern Connecticut. The sweetness of the onions, the creaminess of the ricotta cheese, and the clean, concentrated intensity of roasted tomatoes are fabulous with crusty bread. Beyond brunch, remember this dish next time you grill steak or lamb chops.

> 8 medium onions, sliced 1/4 inch thick
> 1 cup extra-virgin olive oil
> 16 small ripe plum or heirloom tomatoes,
>   halved lengthwise
> 1 pound fresh ricotta or goat cheese
> Salt and coarsely ground black pepper, to taste
> 1 cup slivered fresh basil leaves
> Peasant bread, for serving

1. Preheat the oven to 425°F.

2. Arrange the onion slices in one layer on two to four baking sheets and brush both sides with olive oil.

3. Place the tomatoes in one or two small shallow pans, cut side up, and brush the cut side with olive oil.

4. Place the onions in the oven and roast them for 25 minutes, turning them after 15 minutes. When they are done, the onions will be a deep golden brown. Remove and set aside. Place the tomatoes in the oven and roast them until the centers are soft and the skin charred, 25 minutes.

5. To serve, spoon the ricotta in the center of a platter. Separate the onion slices into rings, and place them in four even piles around the ricotta on each plate. Arrange the tomatoes between the onions. Season with salt and pepper and sprinkle with the basil. Drizzle with any remaining olive oil if desired. Serve with a crusty peasant bread to soak up the juices and oil.

Note: If you like, you can roast the onions and tomatoes a couple of hours ahead of time. Cover the pans loosely with aluminum foil and store at room temperature.

RUSTIC CHICKEN SALAD

This vegetable and chicken medley is a crunch-fest of vegetables accented with capers, vinaigrette, and olives—bold flavors not usually associated with brunch. Make a lot! It will be a most welcome surprise.

FOR THE CHICKEN

1 onion, quartered
2 ribs celery, with leaves
2 carrots, peeled and cut in half
6 sprigs fresh parsley
2 bay leaves
1 tablespoon salt
4 whole black peppercorns
8 boneless chicken breast halves
   (about 3 pounds total)

FOR THE SALAD

8 ounces green beans, stem ends
   trimmed
2 fennel bulbs, cored, fronds chopped
   and reserved
3 cups ripe red cherry or grape tomatoes,
   cut in half
1 cup imported black olives (with pits),
   such as Niçoise or Gaeta
3 tablespoons large capers, drained
1/2 cup fresh flat-leaf parsley leaves
Salt and freshly ground black pepper,
   to taste
3/4 cup Lemon Vinaigrette (page 400)

1. Prepare the chicken: Place 4 quarts water in a large pot. Add the onion, celery, carrots, parsley sprigs, bay leaves, salt, and peppercorns and bring to a boil over high heat. Reduce the heat to medium-low and simmer to blend the flavors, 15 minutes.

2. Add the chicken, raise the heat, and return the water to a boil. Then reduce the heat to medium-low and simmer until the chicken is cooked through, 15 minutes.

3. Remove the chicken from the broth and let it cool to room temperature. Then remove the skin and cut the chicken into 1/2-inch cubes. Place them in a large bowl.

4. While the chicken is cooking, bring a saucepan of lightly salted water to a boil over high heat. Add the green beans and cook until just tender, 2 to 3 minutes. Drain them in a colander, then run them under cold water to stop the cooking. Drain again and pat dry. Set the beans aside.

5. Trim the fennel bulbs and cut them into 1/4-inch-wide lengthwise strips. Add these to the cooled chicken, along with the green beans, tomatoes, olives, capers, parsley, and chopped fennel fronds.

6. Season the salad with salt and pepper. Shortly before serving, toss with the Lemon Vinaigrette.

Note: You can prepare the salad several hours in advance. If you do, cover with plastic wrap and refrigerate until shortly before serving. Do not add the parsley, fennel fronds, or vinaigrette until you are ready to serve the salad.

TOMATOES A LA TAPENADE

In Provence, tapenade is made into a smooth paste with a mortar and pestle. I prefer a somewhat rougher-textured tapenade, so I pulse the olives in a food processor, stopping while there are still some recognizable olive bits. Niçoise olives are called for in the traditional recipe, but they are small and a real chore to pit. If you don't have the time or the patience, Italian Gaeta olives would be my next choice, and Greek Kalamata, third. All of them are pungent and full-flavored. The dark, briny earthiness of the olives plays a rousing counterpoint to thick juicy slabs of ripe tomato. Garnish with nasturtium blossoms and leaves, if available.

> 1 cup pitted Niçoise, Gaeta, or Kalamata olives
> 4 small cloves garlic, coarsely chopped
> 2 tablespoons extra-virgin olive oil
> 2 tablespoons fresh lemon juice
> 2 tablespoons coarsely chopped fresh marjoram, or 1 teaspoon dried
> 2 tablespoons chopped fresh flat-leaf parsley
> 4 ripe tomatoes, cut into 4 slices each

1. Combine the olives, garlic, olive oil, lemon juice, marjoram, and 1 tablespoon of the parsley in a food processor. Pulse the machine on and off until the mixture is nearly smooth, retaining a bit of texture. Transfer the tapenade to a bowl. (It will keep for up to 2 days, covered and refrigerated.)

Tomatoes à la Tapenade

2. To serve, arrange the tomato slices on a large platter. Spread a tablespoon of the tapenade on each slice. Sprinkle the remaining 1 tablespoon parsley over all and serve.

BLACKBERRY SORBET

Some berries are hard to find in the wild, but blackberries grow everywhere. They come into fruit over a long season and they are plentiful. Lucky are those who can find them berry-patch fresh. This sorbet is splendid scooped into a cantaloupe half.

> 2 pints fresh blackberries, or
>   24 ounces frozen unsweetened
>   blackberries, thawed
> 1¼ cups Simple Syrup
>   (page 403)

1. Combine the blackberries with ¼ cup of the Simple Syrup in a food processor or blender and puree until smooth. If desired, strain the puree to remove the seeds.

2. Stir in the remaining 1 cup syrup. Transfer the mixture to an ice-cream maker and freeze according to the manufacturer's instructions. Place in a container, cover, and freeze.

MAKES 1 QUART

RICH PECAN SQUARES

At the start of the food revolution that erupted in New York in the 1970s, the restaurant that got things rolling was The Quilted Giraffe. With such dishes as Caviar Beggar's Purses and their Kaiseki Tasting Menu, Barry and Susan Wine proved to New Yorkers that fine dining doesn't always mean fancy French cuisine. And there was nothing fancy about their take on this down-home American dessert, the pecan square. Susan's is, hands-down, the best one I have ever tasted.

FOR THE CRUST
> 2 cups all-purpose flour
> ⅔ cup confectioners' sugar
> 1 cup (2 sticks) unsalted butter,
>   at room temperature

FOR THE TOPPING
> ⅔ cup (about 11 tablespoons)
>   unsalted butter, melted
> ½ cup honey
> 3 tablespoons heavy (whipping) cream
> ½ cup (packed) light brown sugar
> 3½ cups coarsely chopped pecans

1. Preheat the oven to 350°F. Butter a 13 x 9-inch baking dish.

2. Prepare the crust: Sift the flour and confectioners' sugar together into a bowl. Cut in the butter, using two knives or a pastry blender, until fine crumbs form. Pat the crust onto the bottom of the prepared baking dish. Bake for 20 minutes. Then remove the dish from the oven and set it aside at room temperature for 15 to 20 minutes. Don't turn off the oven.

3. Prepare the topping: Combine the melted butter, honey, cream, and brown sugar in a bowl. Stir in the pecans. Spread the pecan mixture over the crust. Return the baking dish to the oven and bake for 25 minutes. Allow to cool completely in the pan on a wire rack, then cut into squares.

MAKES 36 SQUARES

THE ALL-AMERICAN NUT

The pecan is the only major tree nut that is considered an American native. Pecans were first discovered growing in North America and parts of Mexico in the fifteenth century. The word *pecan*, from an Algonquian Indian word, means "nut requiring a stone to crack." Pecans were a favorite of pre-colonial residents and served as a major food source because they grew in accessible places near waterways and were easier to shell than other North American nut species.

Blackberry Sorbet

Pool

Party

Splashing, giggling, cries of "Don't splash me!" And then someone does a cannonball off the side of the pool and everybody gets splashed anyway. The guys stand around the grill seriously debating the doneness issue. There are endless pitchers of iced tea and plenty of cold beer— it's a hot, hot day. Partying around the pool is as American as drive-in movies and oldies radio stations. It's as relaxing as a long, sun-baked nap or a porch swing. There's no real plan necessary: If you can't stand the heat, it's out of the chaise and into the pool. Once dry, it's time to chow down.

MENU

Pool Party

BUFFET FOR SIXTEEN

Watermelon Daiquiris

Summer Borscht

Cubano Sandwiches

Sumptuous Grilled
Salmon on Focaccia

Madras Lamb Burgers with
Spiced-Up Blueberry Relish

A Little Tomato Salad

Creamy Curry Macédoine

Full of Beans Salad
with Red Wine Vinaigrette

Watermelon, Cucumber,
and Tomato Delight

Roberto Donna's Cherries
in Barbera

Food for a pool party should be lively and playful, and the drinks—like icy daiquiris decorated with watermelon wedges and mint sprigs—should be as well. The Summer Borscht is chilled and just right for sunny-day sipping. Three totally different sandwiches, all with a slight ethnic twist, include a Cubano with mojo-style flavors, Madras burgers enhanced with blueberry relish, and grilled salmon on focaccia. The four festive summer salads are colorful, easily made ahead, and perfect matches for the sandwiches.

For dessert, Cherries in Barbera served with vanilla ice cream sounds like the best cherry ice-cream sundae in the world. . . . which is just what it happens to be. All add up to a bountiful menu designed to allow guests a substantial tapas-size taste of its many offerings. If kids will be coming, have some hot dogs on hand for those with less adventurous palates.

If you have them, place canvas umbrellas around and stack piles of large fluffy striped towels at each corner of the pool. Serve the food buffet-style, under the umbrellas or on the porch. Set out several small tables for easy eating at poolside. Everybody is wearing bathing suits (or they better be!), so easy and relaxed is the order of the day.

You don't want any serious clean-up, so opt for paper napkins and disposable "glassware." Don't stint on quality—choose ones that are very large and heavy. Place them in sturdy containers so they don't fly away.

THE MUSIC

Celia Cruz's *100% Azucar*
Rolling Stones

THE DRINKS

Watermelon Daiquiris
Red Stripe beer
Iced tea

THE EXTRAS

Heavy-duty blender
Paper cocktail parasols and napkins
Poolside furniture
Plastic tableware
Cherry pitter

WATERMELON DAIQUIRIS

There are many legends about the invention of the daiquiri, but in Cuba I learned that the drink originated there near the end of the nineteenth century. To combat the weariness of long treks on horseback and fierce battles, the soldiers of the Liberation Army, then struggling for independence from Spain, tied bottles filled with a traditional stimulating mixture of strong local rum, honey, and lemon juice—which they called *canchachara*—to their saddles. Sometime after U.S. troops arrived in Cuba in 1898, somewhere near the town of Daiquiri in the province of Orinte, the Americans added crushed ice to this concoction, and Daiquiri became the new and lasting name of a terrific cocktail. In the century since, other cocktail fanciers have tried their hand by adding any number of fresh fruits to the original formula. Here is mine, and I guarantee that you will be back for refills. You can substitute any of summer's luscious ripe fruits, such as strawberries, peaches, apricots, or ripe melons. Add a wedge of watermelon along with a mint sprig for garnish, and then spear the watermelon with a hot pink or turquoise paper parasol.

> 8 cups chopped seedless watermelon
> 48 ounces white rum
> 2 cups fresh lime juice
>   (from 12 to 14 large limes)
> 1 cup Simple Syrup (page 403)
> 16 cups crushed ice
> 16 small wedges watermelon, for garnish
> 16 sprigs fresh mint, for garnish

Prepare the daiquiris in batches: Combine some of the chopped watermelon, rum, lime juice, Simple Syrup, and crushed ice in a blender and process at high speed until mixed, 30 seconds. Pour into a large bowl. Repeat until all the ingredients are used up. Stir the bowlful of

Watermelon Daiquiris

daiquiris with a wooden spoon, then ladle into cocktail glasses, garnishing each drink with a watermelon wedge and a mint sprig.

SUMMER BORSCHT

A hot summer day; the air is still, the leaves are hanging down on the trees, even the cicadas have slowed down their metronomic chant. The answer? Borscht. Not any borscht, but a cool beet borscht, sweet and slightly tangy, and silky with sour cream. This recipe is one of my Granny Reeseman's best. Now, should I tempt fate and play with it? Since I love roasted beets and a hint of orange, I've taken the chance. I know Granny would be tolerant.

> 16 beets, scrubbed
> Zest of 2 large oranges, removed from each
>   with a paring knife in 1 strip if possible
> 1½ cups fresh lemon juice
>   (10 large lemons)
> About ½ cup sugar, to taste
> 4 teaspoons salt, or more to taste
> 6 eggs
> 2 cups whole milk
> 2 cups sour cream, for garnish
> 2 hothouse (seedless) cucumbers, peeled,
>   seeded, and diced, for garnish

1. Preheat the oven to 350°F.

2. Cut the greens off the beets, leaving 1 inch of the stems and roots. Wrap the beets individually in aluminum foil and place them on a baking sheet. Bake until they are tender, about 1 hour. When the beets are cool enough to handle, remove the foil and slip off and discard the skins. Trim off the roots and stems.

3. Coarsely grate the beets individually into a large soup pot. (See Note.) Add 16 cups cold water and the orange zest. Bring it to a boil over high heat, skimming off any foam that rises to the surface. Reduce the heat to medium-low, add the lemon juice, sugar, and the 4 teaspoons salt, and simmer, partially covered, for 15 minutes.

4. Remove the pot from the heat and allow the borscht to cool slightly. Remove and discard the orange zest.

5. Beat the eggs and milk together in a large bowl with a fork. Slowly whisk 6 cups of the warm borscht into the milk mixture. Gradually whisk this mixture back into the remaining borscht, whisking constantly.

6. Cover the soup and refrigerate until it is very cold. Taste and correct the seasonings. There should be a good balance between sweet and sour, so add more lemon juice or sugar if necessary.

7. To serve, ladle the soup into glasses. Garnish each serving with a dollop of sour cream and a sprinkling of diced cucumber.

Note: If you would like your borscht to be more liquid, remove some grated beets with a slotted spoon, puree them, and freeze them for later use (for instance, to thicken a sauce for a beef stew or short ribs).

CUBANO SANDWICHES

The cubano is to Cuba what the burger is to the United States: It is an inspired culinary work—mojo sauce, moist roast pork, mild melty cheese, sweet pickles, and salty ham, all packed in a bullet-shaped roll and toasted in a sandwich press. When made with a sweet egg-dough roll, the cubano becomes what Havana night owls call a *medianoche*.

> 6 large cloves garlic, thinly sliced lengthwise
> ⅓ cup thinly slivered red onion
> ¾ teaspoon ground cumin
> Salt and freshly ground black pepper, to taste
> ⅓ cup plus about 4 tablespoons extra-virgin
>   olive oil
> ½ cup plus 1 tablespoon fresh lime juice
>   (from 5 large limes)
> ¾ teaspoon white wine vinegar
> 8 oval rolls, 5 to 6 inches long, halved
>   lengthwise, insides scooped out
> 3 tablespoons Dijon mustard
> 24 thin slices queso blanco or Monterey
>   Jack cheese
> 8 to 16 large sweet gherkin pickles,
>   thinly sliced lengthwise
> 16 thin slices baked Virginia ham
> 24 thin slices roast pork

1. Stir the garlic, onion, cumin, and salt and pepper together in a small bowl.

2. Heat the ⅓ cup olive oil in a small heavy saucepan over low heat. Add the onion mixture and cook, stirring, until the onions are translucent, 10 minutes. Add the lime juice and vinegar and simmer over low heat to mellow the flavors, 5 minutes. Allow the mixture to cool slightly and spoon and brush it on the inside of both halves of each roll, distributing the onions evenly.

3. Dab the bottom half of each roll with about 1 teaspoon of the mustard. Layer each with 3 slices of cheese, then some pickle slices, 2 slices of ham, and 3 slices of pork. Cover with the top of the roll.

4. Heat 1 tablespoon of the remaining oil in a nonstick skillet over medium heat. Place 2 sandwiches, bottom side down, in the skillet and weight them down with the lid of a cast-iron pot. Cook until the sandwiches are browned on the bottom, 1 to 2 minutes. Turn the sandwiches over, weight them down, and cook until that side is browned and the cheese has melted, 1 to 2 minutes. Transfer the sandwiches to a cutting board and cover with aluminum foil to keep warm. Repeat with the remaining sandwiches, adding more oil to the skillet as needed.

5. Cut the sandwiches in half on the diagonal, and serve them wrapped in large paper napkins.

SUMPTUOUS GRILLED SALMON ON FOCACCIA

Combine a simple grilled salmon fillet with crisp sharp arugula, a sweet juicy summer tomato, and cooling crème fraîche, and you have a masterpiece of a sandwich, thanks to the bounty of Mother Nature.

A WHOLE LOT OF GRILLING

This menu relies heavily on the grill—the salmon and lamb burgers are both cooked on it, and you could probably use it to make the Cubano Sandwiches as well, although the recipe calls for the stovetop. Anytime you have plenty of grilling ahead, make sure your propane tank is full (having an extra tank on hand is a good idea) or that you have fresh coals heating up in your chimney starter. Clean the grill before each use.

8 salmon fillets (6 ounces each)
¼ cup fresh lemon juice
  (from 2 large lemons)
¼ cup dry white wine
¼ cup extra-virgin olive oil
2 tablespoons Dijon mustard
2 large cloves garlic, crushed
Salt and freshly ground black pepper, to taste
8 squares (4 inches each) focaccia,
  split horizontally
2 large bunches arugula, tough stems
  removed, washed and patted dry
½ cup crème fraîche
8 slices ripe tomato, cut ½ inch thick

1. Heat a barbecue grill to high. Oil the grill rack well.

2. Place the salmon fillets between two sheets of wax paper and gently flatten them with a metal spatula.

3. Combine the lemon juice, wine, olive oil, mustard, garlic, and salt and pepper in a large bowl. Add the salmon fillets to the bowl and coat them well with the marinade. Let marinate for 15 minutes.

Watermelon Daiquiri,
Sumptuous Grilled Salmon on Focaccia,
and *A Little Tomato Salad*

4. Grill the salmon fillets, flesh-side down, for 3 minutes, basting with the marinade. Then turn and grill on the other side until just cooked through, 3 minutes. Carefully transfer the salmon fillets to a plate (the skin will come off as it grills—discard it).

5. When the salmon comes off the grill, grill the tomato slices for 2 minutes per side, sprinkling them with salt and pepper. Remove them to a large plate, then lightly grill the focaccia, 30 seconds per side.

6. To assemble the sandwiches, place a few arugula leaves on the bottom halves of the focaccia. Cover with a salmon fillet, a dollop of crème fraîche, and a tomato slice. Cover with the top of the focaccia and press down slightly. Carefully cut the sandwiches in half with a serrated knife. Serve immediately.

MADRAS LAMB BURGERS

O f course any self-respecting pool party needs burgers. You can stand up while you're eating them, walk around and talk with one in your hands. You can wash them down with an icy cold beer. For a variation on the traditional beef burger, I went for inspiration to the spiced ground lamb dishes so popular from Greece to India. Curry-accented lamb, curry-laced mayonnaise, and then the classic burger fixings make for a familiar-looking burger with an exciting new taste—and an unusual sweet-tart fruit relish alongside.

FOR THE CURRY MAYONNAISE

1½ cups prepared mayonnaise,
  such as Hellmann's
¼ cup chopped mango chutney
2 tablespoons curry powder

FOR THE BURGERS

¼ cup olive oil
1 cup finely chopped onions
1 cup finely chopped celery
4 tablespoons curry powder
4 pounds ground lamb
8 scallions, white part only, thinly sliced
½ cup coarsely chopped fresh mint
4 tablespoons minced garlic
Salt and freshly ground black pepper,
  to taste
16 hamburger buns, for serving
16 slices ripe tomato, for serving
16 large red-leaf lettuce leaves,
  for serving

Spiced-Up Blueberry Relish (recipe follows),
  for serving

1. Combine the ingredients for the curry mayonnaise in a small bowl and set it aside.

2. Heat the olive oil in a skillet over medium-low heat. Add the onion and celery and cook, stirring occasionally, for 8 minutes. Add the curry powder and cook, stirring, to release the curry aroma, 1 minute more. Transfer this mixture to a large bowl and allow it to cool. Then add the ground lamb, the scallions, mint, garlic, and salt and pepper. Mix with a fork and form into 16 patties.

3. Heat a barbecue grill to high.

4. Grill the burgers 3 to 4 inches from the heat source for 5 minutes on the first side and 4 on the second side for medium-rare.

5. When the burgers come off the grill, lightly grill the buns for 30 seconds per side. Place a burger on each bun and top it with a slice of tomato and a lettuce leaf. Spread 1 tablespoon of the curry mayonnaise on the top bun and then cover the burger. Serve immediately, with a bowl of blueberry relish alongside.

Note: If you prefer, you can spread the blueberry relish on the bottom half of the buns before adding the burgers.

SPICED-UP BLUEBERRY RELISH

Plum relish, tomato relish, quince relish, watermelon rind relish—any fruit or vegetable that is acid and sweet can probably be used in a relish. At the height of blueberry season, baskets of juicy blueberries combined in a relish with pungent aromatics—mace, cinnamon, nutmeg, allspice—balance and complement the most assertive meats, from lamb, to duck, to charbroiled flank steak.

> 2 pounds fresh or IQF
>   (individually quick-frozen)
>   blueberries (6 to 7 cups)
> 1/4 cup cider vinegar
> 1/4 cup red wine vinegar
> 3 cups sugar
> 1/4 teaspoon ground nutmeg
> 1/4 teaspoon ground mace
> 1/4 teaspoon ground cinnamon
> 1/8 teaspoon ground allspice

1. Rinse the berries and drain them well.

2. Place the berries and both vinegars in a heavy saucepan over medium heat. As the juices begin to render, increase the heat slightly and stir gently until the mixture boils. Boil steadily for 10 minutes, stirring occasionally. Skim off the foam as it rises to the surface with a metal spoon.

3. Meanwhile, combine the sugar and spices in a bowl.

4. Skim off the last of the foam from the berries and stir in the sugar mixture all at once. Continue to stir until the mixture returns to a boil. Then boil steadily, stirring occasionally, until all the blueberries have popped and the relish has thickened, 10 minutes more.

5. Remove the pan from the heat. Let the relish cool to room temperature and refrigerate it, covered, for up to 2 weeks.

MAKES 4 CUPS

A LITTLE TOMATO SALAD

In the summer, a visit to a farmstand is pure pleasure, if only for the breathtaking tomatoes. I can never choose among them and always end up taking home a few of each—especially the heirlooms, ranging in color from purple to green-and-white striped, to dark red-and-green. They taste sweet, and they look beautiful when displayed on large platters sprinkled with herbs or fennel fronds. Baby cherry and pear tomatoes add more contrasting shapes and colors. A few summer green beans jazz up the works.

> 1 1/2 cups tender green beans, trimmed and
>   cut into 1-inch pieces
> 3 cups red grape or cherry tomatoes,
>   cut in half lengthwise
> 3 cups yellow pear or cherry tomatoes,
>   cut in half lengthwise
> 6 large ripe heirloom tomatoes, halved
>   lengthwise and cut into very thin wedges
> 3 teaspoons sugar
> Freshly ground black pepper, to taste
> 3 teaspoons red wine vinegar
> 3 tablespoons extra-virgin olive oil
> 1/3 cup chopped fresh fennel fronds

1. Bring a small saucepan of lightly salted water to a boil over high heat. Add the green beans and cook for just 1 minute to blanch them. Drain immediately and rinse under cold water to stop the cooking. Pat them dry.

2. Toss all the tomatoes and green beans together in a decorative bowl. (The recipe can be made up to 4 hours in advance to this point.) Cover the bowl with plastic wrap. Before serving, sprinkle the salad with the sugar, pepper, vinegar, olive oil, and fennel fronds and toss. Serve immediately.

CREAMY CURRY MACEDOINE

Though no pool party would be complete without its poolside barbecue, it's also true that on a hot summer afternoon—when the sun beats down, the air is still, and heat rules the day—a selection of cooling salads can be so satisfying. This one is a mixture of textures and tastes and all kinds of vegetables—that's why it is called a *macédoine*. It's an odd route from Alexander the Great to your table, but Alexander, a Macedonian, had an empire consisting of many disparate states. In his honor, the French call a combination of fruits or vegetables a *macédoine*.

FOR THE VEGETABLES
  1¹/₂ cups diced carrots (¹/₂-inch dice)
  1¹/₂ cups diced boiling potatoes (¹/₂-inch dice)
  1¹/₂ cups diced white turnips (¹/₂-inch dice)
  1¹/₂ cups cut green beans (¹/₂-inch lengths)
  1¹/₂ cups green peas (thawed if frozen)

FOR THE DRESSING
  2 tablespoons canola oil
  ³/₄ cup finely chopped onions
  3 tablespoons curry powder
  3 tablespoons fresh lime juice
    (from 2 large limes)
  2 cups prepared mayonnaise,
    such as Hellmann's
  3¹/₂ tablespoons chopped mango chutney

  4 bunches fresh mint, for garnish
  2 tablespoons coarsely chopped fresh mint,
    for garnish

1. Fill a large bowl with water and ice.

2. Bring a saucepan of lightly salted water to a boil over high heat. Add the carrots and cook until just tender, 2 minutes. Using a slotted spoon, immediately transfer the carrots to the ice water to stop the cooking.

3. Add the potatoes to the same boiling water, cook until just tender, 2 minutes, and add them to the ice water.

4. Repeat this process with the turnips (cook for 2 minutes), the green beans (1 minute), and the peas (1 minute). (If using frozen peas, cook them for just 30 seconds.)

5. Drain the cooled vegetables in a colander, discarding the ice, and pat them dry. Combine the vegetables in a bowl and set it aside. (The recipe can be made up to 24 hours in advance. Cover with plastic wrap and refrigerate until 30 minutes before dressing.)

6. Prepare the dressing: Heat the oil in a small skillet over low heat. Add the onions and cook, stirring, until wilted and translucent, about 10 minutes. Add the curry powder and cook, stirring, for 5 minutes to mellow the flavors. Transfer to a bowl and allow to cool completely. Stir in the lime juice, mayonnaise, and mango chutney.

7. Using a large rubber spatula, fold the dressing into the vegetables. Serve in a shallow bowl, with large bunches of mint placed decoratively around the sides. Sprinkle the chopped mint on top.

FULL OF BEANS SALAD

If you went to a hundred covered-dish suppers, probably ninety of them would feature some variation of a multi-bean salad. Quite often, they emphasize sugar to the detriment of the earthy garden flavors of the beans. A classic vinaigrette will do beautifully, provided you have the secret ingredient: fresh, ripe wax beans, full of freshly picked snap.

> *12 ounces fresh green beans, trimmed*
> * and cut in half*
> *12 ounces fresh yellow wax beans,*
> * trimmed and cut in half*
> *6 scallions, including 3 inches green,*
> * thinly sliced*
> *1½ cups canned dark red kidney beans,*
> * rinsed and drained*
> *1½ cups canned black beans, rinsed*
> * and drained*
> *1½ cups canned chickpeas (garbanzo beans),*
> * rinsed and drained*
> *Salt and freshly ground black pepper,*
> * to taste*
> *Red Wine Vinaigrette (recipe follows)*
> *3 tablespoons chopped fresh flat-leaf parsley*

1. Fill a large bowl with water and ice.

2. Bring a saucepan of lightly salted water to a boil over high heat. Add the green and wax beans and cook until just tender, about 2 minutes. Using a slotted spoon, immediately transfer the beans to the ice water to stop the cooking.

3. Drain the beans in a colander, discarding the ice, and pat them dry. (The recipe can be made up to 24 hours in advance to this point. Place the beans in a bowl and cover with plastic wrap. Refrigerate until 1 hour before serving, then continue with the recipe.) Place the cooked beans, scallions, and canned beans and chickpeas in a large bowl. Season with salt and pepper. Toss with the vinaigrette, sprinkle with the chopped parsley, and serve.

RED WINE VINAIGRETTE

When making a good vinaigrette, you want a perfect emulsion and a good balance of vinegar and oil. All you need is a little sugar to smooth out the taste. This combo should do it.

> *¼ cup red wine vinegar*
> *1 tablespoon Dijon mustard*
> *1 teaspoon sugar*
> *Salt and freshly ground black pepper,*
> * to taste*
> *½ cup extra-virgin olive oil*

Whisk the vinegar, mustard, sugar, and salt and pepper together in a small bowl. Whisking constantly, add the olive oil in a slow steady stream, and continue whisking until thickened. Refrigerate, covered, for 3 to 4 days.

MAKES ¾ CUP

WATERMELON, CUCUMBER, AND TOMATO DELIGHT

Watermelon is red, sweet, and refreshing; tomato is red, sweet and savory, and soft; and cucumber is soothing and crunchy. The combination is as summery as a cotton shirt.

> 3 cups diced seeded watermelon
> (³/₄-inch dice; red, or combination of red and yellow watermelon)
> 6 ripe plum tomatoes, each cut into 8 pieces
> 1¹/₂ hothouse (seedless) cucumbers, peeled, halved lengthwise, and cut into ¹/₂-inch pieces
> 3 tablespoons extra-virgin olive oil
> Generous ¹/₃ cup slivered fresh basil leaves
> Freshly ground black pepper, to taste

1. Prepare all of the ingredients up to 4 hours in advance and set them aside separately in bowls covered with plastic.

2. Just before serving, drain the watermelon, tomatoes, and cucumber in a colander and place them in a decorative serving bowl. Toss with the olive oil, basil, and pepper. Serve immediately.

ROBERTO DONNA'S CHERRIES IN BARBERA

I had the pleasure of eating in chef Roberto Donna's restaurant, Galileo, in Washington, D.C., and enjoyed watching him prepare a multicourse dinner for a small group of awed diners. These luscious cherries are one of his specialties. They're brilliant in June, when cherries

are at their peak, or whenever you are lucky enough to find them in the market. Roberto serves the cherries in a tall glass, topped with whipped cream. For the pool party, serve them over a bowl of Double Vanilla-Bean Ice Cream for a super cherry-vanilla ice-cream sundae.

> 6 pounds fresh Bing cherries,
> rinsed and pitted
> 2 cups sugar
> 4 whole cloves
> 2 cinnamon sticks (each 1¹/₂ inches long)
> Finely grated zest of 2 oranges
> Finely grated zest of 2 lemons
> 2 cups Barbera or other deep purple-red fruity wine
> 2 quarts Double Vanilla-Bean Ice Cream (page 53; also see Notes)

1. Combine all the ingredients except the ice cream in a large pot and bring to a boil over high heat. Remove the pot from the heat and allow the cherry mixture to cool to room temperature. Then transfer to a large container, cover, and refrigerate for 1 or 2 days for the flavors to develop (see Notes).

2. Remove the cloves and cinnamon stick from the cherries, and discard. When you are ready to serve the dessert, spoon the ice cream into dessert bowls. Spoon the cherries, along with some of the juice, over the ice cream. Serve immediately.

Notes: You will need to double the ice-cream recipe in order to make enough to serve 16.

The cherries will keep for up to 2 weeks in a covered container in the refrigerator.

FRESH BLUEBERRY

A t the height of berry-picking season, "dazzling" is an understatement for the deep color and vibrant taste of just-gathered blueberries. Blueberry picking with friends is fun, especially when it culminates in a delicious breakfast. Arrange a time and place to meet, and hand out little baskets for the berries— old-fashioned children's beach pails are fun and handy. Tell the group it's okay to nibble a few, but don't let them fill themselves up! If berries don't grow close by, head for the nearest farm stand instead. Breakfast with good friends—the kind you enjoy seeing during the first half of the day—is a pleasure we don't treat ourselves to often enough.

BREAKFAST

MENU

FRESH BLUEBERRY BREAKFAST

FOR EIGHT

Dazzling Fresh Fruit Salad

Watercress Scrambled Eggs
with Smoked Salmon

Amanda's Blueberry Coffee Cake

Set all the dishes for this charming breakfast on the table at the same time. It features a buttery blueberry coffee cake, and since it takes time to prepare, you'll need to get at least some of your blueberries in advance of the morning berry picking. The cake is delicious when you serve it with a pitcher of freshly squeezed orange juice and, of course, coffee. Watercress Scrambled Eggs are easy to make, and set atop smoked salmon they look lovely as well. And so does the magnificent rainbow fruit salad—gorgeous!

August is prime hydrangea time. There's nothing more decorative than these huge flowers, with their deep green leaves, arranged in large glass vases. Their romantic blooms look like the clouds on a brilliant afternoon, especially alongside blueberry coffee cake, displayed, if possible, on a glass pedestal cake stand. Place a bowl of freshly picked blueberries on the table, with a pitcher of heavy cream or a bowl of clotted cream or sour cream alongside.

Blue-and-white windowpane-check napkins make a charming addition to the breakfast, and they come fully to life when you place them on a rustic table. If you like, be a part of the décor yourself, in a vintage blue skirt or shirt.

THE MUSIC

The Pizzarellis' *Contrast*
Billie Holiday's *Lady Day*

THE DRINKS

Freshly squeezed
orange juice

Freshly brewed coffee
and tea

THE EXTRAS

Little baskets
or beach pails

Pedestal cake stand

Decorative
fruit salad bowl

DAZZLING FRESH FRUIT SALAD

Basically this recipe could be written as "Take everything ripe from the orchard, add everything ripe from the berry patch, mix in everything ripe from the melon garden, and toss with a flourish of mint." Fruit, fruit, and more fruit—the floral scents and flavors and the various juices blending together are downright ambrosial. When they're in season, pluck up some pretty (unsprayed) violets, pansies, and nasturtiums as garnish.

1 cup cubed ripe cantaloupe (1-inch cubes)
1 cup cubed ripe honeydew (1-inch cubes)
1 cup cubed seeded watermelon
    (1-inch cubes)
1 cup cubed ripe pineapple (1-inch cubes)
1 cup ripe strawberries, rinsed, hulled,
    and cut in half
1 cup pitted Bing cherries (if available),
    rinsed
1/2 cup fresh blueberries, gently rinsed
1/2 cup fresh raspberries, gently rinsed
1/2 cup seedless green grapes, rinsed and
    cut in half
1/2 cup seedless red grapes, rinsed and halved
2 blood oranges (if available) or 2 navel
    oranges, peeled and thinly sliced
1 navel orange, peeled and thinly sliced
2 kiwis, peeled, halved lengthwise, and thinly
    sliced
1/2 cup small fresh mint leaves, for garnish

Make sure all the rinsed fruit is well drained. Then combine all the fruit in a large decorative bowl 1 hour before serving, to allow the natural juices to come together (see Note). Sprinkle with the mint leaves and serve.

Note: You can make this up to 3 hours in advance. Cover and refrigerate, then add the mint leaves just before serving.

WATERCRESS SCRAMBLED EGGS WITH SMOKED SALMON

Steamy eggs, soft and fluffy as a feather pillow, served over thin, thin, thin sliced smoked salmon. Top them with a dollop of sour cream and serve on your prettiest plates.

16 large, very thin slices Nova Scotia
    smoked salmon (see Note)
16 large eggs
1/4 cup sour cream, plus 3 tablespoons
    for garnish
Salt and freshly ground black pepper, to taste
1 1/3 cups watercress leaves, plus extra
    for garnish
3 tablespoons unsalted butter

1. Cover the center of each of eight large salad or luncheon plates with two slices of the salmon. Set the plates aside.

2. Whisk the eggs, the 1/4 cup sour cream, and salt and pepper together in a bowl. Stir in the 1 1/3 cups watercress leaves.

3. Cook the eggs in two batches: Melt 1 1/2 tablespoons of the butter in a nonstick skillet over medium-low heat. Add half of the egg mixture and cook, stirring with a spoon and scooping the set eggs in from the sides, until they are just cooked through, 2 to 3 minutes. Set the eggs aside, covered, and keep warm. Repeat with the second batch of eggs.

4. Spoon some of the eggs onto each plate in the center of the salmon. Dollop each with a spoonful of the remaining sour cream and garnish with a few watercress leaves. Serve immediately.

Note: It is important to use smoked salmon (my favorite is Gaspé)—not salty lox, which would overpower the light and elegant eggs.

"*All happiness depends on a leisurely breakfast.*"

—JOHN GUNTHER

Watercress Scrambled Eggs with Smoked Salmon

AMANDA'S BLUEBERRY COFFEE CAKE

A leisurely cup of good coffee and a slice of freshly baked coffee cake moist with just-picked blueberries—now that's a great way to begin a day. Amanda Ross—a good friend and a great baker—shared this super-moist coffee cake, the pièce de résistance of a brunch menu. The crumb topping—traditional on many coffee cakes—is finished off with a light dusting of confectioners' sugar for flavor and eye appeal.

> 12 tablespoons (1½ sticks) cold unsalted butter, cut into small pieces
> 2 cups all-purpose flour
> 1 cup granulated sugar
> 1 teaspoon salt
> ½ teaspoon baking powder
> ½ teaspoon baking soda
> ¾ cup buttermilk
> 1 large egg
> 1 teaspoon pure vanilla extract
> 1½ cups fresh blueberries, picked over, lightly rinsed and patted dry
> ¼ cup (packed) light or dark brown sugar
> Confectioners' sugar, for dusting

1. Position a rack in the center of the oven, and preheat the oven to 350°F. Butter a 9-inch springform pan.

2. Combine the flour, sugar, salt, and 10 tablespoons of the butter in a bowl and mix with an electric mixer until it resembles coarse meal, about 1 minute. Remove 1 cup of this mixture from the bowl and set it aside for the topping.

3. Add the baking powder and baking soda to the remaining mixture in the bowl and stir to combine. With the mixer running on low speed, mix in the buttermilk until combined, followed by the egg and vanilla. Then mix the ingredients for 1 minute on high speed to aerate the batter.

4. Fold in the blueberries, using a rubber spatula. Scrape the batter into the prepared pan.

5. Place the reserved 1 cup topping mixture in a bowl and add the brown sugar and remaining 2 tablespoons butter. Mix with your fingertips until crumbly. Sprinkle this mixture evenly over the cake batter. Bake until a wooden toothpick inserted in the center comes out clean, 1 hour to 1 hour and 10 minutes.

6. Allow the cake to cool in the pan on a wire rack for 20 minutes. Then carefully remove the sides of the springform pan and place the cake on a serving plate. Just before serving, sprinkle the top with confectioners' sugar.

Amanda's Blueberry Coffee Cake

A Big Family

In these days of far-flung families, the old-time custom of the family reunion has once again become popular. Everyone—parents, children cousins, uncles, aunts, grandparents, brothers, sisters, dogs and cats—shows up. Overnighters wake up to giant pancake and sausage blowouts in the morning after late-night gab sessions over Mom's pie. Family legends are dusted off and retold—with embellishments—to the next generation. But it's the main meal that's the big deal; a group effort, resulting in a table

laden with favorites, all of them sure to make this family reunion a major success.

Reunion

MENU

A Big Family Reunion

PICNIC FOR TWENTY-FOUR

Peter's Smoked
Rolled Shoulder of Pork
with
Papaya and
Tomato Relish

———

Betty's Ham Salad

———

Sherried Shrimp Salad

———

Roasted Salmon Salad

———

Reunion Potato Salad

Carrot Slaw with Raisins
and Cherries

———

Rustic Bread Salad

———

Orange-Scented
Cauliflower Salad

———

Summer Corn Salad

———

Jalapeño Corn Muffins

———

Berta's Carrot Cake

A menu for a large gathering requires some careful planning. It's best to have one person designated as coordinator, to deputize family members to bring food, or drinks, or equipment, and to make sure the menu is well balanced. The menu should include something for everyone—as this one does. The pork shoulder is easy to slice and serves a large group nicely. Other main dishes include a vibrant Roasted Salmon Salad and Sherried Shrimp Salad, both of which are easy to serve. Of course, cousin Betty will—as always—bring her ham salad. What a doll! A large variety of vegetable salads are a must for reunions because we're thoroughly modern people. By the way, Glorious Gazpacho, one of the great summer soups, would also be great here (page 133). Besides the Jalapeño Corn Muffins, a nice variety of rolls, different sliced breads, and flatbreads can be served with a cheese board and a basket of seasonal fruits. My mom always brings her carrot cake to our family reunions, cut up in small squares. If you have chocoholic relatives (and who doesn't), bake up a batch of Chocolate Chunk Brownies (page 25) from the Super Bowl Menu.

Summer is the ideal time for a reunion. A big yard, a sunny day, and lots of tables set up are all you really need. If necessary, borrow or rent tables and chairs so there's room for everyone. A tent is not a bad idea if rain is a possibility. Keep it comfy and homey—after all, this is family.

THE MUSIC

Les Paul

Charlie Parker's
April in Paris

THE DRINKS

Lemonade

Sancerre

Gigondas

THE EXTRAS

Outdoor meat smoker

Assortment of serving bowls
and platters

PETER'S SMOKED ROLLED SHOULDER OF PORK

A few years ago, Peter Kaminsky made a pilgrimage to all the stadiums in the National Football League in search of the ultimate tailgate meal. "Anyone who says America has become a total fast-food nation needs to go to the NFL parking lots on any Sunday," Peter says. "There is every nationality making every kind of inventive home-style food." One of the things that he discovered was how wonderfully smoked food works when feeding a crowd and how easy it is to prepare. Here's proof!

FOR THE MARINADE

$1^{1}/_{2}$ bottles dry red wine, such as
    Côtes du Rhône
$^{1}/_{3}$ cup red wine vinegar
$^{1}/_{4}$ cup coarse (kosher) salt
2 large cloves garlic, lightly crushed
Juice of $^{1}/_{2}$ lemon
8 sprigs fresh rosemary
6 sprigs fresh oregano

FOR THE MEAT

2 boneless rolled shoulders of pork
    (about 5 pounds each)
2 tablespoons ground ginger
2 teaspoons paprika
2 teaspoons cracked black pepper
2 teaspoons coarse (kosher) salt
Papaya and Tomato Relish (recipe follows),
    for serving

1. Combine all the marinade ingredients with 2 cups water in a vessel that is large enough to hold the pork (a small turkey roaster works well). Add the pork and turn to coat it well in the marinade. Cover and refrigerate for 24 hours, turning the meat once or twice.

A simple backyard smoker costs about $50, can handle most meats up to and including a full-size turkey, and will serve you for many years. The trick is to fill the water pan, which sits above the coals in the center of the smoker (ideally below the meat), with an aromatic marinade, a flavorful liquid such as wine, apple juice, or beer—or just plain old water—at least 2 inches deep. The steadily simmering liquid moistens and flavors the food during the long smoking process. Check the water pan from time to time to make sure that the liquid level remains at about 2 inches deep, adding liquid as necessary to maintain that level.

2. Prepare an outdoor smoker.

3. Remove the pork from the marinade, reserving the marinade. Combine the ginger, paprika, pepper, and salt in a small bowl and sprinkle this all over the pork shoulders.

4. Place the pork on a rack in a smoker. Pour the reserved marinade into the water pan and, if necessary, top it off with water so the pan is at least half full.

5. Smoke the meat over hot coals for about 6 hours, checking the smoker often to make sure that there is enough liquid in the water pan; it should always be about 2 inches deep. Top it off with water as necessary. Add more charcoal to the hot coals as needed to keep a nice warm fire going (the hot coals should be gray).

6. The pork is done when a meat thermometer inserted in the thickest part of the meat reaches 160°F.

7. Let the pork cool to room temperature. Serve it thinly sliced, with the Papaya and Tomato Relish.

PAPAYA AND TOMATO RELISH

A relish highlights and supports the leading player, and when the leading player is a brawny-tasting meat, the relish can really go for flavor fireworks without the worry of upstaging the main course. Here the sweetness of papaya, the juiciness of ripe tomatoes, the floral top notes of cilantro, and the bite of red onion all help enhance the bold, powerful flavors of the succulent smoky meat.

>*4 ripe papayas (about 1 pound each)*
>*3 ripe plum tomatoes, seeded and*
>*   cut into $1/4$-inch dice*
>*$1^1/2$ tablespoons finely diced seeded*
>*   jalapeño pepper*
>*$3/4$ cup diced red onion ($1/4$-inch dice)*
>*$1/3$ cup chopped fresh cilantro*
>*1 tablespoon finely grated lime zest*
>*$1/3$ cup fresh lime juice*

1. Peel and seed the papayas and cut them into $1/4$-inch dice. Place in a bowl.

2. Gently combine the tomatoes, jalapeño, onion, cilantro, and lime zest with the papaya. Toss with the lime juice. Refrigerate, covered, for no longer than 4 hours before serving.

MAKES 5 CUPS

BETTY'S HAM SALAD

Every member of a family has a special talent, whether it is musical, athletic, or a recipe made to perfection. Ham salad is a perennial—make that eternal—favorite at picnics and potluck dinners, and no one makes it better than my cousin Betty, who can be counted on to show up with a mega-portion of this ham, pasta, and mayonnaise classic. Of course you might say *your* cousin Betty, or Anne, or Victor, makes the best

one, and you would be right . . . for your family. Part of what makes a recipe special are the associations and memories we bring to it.

>*2 cups dried tubetti or ditali pasta*
>*8 cups diced baked Virginia ham ($1/2$-inch dice)*
>*4 cups diced celery ($1/4$-inch dice)*
>*2 cups thinly sliced scallions, including*
>*   3 inches green*
>*$1^1/2$ cups loosely packed fresh flat-leaf*
>*   parsley leaves*
>*$1^1/3$ cups diced sweet gherkin pickles*
>*   ($1/4$-inch dice)*
>*3 cups prepared mayonnaise, such as*
>*   Hellmann's*
>*$1/4$ cup Dijon mustard*
>*1 teaspoon celery seeds*
>*Freshly ground black pepper, to taste*
>*$1/4$ cup chopped fresh flat-leaf parsley, for garnish*

1. Bring a large pot of salted water to a boil over high heat. Add the pasta and cook until just tender, 10 minutes. Drain the pasta into a colander, then run it under cold water to stop the cooking. When it is thoroughly cooled, drain the pasta again and pat dry.

2. Combine the pasta, ham, celery, scallions, parsley leaves, and gherkins in a large bowl. Toss well.

3. In a separate bowl, combine the mayonnaise, mustard, celery seeds, and pepper. Toss the dressing with the ham mixture, coating the ingredients well. Spoon the salad into a large serving bowl and sprinkle with the chopped parsley.

SHERRIED SHRIMP SALAD

Sherry is an oft-overlooked ingredient, which is a shame, because its woodsy tones add depth and character to a recipe without

Sherried Shrimp Salad, Summer Corn Salad, and Peter's Smoked Rolled Shoulder of Pork

weighing it down. In fact, just the opposite happens in this shrimp salad: The sherry actually lightens the effect of the mayonnaise, as do the herbal notes of chervil or dill.

FOR THE SHRIMP

3 cups dry white wine
1 bunch celery, with leaves, coarsely chopped
8 sprigs fresh parsley
8 whole black peppercorns
6 pounds large shrimp, peeled, deveined,
*   and well rinsed (see Note)*

FOR THE SALAD

2 cups diced celery (¼-inch dice)
4½ cups prepared mayonnaise,
*   such as Hellmann's*
6 tablespoons very dry Spanish sherry,
*   such as a fino*
Salt and freshly ground black pepper, to taste
½ cup chopped fresh dill or chervil leaves
Fresh dill sprigs or chervil, for garnish

1. Fill a large pot half full with water. Add the wine, celery, parsley, and peppercorns and bring to a boil over high heat. Reduce the heat to medium-low. Add the shrimp, in batches, and simmer until just done, 1 to 2 minutes per batch. Using a skimmer, remove each batch from the pot to a colander. Drain, then run under cold water to stop the cooking. Drain again and pat dry. Set aside in a large bowl, adding each batch as it is cooked and cooled. When all the shrimp are cooked, discard the cooking stock.

2. Add the diced celery to the shrimp.

3. Combine the mayonnaise and the sherry in a bowl and fold this into the shrimp mixture. Season with salt and pepper.

4. Shortly before serving, add the chopped dill to the salad and fold it in. Spoon the shrimp salad onto a large platter and garnish with the dill sprigs.

Note: Cleaning 6 pounds of shrimp is definitely a family affair. It's a perfect night-before job for the sleep-over contingent. Accompany the task with a selection of oldies-but-goodies CDs and it will be done in no time. Cook the shrimp the night before too. Store in a large bowl in the refrigerator, covered with plastic wrap.

ROASTED SALMON SALAD

Salmon is firm-fleshed, full of flavorful oil, and assertive enough to be combined with as many ingredients as you choose. Here it's flaked into large pieces and gently tossed with a festive mix of bell peppers, tomatoes, celery, cucumbers, and a healthy dose of red onion. Dress the salad lightly—a top-notch red wine vinegar and lots of parsley will do the trick.

8 salmon fillets (8 ounces each)
12 tablespoons extra-virgin olive oil
Salt and freshly ground black pepper,
*   to taste*
12 ripe plum tomatoes, cut into 8 pieces
*   each*
4 yellow bell peppers, stemmed, seeded,
*   and cut into ¼-inch strips*
4 red bell peppers, stemmed, seeded,
*   and cut into ¼-inch strips*
8 ribs celery, cut crosswise into ¼-inch
*   slices*
4 hothouse (seedless) cucumbers, peeled,
*   center scooped out, quartered lengthwise,*
*   and cut into ½-inch pieces*
2 small red onions, cut in half and slivered
*   lengthwise*
¼ cup red wine vinegar
1 cup chopped fresh flat-leaf parsley

1. Preheat the oven to 450°F.

2. Brush each salmon fillet with 1 tablespoon of the olive oil, place them in a large baking dish, and season with salt and pepper. Bake until the salmon is just cooked through and flakes easily with a fork, 12 to 15 minutes. Set it aside to cool.

3. Combine the tomatoes, bell peppers, celery, cucumbers, and onions in a large bowl.

4. Gently flake or cut the salmon into 1- to 1½-inch pieces.

5. Whisk the remaining 4 tablespoons oil with the vinegar in a small bowl and season with salt and pepper.

6. Just before serving, gently toss the salmon, parsley, and vinaigrette with the salad.

REUNION
POTATO SALAD

Family get-togethers demand a stand-out potato salad, and if one is going to shine, this is it! Based on one described by my beloved editor, Suzanne Rafer, this combines the basic vegetables of a classic French macédoine—carrots, green beans, peas—with the best elements of a Southern potato salad: hard-cooked eggs and pickles.

> 12 to 15 russet potatoes (8 pounds total), peeled and cut into ½-inch dice
> 12 carrots, peeled and cut into ¼-inch dice
> 1½ pounds green beans, trimmed and cut into ¼-inch pieces
> 3 cups peas, thawed if frozen
> 12 radishes, cut into small dice
> 12 large sweet gherkin pickles, cut into ¼-inch dice
> 6 hard-cooked eggs, coarsely chopped
> 3 cups prepared mayonnaise, such as Hellmann's
> 3 cups low-fat sour cream
> Coarse (kosher) salt and freshly ground black pepper, to taste
> ¾ cup chopped flat-leaf parsley, for garnish

BEAT THE CLOCK

When you're giving a large party, especially an outdoor event, it's particularly important to be organized. Plan the menu well in advance, and if each person is responsible for a dish, make a list of who's bringing what, or hand out assignments.

Once the menu is established, prepare your shopping lists, and buy all the staple items—pickles, mayonnaise, oil, vinegar, and jarred herbs and spices—early. Keep them together and off-limits so they're still available when you need them. Hold off on the fresh vegetables and seafood until the last day or two.

If the reunion is at your place, and that's where most of the cooking will be done, a few days ahead, lay out your serving pieces (borrow some more if you need them), and begin to prep all the food you can. The pork can be marinated and smoked a couple of days before the reunion. The salads in this menu can be prepared in the morning and refrigerated, covered, until serving time. The morning of the big event, gather your help and toss, toss, toss! If it's hot out, keep salads dressed with mayonnaise cold until serving time, and keep the flowers indoors (or in the shade), as well.

4. Add the peas to the boiling water and cook for 1 minute. Drain them in a colander and repeat the cooling, draining, and drying process. Add them to the other vegetables.

5. Add the radishes, gherkins, and hard-cooked eggs to the bowl of vegetables.

6. Combine the mayonnaise and sour cream in a separate bowl. Add this to the vegetables and gently fold all of the ingredients together with a large rubber spatula, seasoning the salad generously with salt and pepper. Sprinkle with the parsley and serve.

CARROT SLAW WITH RAISINS AND CHERRIES

Carrots, served with dignity in France, North Africa, and India, are often relegated to a supporting role in American cuisine. Here they star, combined with dried fruit providing a sweet, sunny complement to the accompanying dishes. The yogurt adds just the right tang to the mayonnaise in the dressing.

1¹/₂ cups nonfat plain yogurt
1¹/₂ cups prepared mayonnaise,
*   such as Hellmann's*
36 carrots, peeled
1 cup golden raisins
1 cup dried cherries
Salt and freshly ground black pepper,
*   to taste*
³/₄ cup coarsely chopped fresh mint

1. Combine the yogurt and mayonnaise in a mixing bowl and set it aside.

2. Using the grating blade on a food processor, coarsely grate the carrots. As the processor bowl fills, transfer the carrots to a large mixing bowl.

1. Bring a large pot of salted water to a boil over high heat. Add the potatoes and cook until tender, about 8 minutes. Using a skimmer, remove them from the pot to a colander. Run under cold water to stop the cooking. Drain, pat dry, and set aside in a large bowl.

2. Add the carrots to the boiling water and cook until tender, about 2 minutes. Remove them from the pot to a colander with the skimmer and repeat the cooling, draining, and drying process. Set them in the bowl with the potatoes.

3. Add the green beans to the boiling water and cook until tender, 2 to 3 minutes. Remove them from the pot to a colander with the skimmer and repeat the cooling, draining, and drying process. Add them to the potatoes and carrots.

Once all the carrots are grated, add the raisins and cherries, season with salt and pepper, and toss.

3. Just before serving, toss the carrot mixture with the dressing and ½ cup of the mint. Transfer the salad to a decorative bowl and sprinkle with the remaining ¼ cup mint.

RUSTIC BREAD SALAD

O riginally thrown together in Italy as a way to use up day-old bread, *panzanella* has become a favorite summer lunch-eon dish here when the tomatoes are at their prime. As the bread sits it absorbs the flavor of the dressing, and the addition of herbs and other crisp vegetables livens up the colors and textures. Light, flavorful, and fresh—a divine combo.

> 3 thin baguettes, halved lengthwise and
>   cut into 1-inch cubes (about 6 cups)
> 9 tablespoons plus ¾ cup extra-virgin
>   olive oil
> Salt and freshly ground black pepper,
>   to taste
> 1½ hothouse (seedless) cucumbers,
>   peeled, halved lengthwise, and cut into
>   ½-inch pieces
> 3 small red bell peppers, stemmed,
>   seeded, and cut into ¼-inch dice
> 6 ribs celery, cut into ½-inch dice
> 6 carrots, peeled and cut into ½-inch dice
> 1 cup diced red onions (¼-inch dice)
> 24 ripe plum tomatoes, cut into ½-inch pieces
> 3 cups halved yellow cherry or pear tomatoes
> 20 fresh basil leaves, coarsely torn
> 20 fresh mint leaves, coarsely torn
> 9 tablespoons red wine vinegar
> 6 hard-cooked eggs (page 9),
>   coarsely chopped, for garnish

1. Preheat the oven to 350°F.

2. Toss the bread cubes in a bowl with the 9 tablespoons olive oil and season with salt and pepper. Spread the bread cubes in a single layer on baking sheets and bake, shaking the pans every 5 minutes, until slightly toasted and golden, about 15 minutes. Set them aside.

3. Place the cucumbers, bell peppers, celery, carrots, onions, tomatoes, basil, and mint in a large bowl. Season with salt and pepper. Add the bread cubes. Drizzle the remaining ¾ cup olive oil and the vinegar over the salad. Toss, garnish with the chopped egg, and serve.

ORANGE-SCENTED CAULIFLOWER SALAD

T he combination of snappy cauliflower florets, celery, raisins, orange zest, capers, and a vinaigrette dressing fires off a fusillade of tastes that ricochets from assertive to smooth and delicate. The ingredi-ents point to Mediterranean inspiration for this refreshing salad, which works well at a big family gathering.

> 4 cauliflowers (each about 8 ounces)
> ½ lemon
> 8 ribs celery, very thinly sliced
> 2 cups whole inner celery leaves
> 1⅓ cups golden raisins
> ¼ cup tiny capers, drained
> Finely grated zest of 3 oranges
>   (about 3 tablespoons)
> Freshly ground black pepper, to taste
> ¾ cup chopped fresh flat-leaf parsley
> ¾ cup red wine vinegar
> 1 cup extra-virgin olive oil
> Salt, to taste

1. Remove and discard the center core from the cauliflower and break or cut each head into very small florets.

2. Bring a large pot of salted water to a boil over high heat, and squeeze the lemon half into it. Add the cauliflower and cook until just tender, 3 to 4 minutes. Drain in a colander, then run under cold running water to stop the cooking. Drain again and pat dry. Place the cauliflower in a large bowl.

3. Add the celery, celery leaves, raisins, capers, orange zest, pepper, and ½ cup of the parsley. Toss well.

4. Place the vinegar in a small bowl and slowly whisk in the olive oil. Season to taste with salt and pepper.

5. Drizzle the dressing over the salad and toss. Just before serving, sprinkle with the remaining ¼ cup chopped parsley.

SUMMER CORN SALAD

The accent here is on summer. You need summer corn, with every kernel as fresh as a bubble of sunlight. Then throw in the rest of the crunchy vegetables from a summer garden. The cumin vinaigrette accents the nuttiness in the corn and the subtle aromatics that you get only in fresh-picked vegetables.

12 cups fresh corn kernels (from about 24 ears)
3 small zucchini, quartered lengthwise, seeded, and diced
24 cherry tomatoes, quartered
1½ cups diced hothouse (seedless) cucumber (¼-inch dice; see Note)
12 red radishes, cut into small dice
¾ cup chopped fresh flat-leaf parsley
Freshly ground black pepper, to taste
¾ cup Cumin Honey Vinaigrette (page 400)

1. Bring a large pot of lightly salted water to a boil over high heat. Add the corn and cook until just tender, 1 minute. Drain in a colander, then run under cold water to stop the cooking. Drain again, pat dry, and place in a large bowl.

2. Add the other vegetables to the corn, then add the parsley and pepper and toss to mix. Just before serving, toss with the vinaigrette.

Note: If you use cucumbers from your own garden, scoop out the seeds.

JALAPEÑO CORN MUFFINS

Jalapeños add some summery heat to these tempting muffins, but if you think the older (or younger) family members would rather not chance the chiles, bake some up plain as well and make sure the ones with the jalapeños are clearly marked. If your family is big on corn muffins, this recipe is easily doubled—make plenty.

Summer Corn Salad

1 1/2 cups yellow cornmeal
1/2 cup all-purpose flour
3 tablespoons sugar
1 tablespoon baking powder
1/2 teaspoon salt
1/2 cup whole milk
1/2 cup nonfat plain yogurt
2 tablespoons unsalted
  butter, melted
2 tablespoons vegetable
  oil
2 large eggs, lightly
  beaten
1 cup creamed corn (canned is fine)
2 teaspoons minced seeded red and green
  jalapeño peppers or serrano chiles
  (see Note)

1. Position a rack in the center of the oven, and preheat the oven to 400°F. Butter 12 regular or 24 mini muffin cups, or line them with paper liners.

2. Combine the cornmeal, flour, sugar, baking powder, and salt in a mixing bowl. Stir well.

3. In another bowl, combine the milk, yogurt, melted butter, oil, and eggs. Add this to the cornmeal mixture and stir until just combined. Then stir in the creamed corn and the chiles.

4. Spoon the batter into the prepared muffin cups and bake until the tops are golden brown and a toothpick inserted in the center comes out just clean, 20 minutes.

5. Allow the muffins to cool in the pan on a wire rack for 5 minutes before unmolding them. These are delicious served warm, but if that isn't possible, room temperature will be fine.

MAKES 12 REGULAR OR 24 MINI MUFFINS

Note: Canned chopped green chiles may be substituted for the fresh chile peppers.

BERTA'S CARROT CAKE

Wait until you try my mother's carrot cake. This sweet and savory recipe is as irrepressible as my mom herself. There are many, many recipes for carrot cakes, but I keep returning to this one, fine-tuning it here and there. You can do the same, but give this classic rendition a try first, and then let loose your creativity in the future.

FOR THE CAKE
  4 carrots (about 1 pound), peeled
    and cut into 1-inch dice
  4 cups all-purpose flour
  4 cups granulated sugar
  4 teaspoons baking soda
  4 teaspoons ground cinnamon
  2 cups corn oil
  6 large eggs, lightly beaten
  4 teaspoons pure vanilla extract
  2 cups chopped walnuts
  2 cups sweetened shredded coconut
  1 1/2 cups canned crushed pineapple,
    drained

"*Strange to see how a good dinner and feasting reconciles everybody.*"

—SAMUEL PEPYS

FOR THE CREAM CHEESE FROSTING

16 ounces cream cheese, at room
   temperature
12 tablespoons (1 1/2 sticks) unsalted butter,
   at room temperature
6 cups confectioners' sugar
2 teaspoons pure vanilla extract
1/4 cup fresh lemon juice

Confectioners' sugar, for dusting

1. Place the carrots in a large saucepan, add water to cover, and bring to a boil over high heat. Reduce the heat to medium-low and simmer, uncovered, until the carrots are tender, about 20 minutes. Drain. Transfer the carrots, in batches, to a food processor or blender and puree. Set the puree aside.

2. Position a rack in the center of the oven, and preheat the oven to 350°F. Butter two 13 x 9-inch baking pans. Line the bottoms with wax paper and oil the paper.

3. Sift the flour, sugar, baking soda, and cinnamon together into a very large mixing bowl. Add the oil, eggs, and vanilla and beat well. Then fold in the carrot puree, walnuts, coconut, and pineapple. (If you don't have a giant-size bowl, use two bowls, dividing the ingredients between them.)

4. Pour the batter into the prepared pans, and bake the layers until the edges have pulled away from the sides of the pans and a toothpick inserted in the center comes out clean, 1 hour.

Cover the tables with large throws or quilts (not valuable ones!), then decorate them with jugs full of sunflowers or daisies.

Stock ice-filled tubs with beer, wine, soda, water, and juices. Remember to hang a couple of bottle openers from the handles of the tubs so all the guests can help themselves. Also keep a couple of kitchen towels on hand so people can wipe off the bottles and cans.

5. Let the cakes cool in the pans for 10 minutes. Then invert each over a cake rack and unmold. Remove the wax paper, and continue to cool for 1 hour.

6. Prepare the cream cheese frosting: Cream the cheese and butter together in a bowl, using an electric mixer, until fluffy, 5 minutes. Slowly sift in the confectioners' sugar and continue beating until fully incorporated (there should be no lumps), about 5 minutes more. Stir in the vanilla and lemon juice.

7. Place each cooled cake on a large platter or on a baking sheet. Frost the top and sides of the cakes with the cream cheese frosting and then dust the top of each one with confectioners' sugar. Just before serving, cut each cake into 12 pieces, about 3 inches square.

A Birthday

T Bash

There's no official rule that says birthday celebrations must end once we reach the age of eighteen (with a special dispensation at twenty-one), but it seems that as we get older, it's one we follow. How silly is this? I say, "It's your birthday and you should raise the roof."

Invite your best friends over for a celebration dinner, or better still, copy down this menu and ask *them* to cook it up. After all, it is your special day, and you can always return the favor when their birthdays roll around. And as for your age, who's counting?

> "*Age* is an issue of mind over matter. If you don't mind . . . it doesn't matter."
>
> —MARK TWAIN

MENU

A Birthday Bash
DINNER FOR SIX

MOJITOS

SWEET CORN GAZPACHO

CHILEAN SEA BASS MOJO AND MORE
OR HONEY-LIME ROAST PORK

OVEN-DRIED PLUM TOMATOES

FIESTA CHOPPED SALAD

CHOCOLATE BIRTHDAY CAKE
WITH ORANGE BUTTERCREAM

When you're celebrating a birthday or an anniversary, it's nice to plan your event around a theme. For this birthday party, a dash of nuevo Latino pizzazz begins with a totally cool mojito, refreshing with plenty of mint and lime. Dazzling color permeates all the food, from the Sweet Corn Gazpacho to the oven-dried tomatoes. The entree is your choice—a sumptuous Chilean sea bass or succulent roast pork. If a lot of friends are coming, make both. The chopped salad adds to this culinary rainbow, and even the terrific chocolate cake has an orange accent.

The colors and flavors of Chilean sea bass laced with mojo, the all-purpose citrus-based sauce, and the great minty mojito cocktails are the jumping-off points for the dinner party décor. Whether it's fancy or not, get colorful! Look for paper napkins in turquoise, lime green, raspberry, tangerine, hot pink, and yellow. Heavy glass plates go a long way toward creating atmosphere. Party stores have a lot of fun glitters and sparkles to jazz up a party. Multicolored streamers will look festive tossed all over. Confetti always adds a happy air. And since this is a birthday bash, balloons are a must.

Black-eyed Susans arranged in a variety of colorful vases or containers will be just right. Look around your home for fun containers that are suitable for vases. Also look for any colorful shawls or throws to spiff up a table or the back of a couch.

Finally, don't forget to place a candle in the chocolate cake for the best birthday party ever.

THE MUSIC

Miles Davis
Dinah Shore
Rod Stewart

THE DRINKS

Mojitos
Roussanne
Argentine Malbec

THE EXTRAS

Colorful tall glasses
Ice crusher

MOJITOS

The mojito, the Cuban national cocktail, was originally mixed with Bacardi rum in the mid-nineteenth century, when Don Facundo Bacardi made the world's first light rum in nearby Puerto Rico. Earlier there was a cocktail called the *draque*, made with mint, sugar, and *aguardiente*, which is freshly distilled cane juice—a raw and fiery potion. Rum makes a smooth cocktail, and soda and mint give it lively effervescence and a cooling bouquet.

*6 tablespoons chopped fresh mint,
  plus several small whole mint leaves
1 tablespoon superfine sugar
3 tablespoons fresh lime juice
Crushed ice
12 ounces white rum
Club soda
6 sprigs fresh mint, for garnish*

Combine the chopped mint, whole mint leaves, superfine sugar, and lime juice in a pitcher and stir well. Fill six tall glasses with crushed ice. Pour the mint mixture over the ice. Add 2 ounces of rum to each glass and top with club soda. Gently stir, then garnish each drink with a mint sprig.

SWEET CORN GAZPACHO

Gazpacho tastes like a garden-fresh salad, and although corn is not in the traditional mix, it elevates the sweetness and enhances the texture. Yellow bell pepper, instead of green, adds to the look of the soup—and in food, as in beauty contests, looks count! For an extra special effect, garnish each bowl with a fresh nasturtium blossom—preferably yellow. Nasturiums are great garnishes because they are both beautiful and—when untreated—edible.

*1½ cups fresh sweet corn kernels
  (from about 3 ears), lightly blanched,
  or 1½ cups frozen corn kernels, thawed
1½ cups diced ripe tomatoes (¼-inch dice)
1½ cups diced peeled hothouse (seedless)
  cucumber (¼-inch dice)
1½ cups diced yellow bell peppers (¼-inch dice)
⅔ cup diced red onion (¼-inch dice)
2½ cups tomato juice
½ cup red wine vinegar
6 tablespoons extra-virgin olive oil
½ teaspoon sugar
3 dashes Tabasco sauce
Salt and freshly ground black pepper, to taste
⅓ cup finely slivered fresh basil leaves
6 nasturtium blossoms, for garnish (optional)*

1. If you are using fresh corn, bring a saucepan of water to a boil over high heat, add the corn, and cook for 1 minute. Drain in a colander, rinse under cold water to stop the cooking, and set the colander aside to drain.

2. Place the tomato, cucumber, bell pepper, and onion in a large bowl. Add the tomato juice, vinegar, olive oil, sugar, Tabasco sauce, and salt and pepper. Mix well.

3. Transfer half of the mixture to a blender or food processor and coarsely puree, pulsing the machine on and off. Return the puree to the bowl and stir to combine. Adjust the seasonings, if necessary, and stir in the corn kernels. Refrigerate for 4 to 6 hours before serving.

4. To serve, place about 1 cup of the soup in each of six shallow bowls. Garnish with the basil slivers and a nasturtium blossom, if desired.

CHILEAN SEA BASS MOJO AND MORE

Delicious Chilean sea bass; its real name is Patagonian toothfish. Since it has become quite popular, Chilean waters have been

"*In the hands of an able cook, fish can become an inexhaustible source of perpetual delight.*"

—JEAN ANTHELME BRILLAT-SAVARIN

Chilean Sea Bass Mojo, Fiesta Chopped Salad, and a *Mojito*

nearly overfished, so save this tasty white-fleshed cold-water fish for a treat like this one.

FOR THE MOJO SAUCE

6 large cloves garlic, thinly sliced lengthwise
1/3 cup thinly slivered onion
3/4 teaspoon ground cumin
Salt and freshly ground black pepper, to taste
1/4 cup extra-virgin olive oil
1/2 cup plus 1 tablespoon fresh lime juice
  (from about 5 limes)
3/4 teaspoon white wine vinegar

FOR THE FISH

3 fillets Chilean sea bass (about 1 pound each)
6 tablespoons fresh lime juice
  (from about 3 limes)
8 tablespoons extra-virgin olive oil
Salt and freshly ground black pepper, to taste
3 large cloves garlic, passed through
  a garlic press
2 ripe avocados, preferably Hass, for serving
1 1/2 cups coarsely chopped fresh cilantro,
  or cilantro sprigs, for serving

1. Prepare the mojo sauce: Combine the garlic, onion, cumin, and salt and pepper and toss to mix.

2. Heat the olive oil in a small heavy saucepan over low heat. Add the onion mixture and cook, stirring, until softened and fragrant, 10 minutes. Add the lime juice and vinegar, raise the heat to medium-low, and simmer to blend the flavors, 5 minutes. Set the mojo aside.

3. Cut the sea bass fillets in half crosswise.

4. Whisk the lime juice, 5 tablespoons of the olive oil, the salt and pepper, and the garlic together in a large shallow bowl. Add the fish and coat the pieces well. Set aside to marinate for 15 minutes. Then remove the fish from the marinade and pat dry.

5. Preheat the oven to 450°F.

6. Using a very sharp knife, score the skin side of the fish twice on the diagonal to prevent curling.

7. Heat the remaining 3 tablespoons oil in a large nonstick skillet over medium heat. Sear the fish, skin side down, pressing on it with a spatula until the skin is crisp and golden brown, 5 minutes.

8. Transfer the fish to an ovenproof dish or skillet, arranging it skin side down, and bake it in the oven until cooked through, 8 minutes.

9. Meanwhile, gently heat the mojo sauce over very low heat.

10. Cut the avocadoes in half and remove the pits. Peel all four halves, and cut them into thin lengthwise slices.

11. To serve, place a piece of fish in the center of each dinner plate. Spoon 1 to 2 tablespoons mojo sauce atop each piece. Fan 2 or 3 slices of avocado over each serving and sprinkle with some of the cilantro. Place the remaining cilantro and the remaining sauce in bowls, to pass at the table.

HONEY-LIME ROAST PORK

The seductive aroma of Latino flavorings combine wonderfully with roast pork. With pork being bred so lean these days, it is important to baste it often while it cooks. Note that you need to marinate the pork a day ahead.

1 boneless pork loin (3 1/2 pounds)
1 large clove garlic, cut into thin slivers
1/3 cup fresh lime juice (from about 3 limes)
3 tablespoons honey
2 tablespoons sherry vinegar
2 tablespoons extra-virgin olive oil
2 teaspoons ground cumin
Salt and freshly ground black pepper,
  to taste

1. Using the tip of a small sharp knife, make slits about 1/2 inch deep all over the pork loin. Insert the garlic slivers into the slits. Place the pork in a shallow baking dish.

2. Combine all the remaining ingredients in a bowl, mix well, and pour over the pork loin. Marinate, covered, in the refrigerator overnight, turning the pork twice.

3. Remove the pork from the refrigerator 30 minutes before roasting. Preheat the oven to 350°F.

4. Roast the pork, basting it about every 15 minutes, until it is cooked through (150° to 160°F on a meat thermometer), about 1 hour and 10 minutes, or 20 minutes per pound. Let the roast rest for 15 minutes, then slice and serve.

OVEN-DRIED PLUM TOMATOES

After this low-heat roasting, the tomatoes are wrinkled-looking but voluptuous. The sweet acidity of fresh orange juice enhances the taste, and mint leaves round out all the flavors.

*12 to 18 ripe plum tomatoes, halved
  lengthwise and seeded
1/3 to 1/2 cup extra-virgin olive oil
1 1/2 tablespoons sugar
Freshly ground black pepper, to taste
1/4 cup strained fresh orange juice
25 whole small fresh mint leaves,
  for garnish*

1. Preheat the oven to 250°F.

2. Line a baking sheet with aluminum foil and arrange the tomatoes on it in a single layer. Drizzle them lightly with the olive oil. Sprinkle with the sugar and pepper.

3. Bake until wrinkled yet still supple, about 3 hours.

4. Transfer the tomatoes to a small decorative plate. Drizzle the orange juice over them, and scatter the mint leaves over all just before serving.

FIESTA CHOPPED SALAD

This Latin-influenced, colorful chopped salad, tossed with fresh cilantro and a little cumin vinaigrette, complements a menu of roast loin of pork or succulent sea bass.

*1/2 cup corn kernels, fresh or frozen (thawed)
1 Granny Smith apple, unpeeled, cored and
  cut into 1/2-inch dice
1 ripe avocado, preferably Hass, halved,
  pitted, peeled, and cut into 1/2-inch dice
1 tablespoon fresh lemon juice
8 cups chopped inner leaves of romaine lettuce
1 small firm cucumber, cut into 1/2-inch dice
1 large or 2 medium-size ripe tomatoes,
  cut into 1/2-inch pieces
1/2 cup canned dark red kidney beans,
  rinsed and drained
1/2 cup pitted manzanilla green olives,
  coarsely chopped
1/4 cup diced red onion (1/4-inch dice)
1/4 cup coarsely chopped fresh cilantro
Salt and freshly ground black pepper, to taste
3 to 4 tablespoons Cumin-Honey
  Vinaigrette (page 400)*

1. If you are using fresh corn, bring a saucepan of water to a boil over high heat, add the corn, and cook until tender, 1 minute. Drain into a colander, rinse under cold water to stop the cooking, and set the colander aside to drain.

2. Toss the apple and avocado with the lemon juice in a bowl to prevent discoloration. Set it aside.

3. Place the romaine in a large bowl and add the cucumber, tomatoes, kidney beans, corn, olives, onion, and cilantro.

4. Just before serving, add the diced apple and avocado and season with salt and pepper. Toss all the ingredients together, then gently toss with the dressing. Place in a salad bowl and serve immediately.

CHOCOLATE BIRTHDAY CAKE

Here is the ultimate birthday dessert—a big chocolate cake slathered in orange buttercream—a grand finale to a festive meal.

Melted butter, for greasing the pans
Flour, for dusting
3 ounces good-quality unsweetened chocolate
1 cup (2 sticks) unsalted butter,
   at room temperature
2¼ cups (packed) dark brown sugar
3 large eggs
2¼ cups cake flour, sifted
2 teaspoons baking soda
½ teaspoon salt
½ cup buttermilk
1 cup boiling water
2 teaspoons pure vanilla extract
Orange Buttercream (recipe follows)

1. Preheat the oven to 375°F. Butter the bottom and sides of two 9-inch cake pans with melted butter. Line the bottoms with circles of wax or parchment paper, and butter the paper. Dust with flour, tapping out any excess, and set the pans aside.

2. Melt the chocolate in the top of a double boiler over simmering water. Set it aside.

3. Using an electric mixer, cream the butter and brown sugar together in a bowl until light and fluffy. With the mixer on low speed, add the eggs, one at a time, beating well after each addition. Stir in the melted chocolate.

4. Sift the cake flour, baking soda, and salt into another bowl. With the mixer on low speed, and alternating between the two, add the flour mixture (one third at a time) and the buttermilk (¼ cup at a time) to the chocolate mixture, starting and ending with the flour. Scrape down the sides of the bowl and beat on medium speed for 2 minutes. Then slowly add the boiling water and vanilla and continue mixing until combined, 1 minute more.

5. Pour the batter evenly into the prepared pans and bake until a wooden toothpick inserted in the center of the layers comes out clean, 45 to 50 minutes. Let the layers cool in the pans on wire racks for 10 minutes. Then remove the layers from the pans and place them on the racks to cool completely. Carefully peel off the paper.

6. Assemble the cake: Place one layer on a serving plate top side up. Spread it with one third of the buttercream. Top with the remaining layer, top side up. Frost the sides and top with the remaining buttercream.

ORANGE BUTTERCREAM

It's your birthday, so bowl-licking rights are yours—and with this buttercream, you won't want to share.

4 large egg whites, at room temperature
½ cup sugar
Pinch of salt
1¼ cups (2½ sticks) unsalted butter,
   cut into pieces, at room temperature
3 tablespoons Cointreau or other
   orange-flavored liqueur
1 tablespoon finely grated orange zest

1. Place the egg whites, sugar, and salt in a heatproof mixing bowl. Set the bowl over a pot of simmering water and whisk constantly until the egg whites are hot (about 140°F on an instant-reading thermometer) and the sugar has completely dissolved, about 4 minutes.

2. Remove the bowl from the heat and beat with an electric mixer on high speed until the egg whites are thick, glossy, and completely cooled, about 7 minutes.

3. Still beating, add the butter, a few pieces at a time. Continue to beat until the buttercream is thick and spreadable, about 3 minutes. Beat in the Cointreau and the orange zest and frost the cake.

MAKES ABOUT 3 CUPS

Celebrate a

Ripe Tomato

How did we get along before we had tomatoes? While the Aztecs were enjoying this New World plant, the rest of the world was tomato-less. No tomato sauce, no ketchup, no BLTs, no sun-drieds, no pizza. Provençal food would be unthinkable without tomatoes. The rich cuisines of Mexico would be that much poorer. And Italy? Mamma mia, what a catastrophe. But fortunately we don't have to consider such a bleak scenario. There is nothing more delicious than a tomato in season, and a luncheon featuring them when they are at their peak makes perfect sense.

MENU

Celebrate a Ripe Tomato

LUNCHEON FOR EIGHT

OVEN-DRIED
TOMATO CHIPS

CREAMY
TOMATO SOUP

GARDEN
TOMATO TART

HOT TOMATOES!

HONEY-ROASTED
PEACHES

There are marvelous tomato dishes in menus throughout this book—consider these some bonuses, a "hats-off to tomatoes" luncheon. Dessert strays from the tomato theme, but not too far. Peaches, another summer favorite, make for a lovely finish. One, or actually two, pieces of advice: Use as many heirloom tomatoes as you can find, and don't refrigerate them.

Nothing shows off tomatoes better than chartreuse, turquoise, or yellow-gold dishes. The small round Garden Tomato Tart is spectacular when centered on a chartreuse plate. Serve the Creamy Tomato Soup in a Provençal yellow soup tureen for tones that are modern and inviting. Hot Tomatoes!—with

its gooey cheese—looks irresistible in a small yellow oven-to-table baking dish.

Daisies informally placed in colorful flea-market pitchers highlight the stars of this meal. As an homage to Andy Warhol, arrange them in a grouping of clean Campbell's Tomato Soup cans. Red dahlias also look wonderful with tomatoes. Arrange large bunches of

opal basil in a short green pitcher.

For the centerpiece, consider arranging a wide variety of tomatoes on a large pedestal dish or in an antique bowl. Drape on-the-vine cherry tomatoes off the pedestal.

THE MUSIC

**Rosemary Clooney's
*16 Most Requested Songs***

THE DRINKS

**White wine from Languedoc
Chianti or Sangria**

THE EXTRAS

**Soup tureen
Oven-to-table baking dish**

Garden Tomato Tart

OVEN-DRIED TOMATO CHIPS

If you have ever wondered what to serve with a Bloody Mary, try these toothsome savory chips. Not exactly like a potato chip, they are slightly chewy with a little snap to them. Spread some chèvre on a thin cracker with a chip atop for a superb canapé.

3 pounds (about 14) ripe plum tomatoes
About ¼ cup extra-virgin olive oil
1 tablespoon sugar
Freshly ground black pepper, to taste

1. Preheat the oven to 250°F. Line three baking sheets with aluminum foil.

2. Cut the tomatoes into ¼-inch-thick rounds, discarding the stem end. Lay the tomatoes on the prepared baking sheets without overlapping, and drizzle them lightly with the oil. Sprinkle with the sugar and lightly with pepper.

3. Bake until well dried and caramelized, 3 hours. Remove the tomato chips from the oven and allow them to cool to room temperature.

MAKES ABOUT 40 CHIPS

Note: The tomato chips will keep for 1 day in an airtight container.

The famous tomato soup, the one from Campbell's, first appeared in 1895 from the Joseph Campbell Preserve Company. It was called Beefsteak Tomato Soup. Two years later, John T. Dorrance was hired as a company chemist. The president of the company, John's uncle Arthur, gave his out-of-work nephew a "take it or leave it" offer of $7.50 a week. He took it and developed the now famous line of condensed soups in the 10-ounce can. The five original varieties were Tomato, Consommé, Vegetable, Chicken, and Oxtail. More than a century later, Campbell's Tomato Soup is still one of the top ten best-selling items in grocery stores and supermarkets.

CREAMY TOMATO SOUP

When I was a child, it was my opinion—as well as the opinion of many of my friends—that nobody but Campbell's knew how to make creamy tomato soup. Their recipe is still a big favorite, but in summer when the tomatoes are at their peak, I urge you to try this one—pure luxury!

2 tablespoons unsalted butter
2 tablespoons olive oil
1 large onion, chopped
1 tablespoon all-purpose flour
1 tablespoon minced garlic
3½ pounds ripe tomatoes, cored and coarsely chopped
2 tablespoons tomato paste
1 teaspoon sugar
3 cups Vegetable Broth (page 398) or Basic Chicken Broth (page 397)
⅛ teaspoon ground cloves
Salt and freshly ground black pepper, to taste
½ cup half-and-half

1. Melt the butter in the olive oil in a saucepan over low heat.

2. Add the onion and cook until almost softened, 6 to 8 minutes. Sprinkle the flour over the onion and stir to combine. Add the garlic and cook, stirring constantly, for another 2 minutes.

3. Add the tomatoes, tomato paste, sugar, and broth and raise the heat to medium-high. Bring the mixture to a boil, then reduce the heat to medium-low and simmer, covered, until the tomatoes have cooked down and the soup has thickened, 30 minutes. Season with the cloves and salt and pepper. Remove from the heat and allow to cool slightly.

4. Puree the soup, in small batches, in a food processor or blender. Pour the pureed soup through a strainer into a saucepan. Stir in the half-and-half.

5. Just before serving, warm the soup through. Do not let it boil.

GARDEN TOMATO TART

As bright as a Provençal sunset, this tart is so inviting, so satisfying. When dolloped with a fresh pesto, it makes a lovely luncheon dish, and a fine partner for a crisp and ultra-fruity white wine.

*2 sheets frozen puff pastry, thawed according
    to package directions*
2 large egg yolks
2 teaspoons corn oil
4 ripe tomatoes, sliced 1/4 inch thick
1/2 teaspoon extra-virgin olive oil
1/2 teaspoon sugar
Freshly ground black pepper, to taste
1/2 cup Garden Pesto (page 272)

1. Position a rack in the center of the oven, and preheat the oven to 400°F.

2. Place the puff pastry on a lightly floured surface. Using a salad-size plate as a guide and a sharp knife, trim each sheet to form an 8-inch round. Transfer the rounds to an ungreased baking sheet with a large metal spatula. Prick the pastry all over with the tines of a fork.

3. Make an egg wash by whisking the egg yolks, corn oil, and 2 teaspoons water together in a small bowl. Brush the egg wash lightly over the pastry. Leaving a 1/2-inch border around the edge, arrange the tomato slices in overlapping circles on the pastry rounds, covering the surface and tucking a slice in the center.

4. Drizzle each tart with 1/4 teaspoon olive oil, and sprinkle each with 1/4 teaspoon sugar. Season with pepper. Bake until the tarts are golden and the tomatoes are caramelized, about 25 minutes.

5. Serve immediately, with the pesto alongside in a small bowl for dolloping.

HOT TOMATOES!

How many ways can you combine tomatoes and cheese and still come up with something special? That's probably an unanswerable question, but I'm always glad to run across a new marriage of these favorite ingredients. This recipe is inspired by a real conversation-stopper at the restaurant St. John in London. Garlic, mint, cheese, olive oil, and roasted tomatoes join forces here in a powerhouse dish.

12 cloves garlic
5 tablespoons extra-virgin olive oil
*8 ripe tomatoes, still connected on
    the vine*
*Salt and freshly ground black pepper,
    to taste*
8 crottins de chèvre (goat cheese rounds)
2 cups fresh mint leaves
Juice of 2 lemons
12 to 16 slices peasant bread, toasted

1. Position a rack in the center of the oven and preheat the oven to 350°F.

Hot Tomatoes!

2. Place the garlic cloves on a piece of aluminum foil and drizzle 1 tablespoon of the olive oil over them. Close the foil, forming a sealed packet, and place it in a small ovenproof dish. Bake to soften slightly, 10 minutes. Remove the packet from the oven and set it aside. Raise the oven temperature to 400°F.

3. Carefully arrange the tomatoes (still on the vine) in an oven-to-table baking dish. Season them generously with salt and pepper. Arrange the garlic cloves around the tomatoes. Drizzle with 3 tablespoons of the olive oil, and bake until the tomatoes are softened and runny, 25 minutes.

4. Arrange the *crottins* around the tomatoes, and return the dish to the oven. Bake until the cheese softens, another 5 minutes. Watch carefully—you don't want them to melt.

5. Meanwhile, coarsely tear the mint leaves and place them in a bowl. Sprinkle with the remaining 1 tablespoon olive oil and the lemon juice.

6. To serve, pass the dish of tomatoes and cheese. Everybody helps themselves to a tomato and a cheese and plenty of the sauce. Spread the cheese and tomato on the toasts and pass the mint salad to scoop on top or eat on the side.

HONEY-ROASTED PEACHES

When peaches are at their best, they are exquisite tasting, with each bite dripping juice. There's no hint of mealyness in the texture, and the fragrance is sweet and indescribably peachy. This happens much too briefly in midsummer, and coincides with the peak of the tomato harvest. Nothing less than a sensuous peach dessert would best complement a celebration of tomatoes.

8 ripe freestone peaches
1 cup freshly squeezed lemon juice
  (from about 6 lemons)
¼ cup (packed) light brown sugar
1 cup honey
1 pound Robiola Piemonte cheese (see Note)
½ cup chopped unsalted pistachio nuts
8 small fresh mint sprigs

1. Preheat the oven to 350°F.

2. Have ready a large bowl of ice water. Bring a large pot of water to a boil over high heat, then reduce the heat to medium-low so that the water simmers. Lower the peaches into the water for 30 seconds to loosen the skin, then using a slotted spoon, remove them and plunge them into the ice water to stop the cooking. Peel off the skin, then cut the peaches in half and remove the pits.

3. Place the peaches, cut side down, in a shallow baking dish large enough to just hold them. Pour over the lemon juice and sprinkle with the brown sugar. Bake the peaches until they have softened and the liquid in the dish has turned syrupy, about 30 minutes. Cool the peaches to room temperature in the baking dish.

4. To serve, place 2 peach halves on each of 8 dessert plates. Drizzle each portion with 2 tablespoons of the honey and then place a portion of Robiola alongside the peaches. Sprinkle each portion with a tablespoon of the chopped pistachios and garnish with a sprig of mint.

Note: Robiola Piemonte is sold in a variety of paper-wrapped shapes, weighing between 6 and 14 ounces.

CELEBRATE

FRANCE

Everyone who travels in France falls in love with its food. To understand the pleasures of the table, stroll the rue de Seine and the rue de Buci in Paris's sixth arrondissement, lined with sidewalk stalls displaying impeccably fresh vegetables, glistening fish, and bushel baskets of oysters. In the fairyland Loire Valley, visit the majestic châteaux and sample the wines in cool *caves*. In Provence, begin a sunny day with ripe figs plucked off the trees, warm croissants, a perfect confiture, and fresh *fromage blanc* from the market in the square. France is a culinary celebration. Now invite your friends over to share its pleasures.

MENU

This menu is a blend of flavors inspired by different regions of France. The sweet-and-pungent Red Onion Marmalade is reminiscent of Bordeaux, and the tomato tart sings of the sunshine of Provence. The Duck and Carrot Ragoût is actually a dish I first sampled in London, but it is French in spirit and that's what counts. Creamy mashed potatoes are the perfect accompaniment. And to finish off the dinner with a touch of panache—what could be more classically French than a Tarte aux Pommes?

Freshly ironed napkins on a wooden table in the kitchen, or your best china set in the dining room—this meal is happy in either setting. Bright yellow or coral Provençal-type linens would give the room warmth. If you have any brass or pewter pitchers, arrange a variety of pink or coral roses, or zinnias, or other flowers in them. To be truly French, offer some cheese before the dessert—a marble slab can hold a selection of three or four. Pass a warmed sliced baguette, tucked into a napkin-lined basket. Then serve your made-ahead tart with a small bowl of crème fraîche. *Bon appétit!*

CELEBRATE FRANCE

DINNER FOR SIX

Red Onion Marmalade

Fancy Tomato Tart

Duck and Carrot Ragoût

Creamy Shallot Mashed Potatoes

Tarte aux Pommes

THE MUSIC

Edith Piaf
Jacques Brel
Charles Aznavour

THE WINE

Marsannay
Beaujolais Cru Fleurie

THE EXTRAS

Tart pan
Flan ring

RED ONION MARMALADE

Americans tend to think of marmalade as something to spread on their morning toast, but Europeans know that the long syrupy cooking-down of myriad ingredients yields a chutneylike savory that enhances any meal. And this is never truer than with the miracle vegetable, the onion. Its ability to pull out the flavors in other foods is unrivaled. Serve this sweet-tart marmalade as an hors d'oeuvre on toasts, or on small puff pastry rounds.

> 1 tablespoon unsalted butter
> 3 tablespoons extra-virgin olive oil
> 1 1/2 pounds red onions, cut in half lengthwise
>   and slivered
> 2 teaspoons sugar
> 1 teaspoon salt
> Pinch of freshly ground black pepper
> 3 tablespoons balsamic vinegar
> 12 to 18 thin slices baguette, lightly toasted,
>   for serving

Melt the butter in the olive oil in a heavy saucepan over medium-low heat. Add the onions, sugar, salt, and pepper. Partially cover the pan and cook, stirring occasionally, until the onions are completely soft, about 30 minutes. Add the vinegar and cook, uncovered, stirring occasionally, for another 30 minutes. The onions should be thick and resemble a marmalade. Serve with the toasts.

MAKES 2 CUPS MARMALADE

FANCY TOMATO TART

If it were possible to put the sun-drenched bounty of Provence on a plate, you could not come closer than this. The intensity of ripe garden vegetables oozes from the depths of this lush tart. As the tomatoes and peppers cook, they caramelize, releasing their natural sugars. Fresh herbs, showered over the tart just before serving, add an invigorating top note.

FOR THE CRUST

> 1 1/4 cups all-purpose flour
> 1 tablespoon fresh thyme leaves, chopped,
>   or 1 teaspoon dried
> 1/2 teaspoon salt
> Freshly ground black pepper, to taste
> 8 tablespoons (1 stick) cold unsalted butter,
>   cut into small pieces
> 2 teaspoons Dijon mustard
> About 4 tablespoons ice water

FOR THE FILLING

> 6 tablespoons olive oil
> 1 large onion, cut in half lengthwise and
>   slivered
> 2 yellow bell peppers, stemmed, seeded,
>   and thinly sliced
> 2 red bell peppers, stemmed, seeded,
>   and thinly sliced
> 1 tablespoon dried thyme
> 1 tablespoon dried rosemary, crumbled
> Salt and freshly ground black pepper, to taste
> 1/2 cup finely slivered fresh basil leaves
> 1/4 cup chopped fresh flat-leaf parsley
> 4 cloves garlic, minced

FOR THE TOPPING

> 1 cup grated fresh mozzarella cheese
> 2 to 3 large ripe tomatoes, cut into
>   1/4-inch-thick slices
> 1/4 teaspoon freshly ground black pepper
> 2 tablespoons fresh thyme leaves
> 1 tablespoon chopped fresh flat-leaf parsley
> 1 tablespoon extra-virgin olive oil

1. Prepare the crust: Combine the flour, thyme, salt, and pepper in a bowl. Add the butter and mix together with your fingertips or with a pastry

A STUDENT IN PARIS

I could not love any place more than I love Paris. As a young artist, I was drawn to that city like generations of artists before me; it was, quite simply, the only place to be. Every morning I spent three hours studying French, which I then practiced in the afternoons in the atelier where I worked on my etchings. One of them, a print of a cauliflower, was exhibited and filled me with pride. From the atelier I went *très rapidement* to Madame Bergaud's cooking class. There in her tiny kitchen I learned the sauces and skills that make French cuisine the breathtaking art that it is. And what food we ate! At Allard, in the sixth arrondissement, we ordered duck with olives, pigeon, escargots, and turbot, and washed it all down with marvelous red wine. Every Sunday night there was the ineffable couscous steeped in aromatic spices and seasonings, in the North African places around Place Pigalle. . . . And then, once we had saved our francs, we treated ourselves to Taillevent, which then, as now, was a true temple of gastronomic tradition.

cutter until the mixture resembles coarse meal. Stir in the mustard and enough ice water for the mixture to hold together. (Start with 3 tablespoons and if you need more than 4 tablespoons, add it 1 teaspoon at a time.) Form the dough into a thick disk. Wrap it in plastic wrap and chill it in the refrigerator for at least 1 hour.

2. Meanwhile, prepare the filling: Heat the olive oil in a large pot over medium-low heat. Add the onion, bell peppers, thyme, rosemary, and salt and pepper. Cook, uncovered, stirring frequently, until the vegetables are soft and the mixture resembles a thick marmalade, about 45 minutes.

3. Add the basil, parsley, and garlic and cook, stirring constantly, for another 5 minutes. Adjust the seasonings, if necessary. Drain the vegetables in a strainer and set aside.

4. Preheat the oven to 375°F.

5. On a lightly floured surface, roll out the chilled dough to form a 12-inch round, about ⅛ inch thick. Transfer the dough to an 11-inch tart pan with removable bottom, and press the pastry into the bottom and sides. Prick the bottom of the crust all over with a fork, and line it with aluminum foil. Fill the foil with dried beans or pie weights. Bake the crust for 10 minutes. Then carefully remove the foil and beans and bake for 10 minutes more. The crust will be very slightly golden and partially cooked. Allow the crust to cool slightly. (Leave the oven on.)

6. Scatter the cheese evenly over the bottom of the tart shell and spread the vegetable filling over the cheese. Arrange the tomatoes over the filling, overlapping them in a circular pattern, covering the surface. Sprinkle with the pepper, fresh thyme, and parsley. Drizzle the top with the olive oil.

7. Bake the tart for 40 minutes. The cheese will have melted and the tomatoes will be caramelized. Remove it from the oven and let it rest for 10 minutes. Carefully remove the sides of the tart pan and run a thin spatula under the crust to loosen it from the bottom. Use a wide spatula to transfer the tart to a platter, and serve hot or at room temperature.

Note: You can prepare the dough a day ahead and store it, wrapped in plastic wrap, in the refrigerator.

DUCK AND CARROT RAGOUT

In this luscious ragoût, the slow cooking transforms the duck into a meat more succulent than any confit you have ever tasted. What seems like extravagance—buying three whole ducks to get six legs—is well worth it when you taste this amazing dish. And anyway, you can freeze the boned breasts for another meal. In fact, I tucked a recipe for an Aromatic Duck Salad in a box at the end of this menu. It's a wonderful way to prepare duck breasts, so you need look no further.

1 tablespoon olive oil
6 whole duck legs (about 6 ounces each)
1 large onion, cut in half lengthwise and slivered
2 large leeks, including 3 inches green, rinsed well, halved lengthwise, and slivered crosswise
8 cloves garlic
12 carrots, peeled and cut into ¼-inch-thick slices
1 bouquet garni: 3 sprigs fresh rosemary and 10 sprigs fresh parsley tied together with string
2 bay leaves
Salt and freshly ground black pepper, to taste
5 cups Basic Chicken Broth (page 397)
2 tablespoons chopped fresh flat-leaf parsley, for garnish

1. Preheat the oven to 350°F.

2. Heat the olive oil in a large deep flameproof casserole over medium heat. Add 2 duck legs and brown them well, 5 to 6 minutes. Transfer them to a plate and repeat with the remaining duck legs. Discard all but 3 tablespoons of the fat in the casserole.

3. Add the onion, leeks, garlic, and carrots to the casserole and cook, stirring, over medium heat until the onion and leeks are very soft, 10 to 15 minutes. Tuck in the bouquet garni and the bay leaves. Arrange the duck legs among the vegetables, skin side up. Sprinkle with salt and pepper and add the broth.

4. Transfer to the oven and bake, uncovered, for 1 hour. If the dish is browning too quickly at this point, cover the casserole with aluminum foil. Continue to bake until the meat is tender, 30 minutes more.

5. Transfer the duck legs to a plate. Using a slotted spoon, transfer the vegetables to an oven-to-table serving dish that is large enough to also hold the duck. Discard the bouquet garni and the bay leaves. Arrange the duck legs on top of the vegetables. Pour the pan juices through a gravy separator, or allow the juices to cool slightly and then skim the fat from the top.

6. Pour 1 cup of the defatted pan juices over the duck and vegetables. If necessary, reheat the dish in a 350°F oven for 20 minutes. Sprinkle with the parsley and serve immediately.

CREAMY SHALLOT MASHED POTATOES

Lumpy, creamy, moist, or buttery—we all have a preference for how we like our potatoes mashed, but we all seem to agree they are a truly pleasing food. When made with Yukon Gold potatoes, they are outstanding. Slightly yellow in color, these buttery-flavored potatoes hold their shape when boiled and are delicious mashed. Shallots, caramelized to a soft sweetness, give them a French feel.

3 pounds Yukon Gold potatoes, peeled and cut in half
6 tablespoons (¾ stick) unsalted butter
1½ tablespoons olive oil
4 shallots, cut in quarters
¾ cup half-and-half
Salt and freshly ground black pepper, to taste

1. Place the potatoes in a saucepan of lightly salted water to cover. Bring the water to a boil over high heat and cook until the potatoes are very tender, about 30 minutes.

2. Meanwhile, melt 2 tablespoons of the butter in the olive oil in a nonstick skillet over low heat. Add the shallots and cook, shaking the pan, until they are golden brown, about 10 minutes. Set them aside.

3. Heat the half-and-half and the remaining 4 tablespoons butter in a small saucepan over low heat. Keep warm.

4. Drain the potatoes, return them to the pot, and cook over very low heat for 10 seconds, shaking the pot, to dry the potatoes well. Put the potatoes through a ricer, or mash them by hand, in a large bowl.

5. Add the half-and-half mixture to the potatoes and stir until fluffy. Season with salt and pepper and stir in the shallots. Serve immediately.

Duck and Carrot Ragoût

TARTE AUX POMMES

I t is one of the iconic experiences of the first-time visitor to France to taste the round tart with its fan of sugary, buttery, browned apple slices shaped like a half-moon. As your fork cuts into a piece, it breaks away and yields up a sweet slice of apple and a piece of crisp buttery crust that leaves you swooning with satisfaction.

> *1 sheet frozen puff pastry, thawed according*
>   *to package directions*
> *1 cup vanilla wafer or butter cookie crumbs*
>   *(about half a 12-ounce box of Nilla Wafers)*
> *4 apples, preferably Ida Reds, Macoun,*
>   *McIntosh, or Golden Delicious, peeled,*
>   *cored, and halved*
> *½ cup granulated sugar*
> *4 tablespoons (½ stick) unsalted butter*
> *3 tablespoons confectioners' sugar*
> *Crème fraîche, for serving*

1. Line a baking sheet with a piece of parchment paper.

2. Roll the puff pastry out on a lightly floured surface to form a 12-inch circle (or if it is larger than 12 inches, cut it to size). Prick the pastry all over with the tines of a fork. Place a 9½-inch flan ring (see Note) on the prepared baking sheet and line it with the pastry, pressing it up the sides of the ring. Use a rolling pin to roll across the top of the flan ring, cutting off the excess pastry. Cover the pastry and refrigerate it for 1 hour, or wrap it in plastic wrap and chill overnight.

3. Position a rack in the center of the oven, and preheat the oven to 450°F.

4. Scatter the wafer crumbs over the pastry shell. Slice the apple halves lengthwise, as thin as possible, and fan the slices around the flan ring, starting at the outer edge and covering the whole surface. Sprinkle the apples evenly with the granulated sugar and dot with the butter.

5. Bake the tart for 15 minutes. Then reduce the heat to 400°F and bake until the apples are soft, golden brown, and caramelized, about 50 minutes more.

6. Sift the confectioners' sugar over the tart and return it to the top shelf of the oven. Cook until it is a deep golden brown, about 10 minutes. Slip off the flan ring. Use two wide spatulas to transfer the tart to a serving platter. Serve warm, topped with a generous dollop of crème fraîche.

Note: A flan ring resembles a tart pan without a bottom: a metal band or ring, 7 to 9½ inches in diameter, with sides that are 1 to 1½ inches high. It is placed on a baking sheet and then the pastry is fitted into the ring. Because the pastry shrinks slightly during baking, the ring slips right off the finished tart.

AROMATIC DUCK SALAD

Turn the duck breasts you didn't use in the Duck and Carrot Ragoût recipe into this hearty aromatic salad.

FOR THE DUCK AND MARINADE
*3 whole duck breasts, deboned
    (about 1 pound each)
6 tablespoons sherry vinegar
3 tablespoons extra-virgin olive oil
1½ teaspoons ground cardamom
¾ teaspoon ground cinnamon
Salt and freshly ground black pepper, to taste*

FOR THE SALAD
*3 ripe freestone peaches
1½ tablespoons fresh lemon juice
1½ cups diced seeded watermelon
    (½-inch dice)
¾ cup Sherry Vinaigrette (page 263)
6 cups frisée lettuce leaves, rinsed and
    patted dry
4 tablespoons finely diced shallots
Salt and freshly ground black pepper, to taste
¾ cup (loosely packed) fresh basil leaves,
    slivered*

1. Cut each duck breast in half lengthwise. Trim off any excess fat and skin from around the meat. Fan out the fillet pieces from underneath the breast, if they are large. Using a sharp knife, carefully score the skin on each breast three times on the diagonal.

2. Combine the marinade ingredients in a large bowl. Add the duck breasts, flesh side down, and marinate, covered, in the refrigerator for 2 hours.

3. Heat a large nonstick skillet over medium heat. Add the duck breasts, skin side down, and sear until golden brown, about 7 minutes. Carefully pour off some of the excess fat if necessary. Turn the breasts over, sprinkle with salt and pepper, and cook for 2 to 3 minutes for medium-rare. Transfer the duck to a cutting board and let the meat rest for 5 minutes. Then cut each breast into ¼-inch-thick diagonal slices. Set them aside.

4. Pit, peel, and cut the peaches into thin lengthwise slices. Toss with the lemon juice in a bowl (to prevent the peaches from discoloring). Add the watermelon to the bowl. Toss the fruit gently with ¼ cup of the Sherry Vinaigrette. Set aside.

5. Place the frisée and the shallots in another bowl. Season with salt and pepper, and toss with ¼ cup of the Sherry Vinaigrette.

6. To assemble the salad, fan a sliced duck breast in the center of each dinner plate. Drizzle each portion with about 1½ teaspoons of the remaining vinaigrette. Arrange a handful of the frisée salad alongside each duck breast. Spoon equal portions of the fruit salad on top of each duck breast. Garnish each with a generous tablespoon of the basil and serve immediately.

New Cheese &

Fruit Collection

Cheese and fruit are an extra pleasure at the end of a special dinner, at tea time, or as a light lunch. Some combinations were born to be enjoyed with a little glass of sherry, or port, or even champagne. Now that there are so many exquisite cheeses available, a tasting of fruit "sweets" matched with a selection of cheese is one of the new favorite traditions in my home.

Prepare fruit compotes and butters ahead of time, then spoon them alongside some favorite cheeses for a quick and easy celebration.

> *Wine and cheese are ageless companions, like aspirin and aches, or June and moon, or good people and noble ventures.*
>
> —M.F.K. FISHER

MENU

Matching fruit and cheese is often instinctive, visual, or visceral. Although it's hard not to leave well enough alone when it comes to ripe summer cherries, a Bing Cherry Compote served with a creamy Fourme d'Ambert is a good reason to save some of the fruit for cooking. And no longer does a cheese course mean only French cheese. Incorporate Spanish cheeses as well as Italian and American farmstead cheeses. The new American Cheddars and goat cheeses match well with aromatically flavored sweets such as Spiced Cranberry Ketchup and Spiced-Up Blueberry Relish.

A block of Cheddar cheese, a handcrafted bowl filled with apples nearby, and the aroma of mulled wine wafting through the air: a moment of culinary reverie. Or a white plate setting off the deep blue veins of Roquefort along with dried muscats, walnuts, and red wine; or with Stilton, matched with port and pears.

Don't go overboard with quantity. There is so much brilliant cheese available today that visiting a cheese shop or the cheese department of a specialty food store can be a thrilling, and sometimes an awe-inspiring, experience. You definitely want to taste before you buy.

A mild-flavored cheese, followed by one with more depth, followed by something hard—an aged Gouda, perhaps—one of each will do it. Small cheese spreaders and delicate spoons are helpful. Rather than bread, which might be too heavy, provide a basket of mixed crisps and toasts, both sweet and savory.

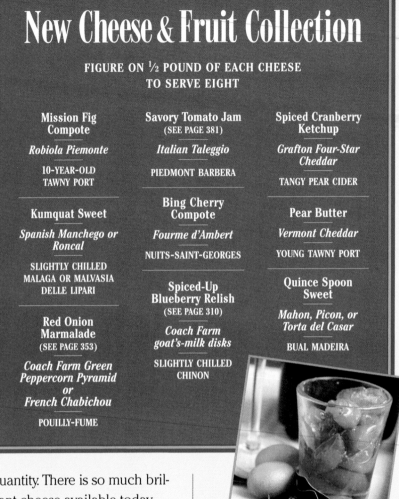

New Cheese & Fruit Collection

FIGURE ON ½ POUND OF EACH CHEESE TO SERVE EIGHT

Mission Fig Compote

Robiola Piemonte

10-YEAR-OLD TAWNY PORT

Kumquat Sweet

Spanish Manchego or Roncal

SLIGHTLY CHILLED MALAGA OR MALVASIA DELLE LIPARI

Red Onion Marmalade
(SEE PAGE 353)

Coach Farm Green Peppercorn Pyramid or French Chabichou

POUILLY-FUME

Savory Tomato Jam
(SEE PAGE 381)

Italian Taleggio

PIEDMONT BARBERA

Bing Cherry Compote

Fourme d'Ambert

NUITS-SAINT-GEORGES

Spiced-Up Blueberry Relish
(SEE PAGE 310)

Coach Farm goat's-milk disks

SLIGHTLY CHILLED CHINON

Spiced Cranberry Ketchup

Grafton Four-Star Cheddar

TANGY PEAR CIDER

Pear Butter

Vermont Cheddar

YOUNG TAWNY PORT

Quince Spoon Sweet

Mahon, Picon, or Torta del Casar

BUAL MADEIRA

THE EXTRAS

Long, narrow ceramic plates

Cheese knives

Small serving spoons

Cherry pitter

MISSION FIG COMPOTE

Enjoy rich, black figs simmered to a honey-thick consistency with a slightly tart creamy Robiola Piemonte. If necessary, when simmering the fruit, add a little extra liquid to keep it from thickening up too much.

8 ounces dried black Mission figs
Finely grated zest of 1 orange
1/3 cup fresh orange juice, or more if needed
1/4 cup sugar

1. Cut the figs into quarters and combine them with all the other ingredients in a heavy saucepan. Add ½ cup water and bring to a boil over medium-high heat. Reduce the heat to medium-low and simmer, partially covered, stirring occasionally, until the figs are softened and mashable, 8 to 10 minutes. Remove the pan from the heat, cover, and let the mixture rest for 5 minutes.

2. Transfer the mixture to a small bowl, and mash it lightly with a large spoon. Allow the compote to cool to room temperature. Store, covered, in the refrigerator for up to 2 weeks.

MAKES 2 CUPS

KUMQUAT SWEET

Traditionally served with cold meats, breads, or tea, this sweet is also a delight with a cheese course.

1 pound fresh kumquats, well washed, stems and leaves removed, and cut in half crosswise
1¾ cups sugar
1/4 cup crystallized ginger, rinsed
1 piece (1 inch) fresh ginger
1½ tablespoons fresh lemon juice
Pinch of salt

1. Pit the kumquats carefully and place the fruit in a heavy saucepan. Add all the remaining ingredients and 1 cup water and bring to a boil over medium-high heat. Reduce the heat to medium-low and simmer until the kumquats are just tender, 12 to 15 minutes.

2. Remove the pan from the heat and allow the sweet to cool to room temperature. Discard the fresh ginger. Store, covered, in the refrigerator for up to 2 weeks.

MAKES ABOUT 2½ CUPS

BING CHERRY COMPOTE

June ripens two favorite fruits: flaming red strawberries and juicy black cherries. Cooking Bing cherries into preserves, pies, and even Grecian-style spoon sweets intensifies the pleasure of this intoxicating fruit. The addition of almond extract enhances the flavor.

1½ pounds Bing cherries, rinsed, stems and pits removed
3 cups sugar
Zest of 1 orange, removed in 1 long strip with a paring knife
1 vanilla bean pod, split lengthwise
1/4 teaspoon almond extract
1 tablespoon fresh lemon juice

1. Layer half of the cherries in a heavy non-reactive saucepan and top them with half of the sugar in an even layer. Place the orange zest and vanilla bean on top. Cover with the remaining cherries. Sprinkle the almond extract over the cherries, and top with the remaining sugar. Set the saucepan aside and allow the cherries to macerate for at least 1 hour.

2. Add ¾ cup water to the pan and bring to a boil over high heat, stirring occasionally. Reduce the heat to medium and simmer, skimming off

mine is replete with aromatic spices of the South Seas as well as the tangy, sweet, bitter thrust of cranberries. It makes a superb accompaniment for a full-flavored Cheddar.

1 pound fresh cranberries, rinsed and
*   picked over*
¹/₂ cup chopped onion
¹/₂ cup cider vinegar
1 cup sugar
¹/₂ teaspoon ground cloves
¹/₂ teaspoon ground cinnamon
¹/₂ teaspoon ground allspice
¹/₂ teaspoon celery seeds
¹/₂ teaspoon salt
¹/₂ teaspoon freshly ground black pepper
¹/₂ cup apple cider

1. Combine all the ingredients except the apple cider in a heavy saucepan with ¹/₂ cup water and bring to a boil over medium-high heat. Reduce the heat to medium-low and simmer until the berries pop open, about 10 minutes. Skim off any foam that forms on the surface. Set aside to let the mixture cool slightly.

2. Place the mixture in a food processor. With the motor running, drizzle the cider in through the feed tube and process until completely smooth. Pass the ketchup through a fine-mesh strainer. Serve at room temperature. Store the ketchup, covered, in the refrigerator for up to 1 week.

MAKES 3¹/₂ CUPS

any foam that rises to the surface, until the mixture starts to thicken, about 15 minutes. Then stir in the lemon juice and remove the pan from the heat. Remove the vanilla bean pod. Allow the compote to cool to room temperature; then refrigerate until ready to serve. Store, covered, in the refrigerator for up to 2 weeks.

MAKES 4 CUPS

SPICED CRANBERRY KETCHUP

Ketchup has as many stories about its origin as it has uses in the kitchen. Some think it comes from Indonesian *kecap manis*, a kind of thick gussied-up soy sauce. The Chinese claim that it comes from their word *fan-kei-cheop* ("foreign-vine-vegetable juice"). I'll leave it to the historians. What I do know is that

PEAR BUTTER

Long-cooked fruit butters get to the very core of a fruit's sweetness. This pear butter matches up well with some sharp Vermont Cheddar and a tawny port alongside. Cooking it in the oven avoids the tendency of fruit butters to scorch.

>6 pounds assorted pears (such as Bosc, Anjou, and Comice), well washed
>2 tablespoons fresh lemon juice
>1 cup apple juice
>$2^1/_2$ teaspoons ground cinnamon
>$1/_4$ cup cider vinegar
>2 cups (packed) dark brown sugar
>Salt, to taste

1. Cut the pears in half, then core, peel, and quarter them. Place them in a large bowl and toss with the lemon juice.

2. Combine the pears and the apple juice in a flameproof casserole and bring to a boil over medium heat. Reduce the heat to medium-low and cook, covered, until the pears are very soft, about 30 minutes.

3. Meanwhile, preheat the oven to 350°F.

4. Place the pears, along with any liquid, in a food processor and puree (you may have to do this in batches). Pass the puree through a strainer into a bowl, using the back of a large metal spoon to press any remaining puree through the strainer. Return the mixture to the casserole. Stir in the cinnamon, vinegar, and brown sugar and place the casserole in the oven. Bake, uncovered, stirring occasionally, until the puree has darkened and thickened, 3 hours.

5. Season the pear butter lightly with salt to bring out the flavors, and allow it to cool to room temperature. Store, covered, in the refrigerator for up to 3 weeks.

MAKES 5 CUPS

QUINCE SPOON SWEET

Quince paste, relatively new to American markets, is an extremely popular accompaniment to Spanish cheeses, such as Manchego and the vibrant blue Cabrales. Look for it in specialty food markets. For my *All Around the World Cookbook* I created a Quince Spoon Sweet recipe, and a delicate portion of it would be delicious served along with the cheese, so I've included it in this menu as well.

>6 quinces (about 3 pounds), cut in quarters, peeled, and cored
>Juice and finely grated zest of 2 lemons
>2 cups sugar
>1 piece (1 inch) fresh ginger
>2 cinnamon sticks (3 inches long)
>4 whole cloves

1. Place the quinces in a large heavy nonreactive pot with the lemon juice, lemon zest, and 3 cups water. Add the sugar, ginger, cinnamon sticks, and cloves. Bring the mixture to a boil over high heat, then reduce the heat to medium-low and simmer until the fruit is tender and the color has changed to pale orange, about $1^1/_4$ hours. The texture will be similar to a homemade applesauce.

2. Allow the sweet to cool to room temperature. Then remove the ginger, cinnamon sticks, and cloves. Store, covered, in the refrigerator for up to 2 weeks.

MAKES ABOUT 3 CUPS

A Gracious

Housewarming

Moving into a new house or apartment is a monumental event. It's a time when your life pauses, you take a deep breath, and you begin again. It's where your "stuff" goes, where your memories are born, where your kids grow up, where you can be you. Never mind that no matter how big the place is, you will run out of space at some point—right now it's freshly painted, beautiful in the morning light that streams through the windows, and alive with the promise that calls for a housewarming celebration. Everything in this meal can be made in advance and set out nicely on your just-unpacked table. Guests can help themselves as they arrive. Housewarmings are informal, and so is this menu.

MENU

Coaxing the deep flavor out of vegetables by roasting them slowly and then spinning them into a soup makes a delicious beginning for a great evening. Follow it up with a colorful salad of slightly bitter greens that are robust and refreshing. Next, an easy roast of chicken and peppers is full-flavored, not too dressy, and complements the other flavors nicely. Fruit and cheese are easy to put together and feel just the right amount of luxurious. Blackberry-Lemon Tart is a delicious dessert, but if it's easier, just go out and buy one—a nut or lemon tart will be just fine. However you choose to serve dessert, you've greeted your guests with a warm meal, a warm heart, and open arms.

Keep the table simple—use whatever you have unpacked. (Some people I know take a good year to toss all the cartons away, so they keep draping them more and more creatively.)

Because the food is colorful, use white or off-white linens. Clear glass dinner plates with white china bowls for both the soup and chicken will show off the food nicely. To keep things simple, place votive candles here and there. One or two small rosemary plants in clay pots will add much more than any scented candle. Set out small delicate tumblers for wine and water. A pitcher or a bottle of water is a good idea too.

Place the pears in a bowl to add color and life to the room. Now enjoy. May you have long years and the best of luck in your new home.

A Gracious Housewarming

BUFFET FOR EIGHT

Slow-Roasted Tomato and Fennel Soup

A Crisp Winter Greens Salad

Rainbow Peppers and Chicken with Herbed Lemon Orzo

Pears and Figs with Parmigiano-Reggiano

Blackberry-Lemon Tart

THE MUSIC

Miles Davis
Burt Bacharach
Elvis Costello
Glenn Gould's *Goldberg Variations*

THE WINE

Orvieto Classico

THE EXTRAS

Several baking sheets
Tart pan

*"...in the composure of a sallet,
every plant should come
in to bear its part,
without being overpower'd
by some herb of a stronger taste,
so as to endanger the native
sapor and virtue of the rest;
but fall into their places,
like the notes in music...."*
—JOHN EVELYN

A Crisp Winter Greens Salad

SLOW-ROASTED TOMATO AND FENNEL SOUP

Slow-roasting seduces all the deep garden flavor out of the tomatoes and the sweet, slightly licorice hint out of the fennel. If you roast some tomatoes at their peak of flavor in the early fall and freeze them, you can serve this dish through the winter for a hearty yet summery starter.

4 pounds ripe plum tomatoes, cut in half
*   lengthwise*
2 fennel bulbs (1 pound total), trimmed,
*   fronds reserved*
¼ cup extra-virgin olive oil
¼ cup sugar
Salt and freshly ground black pepper, to taste
12 cups Basic Chicken Broth (page 397)
½ cup slivered fresh basil leaves

1. Preheat the oven to 250°F. Line two or three baking sheets with aluminum foil.

2. Scoop the seeds out of the tomatoes and place the tomatoes, skin side down, on the prepared baking sheets. Remove the core from the fennel and slice the bulbs lengthwise into strips. Arrange the fennel around the tomatoes. Brush the vegetables with the olive oil. Sprinkle evenly with the sugar and with salt and pepper. Bake until soft and slightly caramelized, 2 hours.

3. Transfer the vegetables to a heavy pot, add the broth, and bring to a boil over high heat. Then reduce the heat to medium-low and simmer, partially covered, to blend the flavors, 10 minutes.

4. Coarsely chop the reserved fennel fronds and stir them into the soup. Let the soup cool slightly.

5. Puree the soup, in batches, in a blender or food processor until just smooth. Return it to the pot and heat it through. Stir in the basil and serve immediately.

A CRISP WINTER GREENS SALAD

Bitter greens add refreshing peppery flavors and crisp colors to a meal, as do the radish slices. Match them up with a dressing of rich extra-virgin olive oil from Spain or Italy, which will round out the flavors. If your housewarming is near the Christmas holidays, you may be able to find red endive. Use it—it adds a dazzling effect.

2 heads radicchio, cored, outer leaves
*   discarded*
2 Belgian endives, stems trimmed
2 large bunches arugula, tough
*   stems trimmed*
4 large red radishes, trimmed
*   and thinly sliced*
2 tablespoons snipped fresh chives
¼ cup red wine vinegar
Salt and freshly ground black pepper,
*   to taste*
3 tablespoons extra-virgin olive oil

1. Separate the radicchio and endives into leaves. Fill a large bowl or the sink with cold water and add the radicchio, endives, and arugula. Swirl the greens around to remove any sand. Drain them well and pat dry.

2. Shred the radicchio and place it in a large bowl. Cut the endives into thin crosswise slivers and add them to the bowl. Add the arugula, radishes, and chives.

3. In a separate bowl, whisk the vinegar with the salt and pepper. Whisking constantly, slowly drizzle in the olive oil. Continue whisking until well combined.

4. Before serving, season the salad with salt and pepper. Drizzle lightly with the dressing and toss well. Serve immediately.

RAINBOW PEPPERS AND CHICKEN

This rustic dish is as appropriate for entertaining as it is for family meals. The long-cooked peppers develop sweetness and just the right amount of tang for a gutsy sauce. Though the flavors are deep and complex, at its heart this is a simple dish that doesn't require a lot of fuss. After you've spent all those days unpacking boxes and hanging pictures, you want a dish that looks nice and is easy for guests to serve themselves. It's great with Herbed Lemon Orzo and crusty bread to soak up all the juices.

*2 chickens (about 3½ pounds each),
    each cut into 8 serving pieces,
    rinsed and patted dry
Salt and freshly ground black pepper, to taste
8 tablespoons olive oil
2 onions, cut in half lengthwise and slivered
4 red bell peppers, stemmed, seeded,
    and cut into 1-inch strips
4 yellow bell peppers, stemmed, seeded,
    and cut into 1-inch strips
2 green bell peppers, stemmed, seeded,
    and cut into 1-inch strips
2 tablespoons minced garlic
1 cup dry red wine
2 pounds ripe plum tomatoes, peeled, halved
    lengthwise, seeded, then cut in half crosswise
1½ cups torn fresh basil leaves
2 teaspoons sugar
Herbed Lemon Orzo (recipe follows),
    for serving*

1. Preheat the oven to 350°F.

2. Season the chicken with salt and pepper. Heat 2 tablespoons of the olive oil in a large non-stick skillet over medium-high heat and sauté the chicken pieces, in batches, until browned, about 5 minutes per side. Add up to 2 more tablespoons of oil as necessary. Transfer the chicken to a plate.

3. Heat the remaining olive oil in a large flameproof casserole over medium-low heat. Add the onions and bell peppers and cook, stirring, until softened, 7 minutes. Add the garlic and wine and cook until the vegetables are very soft, about 3 minutes more.

4. Add the tomatoes, basil, and sugar to the casserole and cook to soften the tomatoes and incorporate the sugar, 2 minutes. Return the chicken to the pot, smothering it in the sauce. Cover, transfer to the oven, and bake until the chicken is tender, 1¼ hours, basting occasionally. Serve with the Herbed Lemon Orzo.

HERBED LEMON ORZO

Orzo is a petite pasta that looks like rice. In Italian it means "barley," no doubt because its shape reminds Italians of a grain of cooked barley. In much the same way that you would add herbs to rice for a light savory accompaniment to more powerful entrees, this orzo provides the sensual pleasure of pasta with light floral notes.

*10 cups Basic Chicken Broth (page 397)
4 cups orzo
½ cup chopped fresh lemon thyme leaves
    (see Note)
4 teaspoons grated lemon zest
4 teaspoons peanut oil
4 teaspoons fresh lemon juice*

1. Bring the broth to a boil in a large saucepan over high heat. Add the orzo, reduce the heat to medium, and cook until just tender, 9 minutes. Drain, and return the pasta to the pan.

2. Add the remaining ingredients and toss well to combine. Serve hot.

Note: If lemon thyme is unavailable, substitute ¼ cup chopped fresh regular thyme or ½ cup chopped fresh parsley or oregano.

Rainbow Peppers and Chicken

PEARS AND FIGS
WITH PARMIGIANO-REGGIANO

The taste and texture of fresh sweet figs match up well with the aged ripeness of Parmigiano-Reggiano, the king of Parmesan cheeses. Pears, by contrast, are soft, succulent, and juicy. A bite of cheese, a slice of fig, and one of pear—it doesn't get much better than that.

Wedge of Parmigiano-Reggiano cheese
(about 1 pound)
8 ripe pears
8 ripe figs

Arrange the cheese on a wooden board, with a sharp knife next to it. Place the fruit in a shallow bowl. Offer each guest a dessert plate and a sharp knife, and invite them to help themselves.

BLACKBERRY-LEMON TART

Sweet, creamy, tangy lemon tart has always been one of my favorite meal-enders. A handful of blackberries, dark as vintage port, set against a light lemon custard makes for a lovely combination of flavors and colors.

8 tablespoons (1 stick) cold unsalted butter
3/4 cup sugar
1/2 teaspoon pure vanilla extract
1 cup all-purpose flour
1/8 teaspoon salt
2/3 cup fresh lemon juice (from 4 lemons)
2 tablespoons heavy (whipping) cream
3 large eggs
2 large egg yolks
9 large blackberries

1. Place the butter in a food processor and process for a few seconds until creamy. Add 1/4 cup of the sugar and process until the mixture is light and fluffy, about 20 seconds, stopping to scrape the sides of the bowl once or twice. Add the vanilla. Combine the flour and the salt and add this to the food processor. Process until the dough comes together, then scrape the sides of the bowl and process for a few seconds more.

2. With lightly floured hands, press the dough evenly over the bottom and up the sides of a 9-inch tart pan with removable bottom. Press around the bottom edge of the tart and make sure that the dough is not too thick.

3. Trim off any excess dough at the top of the tart pan with a knife. Lightly press the dough around the inside of the rim with your thumb so that it extends about 1/8 inch above the pan. Prick the bottom of the dough all over with a fork. Chill in the freezer for at least 30 minutes, or cover with plastic wrap and freeze it for as long as overnight.

4. Preheat the oven to 375°F.

5. Bake the partially or fully frozen tart shell until golden brown, about 25 minutes. Allow it to cool on a wire rack. Leave the oven on.

6. Whisk the remaining 1/2 cup sugar and the lemon juice together in a bowl. Gradually whisk in the cream, then the eggs and the egg yolks. Combine thoroughly. Pour the mixture into a saucepan and cook over medium heat, whisking constantly, until the filling thickens and the whisk leaves a trail when lifted, about 4 minutes. Do not let it boil.

7. Strain the filling into a bowl, then pour it into the baked tart shell. Place a blackberry in the center of the tart and then place the remaining 8 berries evenly around the tart. Bake for 4 minutes. (The filling will be starting to set around the edges and will still be a bit loose toward the center; it will set completely as it cools.)

8. Cool the tart thoroughly on a wire rack. Before serving, carefully remove the sides and bottom of the pan, and slide the tart onto a decorative plate. Serve at room temperature.

A Cozy

Dinner for Two

It needn't be Valentine's Day to have a magical evening. It needn't be an anniversary or birthday, either. A comforting flame in the fireplace, candlelight on the table, champagne in a silver bucket . . . A meal for two only need emphasize that the two of you are special—especially to each other. This menu comes together without hours spent in the kitchen—so you can both relax and enjoy it.

> *"Wine comes in*
> *at the mouth*
> *And love comes in*
> *at the eye. . . . "*
> —WILLIAM BUTLER YEATS

MENU

B e sure the lights are well dimmed. Then begin. Frisée and carrots make a delectable salad on which to bed the perfectly seared scallops. A small roasted venison tenderloin, served with a rich red wine-cherry sauce, serves two people perfectly. Rutabaga and Carrot Whip is a slightly bitter foil for the sweet meat. Top off the meal with sinful Fudge Whip Parfaits, dolloped with Sweetened Whipped Cream.

This is a time to forsake fanfare and celebrate the intimacy of home. Just bring out your favorite things—dishes, glasses, serving pieces, and a sweet bud vase for a single stem of your favorite flower. If you want a more formal tone, light some candles. It should be a comfortable evening, but not so comfortable that you would use paper napkins.

Slice the venison in the kitchen and present it at the table on a small oval or rectangular platter. It is much more elegant to spoon just a bit of the sauce over each portion to enhance the meat, rather than smothering it. Serve the remainder of the sauce in a small gravy boat with an equally small ladle. You might want to add multigrain rolls in a small napkin-lined basket, along with a crock of sweet butter. For a sweet dessert presentation, the Fudge Whip Parfaits are served in the homey ramekins in which they were baked, dolloped with Sweetened Whipped Cream for added dazzle.

To change the dynamics, move to the living room for coffee and an after-dinner drink. Set out some small candies—I like to keep chocolate espresso beans on hand for just this purpose.

A Cozy Dinner For Two

SEA SCALLOPS ON A SALAD MEDLEY

VENISON WITH RED WINE-CHERRY SAUCE

RUTABAGA AND CARROT WHIP

FUDGE WHIP PARFAITS

THE MUSIC

The tangos of Astor Piazzolla

Django Reinhardt and Stephane Grappelli's
Quintette du Hot Club de France

THE WINE

Corton-Charlemagne

Pommard

THE EXTRAS

Ramekins

Bud vase

SEA SCALLOPS ON A SALAD MEDLEY

The scallop's texture is exceedingly sensual. Oysters may have the reputation of being a mild aphrodisiac, but I think scallops also make the heart go pitter-pat. Remember that famous scene in the movie *Tom Jones* when Albert Finney and his love of the evening stare lasciviously into each other's eyes as they slurp oysters and chew juicy pears? They might have cut to the chase even more quickly if they had had some delicate-fleshed scallops.

Juice of 1 lime
3 tablespoons olive oil
Salt and freshly ground black pepper,
  to taste
6 sea scallops
2 tablespoons fresh lemon juice
2 carrots, peeled and grated
1 small head frisée lettuce,
  leaves washed and separated,
  or 2 cups mesclun
1 shallot, finely chopped
2 tablespoons chopped fresh flat-leaf
  parsley or mint leaves

1. Combine the lime juice, 2 tablespoons of the olive oil, and the salt and pepper in a bowl and stir well. Add the scallops and coat them well. Set aside to marinate for 15 minutes.

2. Remove the scallops from the marinade. Place a nonstick skillet over medium-high heat and sear the scallops for 2 minutes per side (4 minutes total), adding more oil if necessary. Set them aside.

3. Whisk the lemon juice with the remaining 1 tablespoon olive oil in a bowl. Add the carrots, frisée, and shallot and toss. Season with salt and pepper. Divide the salad between two dinner plates and place 3 scallops atop each salad. Sprinkle with the parsley and serve.

Sea Scallops on a Salad Medley

VENISON WITH RED WINE-CHERRY SAUCE

Game, wine, and fruit—the combination makes me think of the comfort and warmth of a romantic country weekend. Since venison is a lean meat, you never cook it very long, which means you have more time to spend on each other. Because there is not a lot of fat and the meat itself has a big flavor, it complements the forward tastes in the red wine-cherry sauce. In the winter, there is no better choice to serve for a romantic dinner for two than this luscious meat. But if you can't get venison, by all means substitute a pork tenderloin—the preparation works equally well (see Note). Arrange each plate with as much attention as you would give to a plate at a formal meal for ten.

1 venison tenderloin (about 1 pound)
1 large clove garlic, cut into thin slivers
1 teaspoon chopped fresh thyme,
*   plus 6 sprigs*
Salt and freshly ground black pepper,
*   to taste*
1 to 2 tablespoons olive oil
½ cup dry red wine or cranberry
*   juice*
½ cup dried cherries
1 tablespoon red currant jelly
2 tablespoons unsalted butter

Venison with Red Wine-Cherry Sauce and Rutabaga and Carrot Whip

1. Position a rack in the center of the oven, and preheat the oven to 450°F.

2. Pat the venison dry with a paper towel.

3. With the tip of a sharp knife, make inch-deep slits in the meat and insert the garlic slivers. Pat the chopped thyme and the salt and pepper well onto the venison.

4. Heat the olive oil in a nonstick skillet over medium heat and brown the meat well, turning it once, 5 to 6 minutes. Transfer the venison to a baking pan and place it in the oven.

5. Roast the venison until it is medium-rare (about 125°F on an instant reading thermometer), 7 to 9 minutes. Transfer the meat to a cutting board and let it rest for 4 to 5 minutes before serving.

6. While the meat is resting, place the wine, cherries, and 2 of the thyme sprigs in the skillet and bring to a boil, scraping up any brown bits. Whisk in the red currant jelly and then swirl in the butter.

7. Slice the tenderloin ½ inch thick, and arrange the slices decoratively on two dinner plates. Spoon the hot cherry sauce on top and garnish with the remaining fresh thyme sprigs. Serve immediately.

Note: If you are substituting pork tenderloin for the venison, preheat the oven to 400°F in step 1. Continue with the recipe, searing the meat for 10 minutes in step 4 and roasting it until pale pink, 10 minutes, in step 5. Let the meat rest for 10 minutes before serving. All else remains the same.

RUTABAGA AND CARROT WHIP

A creamy, steamy, sweet, and aromatic puree—the rutabaga may not be the most romantic-sounding vegetable, but it makes a truly passionate puree. Lightly sweet, lightly sharp, rutabaga goes beautifully with the underlying sweetness of carrots.

1 pound rutabaga
2 carrots, peeled and cut into
   2-inch lengths
1 small onion, thinly sliced
1 tablespoon light brown sugar
$1/2$ teaspoon ground ginger
$1/4$ teaspoon ground mace
Pinch of cayenne pepper
Salt, to taste
2 tablespoons unsalted butter
1 cup Basic Chicken Broth (page 397)
   or Vegetable Broth (page 398)

1. Preheat the oven to 350°F.

2. Carefully peel the rutabaga and cut it into small chunks.

3. Combine the rutabaga with the carrots and onion in a heatproof casserole. Sprinkle with the brown sugar, ginger, mace, cayenne, and salt. Dot with the butter and pour the broth over the vegetables. Cover and bake for 2½ hours.

4. Puree the vegetables with their liquid, in batches, in a food processor or blender, leaving some texture. Serve immediately, or reheat, covered, in a 350°F oven for 15 to 20 minutes.

FUDGE WHIP PARFAITS

After dinner in the summer, when the sun was still out and bedtime felt far off, the kids in the neighborhood I grew up in used to go outside and play ball while waiting for the ice-cream man to drive his truck down our street. Fudgsicles were favorite pops on a stick, and nostalgia for that flavor went into the creation of this special dessert.

$2/3$ cup heavy (whipping) cream
$1/3$ cup whole milk
2 tablespoons (packed) light brown sugar
3 ounces bittersweet chocolate, coarsely chopped
2 large egg yolks
$3/4$ teaspoon pure vanilla extract
$1½$ teaspoons cognac
Sweetened Whipped Cream (page 403),
   for serving

1. Position a rack in the center of the oven and preheat the oven to 300°F.

2. Combine the cream, milk, and brown sugar in a saucepan and bring to a simmer over medium heat, whisking lightly until the sugar has melted. Remove the pan from the heat, stir in the chocolate, and cover the pan. Allow the mixture to sit undisturbed for 10 minutes. Then uncover and whisk until smooth. Set it aside.

3. Whisk the egg yolks together with the vanilla in a mixing bowl until light, about 2 minutes.

4. Whisking constantly, add the cream mixture to the egg yolks in a slow steady stream and continue whisking until just incorporated. Whisk in the cognac. Strain the mixture through a fine-mesh sieve into a bowl.

5. Pour the mixture into two 4-ounce ovenproof ramekins (they should be three-fourths full). Place the ramekins in a deep baking dish and pour boiling water into the dish so that it comes two thirds of the way up the sides of the ramekins. Lightly cover the baking dish with aluminum foil and cut about eight slits in the foil so the steam can escape. Bake until the whip is almost set (there will be a dime-sized area in the center that will not be completely set), about 1 hour.

6. Remove the ramekins from the water bath and allow to cool to room temperature (this will take 4 to 6 hours). Then chill completely in the refrigerator. Serve with Sweetened Whipped Cream.

"**C**ome with me to the casbah," Charles Boyer, as romantic underworld figure Pepe le Moko, says to sultry Hedy Lamarr in the movie *Algiers*. Or does he? Alas, no such words were uttered in the movie, but so

Morocco

strong is our image of the casbah, with its dens of pleasure, its mounds of spices, its yards of flowing silks, its lovers and world-weary poets, that we all swear we heard it said. Perhaps it is an unspoken invitation that rides on the breezes and in the alleys and palaces of Tangier, Morocco. Is there a place more made for moonlight, more perfumed with the fragrance of seductive spices and luscious food worthy of celebration? Come with me to the casbah. . . .

MENU

The flavors, sights, colors, and smells of Morocco are all inspirations for this menu. The hors d'oeuvres reflect the brilliance of the market-place at the Jemaa el Fna in Marrakech. The Savory Tomato Jam, a vibrant red, and the verdant green zucchini, showered with mint, are particularly delectable alongside Merguez Bites. Bright orange carrot soup fired up with harissa leads the palate into the main courses of rich Lamb Tagine and a lighter but equally flavorful roasted halibut. Both are accompanied by a delicate couscous and a robust tabbouleh. End the meal with cool, crisp, and delicious Orange-Blossom Sorbet.

Moroccan hosts are particularly adept at setting a magnificent table. Begin by polishing up any brass you may have (don't polish too hard—leave a slight patina of age). Old brass candlesticks, the more ornate the better, are my pick to hold ivory or pale pink candles. If you want more light, add votive candles to the mix, and if you have a sparkly shawl in your closet, drape it over a white tablecloth. Cranberry, blue, or green wineglasses are perfect set next to long-neck pitchers.

In Morocco many people eat with their fingers, but since this is unlikely to happen at your home, use whichever flatware best matches your dishes. The magic touch—to make your table so Moroccan and so magnificent—is to scatter red and pink rose petals all over the table. When you begin to think you are over-doing it, you have enough.

Finally, offer finger bowls of water scented with rose water between dinner and dessert, so everyone will feel fresh and the air will be perfumed.

Celebrate Morocco

DINNER FOR SIX

Savory Tomato Jam, Sweet Mint Zucchini, and Merguez Bites

Moorish Carrot Soup with Harissa

Moroccan Roasted Halibut

Lamb Tagine

Fluffy Couscous

Tabbouleh with Roasted Peppers

Orange-Blossom Sorbet

A Moroccan Fruit Tray

THE MUSIC

The Master Musicians of Jajouka

Soundtrack from
The Sheltering Sky

THE WINE

Greco di Tufo

Alentejo

THE EXTRAS

Small oval dishes for appetizers

Ice-cream maker

PITA CHIPS FOR DIPS AND SPREADS

To prepare pita chips, preheat the oven to 350°F. Cut 7-inch pita breads into 8 wedges each, and arrange the wedges on baking sheets. Bake until just crisp, about 5 minutes—or if you want them really crisp, bake for 10 minutes. Place in a napkin-lined basket and serve.

SAVORY TOMATO JAM

With all their delicious varieties, from the heirlooms in their gorgeous rainbow colors to the grapes, pears, plums, and cherries, tomatoes eaten out of hand are pleasurable enough. When it comes to tomatoes, however, enough is never enough, and I'm always looking for more ways to prepare them. I first tasted this sweet and tangy tomato jam on the roof of the Yacout Restaurant in Marrakech. It makes a wonderful foil for spicy hot dishes. Serve it on pita crisps (see box) or on store-bought onion or caraway crisps.

> *3 pounds ripe plum tomatoes,*
> *seeded and coarsely chopped*
> *¼ cup sugar*
> *2 tablespoons honey*
> *Salt, to taste*

1. Combine the tomatoes, sugar, and honey in a saucepan. Cook, uncovered, over low heat, stirring occasionally, until thick and jamlike, about 1½ hours, depending on how watery the tomatoes are. If necessary, raise the heat toward the end of the cooking time to speed up the process. Add a pinch of salt to accentuate the sweetness, and allow the jam to cool to room temperature.

2. To serve, spread the tomatoes on a small oval plate, flattening them slightly with the back of a spoon. Serve at room temperature.

Note: This will keep, covered and refrigerated, for up to 2 days.

SWEET MINT ZUCCHINI

Cooked zucchini sometimes has a slightly bitter overtone, but the Moroccan style of cooking it, in sugared water, removes any harshness and brings out the sweetness. Enjoy this small plate as part of your appetizer selection, along with the Savory Tomato Jam.

> *2 zucchini (about 1 pound total)*
> *¼ cup sugar*
> *¼ cup chopped fresh mint*

1. Trim off the ends of the zucchini and discard them. Quarter the zucchini lengthwise and cut them into 1-inch pieces.

2. Combine the sugar and 2 tablespoons water in a saucepan. Bring to a boil over medium-high heat and cook until the sugar has dissolved, about 1 minute. Then reduce the heat to low, add in the zucchini, cover, and simmer, stirring occasionally, until the zucchini is tender but not mushy, 7 to 8 minutes. Drain the zucchini, reserving the syrup.

3. Toss the zucchini in a bowl with the mint and 2 tablespoons of the reserved syrup. Allow it to cool to room temperature. Serve as an appetizer salad on small plates.

MERGUEZ BITES

The ideal accompaniment to the intensely flavored tomato jam and sweetened zucchini is merguez. These fresh and spicy sausages, which originated in Algeria and Spain in the eighteenth century, are made of lamb and delicately spiced with cumin and hot pepper, which lends the sausage its rosy hue. Pan-fried or grilled, merguez is often served along with couscous or on brochettes. It is sold in a coil or sometimes in links. If you can't find merguez, chorizo makes a good substitute.

1 teaspoon olive oil
12 ounces merguez or chorizo sausage,
*   cut into 3-inch lengths*

Heat the olive oil in a nonstick skillet over medium-low heat. Add the sausage, raise the heat to medium, and sauté until it is a nice brown color all over, 12 to 15 minutes. Serve immediately on a small oval plate.

Note: If you prefer, the sausage can be grilled whole over high heat, 3 inches from the heat source, for about 12 minutes. Let it rest for 10 minutes before slicing it into 3-inch lengths.

MOORISH CARROT SOUP

In this deep-orange soup, the subtle insistence of cumin and the explosion of a dollop of harissa warm up a cool autumn night. Close your eyes; the sound of November's frigid gale might just become the summer wind off the Sahara.

2 tablespoons olive oil
1 onion, chopped
8 carrots, peeled and cut into 1-inch-thick slices
1 tablespoon minced garlic
1 tablespoon ground cumin
6 cups Basic Chicken Broth (page 397)
¼ cup pearl barley
Salt and freshly ground black pepper,
*   to taste*
Harissa (recipe follows), for garnish

1. Heat the olive oil in a heavy pot over low heat. Add the onion, carrots, and garlic and cook until the vegetables have softened, about 15 minutes.

2. Add the cumin and stir to coat the vegetables for 3 minutes.

3. Add the broth and barley and bring to a boil over high heat. Reduce the heat to medium-low and simmer, partially covered, until the carrots are tender and the barley is cooked, 35 minutes. Season with salt and pepper. Allow the mixture to cool slightly.

4. Process the soup in a blender or food processor, in batches if necessary, until mostly pureed but not completely smooth. Return the soup to the pot and heat it through over low heat. Ladle the soup into individual bowls, topping each serving with no more than ½ teaspoon of the warming harissa.

HARISSA

The Berbers, the nomadic tribesmen of North Africa, gave us that most typical of Moroccan and Tunisian condiments, harissa. This variation comes via my colleague Laurie, and was inspired by the mother of her friend in Tunis, Khaled Kouhen. His mother serves it at every meal. It is particularly delicious on Moorish Carrot Soup, as well as on grilled vegetables, omelets, and, of course, couscous.

1 ounce (about 3) large dried chiles,
*   such as ancho chiles*
3 roasted red bell peppers (page 399)
4 cloves garlic, cut in half
1 teaspoon coarse (kosher) salt
1 teaspoon caraway seeds
1 teaspoon coriander seeds
1 teaspoon ground cumin
¼ cup olive oil

1. Rinse the chiles and remove the stems and seeds. Soak them in a bowl of hot water for 1 hour to rehydrate. Then drain them thoroughly.

2. Place the rehydrated chiles, roasted bell peppers, garlic, salt, caraway, coriander, and cumin in a food processor. Pulse the machine on and off until the mixture is well combined but not completely smooth.

3. With the machine running, drizzle in the olive oil through the feed tube. Continue processing until the oil is incorporated and the mixture is just smooth, about the consistency of mayonnaise.

4. Transfer the harissa to a glass jar and keep refrigerated for up to 4 days.

MAKES 1¼ CUPS

MOROCCAN ROASTED HALIBUT

The classic Moroccan combination of aromatic spices and herbs with the concentrated sweetness of dried fruits—here, golden raisins—has an almost alchemical effect on simple halibut.

⅓ cup extra-virgin olive oil
1 cup diced onions (¼-inch dice)
4 cloves garlic, very finely minced
1 teaspoon ground cardamom
¼ teaspoon crumbled saffron threads
¼ cup fresh lemon juice (from 2 lemons)
1 cinnamon stick (3 inches long)
2 long strips of orange zest removed
*   with a paring knife*
¾ cup Basic Chicken Broth (page 397)
Salt and freshly ground black pepper, to taste
¾ cup canned chickpeas (garbanzo beans),
*   drained and rinsed*
½ cup golden raisins
6 ripe plum tomatoes, seeded and cut into
*   ½-inch dice*
¼ cup chopped fresh flat-leaf parsley
¼ cup chopped fresh mint, plus 2 tablespoons,
*   for garnish*
6 halibut steaks (6 to 8 ounces each),
*   1½ inches thick*
Fluffy Couscous (page 386), for serving

Moroccan Roasted Halibut

Lamb Tagine with Fluffy Couscous

> *"Cookery means ...*
> *English thoroughness,*
> *French art, and*
> *Arabian hospitality;*
> *it means the knowledge*
> *of all fruits and herbs*
> *and balms and spices;*
> *it means carefulness,*
> *inventiveness,*
> *and watchfulness."*
>
> —JOHN RUSKIN

1. Place the olive oil, onion, and garlic in a heavy pot over low heat and cook, stirring, until the onions are very soft, 15 minutes.

2. Add the cardamom, saffron, lemon juice, cinnamon stick, orange zest, broth, and salt and pepper. Raise the heat to medium-high and bring to a boil. Reduce the heat to medium-low and simmer, partially covered, for 10 minutes. Then stir in the chickpeas, raisins, and tomatoes. Add the parsley and the ¼ cup mint and simmer, partially covered, shaking the pan occasionally, for 15 minutes.

3. Meanwhile, preheat the oven to 400°F.

4. Remove the cinnamon stick and the orange zest from the vegetable mixture. Place the cooked vegetables in a 13 x 9-inch baking dish and arrange the halibut steaks on top. Spoon some of the vegetable liquid over the fish. Bake until the fish is cooked through and flakes easily when tested with a fork, 15 minutes.

5. Serve the fish and vegetables over couscous and sprinkle with the remaining 2 tablespoons chopped mint.

LAMB TAGINE

The two intoxicating flavor traditions in Morocco—aromatic spices and fruits—are combined in this subtle, succulent, and complex recipe built upon a foundation of fork-tender braised lamb. When you order a tagine in a Moroccan restaurant, it is most often served in an impressive deep clay plate with a cover shaped like a large conical hat—also called a tagine. Very exotic, very delicious—true Moroccan comfort food.

3 pounds boneless lamb shoulder,
  cut into 2-inch pieces
1 cup fresh orange juice
½ cup sherry vinegar
4 cloves garlic, finely minced
¼ cup extra-virgin olive oil, plus more
  if needed
1 onion, chopped
3 carrots, peeled, halved lengthwise,
  and cut into 2-inch lengths
1 teaspoon saffron threads
2 teaspoons ground cumin
2 teaspoons dried thyme
1½ teaspoons ground coriander
1 tablespoon all-purpose flour
1 cup canned chickpeas (garbanzo beans),
  rinsed and drained
½ cup pitted prunes
½ cup dry red wine
Salt and freshly ground black pepper,
  to taste
3 ripe tomatoes, seeded and cut into
  ½-inch pieces
½ cup imported black olives
  such as Gaeta, Kalamata, or
  Niçoise, pitted
1 tablespoon fresh lemon juice
Fluffy Couscous (page 386)
  or Rutabaga and Carrot Whip
  (page 376), for serving
Fresh mint leaves, for garnish

1. Place the lamb in a large nonreactive bowl and add the orange juice, vinegar, and garlic. Toss to combine. Let the lamb marinate, covered, in the refrigerator for 2 hours, turning the pieces once or twice. Then drain the lamb, reserving the marinade.

2. Heat 2 tablespoons of the olive oil in a flameproof casserole over medium-high heat. Add the lamb, in batches, and cook until browned, about 10 minutes per batch, adding more oil as needed.

3. As the lamb is browned, remove the pieces to another bowl. Set the lamb aside. Reduce the heat to medium-low and add the onion and carrots to the casserole. Adding more oil if necessary, cook the vegetables until softened, about 8 minutes. Then stir in the saffron, cumin, thyme, and coriander and cook over low heat for 5 minutes to blend the flavors.

4. Sprinkle the flour over the vegetables and cook, stirring, for 1 minute. Add the chickpeas, prunes, wine, and the reserved marinade. Season with salt and pepper.

5. Return the lamb to the casserole and add the tomatoes and olives. Simmer, covered, over medium-low heat, stirring occasionally, for 1¼ hours. Stir in the lemon juice (this brightens the flavors). Serve over couscous, garnished with the mint.

FLUFFY
COUSCOUS

Couscous is the starch of choice with a Moroccan meal, but it is so easy to prepare, think of it anytime braised lamb or chicken is on the menu. It has a delicate texture that marries well with stewed meats and vegetables. Serve it as is, or stir in some currants or almonds—or both—before serving.

3 cups Basic Chicken Broth (page 397)
   or water
¾ teaspoon salt
2 tablespoons olive oil or unsalted butter
2¼ cups couscous
½ cup currants or golden raisins (optional)
⅓ cup slivered almonds (optional)

Place the broth, salt, and olive oil in a large saucepan and bring to a boil over high heat. Stir in the couscous, cover, and remove the pan from the heat. Let stand for 5 minutes, then add the currants or almonds, if desired, fluff the couscous lightly with a fork, and serve.

A MOROCCAN FRUIT TRAY

Opulence comes first when arranging a fruit platter for a Moroccan meal. When selecting the fruit, think color, shape, and always, ripeness. Next come the serving pieces. If you own a tiered *petit four* dish, that would work beautifully with small fruit. Place luscious ripe apricots on the lowest tier, cherries on the center tier, and peeled sections of tangerine on the top tier, with perfect strawberries, almonds, and rose petals.

Two elegant deep conical bowls can look stunning arranged with pyramids of tangerines or clementines. Tuck in some lemon leaves here and there. Tangerines, cascading grapes (cut into small bunches), and masses of cherries, all arranged by fruit on a round decorative brass tray or crystal platter, also make for an appealing display. Scatter red and pink rose petals all over the fruit, and be sure to place a few small bowls nearby for the cherry pits.

TABBOULEH
WITH ROASTED PEPPERS

Traditionally we've enjoyed tabbouleh combined with a mix of crisp salad ingredients, but here it does a more substantial star turn dressed up with roasted peppers.

> $1^1/_3$ cups bulgur wheat
> 2 cups boiling water
> $^1/_2$ cup fresh lemon juice
> $^1/_2$ cup extra-virgin olive oil
> 4 roasted red bell peppers (page 399)
> 2 roasted yellow bell peppers (page 399)
> 4 ripe plum tomatoes, cut into $^1/_2$-inch pieces
> $^1/_4$ cup chopped fresh mint
> Salt and freshly ground black pepper, to taste

1. Place the bulgur in a bowl and stir in the boiling water, lemon juice, and olive oil. Cover and refrigerate for 30 minutes. Remove and fluff with a fork.

2. Coarsely chop the roasted peppers and add them to the bulgur. Using a fork, mix in the tomatoes and mint leaves. Season well with salt and pepper. Serve chilled or at room temperature.

ORANGE-BLOSSOM SORBET

The mysterious flavors of Morocco are always dappled with a hint of romance, often in the form of the subtle perfume of rose water or orange-flower water. Called *mazhaar* in Morocco, orange-flower water is made from the flowers of the bitter bergamot orange. This subtle addition raises orange sorbet to the sublime. Molasses Cookies (page 23) or Rich Pecan Squares (page 300) alongside make for a grand accompaniment.

> 2 cups fresh orange juice
>   (from about 8 oranges)
> 2 cups Simple Syrup (page 403)
> $^1/_2$ teaspoon orange-flower water
>   (see Sources, page 405)

Place the orange juice, Simple Syrup, and orange-flower water in an ice-cream maker and freeze according to the manufacturer's instructions. Transfer the sorbet to a container, cover, and freeze.

MAKES ABOUT 1 QUART

The

Big Raise

A big raise is a big thank-you for a job well done. Because money is just about the hardest thing for bosses to part with, a raise is significant. Who wouldn't want to celebrate? Maybe now you can plan that exotic vacation, put some money in the college account, think about a new car. Most raises won't cover a major change in lifestyle, but they are definitely a reason to enjoy a great meal with a few close friends. So go ahead, live it up! After all, you earned it.

"At a dinner-party one should eat wisely but not too well, and talk well but not too wisely."

—W. SOMERSET MAUGHAM

MENU

The Big Raise

DINNER FOR SIX

Blushing Lobster Cocktail

———

Fennel and Apple Slaw
with Honey-Mustard Vinaigrette

———

Rich Man's Burgers

———

Lemon-Caviar Potato Salad

———

An Elegant Raspberry Tart

A celebration for the big raise is a big deal, so go for it! Set the tone with sumptuous Blushing Lobster Cocktails. Then follow them with Rich Man's Burgers made from all the ingredients that go into steak tartare. By adding a Béarnaise Mayonnaise, the menu layers one luxury with another. Lemon-Caviar Potato Salad takes the prize for sheer indulgence. And An Elegant Raspberry Tart is the ideal finale to celebrate your new prosperity.

Be sure to dress up, and dress up the house, too. This calls for your best linen, flatware, and dishes.

The menu is a wonderment of extravagant food, but it should be served with a sense of humor—and the flowers should be chosen with one, too. If it's a man who's celebrating, a boutonniere perhaps: a small rose or orchid is nice. For a woman, the same, or a gardenia as a corsage or as a hair ornament. Since you'll be toasting your raise with Champagne, flutes are a must. And you'll need good red wine glasses for the excellent wine that will accompany the Rich Man's Burger.

THE MUSIC

Dean Martin
Sammy Davis Jr.

THE WINE

Champagne
Côtes du Rhône
Pauillac

THE EXTRAS

Champagne flutes
Tart pan

Blushing Lobster Cocktail

BLUSHING LOBSTER COCKTAIL

L obster was not always thought of as a lux-ury food. In fact, in early colonial America, lobsters were so plentiful they were used as fertilizer. I remember lobsters washing up on the beach in Connecticut after a fierce southwesterly storm when I was a kid. Somewhere along the line—after we started to fish them out—they became rare and prized. But to my way of think-ing, lobsters were always delicious enough to be prized. And what good is a raise if you can't luxu-riate and splurge a little? The dressing for the salad uses the popular combination found in Russian dressing—mayonnaise and ketchup—but the additions give it a little more of a kick. In fact, next time you make a turkey sandwich, consider spreading this spicier variation on the bread.

1½ pounds cooked lobster meat, chilled
(see page 152)
¾ cup prepared mayonnaise,
such as Hellmann's
2 tablespoons fresh lemon juice
1½ tablespoons ketchup
1 teaspoon Worcestershire sauce
6 leaves Boston lettuce, rinsed and
patted dry
6 small sprigs fresh flat-leaf parsley,
for garnish

1. Cut the lobster meat into 1-inch chunks.
2. Combine the mayonnaise, lemon juice, ketchup, and Worcestershire sauce in a medium-size bowl. Add the lobster and fold everything together.
3. To serve, line each of six margarita or mar-tini glasses with a lettuce leaf. Spoon the lobster salad over the lettuce and garnish with a sprig of parsley.

FENNEL AND APPLE SLAW

T his crunchy sweet slaw complements the richness of the lobster and the burger with its fruity tang. The licorice taste of the fen-nel helps boost the sweetness the apple.

3 Granny Smith apples, cored and
cut in half
Juice of 1 lemon
2 fennel bulbs, trimmed and cored,
fronds reserved
½ cup coarsely chopped fresh mint leaves
½ cup Honey-Mustard Vinaigrette
(recipe follows)

1. Cut the apples into matchstick pieces. Place them in a large decorative bowl and toss with the lemon juice to prevent discoloration.
2. Cut the fennel into matchstick pieces and combine with the apple. Chop the fennel fronds and set them aside.
3. Toss the mint with the apples and fennel.
4. Add the Honey-Mustard Vinaigrette, coat-ing the apples and fennel thoroughly. Garnish with the fennel fronds and serve.

HONEY-MUSTARD VINAIGRETTE

H oney in a vinaigrette may come as a bit of a surprise, but its soft sweet flavor is just what the slaw needs.

1 tablespoon Dijon mustard
2 tablespoons clover honey
2 tablespoons red wine vinegar
Salt and freshly ground black pepper,
to taste
¼ cup extra-virgin olive oil

Whisk the mustard, honey, vinegar, and salt and pepper together in a small bowl. Whisking constantly, slowly drizzle in the olive oil. Continue whisking until the vinaigrette thickens. Refrigerate, covered, until 30 minutes before you're ready to use it. Let the vinaigrette come to room temperature before dressing the slaw.

MAKES ½ CUP

Rich Man's Burgers

2 pounds top-quality ground beef round
½ cup finely diced red onion
¼ cup chopped fresh flat-leaf parsley
2 tablespoons tiny capers, drained
2 tablespoons cognac
2 teaspoons Worcestershire sauce
2 or 3 dashes Tabasco sauce
Salt and freshly ground black pepper, to taste
2 tablespoons unsalted butter, or more if needed
6 fresh-baked hamburger buns
½ cup Béarnaise Mayonnaise (page 401)
6 slices ripe tomato
6 leaves Boston lettuce

1. Place the ground beef in a mixing bowl. Add the onion, parsley, capers, cognac, Worcestershire sauce, and Tabasco sauce. Season generously with salt and pepper. Blend everything together lightly and form the mixture into 6 patties.

2. Melt the butter in a large nonstick skillet over medium heat. Add the burgers and cook for 5 minutes on the first side. Turn, and cook for 3 minutes longer for medium-rare. (If you prefer a more well-done burger, cook for 1 to 2 minutes more on the second side.)

3. While the burgers cook, toast the buns.

4. Spread a heaping tablespoon of Béarnaise Mayonnaise on the bottom half of each bun. Add the burger, a slice of tomato, a lettuce leaf, and the top of the bun. Serve immediately.

RICH MAN'S BURGERS

Now, if you think a burger isn't swank enough to serve at a dinner celebrating a raise, you would be wrong. This burger is pure luxury. It has all the taste extras of steak tartare and is worthy of any special occasion. I like it with a dollop of Béarnaise Mayonnaise.

LEMON CAVIAR POTATO SALAD

At cocktail parties, trays of small potatoes micro-dotted with sour cream and caviar are often passed. Those three ingredients make a terrific combination, so I dreamed up a potato salad with lots of caviar and a smooth, creamy mayonnaise.

An Elegant Raspberry Tart

1¼ cups prepared mayonnaise,
   such as Hellmann's
1¼ cups sour cream
Finely grated zest of 1½ lemons
4½ tablespoons fresh lemon juice
   (from 2 large lemons)
4½ tablespoons (about 2 ounces)
   osetra caviar (red salmon or American
   sturgeon caviar are also fine)
3 pounds Yukon Gold potatoes (about 9),
   unpeeled, scrubbed

1. Combine the mayonnaise, sour cream, lemon zest, and lemon juice in a large decorative bowl. Gently fold in the caviar and set aside, covered, in the refrigerator.

2. Place the potatoes in a large heavy saucepan, cover with cold water, and bring to a boil over high heat. Reduce the heat to medium and cook until tender, 25 to 30 minutes.

3. Drain well, return the potatoes to the pot, and place over very low heat for about 30 seconds to dry the potatoes well. When they are cool enough to handle, peel and quarter them. Cut each quarter crosswise into ¼-inch slices. Gently fold together with the lemon caviar mayonnaise and refrigerate until ready to serve, up to 4 hours ahead.

AN ELEGANT RASPBERRY TART

O f all the berries, the raspberry is my favorite. It is the Audrey Hepburn of berries. Such elegance wants a bit of lace to go with it— creamy lemon curd with accents of intense almond.

FOR THE LEMON CURD
¾ cup fresh lemon juice
   (from about 6 lemons), strained
2 large eggs
3 large egg yolks
½ cup sugar

FOR THE ALMOND CREAM
⅓ cup almond paste
3 tablespoons unsalted butter,
   at room temperature
½ large beaten egg
½ teaspoon pure vanilla extract

Easy Tart or Pie Crust (page 402)
   for a 1-crust tart
2 cups fresh raspberries, rinsed and
   patted dry

1. Prepare the lemon curd: In the top of a double boiler over simmering water, whisk together the lemon juice, eggs, egg yolks, and sugar. Whisk vigorously until the mixture thickens, about 15 minutes. (Do not stop whisking, or the eggs will cook.) Scrape the mixture into a bowl and lay plastic wrap directly on the surface to prevent a skin from forming. Let it cool completely and use immediately, or refrigerate.

2. Prepare the almond cream: Combine the almond paste and the butter in a bowl and cream with an electric mixer. Add the egg and the vanilla and beat the mixture on high speed until it is light and fluffy, 4 to 5 minutes. Use immediately, or cover and refrigerate.

3. Preheat the oven to 350°F.

4. Roll the tart dough out on a lightly floured surface to form a 12-inch round, about ⅛ inch thick. Fit the dough into a 10-inch tart pan with removable bottom and trim the overhang.

5. Spread the almond cream over the bottom of the crust. Bake the tart until it is very lightly browned, about 30 minutes. Let it cool completely in the pan on a wire rack.

6. When the tart is cool, carefully remove the ring. Spread ¾ cup of the lemon curd over the tart. Cover the surface with a single layer of raspberries, all standing on their stem ends. Refrigerate until ready to serve. The tart tastes best served the day it is made.

Note: Extra lemon curd is delicious spread on biscuits or scones.

The Basics

BASIC CHICKEN BROTH

Broth is fundamental to many sauces, soups, and stews. Without question, the secret to great chicken broth is a good stewing hen, not too much water in the pot, parsnips, dill, and slow simmering. Boiling will result in a cloudy broth and a confused taste. Keep plenty of broth on hand.

1 soup chicken (5½ to 6 pounds),
  preferably a stewing hen
2 onions, unpeeled, cut in half
4 whole cloves
3 ribs celery with leaves, cut in half
2 carrots, unpeeled, cut in half
2 parsnips, unpeeled, cut in half
3 cloves garlic, unpeeled, lightly crushed
1 large ripe tomato, halved and seeded
8 sprigs fresh dill
4 sprigs fresh flat-leaf parsley
8 whole black peppercorns
2 tablespoons coarse (kosher) salt

1. Remove the giblets from the chicken and reserve for another use. Rinse the chicken well and trim off all excess fat. Cut the chicken into 6 pieces and place them in a large soup pot.

2. Stud the onions with the cloves and place them in the pot, along with all the remaining ingredients. Add 12 cups water.

3. Bring to a boil over high heat, skimming off any foam that rises to the top. Reduce the heat and simmer, partially covered, until the chicken is cooked through, about 1 hour.

4. Remove the chicken pieces from the pot. If it is not a stewing hen, which would be tough, reserve the meat for another use. Discard the large vegetables and strain the broth through a fine-mesh sieve into a bowl. Adjust the seasonings if necessary. Allow the broth to cool to room temperature.

5. If the broth is to be used immediately, allow the fat to rise to the surface; then degrease the broth by skimming off the fat with a metal spoon or by pouring the broth through a gravy separator. If it is not for immediate use, transfer the broth to a storage container and refrigerate it, covered, until the layer of fat has solidified on top, 4 hours or overnight. Remove the fat before using. Refrigerated, the broth will keep for up to 4 days; frozen, for up to 3 months.

MAKES ABOUT 3 QUARTS

BEEF BROTH

The time you put into a rich homemade beef broth always pays off. Look for nice soup beef with bones, such as flanken, or short ribs. Roasting the meat and bones on top of the vegetables caramelizes everything and begins the melding of flavors. Simmering slowly for several hours completes this marriage of essences. The flavors concentrate (you start off with a lot more liquid than you wind up with), so hold off on the salt until the end when you can accurately gauge the taste.

4 onions, unpeeled
4 ribs celery with leaves
4 carrots, unpeeled
4 tomatoes
3 parsnips, unpeeled
3 leeks, including 3 inches green,
  well rinsed
4 cloves garlic, unpeeled, lightly crushed
3 pounds soup beef with bones
3 pounds beef bones
8 whole black peppercorns
6 whole cloves
4 large sprigs fresh thyme
1 bay leaf
Coarse (kosher) salt, to taste

1. Preheat the oven to 450°F.

2. Rinse and coarsely chop the onions, celery, carrots, tomatoes, parsnips, and leeks. Place them in a flameproof roasting pan, add the garlic, and arrange the meat and bones on top. Roast, uncovered, for 1 hour.

3. Transfer the meat, bones, and vegetables to a very large soup pot.

4. Pour 4 cups water into the roasting pan and bring it to a hard boil on top of the stove over high heat, scraping up any brown bits in the bottom of the pan. Pour this into the soup pot and add 12 cups more water.

5. Add the peppercorns, cloves, thyme sprigs, and bay leaf. Bring to a boil over high heat, skimming off any foam that rises to the surface. Reduce the heat to medium-low and simmer, partially covered, for 2 hours. Then uncover and simmer for 30 minutes. Add salt to taste, and simmer for another 30 minutes to reduce the liquid and concentrate the flavors.

6. Remove the meat (see Note) and bones. Strain the broth through a sieve into a large bowl. Then line the sieve with a double thickness of dampened cheesecloth and strain the broth again. Allow it to cool to room temperature.

7. If the broth is to be used immediately, allow the fat to rise to the surface, then degrease the broth completely by skimming off the fat with a metal spoon or by pouring the broth through a gravy separator. If it is not for immediate use, transfer the cooled broth to a storage container and refrigerate it, covered, until the layer of fat has solidified on top, 4 hours or overnight. Remove the fat before using. Refrigerated, the broth will keep for up to 2 days; frozen, for up to 3 months.

MAKES ABOUT 6 CUPS

Note: The meat is delicious trimmed of fat and served with mustard and horseradish alongside.

VEGETABLE BROTH

This is an intensely flavored broth. Don't wash the mushrooms; clean them with a brush or damp cloth to keep their intense taste intact. The skin on the onion and the other vegetables adds both color and nutrients to the broth. Tomatoes and a parsnip sweeten the broth with a rich deep flavor.

1 onion, unpeeled
1 parsnip, unpeeled
2 cloves garlic, unpeeled, lightly crushed
*2 ribs celery with leaves, cut into
    large chunks*
2 carrots, unpeeled, cut into large chunks
*2 leeks, trimmed, well rinsed, and cut into
    large chunks*
8 white mushrooms, cut in half
2 tomatoes, cut in quarters
4 new potatoes, unpeeled, cut in half
4 whole cloves
*8 sprigs fresh flat-leaf parsley, stems
    lightly crushed*
2 sprigs fresh dill
1 bay leaf
8 whole black peppercorns
1 teaspoon coarse (kosher) salt

1. Rinse all the vegetables well. Stud the onion with the cloves.

2. Place all the ingredients in a large heavy pot, add 10 cups water, and bring to a boil over high heat. Reduce the heat to low and simmer, uncovered, for 1 hour. Taste, adjust the seasonings, and simmer for 30 minutes more.

3. Strain the broth and allow it to cool to room temperature. Then refrigerate it, covered, or freeze it. Refrigerated, it will keep for up to 4 days; frozen, for up to 3 months.

MAKES ABOUT 4 CUPS

Note: This recipe is easily doubled.

MARINARA SAUCE

Having a good marinara sauce on hand means you're ready for even the most spur-of-the-moment celebration. Boil up a pot of pasta, toss together a green salad, slice up a crusty loaf of garlic bread, and it's party time.

¼ cup extra-virgin olive oil
4 large cloves garlic, lightly crushed
4 cans (28 ounces each) plum tomatoes,
  drained and coarsely chopped
½ cup dry red wine
½ cup coarsely chopped fresh flat-leaf parsley
½ cup fresh basil leaves, torn in half
2 teaspoons dried oregano
Salt and freshly ground black pepper, to taste
Pinch of sugar

1. Heat the olive oil in a large heavy pot over medium-low heat. Add the garlic and cook until it colors slightly but does not burn, 3 to 4 minutes. Remove the pot from the heat and carefully stir in the tomatoes and wine.

2. Return the pot to medium heat. Stir in the parsley, basil, oregano, salt and pepper, and sugar. Simmer, uncovered, stirring occasionally, for 30 minutes. Serve immediately, or cool and store, covered, in the refrigerator for up to 2 days. This will also keep frozen for up to 3 months.

MAKES 7 CUPS

ROASTED BELL PEPPERS

The secret when charring bell peppers is to get them black, but not so much so that the skins are impossible to slip off. All the different colored peppers arranged on a large platter, drizzled with olive oil and lemon juice, and topped with a sprinkling of basil, is a beautiful sight. Roasted peppers are a marvelous addition to any buffet and splendid for sandwiches and slivered on pastas.

Red, green, yellow, or orange bell peppers,
  stemmed, cut in half lengthwise, and seeded
Extra-virgin olive oil, for drizzling

1. Preheat the broiler. Line a baking sheet with aluminum foil.

2. Flatten each pepper half slightly with the palm of your hand. Lay the peppers, skin side up, in a single layer on the prepared baking sheet. Place under the broiler, 3 to 4 inches from the heat source, and broil until the skins are just charred black, 12 to 15 minutes. Transfer the peppers to a paper or plastic bag, close it tight, and let the peppers steam for about 15 minutes. Then slip off the charred skins and use the peppers as directed in the recipe.

3. To store, drizzle the peppers lightly with olive oil and place in an airtight container in the refrigerator. They will keep for 10 days.

ROASTED BEETS

Oven-roasted beets, with their sweet concentrated flavor, are one of my favorite standbys. They look beautiful, and they liven up so many dishes. Most salads benefit from them, as do robust meats and game of all kinds.

Beets, leaves removed

1. Preheat the oven to 350°F.

2. Scrub the beets well, and trim the stems and roots, leaving 1 inch of each. Wrap the beets individually in aluminum foil, place on a baking sheet, and bake until tender, 1 to 1½ hours, depending on size. Remove them from the oven and slip off the skins, using rubber gloves. Use in recipes or serve as is.

3. Store the beets in an airtight container in the refrigerator. They will keep for up to 1 week.

CUMIN-HONEY VINAIGRETTE

The honey mellows the vinegar just enough to make this an ideal dressing for vegetables and grains. It is particularly delicious with fresh corn kernels.

2 tablespoons red wine vinegar
1 teaspoon ground cumin
1 teaspoon Dijon mustard
1 teaspoon honey
Salt and freshly ground black pepper,
  to taste
½ cup extra-virgin olive oil

Whisk the vinegar, cumin, mustard, honey, and salt and pepper together in a small bowl. Whisking constantly, drizzle in the olive oil. Continue whisking until the dressing is slightly thickened. Store in a covered container in the refrigerator for up to 3 days. Bring to room temperature before use, rewhisking as necessary.

MAKES ½ CUP

LEMON VINAIGRETTE

Vinaigrette, to be literal, requires vinegar. But who says a vinaigrette has to be literal? Lemons add a wonderful tang to dressings. Use this one on sweet fruit salads and salads of delicate silky greens, like Boston lettuce.

7 tablespoons fresh lemon juice
2 teaspoons Dijon mustard
1 teaspoon sugar
Salt and freshly ground black pepper, to taste
½ cup extra-virgin olive oil

Combine the lemon juice, mustard, sugar, and salt and pepper in a small bowl. Whisking constantly, slowly drizzle in the olive oil and continue whisking until the dressing has thickened. Store in a covered container in the refrigerator for up to 3 days.

MAKES 1 CUP

LEMON MINT DRESSING

A lovely light dressing, the lemon-mint combination sparks up a Savory Lentil Salad (page 159) and would also taste delicious spooned over roasted beets or freshly steamed green beans.

1 cup low-fat plain yogurt
1 tablespoon fresh lemon juice
1 teaspoon finely grated lemon zest
¼ cup extra-virgin olive oil
¼ teaspoon coarsely ground
  black pepper
2 teaspoons chopped fresh mint

Mix the yogurt, lemon juice, and lemon zest together in a small bowl. Slowly drizzle in the olive oil, whisking constantly until smooth and slightly thick. Add the pepper, then the mint leaves. Dress the salad within 1 hour of adding the mint leaves.

MAKES 1¼ CUPS

BEARNAISE MAYONNAISE

Luxurious and rich, this is a quickie interpretation of the classic French béarnaise sauce. Use it as a condiment for everything from burgers to *steak frites*. Don't hesitate for a minute to slather a chicken and Boston lettuce sandwich with this, or, come to think of it, a BLT.

4 teaspoons white wine vinegar
2 teaspoons dried tarragon, crushed
¼ cup minced shallots
2 tablespoons chopped fresh
*   tarragon leaves*
1½ cups prepared mayonnaise,
*   such as Hellmann's*
Salt and freshly ground black pepper, to taste

Combine the vinegar and dried tarragon in a small bowl and set aside for 5 minutes to soak. Stir in the shallots and fresh tarragon. Whisk in the mayonnaise. Season with salt and pepper. Cover and refrigerate for up to 3 days.

MAKES ABOUT 1½ CUPS

SHALLOT HERB BUTTER

Compound butters are easy to make and add intense flavor to everything from vegetables to grilled meats. This is a case where a little dab will do you. Once the butter is made, freeze it and then slice off a pat as needed.

8 tablespoons (1 stick) unsalted butter,
*   at room temperature*
2 tablespoons finely chopped shallots
1 tablespoon finely chopped garlic
1 tablespoon chopped fresh flat-leaf parsley

1. Melt 1 teaspoon of the butter in a skillet over low heat. Add the shallots and garlic and cook, stirring, until tender, 3 to 4 minutes. Cool to room temperature.

2. Place the remaining butter in a small bowl and cream it well until smooth. Add the cooked shallot mixture and the parsley and stir well. Mound the butter in the center of a large piece of wax paper. Cover the top of the butter with the paper and roll the butter into a log about 1 inch in diameter. Fold the ends of the paper under to seal and store, in the refrigerator for up to 1 week. For longer storage, double-wrap the log in aluminum foil and freeze for up to 2 months.

MAKES ½ CUP

BASIC PIE CRUST

Making pie dough by hand is easy and fast, and it gives you much more control over the dough. The result is a crust that is flaky and tender. This one is good for both sweet and savory pies.

2½ cups all-purpose flour
½ teaspoon salt
12 tablespoons (1½ sticks) cold unsalted
*   butter, cut into tablespoon-size pieces*
½ cup solid vegetable shortening, chilled
¼ to ½ cup ice water

1. Combine the flour and salt in a large bowl. Add the butter and mix together with your fingertips, or with a pastry cutter, until the mixture is very coarse—the size of peas. Then add the shortening and continue blending with your fingertips. The mixture should still be very coarse.

2. Add ¼ cup of the ice water and toss the mixture together. If the dough does not hold together when gathered in your hand, add more water, 1 tablespoon at a time (but no more than an additional ¼ cup). Do not overwork the dough. Divide the dough in half and form it into thick disks. Wrap each disk in plastic wrap and chill in the refrigerator for at least 1 hour or as long as 2 days (see Note).

3. Remove one disk of dough from the refrigerator. Unwrap it and roll it out on a lightly floured work surface, or between two sheets of wax paper, to form a round about ⅛ inch thick and 2 inches larger than the pie plate. Work quickly, as the dough can become sticky. Using a spatula to help lift the dough, fold it loosely in half and then into quarters. Gently transfer it to the pie plate, centering the corner of the dough in the center of the pie plate. Open up the dough and press it lightly into the plate to fit. If the dough should tear, just press it gently together. Trim the dough, leaving a 1-inch overhang. If making a single-crust pie, turn the edge under and flute it decoratively.

4. Repeat the rolling process for a top crust or for another bottom crust. The dough for a top crust should be 9 inches for an 8-inch pie, 10 inches for a 9-inch pie.

5. Follow the individual pie recipe for filling and baking.

MAKES ENOUGH FOR **1** DOUBLE-CRUST PIE, **8** TO **9** INCHES IN DIAMETER, OR **2** SINGLE-CRUST PIES

Note: If you wish to freeze this dough, wrap each disk separately in heavy-duty aluminum foil. It will keep for up to 2 months in the freezer. Let thaw in the refrigerator overnight.

EASY TART OR PIE CRUST

This crust is an excellent one to have in your repertoire. It's a little richer than the Basic Pie Crust (above) and easy to make in a food processor. Use it for both sweet and savory pies and tarts.

1½ cups all-purpose flour
1 teaspoon sugar
1 teaspoon salt
10 tablespoons (1¼ sticks) cold unsalted
   butter, cut into small pieces
¼ cup ice water, or more as needed

1. Combine the flour, sugar, and salt in a food processor, and pulse to mix. Add the butter and pulse the machine until the mixture resembles coarse meal.

2. With the machine running, trickle in the ¼ cup ice water through the feed tube, just until the dough gathers together. (If the dough seems dry, add up to 1 tablespoon more water, ½ teaspoon at a time.) Remove the dough from the machine and flatten it with the palm of your hand to form a thick disk. Wrap the disk in plastic wrap and chill in the refrigerator for at least 1 hour or as long as 2 days (see Note).

3. Use the dough as directed for a tart, or prepare it for a double-crust pie: Remove one disk of dough from the refrigerator. Unwrap it and roll it out on a lightly floured work surface, or between two sheets of wax paper, to form a round about ⅛ inch thick and 2 inches larger than the pie plate. Work quickly, as the dough can become sticky. Using a spatula to help lift the dough, fold it loosely in half, and then into quarters. Gently transfer it to the pie plate, centering the corner of the dough in the center of the plate. Open up the dough and press it lightly into the plate to fit. If the dough should tear, just press it gently together. Trim the dough, leaving a 1-inch overhang. Turn the edge under and flute it decoratively.

4. Follow the individual tart or pie recipe for filling and baking.

MAKES ENOUGH FOR **1** TART UP TO **10** INCHES IN DIAMETER, OR **1** SINGLE-CRUST PIE, **8** TO **9** INCHES IN DIAMETER

Note: If you wish to freeze this dough, wrap it in heavy-duty aluminum foil. It will keep for up to 2 months in the freezer. Let thaw in the refrigerator overnight.

SWEETENED WHIPPED CREAM

This whipped cream is divine scooped on cakes and pies (especially pumpkin), and don't forget it for your Irish coffee!

1 cup heavy (whipping) cream
2 tablespoons sugar
½ teaspoon pure vanilla extract

Beat the cream in a large bowl with an electric mixer at medium speed until it becomes frothy. Add the sugar and vanilla and continue beating until the cream holds soft peaks. Do not overbeat. Refrigerate the whipped cream, covered with plastic wrap, for no more than 1 hour, if not using it immediately.

MAKES 2 CUPS

SIMPLE SYRUP

Simple Syrup is excellent to have on hand to use in drinks or sorbets. It will keep in the refrigerator for weeks.

2 cups sugar
2 cups water

Combine the sugar and the water in a saucepan and bring to a boil over high heat. Reduce the heat and simmer gently until the sugar has dissolved, about 5 minutes. Allow the syrup to cool to room temperature. The syrup can be used immediately, or stored in a covered container in the refrigerator until use.

MAKES 2½ CUPS

sources

Most of the ingredients used in the recipes in *Celebrate!* are easy to find in your local markets, especially now that our larger supermarkets carry lines of ethnic spices and pastes that were once considered exotic. Still, there are a few things that you might have trouble locating, so I've listed them here with a source.

CANDIED ROSE PETALS (used in the Frozen Lime Soufflé in *A Toast to the New Year* menu) are available from:
Chefshop.com; (877) 337-2491;
www.chefshop.com
A ½-ounce package of petals costs $6.79. They will ship by mail.

FOIE GRAS (Foie Gras and Thinly Sliced Fig Log in *The Night Before Christmas* menu) is available from:
D'Artagnan,
Newark, NJ; (800) 327-8246
(in the Continental U.S.),
(973) 344-0565;
www.dartagnan.com
They supply many food shops in the United States, so inquire about suppliers in your area. An 8-ounce terrine of duck foie gras costs $63.75. They will ship by mail.

INDIAN SPICES (if you want to make your own curry powder for the *Celebrate India* menu) are available at:
Penzeys Spices,
Brookfield, WI;
(800) 741-7787;
FAX (262) 785-7678;
www.penzeys.com
They will ship by mail.

ORANGE-FLOWER WATER (used in Orange-Blossom Sorbet in the *Celebrate Morocco* menu) is available from:
Chefshop.com; (877) 337-2491; www.chefshop.com
A 3-ounce bottle costs $3.29. They will ship by mail.

PANKO (Japanese bread crumbs, used in Panko Soft-Shell Crabs in the *When Spring Has Sprung* menu) are sold in many gourmet markets and food stores, but if you can't find them in your area, they are available from:
Uwajimaya, Seattle, WA;
(800) 889-1928 (in the Continental U.S.),
(206) 624-6248; www.uwajimaya.com
An 8-ounce package costs $.99. They will ship by mail.

PISTACHIO PASTE (used in Pistachio Ice Cream in the *St. Patrick's Day Feast* menu) is available from:
The Baker's Catalogue, Norwich, VT;
(800) 827-6836; www.kingarthurflour.com
A 15-ounce can costs $11.95. They will ship by mail.

RICE PAPER (spring roll) wrappers (used in Starlet Summer Rolls in the *Academy Awards Bash* menu) are available from:
Pacific Rim Gourmet (i-clipse, Inc.),
San Diego, CA;
(800) 910-9657 (in the Continental U.S.),
(858) 274-9013; FAX (858) 274-9018;
www.i-clipse.com
A 12-ounce package (8½ inches in diameter) contains 24 to 30 wrappers and costs $2.79. They will ship by mail.

SMITHFIELD HAM (served in *A Run for the Roses* menu) is available from:
The Smithfield Collection, Smithfield, VA;
(800) 628-2242; FAX (757) 673-3719;
www.smithfield.com
An uncooked 13- to 16-pound Smithfield ham costs $62.00. They will ship by UPS.

Thanks to some good friends with good books and Websites, I was never at a loss when I needed to double check a fact. Here is who I turned to in researching *Celebrate!*

Ehler, James T.
"Food Reference Website."
www.foodreference.com

Jones, Evan.
A Food Lover's Companion.
New York: Harper & Row, 1979.

Kasper, Lynne Rossetto.
The Splendid Table.
New York: William Morrow, 1992.

Mariani, John.
The Dictionary of American Food and Drink.
New York: Hearst Books, 1994.

Nathan, Joan.
The Foods of Israel Today.
New York: Alfred A. Knopf, 2001.

Rodin, Claudia.
The Book of Jewish Food.
New York: Alfred A. Knopf, 1996.

Root, Waverly.
Food.
New York: Konecky & Konecky, 1980.

Wolf, Burt, Emily Aronson,
and Florence Fabricant, eds.
The New Cooks Catalogue.
New York: Alfred A. Knopf, 2000.

Wolfert, Paula.
Couscous and Other Good Food From Morocco.
New York: Harper & Row, 1973.

conversion tables

APPROXIMATE EQUIVALENTS

1 STICK BUTTER = 8 tbs = 4 oz = ½ cup

1 CUP ALL-PURPOSE PRESIFTED FLOUR OR
DRIED BREAD CRUMBS = 5 oz

1 CUP GRANULATED SUGAR = 8 oz

1 CUP (PACKED) BROWN SUGAR = 6 oz

1 CUP CONFECTIONERS' SUGAR = 4½ oz

1 CUP HONEY OR SYRUP = 12 oz

1 CUP GRATED CHEESE = 4 oz

1 CUP DRIED BEANS = 6 oz

1 LARGE EGG = about 2 oz or about 3 tbs

1 EGG YOLK = about 1 tbs

1 EGG WHITE = about 2 tbs

*Please note that all conversions are approximate but close
enough to be useful when converting from one system to
another.*

WEIGHT CONVERSIONS

US/UK	METRIC	US/UK	METRIC
½ oz	15 g	7 oz	200 g
1 oz	30 g	8 oz	250 g
1½ oz	45 g	9 oz	275 g
2 oz	60 g	10 oz	300 g
2½ oz	75 g	11 oz	325 g
3 oz	90 g	12 oz	350 g
3½ oz	100 g	13 oz	375 g
4 oz	125 g	14 oz	400 g
5 oz	150 g	15 oz	450 g
6 oz	175 g	1 lb	500 g

LIQUID CONVERSIONS

U.S.	IMPERIAL	METRIC
2 tbs	1 fl oz	30 ml
3 tbs	1½ fl oz	45 ml
¼ cup	2 fl oz	60 ml
⅓ cup	2½ fl oz	75 ml
⅓ cup + 1 tbs	3 fl oz	90 ml
⅓ cup + 2 tbs	3½ fl oz	100 ml
½ cup	4 fl oz	125 ml
⅔ cup	5 fl oz	150 ml
¾ cup	6 fl oz	175 ml
¾ cup + 2 tbs	7 fl oz	200 ml
1 cup	8 fl oz	250 ml
1 cup + 2 tbs	9 fl oz	275 ml
1¼ cups	10 fl oz	300 ml
1⅓ cups	11 fl oz	325 ml
1½ cups	12 fl oz	350 ml
1⅔ cups	13 fl oz	375 ml
1¾ cups	14 fl oz	400 ml
1¾ cups + 2 tbs	15 fl oz	450 ml
2 cups (1 pint)	16 fl oz	500 ml
2½ cups	20 fl oz (1 pint)	600 ml
3¾ cups	1½ pints	900 ml
4 cups	1¾ pints	1 liter

OVEN TEMPERATURES

F	GAS MARK	C	F	GAS MARK	C
250	½	120	400	6	200
275	1	140	425	7	220
300	2	150	450	8	230
325	3	160	475	9	240
350	4	180	475	9	240
375	5	190	500	10	260

*Note: Reduce the temperature by 20°C (68°F) for fan-assisted
ovens.*